PRECIOUS RECORDS

PRECIOUS RECORDS

Women in China's Long Eighteenth Century

SUSAN MANN

Stanford University Press
Stanford, California

Stanford University Press
Stanford, California

Printed in the United States of America

CIP data are at the end of the book

Parts of Chapter 6 were adapted from Susan Mann, "Household Handicrafts and State Policy in Qing Times," in Jane Kate Leonard and John R. Watt, eds., *To Achieve Security and Wealth: The Qing Imperial State and the Economy, 1644–1911*, Cornell East Asia Series no. 56 (Ithaca: Cornell University East Asia Program, 1992), pp. 75–91. Translations of poems and portions of text have been reproduced, with some revisions, from Susan Mann, "Learned Women in the Eighteenth Century," in Christina K. Gilmartin, Gail Hershatter, Lisa Rofel, and Tyrene White, eds., *Engendering China: Women, Culture, and the State* (Cambridge, Mass.: Harvard University Press, 1994), pp. 27–46. Quotations from Zhang Xuecheng's "Fu xue" and Yun Zhu's preface to her anthology *Correct Beginnings* are drawn from Susan Mann's translations of these works in Kang-i Sun Chang and Haun Saussy, eds., *Chinese Women Poets: An Anthology of Poetry and Criticism from Ancient Times to 1911* (Stanford: Stanford University Press, forthcoming).

To the memory of

Wanyan Yun Zhu

萬歲

Acknowledgments

MANY LONG CONVERSATIONS WITH Dorothy Ko, Ann Waltner, and Gail Hershatter kept this book unfolding, and it is my pleasure to thank these colleagues here, with affection and respect. William Skinner listened to arguments and prodded my thinking for years while I worked on subjects related to this project, and he commented astutely on parts of the final draft. I received gracious assistance from librarians at the Lou Henry Hoover East Asia Collection at Stanford University and the East Asiatic Library at the University of California, Berkeley; from Mi Chü Wiens at the Library of Congress; from the staff in the classics section of the Shanghai Municipal Library; and from many scholars at the Institute of Modern History, Academia Sinica, Taiwan, where I was privileged to participate in a three-year project on women in modern Chinese history. Closer to home, I have relied on the indispensable help of Phyllis Wang, head of the East Asia collection in Shields Library at the University of California, Davis.

Comments, suggestions, and help of other kinds came from so many people that I can mention only a few here, especially Kwang-Ching Liu, Francesca Bray, Ellen Widmer, Beverly Bossler, Lynn Struve, Margaret B. Swain, William T. Rowe, James Cahill, Lisa Rofel, Emily Honig, Cynthia Brokaw, Evelyn Rawski, Tobie Meyer, Angela Leung, Hsiung Ping-chen, Chen

Yung-fa, Chün-fang Yü, and Nancy Price. At various times I have benefited from the expert research assistance of Yu-yin Cheng, Chi-kong Lai, Chris Hamm, and Wing-kai To. Zumou Yue and Zhiyuan Lü compiled computer databases for the regional analysis of women writers. My translations owe much to Ms. Cheng's encyclopedic sinological knowledge; Wang P'ei-chün, Tsao Jr-lien, and my colleague Michelle Yeh also corrected many translation errors. In addition, midway through the writing of the manuscript, I was fortunate to have a chance to read and discuss texts with Tu Wei-ming during breaks at a workshop at the East-West Center, University of Hawaii. Stephen West, with great generosity, patiently read many poems with me, and, while correcting my errors, he also confirmed my sense that—in some cases, at least—I was reading works of genius. At the Inter-University Program for Chinese Language Studies in Taipei, where I received a generous fellowship from the Chiang Ching-kuo Foundation in the summer of 1992, the learned Wu Hsien-i guided me through the difficult texts describing courtesans and their world. I am responsible for the errors that remain, despite the combined efforts of so many people.

Research support over the years came from the Academic Senate Research Committees at two University of California campuses: Santa Cruz and, since 1989, Davis. Preparation of the first draft of this book was made possible by a National Endowment for the Humanities Fellowship for University Teachers (FA-31423-92), which supplemented a sabbatical leave provided by U.C. Davis in 1992–93. I am especially grateful to Charlotte Furth for her candid and insightful comments on the first complete draft and to Harold Kahn for an interminable and invaluable afternoon spent reviewing the manuscript page by page. Ann Waltner gave the final draft the painstakingly close reading that every sinological scholar imagines her work deserves. I am indebted for final editing to the meticulous and sympathetic eye of Amy Klatzkin of Stanford University Press. Thanks finally to the members of my extended family, who remained enthusiastic, impatient, and confident that one day they would have this book in their hands.

S.M.

Contents

TABLES

ILLUSTRATIONS

Maps

Figures

PRECIOUS RECORDS

1 *Introduction*

OUTSIDE OF CHINA, RESEARCH ON the history of Chinese women is just beginning, and scholars everywhere have barely tapped the wealth of work left by China's women writers. This book presents no more than a preliminary sense of what women felt and believed, and what they actually did, during one short period. My most important sources have been women's writings, mainly poetry. I have also drawn on familiar historical sources written by men: biography and epitaphs, local histories and government documents. Women and gender relations figure in men's essays on statecraft—policy recommendations written by bureaucrats for practical use in local administration—and in their scholarly studies of ritual, art, and literature. Analyzing these familiar sources, written by men, in conjunction with women's own writings opens a new window on the world of Chinese women.

Among these many sources, biography is the richest. Biographies of Chinese women were published by the thousands. They can be found as epitaphs and short anecdotal sketches, in local histories (called gazetteers), and in the collected literary works of published scholars, who regularly wrote about women they loved or admired. Most often honored in these writings were mothers, grandmothers, aunts, and stepmothers—the writer's own or those of a close friend. Also included were individuals we might call saints (Daoist adepts or Buddhist nuns) and special heroines who distinguished themselves by their courage (defending father, wrongfully jailed on a trumped-up charge, for instance, or saving mother from a charging tiger). In the late imperial period, loosely defined as the Ming (1368–1644) and Qing (1644–1911) dynasties, virtually all biographies of so-called exemplary women told stories about martyrs (women who died or committed suicide resisting rape) or widows who scorned remarriage and remained celibate.

Special collections of biographies of model women supplied the archetypes for these biographical forms.[1] The earliest surviving collection, *Biographies of Exemplary Women* (*Lienü zhuan*), was compiled during the early Han period by the scholar Liu Xiang (77–6 B.C.E.). Stories in Liu Xiang's collection illustrate the virtues associated with proper womanly behavior in Confucian families and warn against the vices of jealous, vindictive, and evil women. Another early collection, the *Biographies of Nuns* (*Biqiuni zhuan*), compiled in 517 by Shi Baochang, tells the life histories of the cultivated religious women of the Six Dynasties era (C.E. 220–589).[2] Both these traditions of female biography—the Confucian and the Buddhist—were carried on by eighteenth-century scholars, as we shall see.

Confucian scholars favored biography as the quintessence of historical writing because, they believed, individual lives illustrated the basic principles of praise and blame that made the historical record instructive for future generations. As Denis Twitchett has pointed out, Chinese historians wrote biography to "illustrate the Confucian virtues of their subject" by linking the subject with a paragon of virtue from the ancient past.[3] Confucian biography could be negative as well as positive, as in Liu Xiang's collection. But as time passed, negative models disappeared from didactic works, while positive models for womanly behavior changed. After the Tang dynasty (618–906), individualized tales of ascetics, mystics, and bold, independent filial daughters fade from the historical record. In their stead we find myriad repetitious formulaic stories of women who commit suicide in the name of chastity or who dedicate their lives to serving their parents-in-law in the name of celibate widowhood.

This distinctive style in late imperial biographies of women was partly a response to aggressive government campaigns promoting Confucian models of moral behavior among the common people. The Mongol Yuan dynasty was the first to construct monumental arches honoring chaste women and the first to offer imperial inscriptions of merit to families of chaste widows and female martyrs. Government campaigns promoting female chastity began in earnest under the first Ming emperor. Although, like all imperial policies, these campaigns waxed and waned, they reached a peak during the High Qing era

(c. 1683–1839).* At the same time, over the course of the Ming and Qing periods, ideals of chaste womanhood shifted slightly. For example, Ming rules honored a local custom that was especially visible in a few localities, a practice much like the practice of *sati* in colonial Bengal in which young widows "followed their husbands in death" by starving themselves, strangling on their own sashes, drowning in wells or rivers, or even hanging themselves publicly on a platform. By contrast, early Qing rulers deplored widow suicide. The Yongzheng emperor published attacks on the custom, deriding women who embraced it as cowards who could not face up to the harsh demands of life as a widow. As a result of these Qing policies, even though martyrdom to preserve chastity remained a prominent theme in the biographies of model women during the eighteenth century, long-suffering celibate widows greatly overshadow dramatic suicides in High Qing women's biographies. In this way, the changing character of female biography points to historical shifts in the ideals for women's behavior in late imperial China.

Valuable as they are to historians of women, however, these biographies written by men grow opaque when we try to understand what women themselves thought or believed. For this reason, the women in High Qing biographies seem to represent quintessential objects of a "male gaze." They are literary subjects constructed for specific historical purposes. We cannot expect to find in these stories traces of women's own subjectivity. At the same time, studies of gender relations in Chinese history have demonstrated that elite women and men shared many assumptions about Confucian virtue and its proper representation in women's lives.[4] Consequently women's biographies, even though written by men, contain invaluable evidence about gender relations in High Qing society and reveal some of the reasons why a young woman might contemplate suicide or deny her sexuality. Fortunately, however, late imperial sources are not limited to writings by men. During the High Qing era, published work by women came into its own. The first anthologies of women's writing, edited by women, appeared in print. Elite families reveled in the achievements of erudite mothers and daughters and published their writing in separate editions, not just as appendages to the collected writings of their kinsmen. These published collections of women's writing without doubt constitute the most valuable source we have for the study of Chinese women in the premodern era. Virtually all of the women's writing that survives is poetry.

As I was beginning my research on this book, some of my colleagues in the United States had begun to explore this territory and write about their

* The phrase "High Qing," as used in this book, is defined and discussed in Chap. 2.

discoveries. Maureen Robertson, Dorothy Ko, Ellen Widmer, and Paul Ropp were among the first to alert me to the possibilities of learning about Chinese women in times past through their poems. Even then, however, few of us realized how much poetry by women had survived. In 1985, when Hu Wenkai's sourcebook on women's writings was reprinted, it seemed that scholars recognized for the first time the magnitude of the corpus available to us. Hu's work first appeared in 1957, too early to claim the attention of China scholars in the United States, for whom gender did not become a category of analysis until the 1970's. But now at last historians and literary critics are studying the thousands of volumes of published books and unpublished manuscripts by women that Hu identified in his anthology, and countless others are still being discovered. As I write, a massive anthology of women's writings in English translation is being compiled under the direction of Kang-i Sun Chang and Haun Saussy.

Despite the abundance of women's writing, these works raise particular problems as a source for the historian of eighteenth-century China. Chinese women writers of this era were part of a tiny elite, far more highly educated than most of us today. Many lived lives of privilege that few of us can imagine, separated as they were by leisure and learning from the other 99.9 percent of women in the late empire. Moreover, more than 70 percent of them came from one small region on China's central coast—the region displayed in Maps 1 and 2. As a window on the world of "Chinese women," then, women's writing itself leaves something to be desired.

That is why this book takes an eclectic approach to sources and to questions about gender in Chinese history. I rely on women's own writings to correct the distortions inherent in the male gaze and to see how women themselves articulate value and meaning in a society dominated by Confucian norms. At the same time, while placing women at the center of my analysis, I have also located them in the context of the High Qing era. Women's roles and gender relations were part of a process of historical production involving state policies, marriage and labor markets, scholarly tastes, and aesthetic sensibilities unique to the eighteenth century. Complex state societies construct tax systems, welfare plans, labor legislation, and warfare strategies that directly affect household composition and the division of labor, the hierarchy of decision making and accountability within the household, the distribution of resources by sex/gender, and the value assigned to the work, reproductive as well as productive, of males and females. The late imperial Chinese state was no exception, and documentation about China's imperial government is second to none in the world. Not surprisingly, the writings of High Qing policy makers yield much evidence about gender relations.[5]

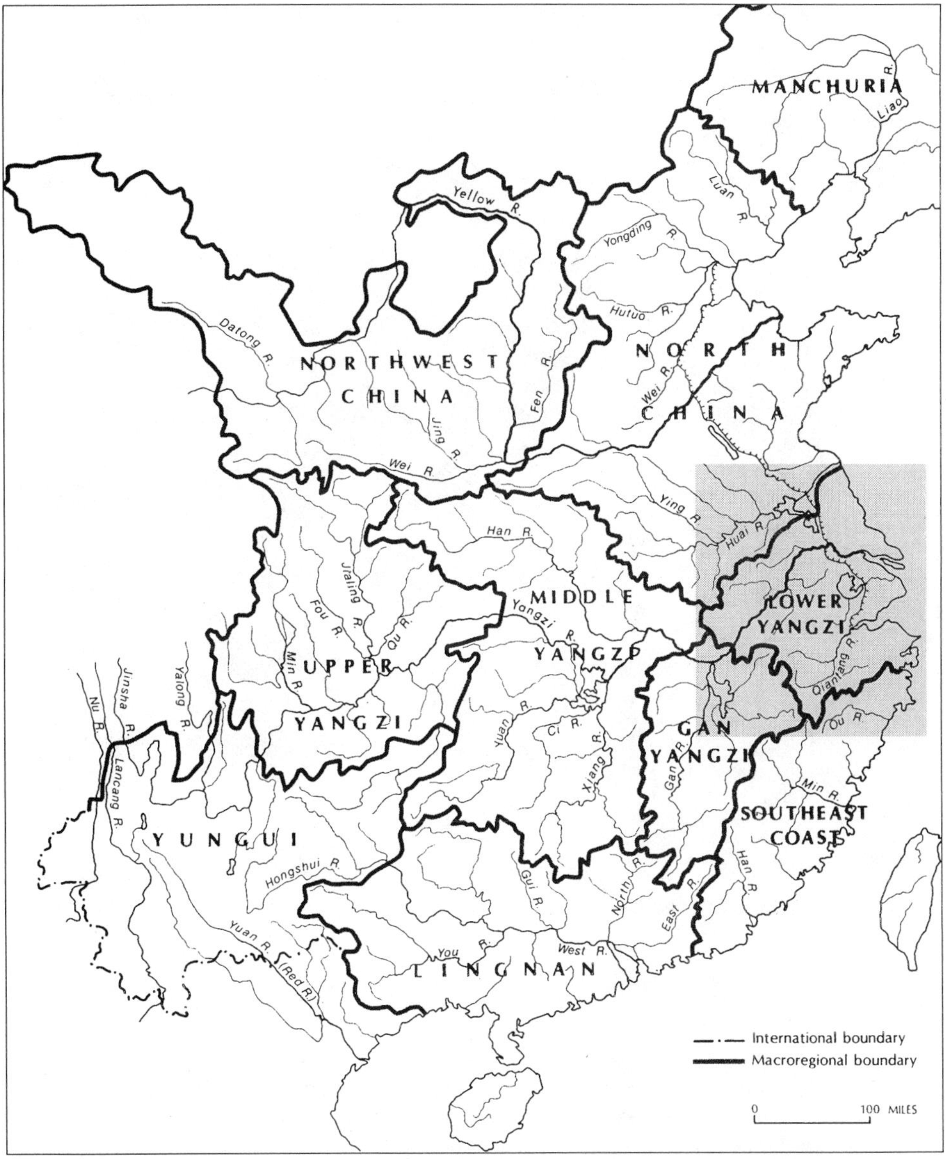

Map 1. China's physiographic macroregions, with the Lower Yangzi region highlighted. From Skinner 1985: 273. Reprinted with permission from the Association for Asian Studies, Inc.

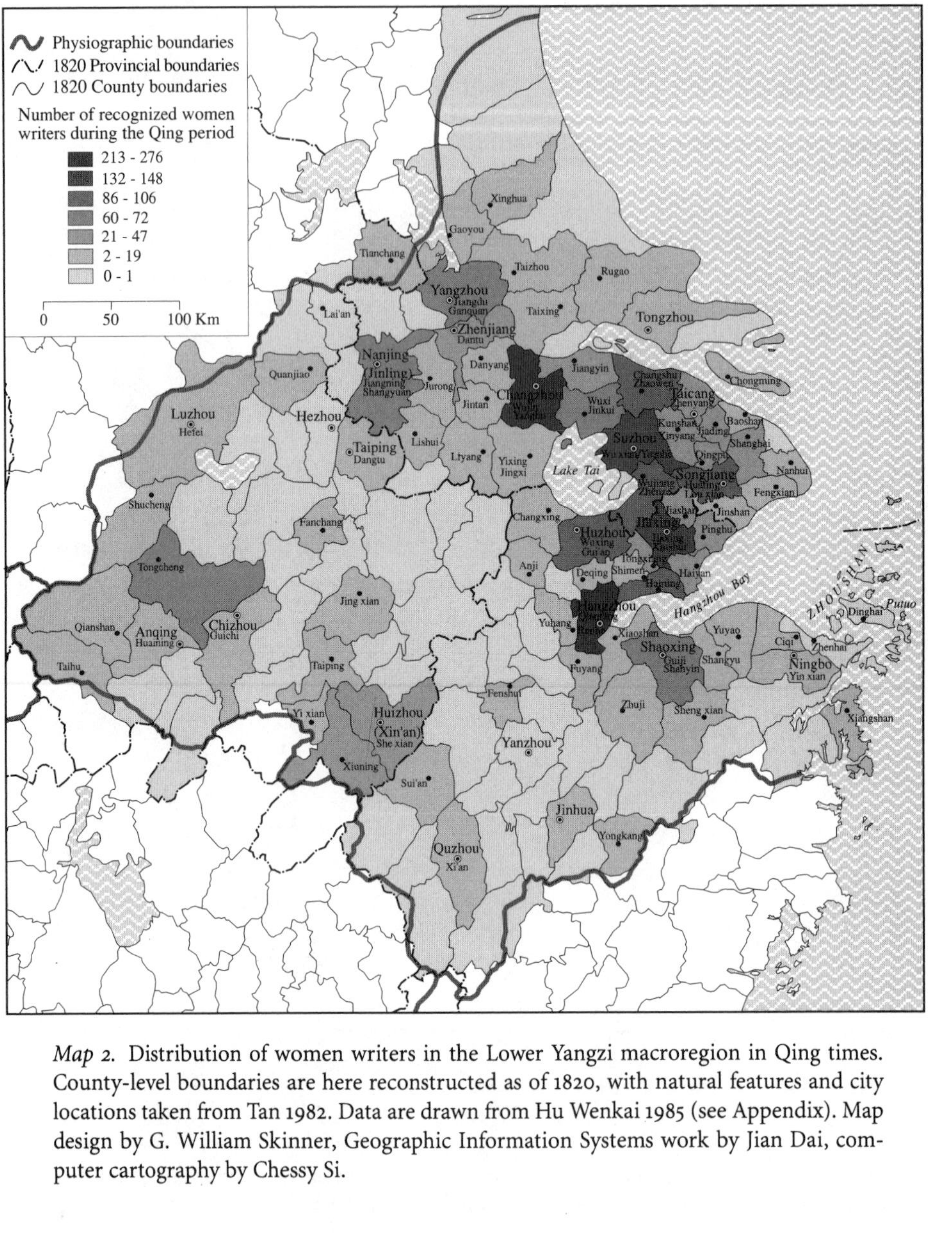

Map 2. Distribution of women writers in the Lower Yangzi macroregion in Qing times. County-level boundaries are here reconstructed as of 1820, with natural features and city locations taken from Tan 1982. Data are drawn from Hu Wenkai 1985 (see Appendix). Map design by G. William Skinner, Geographic Information Systems work by Jian Dai, computer cartography by Chessy Si.

But policies, markets, tastes, and sensibilities were also profoundly affected by women in High Qing times. Only by making our sources talk to one another and by placing women at the center of historical analysis can we study gender and culture in the High Qing era. More than a new understanding of China's long eighteenth century is at stake here. Placing women at the center of any historical inquiry calls into question our conventional models of periodization. Understanding women's place in the High Qing era invites us to consider gender relations in the periods that precede and follow the High Qing—the late Ming era and the late nineteenth century—and to ask how unique the High Qing era really was.

Dorothy Ko's path-breaking study of women and culture in the seventeenth century shows how urbanization, commercialization, and the print culture of late Ming society brought women's voices into the historical record.[6] Through reading and writing, elite women developed new spheres of influence, expanding the domain of kinship and friendship beyond domestic space, mastering the tools of learning that had been the domain of men, and articulating notions of talent and beauty in a dialogue with husbands, lovers, and fathers as well as with teachers, both male and female. Ko stresses that these changes in women's sphere span the seventeenth century, erasing the conventional divide that separates Ming from Qing China, that is, the Manchu conquest of 1644. In fact, as if to acknowledge the importance of the High Qing era, Ko ends her study in 1720, around the beginning of the Yongzheng emperor's reign.

Focusing, like Ko's study, on gender, my research confirms part of her conclusions about periodization, but it also raises new questions. High Qing women writers built on and expanded the domain of learning and creative expression first developed by their seventeenth-century predecessors. But important—indeed, crucial—differences separate Ko's seventeenth-century women writers from those I study in the High Qing era. Most of those differences can be traced, as Chapter 2 shows, to the Manchu conquest. To be sure, the dynastic cycle has no impact on the trajectory of women's learning in late imperial China. That trajectory appears to rise steadily from the late Ming onward, unaffected by the Ming-Qing transition. However, a focus on gender shows that the Manchu conquest marked a cultural disruption that transformed gender relations as Qing hegemony took hold. From this perspective, the history of gender relations in the Qing period marks a break from the late Ming, forcing us to reassess the importance of Manchu identity and Manchu values in the making of Qing society. In other words, for women's learning itself, the advent of the Qing dynasty barely signifies. But when we examine the role of women's learning in social and cultural life during the High Qing era, we shall see that Manchu rule was not just another "dynastic cycle." Instead, the High Qing stands as a unique moment in Chinese women's history, set apart from the late Ming period that preceded it by a particular set of historical conditions.

The unique conditions of the High Qing period can also be read forward in time to illuminate the modern history of Chinese women. Retrospective views of the Qing period, as seen from the vantage point of twentieth-century reformers and revolutionaries, lump it together with the Ming as a "feudal" or "traditional" era when Chinese women were the oppressed subjects of a Confucian patriarchy. Late-nineteenth-century Chinese reformers and foreign missionaries singled out footbinding and women's "lack of education" as hallmarks of China's backwardness in the Ming and Qing periods. Beginning in the 1890's, these critics promoted women's education and protested footbinding as essential first steps toward a strong Chinese nation. By their logic, late imperial China was once again as Hegel imagined it: a civilization without a history, a society where nothing changed until the advent of Western ideas set it on the road to modern nationhood. Thanks to our new understanding of gender relations in Ming and Qing times, this lingering view of late imperial history can be scrapped. Far from being an era of unremitting female oppression, the Ming and Qing periods were dynamic and diverse centuries of social, political, and economic change with profound consequences for gender relations in China, and as such they demand new analysis.

Like Western women's history, then, the history of women in China challenges conventional notions of periodization and invites a nuanced appreciation for shifts in gender relations located carefully in time and space. It is no accident that, in explaining why women are central to our understanding of historical change, historians of China have drawn inspiration from feminist historians of Europe and North America. My study is especially indebted to the stimulating essays by a historian of the Italian Renaissance, the late Joan Kelly, and her critics. In asking herself if women had a Renaissance, Kelly was led to rewrite her own conclusions about Renaissance history. How, I wondered, would the High Qing era look, and how would our understanding of the eighteenth century change, if our historical inquiries placed women at the center? Or, to paraphrase Kelly, did women have a High Qing era? Kelly's work convinced me that by introducing women into conventional historical frameworks, we do not simply change the content of the frame; we may also destroy the framework itself.

So far, so good. But as we begin to rewrite the historical record to take account of these shifts in gender relations through time and space, historians of China encounter other problems. We seem to find ourselves once again "catching up" with paradigms and methods developed by historians of Europe and North America. By embracing gender as a category of analysis, we finally join the ranks of mainstream historians inspired by the work of Gerda Lerner, Joan Kelly, and Joan Scott to defamiliarize familiar historical terrain. At the same time, historians of China know well that the paradigms of Western historiography have always had limited explanatory power for the Chinese historical record. Where gender relations are concerned, the problems with using Western categories of analysis are especially vexing. The structure of the late imperial Chinese family assigned women roles and relationships that are unknown in Euro-North American culture. The social stratification system in Qing times offers no counterpart to the Western bourgeoisie, let alone an emergent "middle class," and the economy did not move toward an industrial revolution. No church vied with the state for the power to define domestic relationships or inheritance law. Not surprisingly, and partly as a result of these great differences, the myths of desire and transcendence in which men and women figured and around which young girls constructed their conceptions of sexuality and gender relations were radically different from those in Europe and North America, posing existential questions that cannot be framed using a Western vocabulary.[7]

This conclusion does not mean that gender is a useless category of historical analysis for China scholars. It means, on the contrary, that studies of gender and culture in Chinese history stand to illuminate the unspoken ethnocentric assumptions that historians of Europe and North America unconsciously bring to their own studies of gender. For example, they tend to assume a family system that is conjugal or stem, to use the anthropological terms. Primogeniture, neolocal marriage, delayed childbearing, and a high proportion of never-married women are all part of the presumptive family systems generally studied by feminist historians of Europe. In addition, Western historians presume a context in which a Christian church offsets the power of secular government to define familial relationships through its control of property, sacred authority, and even marriage and inheritance.

To illustrate, consider two examples of the social space available to learned women in Renaissance and early modern Europe, periods in many ways comparable to the High Qing era. The "book-lined cell" described by Margaret King offered the never-married learned woman a permanent sanctuary where she was free to pursue a life of the mind that was sanctioned by the church and legitimized in the eyes of her peers.[8] A different, public, space was available in the Italian universities Paula Findlen studied, where gifted women like Laura Bassi—married and with five children—taught philosophy and even received university honors.[9] None of these spaces was available to learned women in

High Qing China. The Confucian family system and the absence of a church ruled out the possibility of a book-lined cell. No religious institution offered a legitimate place for never-married women with a fine education, and no family allowed a promising young lady to escape marriage.[10] As for university positions, China's scholarly academies never admitted women because the sole purpose of these institutions was to prepare men to sit for the examinations that would admit them into the imperial bureaucracy.

Such simple but obvious differences call our attention to other kinds of spaces, open not to European women but to late imperial Chinese women, thanks to specific cultural and historical conditions. In this book, the reader familiar with Western women's history will be struck by a singular feature of High Qing society: the importance of publishing—including the role of the family in publishing—women's writings. The printed text, passed in manuscript or hand-copied or block-printed form from family to family, studio to studio, offered learned women in High Qing times a unique place in both the domestic life of the family and the public life of high culture. A brief digression here will point to particular features of High Qing society that help explain the unique cultural context it provided for women as writers.

The women I discuss in this book were part of a joint family system in which the patrilocal "grand family" was the norm.[11] The joint family spanned three—rarely four or five—generations, all sharing the same roof and kitchen. Kinship was reckoned through male descent from a common ancestor. Inheritance was partible. All sons inherited equally, all sons were expected to marry, and all married sons, together with their wives and offspring (married sons and unmarried sons and daughters), resided with surviving parents. Daughters were "married out" to become part of another descent line. In the High Qing period, government policy and Confucian learning made life in such a family the quintessential expression of what it was to be fully human. Monastic Buddhism offered an alternative to Confucian family life, but Buddhist monasteries recruited nuns almost exclusively from the poorest families or among abandoned or orphaned girls. In elite families, extremely rare and eccentric behavior might persuade the parents of a young girl to allow her to pursue a celibate religious life. For the most part, however, the power of Buddhism as a religious teaching reached elite women through lay rituals that promised sons to married women in their childbearing years and spiritual satisfaction following menopause. "Getting to a nunnery," however, was not an appropriate choice for a young woman of elite status. As a member of the great Jia family remarks in the novel *Dream of the Red Chamber*, "It would look very bad for a girl from a family such as ours to enter a nunnery. That really is unthinkable."[12]

The psychological consequences for women of growing up in such a family system have been explored at length by anthropologists. Their work emphasizes the different effects on sons and daughters of Confucian family relationships. Sons were to honor their parents in life by being respectful and by fathering sons; daughters were to marry into another family, bear sons, be faithful to their husbands, and serve their parents-in-law. After death, a son's parents were honored by the son, his wife, and their progeny with rituals in which food offerings reiterated the undying devotion of their offspring and displayed the success of their descendants.

Women in this family system stood both at the margins and at the center. As daughters who married out, they were transient members of their natal families, but as wives who bore sons, they became part of the enduring ancestral cult.[13] This crucial feature of the female life cycle in the Chinese family system presents psychological traumas that directly contradict the gender patterns identified by psychiatrists and psychologists in Western Europe and North America. In most Western European and North American societies, it is sons who undergo traumatic separation from the mother, a separation that becomes the fundamental experience informing their own gender identity. Daughters, by contrast, maintain an unbroken connection to the mother and to the close emotional bonds forged in early childhood.[14] In High Qing families, daughters—not sons—suffered the trauma of separation. Daughters grew up knowing that they must eventually "marry out" and enter another family; sons, by contrast, could count on a lasting, intimate bond with their mothers that would be broken only by death.

Husband-wife relations in the High Qing family system offer another striking contrast to Euro-North American models. The norm in most studies of Western gender relations is a neolocal family in which the husband-wife bond is the core of a nuclear household. Couples delay marriage so they can afford to set up a separate household, and both men and women must achieve some degree of economic independence prior to marriage. By contrast, Chinese marriages were planned by parents through a go-between, making every young couple's marriage a parental, and sometimes a corporate, family investment. In elite grand families, sons and daughters married young and remained dependent on the groom's parents or paternal grandparents throughout the childbearing years. Seeking a bride for a son, elite parents looked for a healthy woman from a comparable family background, sometimes arranging for a betrothal in utero when a good friend's wife became pregnant.

In this context, married couples were not expected to be intimate, and often they spent little time together. Indeed, a Chinese mother was likely to view a son's attraction to his wife as a threat to her own claim on his affection, or, at the very least, as a source of distraction from the work her daughter-in-law was supposed to do for her. In elite families, husbands worked "outside" the home as scholars or officials or businessmen, which meant regular extended periods of travel to examinations or extended sojourning in teaching positions, official posts, or trade centers far from home. The husband's absence required a bride to forge her primary ties with her mother-in-law and with the other women in her husband's family, with whom she would spend most of her time. In this context, fantasies about marital intimacy represented not some romantic ideal of domesticity but resistance to the disciplines of Confucian patriarchy.

In High Qing times, elite parents planning a marriage asked a go-between to negotiate a wedding of "matching doors," that is, a match between a couple of roughly comparable social background. There are many reasons why "matching doors" was desirable. First, elite families tried to avoid the appearance of needing to purchase a spouse for a child through the presentation of bridal gifts or dowry. Bridal gifts (from the groom's family to the bride's) and dowry (items accompanying the bride when she moved from her natal family to the groom's) were supposed to be of roughly equal value. Second, no family wished to give the appearance that its offspring were "marrying down." Marriage was an opportunity to forge kinship ties that would be advantageous or prestigious for both sides. Third, for parents concerned about the welfare of married daughters, matching doors offered some assurance that a daughter would adjust well to her new surroundings and that her mother-in-law would be pleased with her upbringing and favor her.

No matter how much bride-giving parents contrived to "match doors," however, the High Qing marriage market put daughters at special risk. Unbalanced sex ratios, resulting from the preference for sons in the family system, created an insatiable demand for brides, which one demographer has termed a persistent "marriage crunch."[15] The result was that virtually every woman expected to marry and that hypergamy was as common as "matching doors"—that is, bride-giving families could expect their daughters to "marry up." At the same time, declining odds of success in the examination system and rising opportunities for money-making in the commercial economy continually brought nouveaux-riches families into competition with elite scholarly families whose fortunes were declining. A man from a scholarly background took a chance when marrying off his daughter to the son of an arriviste rich peasant, artisan, or merchant, even if the match looked desirable. If the bride was well educated and the groom failed to appreciate her gifts, she would suffer for the rest of her life, as many stories in the pages that follow show. A second source of risk for bride-giving families lay in the likelihood that any family of means would bring in a concubine or two to bear sons or to provide sexual satisfaction for a husband who tired of his wife. Finally, since marriages were arranged through matchmakers whose interest in full disclosure was compromised by their interest in money, marriage was almost always based on incomplete information.

For these and other reasons, arranged marriage—even hypergamous arranged marriage—was a gamble, and losing out was common. Unhappy marriage is a constant theme in women's biographies written by men and in poems by women themselves. Women's loneliness, isolation, and emotional privation in marriage—which men could escape through travel and by seeking other sexual relationships—find expression in nostalgia for childhood and for the siblings and parents and other kinfolk who made up the bride's world before she was wrenched away. A married woman's joy and comfort come from memory, reconstructed again and again in poems; from correspondence and the exchange of poetry with absent loved ones and with "poet friends" (*shi you*); and from children who themselves were growing up to marry.

Matching doors aside, bride-giving families enjoyed a slight edge in the marriage market, since the shortage of women gave them more choices. Moreover, since every family wanted sons to carry on the descent line, young women of lower status could enter elite households as concubines. High Qing writers, especially the women, were acutely conscious of the value and privilege of wives, the lowly and vulnerable status of concubines, and the commercial quality of courtesans' sexual availability. Therefore marital status as wife or concubine was a primary indicator of status for women, setting off wives from concubines within the elite family, creating a rank order among daughters-in-law, with the wife of the first-married eldest son presiding, and marking courtesans as "ill-fated women" tainted by their commercialized bodies.[16] In High Qing times, then, every woman knew that she must marry and understood that being a wife was the best possible marital status she could hope for. Herein lie the pain and paradox of much of High Qing women's history.

If China's family system offers a sharp contrast to those dominating Europe and North America, social stratification in late imperial China is equally unfamiliar to Westerners. In China, as elsewhere, marriage markets served to reproduce status hierarchies, but unlike the situation in preindustrial Europe, hereditary status in China was a privilege only of the imperial clans. No hereditary landed aristocracy ruled the countryside, no incipient bourgeois middle class arose in the cities, and no laboring class of peasants and artisans was barred from the ranks of elite status. Instead, open mobility in and out of broad occupational categories was the basis for defining prestige and privilege. The absence of a hereditary elite, the fluid system of stratification, and the vitality of the commercial economy made marriage and work more important than ever as avenues of upward mobility during the High Qing era. Under Ming rule certain occupations remained formally inherited (such as those of the artisan, the military colonist, and, to some extent, even the merchant), but by Qing times labor markets were completely open, and competition for status was fierce on all fronts. At the broadest level, those who performed manual labor (peasants and artisans) were viewed as "the ruled," while those who labored with their minds (scholars and officials) made up the ruling elite. Access to wealth and leisure modified this scheme. Thus merchants whose occupation tainted them with the quest for profit could affect the trappings of elite life by investing in libraries and fine art to mimic the scholar class, even though peasants and artisans remained nominally superior to merchants because of their honest labor. Imperial rhetoric aptly celebrated peasants, who supplied the grain and paid the land taxes that sustained the elite, as the "foundation" of the polity.

In Qing times, then, peasants, artisans, and merchants alike could rear sons with the hope that one gifted member of the next generation might succeed in the official examination system and begin the family's rise to a place within the scholar-official elite. As in Europe, men and women of the High Qing elite struggled for material wealth, honor, and power. But in China no class system offered a safety net to catch those who found wealth and power slipping away. Moreover, the merchant class continued to purchase scholarly degrees and education for sons, ensuring that a separate bourgeois identity would not develop.[17]

This system of stratification, centered on male mobility patterns, applied to women as well. A woman's status followed that of her natal family (i.e., her father's) before marriage and her marital family (i.e., her husband's) after marriage. The main difference in stratification systems for women and men in the High Qing period lay in their relationship to manual labor. For men, the opportunity to eschew manual labor was the first signal of rising status. For women, by contrast, leisure, or freedom from manual labor, never served as a status marker. On the contrary, diligent productive manual labor, specifically spinning and weaving—and, for upper-class women, embroidery—was the mark of virtue for all women, regardless of class. Idleness in a woman signaled wantonness; it could compromise a woman's status in the marriage market and her standing in her family. Courtesans and prostitutes, like women in pariah occupations such as acting, were lowly precisely because they neither spun nor wove.

China in the High Qing era was a fluid, competitive society markedly different from its counterparts in Europe and North America. Even so, the discourses of desire that pervade the writings of the time invite comparison with the European case. For example, Nancy Armstrong has argued that the authority of women's writing voice in the English novel was part of the process by which a nascent middle class defined its place in society and described an emerging domestic space centered on women's bodies.[18] Readers will find much in High Qing culture that is reminiscent of the English discourse, especially the discourse on moral wives. Readers of this book will also be reminded of the debates about the relationship between women's writing and lapsed virtue that arose in eighteenth-century Italy and France. But they will be very surprised by the Chinese construction of the relationship between public life and domestic life that lies at the heart of Confucian thought and frames these debates. In High Qing times, the distinction between *nei* and *wai*—between women's inner sphere and men's outer sphere—is quite unlike the Western dichotomy separating the "domestic" from the "public" sphere.[19] Instead, in High Qing discourse the principle of *bie*—separate spheres—is invoked to stress that wives and mothers inside the home embody the moral autonomy and authority on which husbands and sons must rely to succeed outside. All are part of a family system that constitutes a seamless, unitary social order centered on the home and bounded by the outer reaches of the imperium.

The unique role of mothers and wives in High Qing elite society is a reminder of the great cultural differences separating the Chinese experience from apparently similar historical experiences in Europe and North America. We cannot assume that the celebration of virtuous wives and the romantic allure of female poets carried similar cultural messages in High Qing China and early modern France or Italy or late-eighteenth- and nineteenth-century England. Because of the structure of the Chinese family and the elevation of learning over wealth and heredity, myths of desire in High Qing China encode particular cultural messages. To men, they hold out the promise of an encounter with a divine woman, someone who will first inspire his passion but who will ultimately enable him to transcend worldly desire and passion. A passionate engagement with a woman was an ephemeral experience, not an all-consuming goal. Men poured their most powerful emotions into lifelong bonds with their mothers or into homosocial relationships with colleagues. Heterosexual passion was reserved for that rare and elusive encounter with the divine woman, someone who would "know the inner self" (*zhi ji*) or "know one's inner sounds" (*zhi yin*)[20] and, in the knowing, show a man how to transcend his worldly passions.

As for womanly desire, direct expressions of it in High Qing China are rare. Festivals, folktales, and religious practice echo the sentiments found in women's writings, which continually reject the promise of desire, cloaking it in sadness, loneliness, and pain. The disciplines of domestic life act as a critique of desire, and relationships with siblings, children, and friends give emotional comfort. Women at mid-life, moreover, develop autonomous spiritual powers through techniques of bodily discipline that promise transcendence. Like men, they may seek transcendence in a divine encounter with another being, a female deity who promises enlightenment. Or they may look to themselves and to their own spiritual discipline to find the power to transcend worldly cares. Studies of eighteenth-century Chinese fiction point to this dialectic between passion and transcendence, or, as one scholar puts it, "enchantment and disenchantment,"[21] especially in the great novel *Dream of the Red Chamber*, from which some of the evidence in this book is drawn. Louise Edwards sums this up best when she says that the world idealized in *Dream of the Red Chamber* is a "merger of the sexual with the maternal in a realm free of social morality."[22] As the reader will see, though wives figure in the literary imagination as authorities in the domestic realm, it is mothers who invoke the most profound feelings. In other words, the particular structure of the Chinese family produces a discourse of desire that, as in England, defines domestic space. The configuration of that space, however, is particular to Chinese culture.

A final arena of difference that any study of High Qing gender relations will immediately foreground is the crucial role of writing as a mark of cultivated humanity. The role of "writer" or "novelist" was not identified as a special social category. The Chinese term for writing, *wen*, is the same as the term for culture.[23] In that sense, it was presumed by all parents in elite families that a fully realized human being would be able not only to read, but also to write, especially to write poetry.[24] To write, in this sense, meant something unusually complex, for mastering classical Chinese required rote memorization from a very early age of hundreds of canonical and historical and literary works. The memorization process produced an immense memory bank,[25] a vast store of prose and poetry containing phrases and allusions that the pupil would encounter and use again and again throughout her reading life. Reading, then, was a cumulative process in which the reader would continually reinforce earlier childhood memorization by calling up from memory the phrases and names of writers through the ages. By the same token, the writer's literary powers relied on the evocative capacity of words to call up those remembered canonical, historical, and literary texts for every reader. By the time a young person had reached the age of eight or nine, it was assumed that she would be trying out her own skills of evocation by writing simple exercises. Gifted children at that age started practicing short four-line, five-character-per-line poems or brief expository notes. In other words, growing up learned in elite households of the High Qing period meant growing up to write. Young women in elite families composed poetry through most of their early years and often into adulthood without necessarily thinking of themselves as "poets."

In explaining the role of writing in High Qing elite culture, I have used female pronouns to emphasize that both little boys and little girls in elite families were expected to learn to read and write. It is important to note, however, that expectations for girls were somewhat special. The reasons for that will become clear as the book unfolds, but briefly stated, writing was a necessary art for boys who aspired to success in the official examinations, which required proficiency in classical prose. By contrast, girls—who were barred from taking examinations or holding office and who were not groomed with these goals in mind—had no clear use for their writing. That is what makes women's writing so powerfully revealing about ideas of gender difference in premodern Chinese society. Whenever a woman wrote, the purpose of writing—not simply the quality of it—was subject to scrutiny and evaluation, praise or blame. Thus in all periods of Chinese history, we find writing women a subject for discussion. They might be honored for exceptional talent, as was Ban Zhao in Han times. They might be emblems of an aristocratic culture like Xie Daoyun, who moved in the esoteric circles of medieval philosophes. They might be criticized and silenced, as were so many of the aspiring poet daughters in Song gentry families.[26] Or they might be the center of bitter controversy, as were the High Qing poets in Yuan Mei's entourage known as the "female followers at the Sui Garden." Whatever her historical position, the woman as a writing subject challenged fundamental conventions of Chinese high culture.

In the High Qing period, these challenges centered on a core set of contradictions. As a human being, a woman ought to develop her aesthetic and moral capacities to the full; this required that she write. As a woman, she ought to work constantly with her hands; this made her writing an abdication of her moral responsibilities. As a woman, her primary responsibilities lay in her roles as wife, mother, and daughter-in-law. As a writer, meanwhile, precisely because she was a woman and therefore untainted by the quest for honor or position, she was capable of an emotional spontaneity and purity of expression that eluded men. That is why you will find this book laced with arguments about women writers. They wrote better than men, but they had no business taking time away from work to do it; they must be educated, but they should never put their learning to use beyond their family duties.

What actually happened during the eighteenth century, as we shall observe, is that writing empowered elite women in ways that made many of these debates superfluous. Through their writing, especially when it was published or copied and exchanged, women created a powerful identity of their own. This identity both represented and reinvented, scrutinized and criticized, the actual life situations in which women found themselves. In that sense, the work of High Qing women writers is much like the orally transmitted lyric poems of Bedouin women: classical verse gave women of High Qing times a vocabulary they could use both to mimic and to create.[27] So they criticized the present and imagined a better future while inscribing and reinscribing the remembered past as a continual source of comfort and continuity. Above all—and this is what makes Chinese women poets different still from their Bedouin counterparts—the women poets of the High Qing period grew up presuming they had the talent to write poetry. No educated woman I have encountered in the documents from this period complains that she cannot write poetry, though many bitterly lament their wasted talent or burn works they feel too embittered to leave behind. Because they presumed that, as cultured human beings, they could write, educated women of the High Qing era poured into poetry all their feelings, revealing to us a lost world.

To understand this world we must revisit the High Qing period by reintroducing some of its most important characteristics—those signs that historians of China have long considered the hallmarks of the age. Chapter 2 surveys three aspects of High Qing history that dramatize the unique character of the period, focusing on the Lower Yangzi region and taking gender as a category of analysis. The most important issues we will examine relate, directly or indirectly, to Manchu imperial policy and its consequences for women and for gender relations. This chapter is followed by an analysis of the female life course (Chapter 3) and then by discussions of women's place in writing (Chapter 4), in entertainment (Chapter 5), at work (Chapter 6), and in religious practice (Chapter 7). The concluding chapter returns to broad historiographic questions about where women figure in space and time and why we should not write histories that leave them out.

2 *Gender*

When my teacher Grand Lady Yun Zhenpu compiled her collection of women's poetry from the Qing dynasty, she titled it *Correct Beginnings*, meaning that the emotions of the wise and pure ones in the women's quarters are correct. Just as Confucius edited the *Odes*, placing the poem "Guan ju" first, so in her own collection she placed elegant refinement (*ya*) before style (*feng*). . . . As an injunction to the woman writer, the meaning of her anthology was both subtle and illuminating. Laboring over several decades, she gathered works by nearly a thousand woman authors, even those living at the margins of the realm or beyond its borders. No talented writer was omitted. Her project truly expanded the transformative influence of this prosperous age; she was not merely collecting women's rhymes.

—Jin Wengying, Preface to *Guochao guixiu zhengshi xuji* (Correct Beginnings: Women's poetry of our august dynasty, continued), 1836

JIN WENGYING, A STUDENT of the woman poet, painter, and anthologist Yun Zhu,* wrote the comments above in her preface for the sequel to the classic anthology of Qing women's poetry that Yun Zhu compiled. Jin viewed women's poetry as a glorious sign of her "pros-

*Yun Zhu's married name, Wanyan, is often dropped by scholars writing about her. Her marriage into the Manchu Wanyan lineage is discussed in Chap. 4 ("Writing"), which draws heavily on her anthology and its sequels.

perous age" (*sheng shi*), which is why her remarks make such an apt introduction to a chapter on women's roles in the High Qing era.

Works by more than three thousand Qing women writers survive, of which perhaps half date from the "prosperous age" known in English as the High Qing era (1683–1839). The rhetorical phrase *sheng shi* was reserved for the peak of each dynastic cycle. Thus the High Qing is considered the high point of Manchu rule. By convention, it is often referred to as China's "long eighteenth century."[1] The "peak" is actually a trajectory that begins to rise in 1683, the year the Manchus eliminated the last remnants of Ming loyalist resistance. It reaches its zenith during the decades after the 1720's and begins a downward turn sometime in the mid 1770's, declining rapidly after the 1790's, when White Lotus and Miao rebellions began to undermine the power of the central government. Though some scholars see the end of the High Qing in the 1790's, perhaps with the death of the Qianlong emperor in 1796, others (myself among them) would push the High Qing into the late 1830's and end it on the eve of the Opium War, which marked the ascendancy of Western military power in China's traditional spheres of influence and the true end of an era. Jin Wengying, writing in the early 1830's, considered herself a beneficiary of a prosperous age. She had no inkling of what was to come.

Whatever their dating schemes, all scholars agree on the hallmarks of the High Qing period. These include explosive population growth, dramatic economic transformation, and high rates of migration and mobility—social as well as geographical.[2] The High Qing was also the age of a great classical revival in scholarship.[3] Finally, the eighteenth century stands out as the time when China's imperial bureaucratic state intervened most directly in the moral and material lives of ordinary people.[4]

Recent studies have tarnished this glowing picture of robust prosperity, adding blights to hallmarks. Philip Kuhn's analysis of the Lower Yangzi sorcery scare of 1768 is an ironic commentary on the dark side of the High Qing "prosperous age" that focuses on the migratory underclass. Kuhn reveals the tensions and anxieties filling official documents and literary writings, especially the fear of "dangerous strangers on the move."[5] Tensions and anxieties bristle as well in the era's greatest novel, *Dream of the Red Chamber*, which traces the collapse of a grand family and the end of a way of life by dissecting the intimate relationships between men and women in a wealthy upper-class household, as Louise Edwards has shown.[6] Probing the roots of tensions offers a different approach to Jin Wengying's celebratory comments, since Jin calls our attention to the debates about women writers that erupted in many spheres during the High Qing era.[7] Debates about women's roles in Qing times have already attracted scholarly analysis, especially among students of fiction, because High Qing fiction writers loved to satirize gender roles.[8] But little attention has been paid to debates about women as writers or to writings by women themselves, which were often the inspiration for these debates. Nor have scholars noticed concurrent discussions in other kinds of documents—for instance, scholarly essays on how to manage the farm economy—that also pay unusual heed to women and their roles in economy and society in High Qing times.[9] These neglected discussions and debates invite historical explanation. Why were women and women's roles so important, and so controversial, in the eighteenth century? If we reexamine the High Qing era with this question in mind—taking as our focus the Lower Yangzi region and using gender as a category of analysis—several key arenas emerge at once.

The most important is Manchu state policy. From the beginning, crucial Manchu policies took aim at family relations and what Americans in the 1990's would call "family values." Many of these policies focused specifically on women and predate the High Qing era. For example, Manchu rulers promoted female chastity, and they sharply curtailed public displays by female entertainers. The Manchus also generally supported measures that broke down barriers in the commoner marriage market and sharpened the differences between free persons and slaves. Starting with edicts issued in 1645, the Qing emperors systematically dismantled hereditary occupational and status groups inherited from the Ming.[10] These policies clearly stem from concerns raised by the Manchus' ethnic background, which unavoidably colored the values Qing rulers brought to the throne, in particular their attitude toward gender roles. Scholars trained in Manchu are now probing the significance of these values;[11] in this book I can only stress that they will prove crucial to our ultimate understanding of gender relations in High Qing times.

A second arena for inquiry in any study of gender relations in High Qing times is the writing of local officials, who reported to the Manchu emperors on their plans for ensuring the welfare of peasant families. Local officials' writings in this period focus on two key gender issues: women's work and women's religious practice. They developed programs to expand the use of female labor in the household economy, especially in sericulture and in cotton spinning and weaving. They also led campaigns to stamp out what they viewed as dangerous religious activities among laywomen.

The classical revival is a third arena where questions about women in High Qing times seem to explode. The revival itself was related to Manchu state policy inasmuch as the High Qing emperors patronized arts and letters, encouraging scholars to throw their energies into the study of ancient texts. However, scholarly tastes independent of Manchu patronage also steered Chinese intellectuals toward "empirical research" (*kaozheng xue*) on the history of classical texts during the eighteenth century. Studies of classical texts drew attention to learned women in times past—with dramatic results, including the gradual empowerment of women writers as moral wives, participants in an emerging discourse of what I call familistic moralism in High Qing times. This discourse clearly distinguishes the High Qing era from the late Ming period studied by Ko, when the cult of *qing*—passion, love, or desire—dominated the literary imagination of elite writers, male and female. In High Qing times, despite dissenting voices like the poet Yuan Mei's and the fiction writer Li Yu's, the cult of *qing* was repressed. Pornographic works and romances remained on the market, but illustrated sex manuals became harder to find,[12] and "unbridled descriptiveness" gave way to "more cerebral" story telling.[13] As Keith McMahon puts it, the chaste Qing couple "replaces sex with words: poems, letters, and polite conversation."[14]

Still another way to probe the distinctive character of the High Qing era in the history of gender relations is to consider demographics, especially the growing competition over status and the rapid upward and downward mobility facing the people of the eighteenth century. The struggle for success placed particular strains on relationships between men and women, creating obsessive dialogues between wives and husbands, mothers and sons.

Finally, we will observe that during this unique era in Chinese history, educated women writers began to identify themselves as emblems of that historic time—as living proof of the fullest realization of the Manchu civilizing project.[15] Jin Wengying is one example.

Despite the special character of the High Qing era, in many respects it continued and expanded earlier shifts in gender relations identified in Dorothy Ko's pathbreaking work,[16] marking the "late imperial era" as a single unit in the history of Chinese women. Ko's analysis of the emergence of a women's writing culture in the late Ming stresses the continuities linking the High Qing period with the century that preceded it. She shows how the late Ming began a process of economic transformation that fundamentally altered the social relation of the sexes in late imperial China. This process of economic transformation persisted almost without interruption after the Manchu conquest, continuing the Ming trends of more urbanization, more print culture, more books for women, more published work by women, and more discussion about companionate marriage and about intellectual companionship between women and among men and women. In sum, Ko's findings illuminate the greatest shift of all in the premodern history of Chinese women: the emergence of female writers as legitimate, powerful aesthetic and even philosophical voices.

The power of the female writing voice in late imperial times contrasts sharply with its weakness during the Song era (960–1279), a problem recently noted in Patricia Ebrey's meticulous study of women and marriage in Song times.[17] Whereas in most respects scholars of late imperial history consider the Song the source of China's "early modernism," the absence of prominent women writers in the gentry families of the Song era calls our attention to sharp cultural breaks that separate the late Ming and Qing periods from the Song. In other words, the late imperial era by one measure—the rise of women writers—marks a distinctive and unitary phase in the history of gender relations in China. Nonetheless, important differences distance High Qing society from the late Ming urban culture that gave rise to it, and to these we now return.

Qing State Policies Affecting Women and the Family

The Manchus conquered China in 1644 and at once began to issue edicts setting standards for female conduct and gender relations. In that some of these policies continued and expanded programs established in earlier dynasties, they seem to signify the Manchus' earnest commitment to Confucian ideals of governance. Mark Elvin, for example, has shown that in promoting Confucian ideals among commoners, the Qing government brought to culmination state programs, long established under previous dynasties, that honored virtuous women.[18] The Manchus' most famous policy on women was their enthusiastic support for the cult of the "chaste widow" (*jie fu*). Significantly, the court practice of honoring chaste widows was begun under an earlier non-Han dynasty, the Mongol Yuan, in 1304 and continued in Ming times.[19] By the end of the High Qing period, the "widow chastity cult" and its grand stone arches (Fig. 1) had become an emblem of Manchu rule, especially in the Jiangnan area.[20]

Government campaigns to promote female chastity, which began in earnest in the Ming, were based on a system of rewards in which leaders of local communities were asked to nominate exemplary women and send their names, along with a brief biographical sketch, to the county magistrate for consideration for imperial honors. To be eligible for recognition as a chaste widow in High Qing times, a woman had to be widowed before the age of 30 *sui* and remain celibate past the age of 50. If the evidence supporting her case passed muster at the capital, where it was examined at the Board of Rites, her family might be rewarded with a commendation written in the emperor's elegant calligraphy, which could be displayed at the entrance to their home. In some cases, the woman's family members or, if appropriate, community leaders were given a sum of money to construct a monumental stone arch

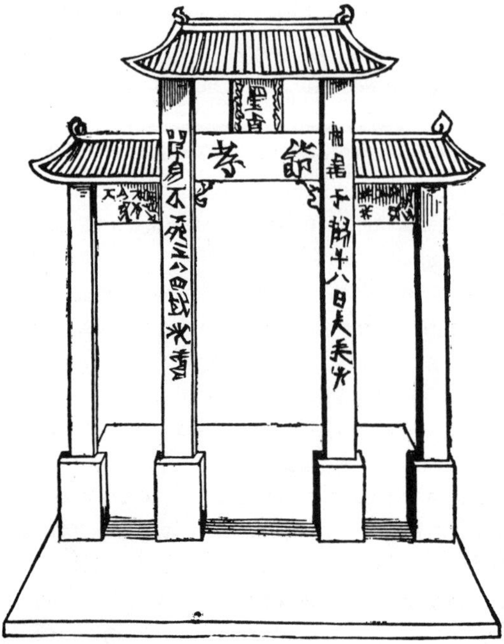

Fig. 1. Stone arch honoring a chaste widow. From Doolittle 1867, 1: 111.

honoring her. The names of all women so honored were inscribed on special lists in shrines to honor the "celebrated officials and local worthies."[21]

During the eighteenth century, the court reviewed thousands of petitions from around the realm each year, granting chaste-widow honors to thousands of Jiangnan women. Between 1644 and 1736, 6,870 Jiangnan widows received imperial honors for their fidelity.[22] In 1733, 120 widows were recognized in Suzhou alone; Jiangsu province in 1749 reported over 200 granted imperial commendations.[23] The High Qing emperors, obsessed with extending the reward system to commoner families and annoyed that elite households were monopolizing it, sponsored special drives exhorting county magistrates to seek out humble commoner widows who could be honored publicly for their virtue.[24] Women from elite families, it was pointed out, already stood to collect honorific titles through their male relatives.[25]

Although the Manchus' commitment to promoting chaste widowhood in the commoner population cannot be doubted, they were not blindly following imperial precedent. In fact, they were selective about the womanly values they wished to encourage. For example, they actively discouraged a local custom dramatizing widow fidelity: suicide by young widows proclaiming their wish to "follow the husband in death" (*xun si*), which in Ming times was admired as a noble display of a woman's fidelity.[26] According to Manchu critics, and indeed by the evidence of countless biographies, widow suicides were often impelled not by fidelity, but by despair. A twice-married woman was considered "unfaithful" and dishonorable, according to Confucian teachings. Consequently if a young widow's in-laws decided to marry her off again, she faced triple jeopardy: the loss of her children's security as members of their patriline; the prospect of a distinctly inferior match, since a previously married woman was not an acceptable partner for families who could afford a never-married bride; and her personal humiliation and moral failure. The many other motives for widow suicide are easy to imagine: loneliness, fear of hardship, unwillingness to face the burdens of caring for a dead husband's aging parents, abusive in-laws, or even the conviction that as a wandering ghost a dead woman could take revenge on living persons who had made her miserable.[27]

During the early Qing period, the Manchus were reluctant to embrace dramatic images of female suicide as emblems of fidelity. In fact, in the Ming-Qing transition, suicides by Han Chinese women were seen as heroic acts of self-sacrifice and dramatic displays of loyalism, inspiring men in the Ming resistance.[28] Meanwhile the Manchus' own tradition of human sacrifice was apparently being debated at court during the first few decades of Qing rule; until the early 1660's, the wives and concubines of Manchu princes were honored for following their husbands in death.[29]

By the High Qing era, however, times had changed. Female suicide was no longer associated with Ming loyalism, and Qing rulers continued to honor female martyrs who died resisting rape, but they declared themselves in firm opposition to widow suicide. A widow who killed herself, concluded the High Qing emperors, was in violation of her wifely commitment to serve her husband's family. Coerced or "voluntary," widow suicide threatened the family system that the Qing government wanted to nurture. The Yongzheng emperor argued in an eloquent edict of 1728 that widow suicide was a cowardly way to escape Confucian family duties. A truly virtuous widow, he intoned, should remain alive to serve the patriline into which she had married.[30]

High Qing campaigns for chaste widowhood complemented other Qing imperial programs promoting the material welfare and social stability of the Chinese family. In addition to providing the preindustrial world's most effective and efficient famine relief,[31] the High Qing government rewarded local leaders who endowed institutions to secure and sustain family relationships. An imperial edict of 1724 ordered the construction of orphanages in every major city in the realm,[32] and the first home for indigent chaste widows, founded in Suzhou in 1774, touched off a movement that spread rapidly throughout the Lower Yangzi region.[33]

High Qing state policies promoting and protecting Confucian family values were implemented in a legal framework designed to reinforce family relationships. The Qing code was primarily a criminal code, not a civil code, yet its provisions regulated both kin relations and sexual behavior. One of the best-known examples of this is the 1646 law, studied by Vivien Ng, which narrowed the definition of rape by setting new rigorous standards for evidence of physical resistance on the part of the victim.[34] The Qing criminal code also protected the status of the first wife and gave parents absolute power of life and death over daughters. A daughter whose behavior was judged so improper that it brought shame on her ancestors could be killed by her parents with impunity. Two men who strangled their daughters to death and another who caused his daughter's death by hacking her flesh all went unpunished under the provisions of this code.[35] The law also protected the family unit by forbidding the pawning, sale, and kidnapping or abduction of wives, concubines, and unmarried daughters from commoner families.[36]

Han Local Officials and Manchu State Policy

Most Qing state policies protecting the family won warm support from the Han Chinese elite, but some proved controversial. As the chaste-widow cult flourished, the Manchu government also launched sharp critiques of eroticism and decadence, including repeated bans on erotic singing and dancing by women in the palace precincts and, eventually, in the quarters of local officials as well. Further research in Manchu records may explain the political and cultural reasons for these bans, which Han local officials initially resisted. Perhaps the Manchus were shocked and offended by the culture of palace life they inherited from their Ming predecessors, especially by the hundreds, even thousands, of women who served as palace entertainers. Perhaps they viewed female entertainments as an insult to their strict martial codes and a threat to the warriors' cultural heritage they sought to preserve. Perhaps palace singers and dancers epitomized the greatest threat of all, the "feminizing" effects of Chinese culture. In any case, by the middle of the nineteenth century, female dancers and singers had vanished from the public processions that heralded the arrival of spring in every county seat (Fig. 2), and the hereditary caste of palace entertainers (*yue hu*) had been dismissed from Beijing to scatter through the northern countryside, where many lived as pariahs well into the twentieth century. Chapter 5 examines these policies and their implications for the commercial market in female sex and entertainment.

Only one Manchu critique of women's behavior truly backfired, and that was the futile attempt to end footbinding in Han Chinese families. Although

Fig. 2. Leading in the clay ox to welcome spring. From Nakagawa [1799] 1983: 62–63.

footbinding is often portrayed as (in Howard Levy's words) "a curious erotic custom,"[37] Chinese women in this period seem to have viewed it as a bodily marker of status, purity, and good breeding. As a result, early Qing rulers' vigorous attacks on the crushing and wrapping of the feet of young girls were simply ignored—in contrast to the enthusiastic reception Han families gave the chaste-widow cult. Ironically, Manchu women, who were strictly forbidden to bind their feet, took to wearing specially made shoes to conceal their natural feet above tiny platforms, which, protruding below the hem of the skirt, gave the illusion of the fabled "three-inch lotus."[38] Scholars have yet to explain why the Manchus were able to force Han Chinese men to wear a queue but were unable to end footbinding. Doubtless resistance from Han Chinese officials actually came from their wives, who refused to comply; moreover, since women who had bound feet were usually cloistered and women who did the binding did it in private, enforcing the proscription was impossible. It may also be that in the Qing period the meaning of bound feet shifted away from eroticism and toward social respectability. Late Ming women's poetry hints at a strong attraction, even an erotic response, to bound feet among upper-class women as well as men.[39] In Qing times, perhaps because of the erosion of the cult of *qing* and its displacement by familistic moralism, the erotic significance of bound feet for elite wives may have diminished. This change in meaning would help explain why the High Qing is the era when critics of bound feet began to appear among the Han scholarly elite.[40]

Footbinding aside, Qing state policies and laws affecting women were implemented by Han Chinese officials, who appear to have fully supported the values promoted at the Manchu court.[41] The distinguished local administrators Yin Huiyi (1691–1748), Wang Huizu (1731–1807), Chen Hongmou (1696–1771), Lan Dingyuan (1680–1733), and Huang Liuhong (1633–93)—all known for their prolific writings on statecraft—wrote texts explicitly addressing women's behavior and female morality. Yin's didactic *Record of Four Mirrors* (*Sijian lu*), which he completed in 1748, gives moral instruction to four groups: rulers (*jun*), ministers (*chen*), scholars (*shi*), and—without regard to status—women (*nü*). The fourth "mirror" for women is modeled after Liu Xiang's Han classic *Biographies of Exemplary Women* (*Lienü zhuan*). Yin records biographies of women judged worthy, pure and virtuous, wise and enlightened, or pure and heroic by their deeds, and he adds his own didactic commentary. His preface to this section explains that women must be included in an instruction book for "those who rule" because "responding to the circumstances of the moment, a woman may establish her merit and make a name for herself, so that her actions affect the whole of the country."[42] As this comment suggests, the stories Yin records are for those who "rule" well precisely because of good women. We see wives and consorts of powerful men who save them from disgrace, advise them in distress, counsel them in crisis, and bring them to their senses when their good judgment lapses.

Wang Huizu, best known to High Qing scholars as a distinguished legal expert, published a different kind of advice book: a homely set of family instructions modeled after earlier examples, full of guidelines and advice about how to manage a successful grand family and how to ensure the perpetuation of the patriline.[43] Named in honor of the two women who reared him,[44] the text includes several sections on relations between men and women in the family. One chapter, titled "Managing the Family," focuses exclusively on women because, Wang points out, "continuing the line requires the guidance of mothers."[45] Together these didactic works by Yin and Wang repeat the message that good women are crucial to the governance of the state and the management of the home.

Chen Hongmou, one of the great provincial governors of the High Qing period, published five collections of "Bequeathed Guidelines": homilies and lessons culled from classic works throughout history. He devoted an entire collection to instructions for women: *Bequeathed Guidelines for Instructing*

Women (*Jiaonü yigui*). This work was in great demand, reprinted in standard editions for use in the homes of elite families through the end of the Qing period.[46] Chen's all-purpose instruction book for women includes practical advice about managing the servants and controlling the temper side by side with idealized biographies of exemplary women of the past.[47] Lan Dingyuan, best known as a county magistrate, wrote a book titled *Women's Learning* (*Nü xue*) that was modeled after the classical text *Instructions for Women* (*Nü jie*), by the Han female scholar Ban Zhao. Echoing the sentiments found in other books on women by contemporaries, his preface explains that "the basis of the government of the empire lies in the habits of the people. The correctness of the habits of the people depends upon the orderly management of the family. The Way (*Dao*) for the orderly management of the family begins with women."[48] In a different vein, Huang Liuhong's classic advice book for county magistrates titled *A Complete Book Concerning Happiness and Benevolence* (*Fuhui quanshu*), widely used in High Qing times, shows that county magistrates had women's issues very much on their minds, mostly because they were expected to regulate as well as reward women's conduct.[49]

These advice books set forth the standards for women's conduct that the High Qing government and its officials idealized: Women must be absolutely chaste in their conduct and their words, work hard with their hands as producers in the peasant household economy (or act as responsible managers of servants in elite households), and take primary responsibility for rearing children and caring for elders. When required, they must go further, reaching out to rescue or advise faltering menfolk. The officials who wrote these hortatory advice books were equally outspoken when it came to female behavior that they deemed heterodox or threatening to the Confucian family and political order. Chen, Lan, and Huang all led campaigns to suppress women's Buddhist religious activities (see Chapter 7, "Piety").

Local officials promoted Qing family values to peasant households in other ways as well. They devised policies to encourage women's home handicraft labor through education, propaganda, and agricultural extension programs in the countryside. Like the Qing granary system, these programs were designed to level seasonal shortages of food and income by ensuring that farm families could keep their land (their *heng chan*, "enduring source of income"). The secret of success was to maximize the year-round value of female and child labor and to absorb labor idled during the off-season by teaching women how to spin and weave at home (see Chapter 6, "Work").

The Classical Revival and the 'Querelle des Femmes'

Qing government support for widow chastity and other government policies affecting women heightened awareness about women's proper roles among officials and commoners. In the scholarly world, concern about women's roles also developed in the course of a classical revival during the eighteenth century, when scholars turned to meticulous studies of early texts in search of the original meaning of the classics. This movement toward philological "empirical" research was probably a response to several factors: disenchantment with the perceived failures of late Ming philosophy, fear of Manchu censorship, a growing interest in ritual practice in its purest forms, and a nativist attraction to the fundamental principles of Han Chinese culture during a period of alien rule.[50] Whatever the motives of Han Chinese scholars, they were encouraged by the Qing court, which sponsored a series of massive scholarly projects culminating in the great Four Treasuries collection, which contained virtually every extant work in the four broad categories of classics, histories, philosophies, and belles lettres.[51] Similar projects in the provinces helped put unemployed scholars to work as compilers, editors, and analysts for local officials and wealthy patrons. The result was tomes of philological research yielding standard annotated editions of thousands of ancient texts, especially texts dating from Han times that were judged pure and untainted by the later influence of Buddhism.[52] Called the "Han learning" movement for this reason, and also dubbed the "textual research" movement because of its philological precision, this massive scholarly enterprise revived scholars' interest in works long neglected in Chinese scholarship, drawing a flurry of fresh attention to the ancient classics and philosophers.

In the course of classical research, scholars rediscovered the prominent female intellectuals of the past. The most brilliant philosopher of the High Qing period, Zhang Xuecheng—struck by these discoveries and shaken by the disparity between what he saw in the classical age and in his own time—wrote a history of "women's learning" in Chinese culture based entirely on his research in the early classics.[53] Zhang's unique essay presented detailed evidence of what he called a lost heritage of female erudition (see Chapter 4, "Writing").

Ironically, classical studies even led some High Qing scholars to criticize the widow chastity cult. Imperial commendations for chaste widows, scholars noted, had no precedent in Han times. (As we have observed, the earliest examples dated from the Yuan dynasty, a period of foreign rule.) To some classicists, the impassioned suicide of faithful widows, and especially the self-denial of bereaved young girls who had lost a fiancé and vowed their fidelity to his spirit, distorted the true meaning of classic ritual texts.[54]

Classical models of learned women posed other challenges to the values and assumptions of eighteenth-century writers. The classics obviously supported ideals dear to High Qing elite families, such as the importance of educating daughters and the celebration of motherly authority. But gifted female poets in ancient times often acted more like courtesans than like respectable young ladies. By the same token, the classic *Book of Poetry* (*Shi jing*) began with poems celebrating the moral authority of the king's wife, but other poems in the same work sounded to Qing ears like lewd invitations to promiscuity, and the apologetic commentaries written to explain their moral purpose were no longer convincing. Contemporaries began to ask, and to argue, about the purpose of educating women. If respectable women were educated and learned to write, what should be their proper voice? Who should be their audience?

The rediscovery of the educated woman in the classics posed yet another problem, given that female erudition itself embodied a critique of High Qing scholarly politics. To a reader like Zhang Xuecheng and to female readers who became acquainted with leading female intellectuals of the past in the course of the Han learning movement, learned women of the classical age exemplified a pure erudition untainted by the competition for degrees and office that had co-opted men's creative energies as China's bureaucratic state expanded. Hence male scholars of the High Qing era could invoke the image of female scholars of the past to criticize corruption and competition in their own society. Their critiques further empowered women writers, who were becoming increasingly conscious of their moral authority, grounded—or so it seemed—in the highest, purest forms of learning. In this manner the classical revival sparked a *querelle des femmes*—a debate about women—that invaded every quarter of Jiangnan's elite society in the High Qing period.[55]

Commercialization, Competition, and Mobility

The vigorous economic recovery that followed the defeat of the Ming dynasty in 1644 and the pacification of the last Ming-loyalist resistance movement in 1683 helped underwrite the scholarly renaissance of the High Qing. Despite ups and downs, China's economy grew steadily throughout the century of what Ho Ping-ti has dubbed *pax sinica*, "Chinese peace." As Ho's classic work on the High Qing era demonstrates, economic recovery spurred massive transformations, including interregional and overseas migration; a revolution in food-cropping accompanied by the expansion, intensification, specialization, and commercialization of agriculture; the proliferation of trade networks sustained by guilds and native banks in urban commercial centers; the rise of new protoindustries and household handicrafts, especially cotton; an increasing concentration of land in the hands of a landlord class favored by Qing dynasty tax policies; and a slow, steady rise in prices.

The Lower Yangzi, in late Ming times already the most highly commercialized and urbanized region in the empire, was the region least damaged by the Qing conquest and the first to rebound into the "peaceful age."[56] In a regional history of the eighteenth century, Susan Naquin and Evelyn Rawski point out that High Qing Jiangnan benefited especially from the rapid expansion of handicraft industries, the explosion of consumerism, and lavish imperial investment.[57] All these features of the Lower Yangzi economy had important implications for gender relations.

The rapid recovery of cotton cultivation and sericulture in Jiangnan accelerated the growth of textile industries and shrank the proportion of land planted in rice. This economic shift drew local officials' attention to the importance of female spinning and weaving in the farm economy and the government fisc. Scholars commissioned to compose policy statements on the administration of the farm economy marked Jiangnan as the imperial model for an ideal gender division of labor in the peasant household (see Chapter 6, "Work"). Jiangnan's exploding consumer economy made the managerial skills and investment strategies of wives and mothers the stuff of family legend. In fact, women themselves became a choice commodity in the entertainment districts of Yangzhou, Suzhou, and Nanjing, fancied by male consumers who paid handsomely to see them and valued by the families who used them as "money trees." Another effect of rising consumerism was extravagance in weddings, which required bride-giving families to lavish huge sums on chests stuffed with commodities that were paraded through the community en route to the bride's new home. As Chen Hongmou complained in a diatribe on dowries—obviously with Jiangnan society in mind—"even the poor will borrow heavily to give the appearance of having property, all for the sake of a single public display." And, he noted pointedly, families with daughters got the worst of this trend because families with sons could delay marriage plans while they saved money; a daughter had to be married young.[58]

In other words, women were central to household production and consumption patterns in Jiangnan's High Qing economic upswing, and rapid economic change called immediate attention to women's roles in production and consumption. Women were also the indirect beneficiaries of the Qing court's investment in the regional economy. Both the Kangxi and Qianlong emperors conducted grand southern tours, spending freely to improve the waterways on which they traveled, while the resulting flood control and irrigation works further increased the productivity of farm households. The High Qing emperors on tour took a particular interest in Jiangnan institutions that were important to women, thanks mainly to the empresses dowager and to the filial devotion they inspired in their sons. The Kangxi emperor's mother and the Qianlong emperor's mother both demanded the restoration and expansion of Jiangnan shrines that were central to women's spiritual lives in the High Qing era. The results for women were practical as well as spiritual (see Chapter 7, "Piety"). Peasant women earned income making spirit money for pilgrims, while crowds of women flocked to the shrines in a ceaseless spiritual quest.

Political, cultural, and economic changes in High Qing times brought concerns about women to the fore, especially in the Lower Yangzi region. Less obvious, however, is how other crucial changes may have affected gender relations. The remainder of this chapter examines three such areas of change: population growth, migration, and mobility.

Demographic Change

The most striking feature of the High Qing era is the demographic explosion. The government's most reliable data show the population growing from approximately 150 million in the early Qing period to perhaps 380 million by the mid-nineteenth century.[59] How these extraordinary changes affected women and gender relations can only be inferred. Improved economic conditions probably meant that more female infants were spared infanticide, releasing more women into the marriage market and enabling more men to marry.[60] In other words, rising life expectancy for females should have produced higher rates of marriage among ordinary commoners. This demographic response to economic prosperity cannot be verified with hard data.[61] But new research, by microdemographers using disaggregated data from genealogies and by cliometricians using new archival sources, suggests that population growth during the High Qing era was made possible by, and in turn promoted, improved life chances for Chinese women.

Above all, rapid population growth was the result of declining mortality. Liu Ts'ui-jung, using lineage data from a region outside Jiangnan, has stressed the broad role of wealthy lineages in providing social services and public goods to the community at large in High Qing times. Specifically with respect to the welfare of females, Liu noticed that as conditions improved, proliferating lineage "family instructions" included measures to prevent or discourage female infanticide.[62] Liu marks the end of these trends in the late eighteenth century, when the proportion of never-married persons began to rise along with mortality rates as birth rates fell.[63]

Research by Ted Telford also suggests that rates of marriage improved slightly in High Qing times.[64] In one study, Telford was able to show that marriage became slightly easier for poorer men at the bottom of the marriage market during the High Qing era. The difference in age at first marriage for lower-class and upper-class males declined by as much as two years (from five to three years) after the Manchu conquest.[65] Telford believes that the economic conditions responsible for the increasing supply of women in the marriage market continued to improve throughout the eighteenth century. As one measure of worsening conditions after the eighteenth century, by contrast, he cites a rise in the frequency of widow remarriage.[66] Even so, Telford finds that no matter how much marriage markets for men improved during the eighteenth century, women were still in such short supply that the population remained locked in a "marriage crunch" in which "the vast majority of all women were married and had begun having children as early as human female physiology could possibly have allowed" throughout the late imperial period, making it "extremely unlikely that more than a handful of women could have remained unmarried as Buddhist nuns, maids, prostitutes or 'marriage resisters' throughout their adult lives."[67]

Rising fertility among couples in the elite families of the lower Yangzi has been demonstrated by Stevan Harrell, using data from four Zhejiang lineages. Harrell's data show that as Jiangnan lineages accumulated wealth in the course of the eighteenth century, their richer members produced more and more children.[68] Moreover, rising fertility in elite families was accompanied by improved social conditions for poorer households, especially stronger safety nets for the poor. Harrell stresses, in other words, that demographic benefits were not confined to the rich alone. Even though richer lineage segments (*fang*) tended to hive off from poorer segments that were less demographically successful, lineage bonds continued to help poorer members of a lineage survive difficult times.

Qualitative evidence from Jiangnan, presented throughout this book, supports the fragmentary demographic evidence that mortality fell and life chances for women improved during High Qing times, at least until the end of the eighteenth century. "Societal investment" in women can be measured in the rising visibility of female writers in the documentary record (rising family investment), the growing attention officials paid to the female labor force (rising government investment), the development of institutions to care for widows and orphans (rising community investment), and the market for female entertainers (rising commercial investment). Attitudes toward women suggest the impact of these changing patterns. Accomplished girls became symbolic capital in elite families, treasured within the home for their lively talents and boasted about to others as an emblem of the family's scholarly credentials. The body of the slight twelve-year-old whose field labor was of negligible value could be put to work spinning, weaving, or—if she was pretty—singing and dancing. Parents could have it both ways: a daughter might be sent out as a maid while she was still a child, then recovered and married off for a suitable brideprice when she matured, entering her married life complete with a wardrobe and gifts from her former employer and the skills and experience gained in an upper-class household. In sum, even without a large base of quantitative data we can make a plausible case linking expanding economic opportunity to demographic shifts that placed women at the center of High Qing transformations in the Lower Yangzi region.

Migration and Mobility

The population explosion in High Qing times accompanied unprecedented population movement. People moved across regions as shifting cropping patterns opened new areas for cultivation; they moved up and down the social ladder as economic opportunities changed and competition for degrees and posts grew. Studies of mobility to date have focused on males, but anecdotal evidence reveals the impact of mobility on gender relations in High Qing Jiangnan.[69]

Migration gave men a double vision of women's roles and morals. At home, women were guarded for chastity, marriage, and reproduction of the family line. On the road or abroad, however, women became part of the traffic in sex and servitude. Therefore in respectable commoner families, parents kept daughters at home and sent sons out to work; wives and mothers remained behind when husbands and sons sojourned abroad.[70]

Male sojourning took many forms. Scholars and officials went sightseeing and traveled to academies and examination halls, in addition to going on the routine circuits that took them to jobs all over the empire. Merchants, artisans, and common laborers migrated to conduct business and seek employment. A man sojourning away from home tried to find relatives or friends or, failing that, lodging through a native-place association or guild that could help provide for his needs. These organizations supplied lodging, meals, health care, and even burial services. They also funded ritual and religious events and festival celebrations. Though little is known about the service staff, they were almost certainly men—cooks, coolies, medical practitioners, and servants—transported from their native place as indentured laborers or contract employees. In other words, native-place associations and guilds, another hallmark of High Qing Jiangnan, housed sojourning men of all classes.[71]

These vast networks of male migration had a contradictory effect on gender relations. On the one hand, they encouraged the rapid growth of sex and entertainment services for male clients and customers in the growing towns and cities of the Lower Yangzi. Having left their wives and daughters safely at home, men bought female company as they traveled. The rich sought out the pleasure boats of exclusive courtesans; the poor, the seamy quarters of cheaper prostitutes.[72] At the same time, migration by men raised the value of female chastity and seclusion, since the women left at home were required to carry on family responsibilities and to supervise the household economy. These mothers, wives, and daughters-in-law "managed everything." Their job was to combine income in cash and in kind from agricultural production and handicrafts and to supplement that with remittances from their menfolk in the city (if any arrived) so that children could be reared, property managed, elders cared for, and rituals conducted. It is no accident that the classical value "tranquillity" or "stillness" (*jing*) in women was much admired by High Qing scholars. *Jing* is one of many signs and symbols, like the widow chastity arch, marking women who served the patriline and were not sexually available to sojourning men.

Sojourning men appear constantly in elite women's writing, enabling us to see how the women imagined themselves at the still point that constituted home. The poet Wang Ren wrote this verse, thinking of her father while he served in a distant office:

> Tired of hearing the noise of this troubled world
> Fixing my gaze, I lean out from the high tower.
> Clouds mass, concealing a thousand peaks;
> Winds sweep, coloring ten thousand trees.
> Our flock of geese has straightened its ragged lines.*
> The nomad flute sings "make your way home."
> Tears spilling, I think of my stern father,
> On the cold frontier, traveling on his official duties, all alone.[73]

As Chapter 4 shows, poems "sent to my husband" (*ji wai*) balance loneliness against other feelings. Echoing classic poems by wives in times past, they upbraid absent husbands for debauchery and neglect of family responsibilities while asserting a wife's autonomy and moral authority. These powerful and ambivalent feelings about separation were imagined and voiced as women

* My brothers have all returned from their travels.

celebrated the Double Seven Festival. Rites of Double Seven, on the evening of the seventh day of the seventh lunar month, honor the Weaving Maid, who was fated to endure a lifetime of labor and separation, broken only by a brief yearly reunion with her beloved Cowherd on Double Seven. As if in counterpoint to wifely poems about the "seventh night," records of courtesans and entertainers who received sojourning men abroad weave the constant themes of transience and impermanence, vulnerability and abuse, through the stories of their lives. In all these ways, as the chapters that follow demonstrate, migration in High Qing times shaped women's literary imagination, constructing the tropes around which women built their emotional and spiritual lives and shaping in turn the emotional and material lives of the men who kept them company.

If migration was a constant, visible force shaping women's lives, mobility cast the shadow of anxieties that men and women of elite families shared. To understand these anxieties is to appreciate the risks every parent took launching children into volatile marriage markets and chancy examination competitions. How real were the risks? They become more palpable when we observe that the High Qing government systematically dismantled the last remaining status barriers in Chinese society, exposing the civil service system and the marriage market to new levels of competition. The remainder of this chapter examines the Qing policies redefining status hierarchies and considers one example from fiction to illustrate the psychological effects of these hierarchies on women.

For elite families, mobility via the civil service examination system was declining in the eighteenth century,[74] and recent research has stressed the downward slide of impoverished people as a telling underside of High Qing affluence.[75] However, among the poorest sectors of the population, mobility may actually have risen in High Qing times, thanks to two government policies. The first was a drive to eliminate the status category "hired laborer" from the Qing legal code; the second, an effort to emancipate households registered as hereditary pariahs.

Documents of the High Qing era show that wealthy households employed huge retinues of menial servants, an unknown proportion of whom worked in relationships of long-term dependency as virtual slaves.[76] The imperial court was the largest employer of slaves and servile persons, but official residences everywhere commanded the labor of "forests" of servants. For county magistrates, retinues of a hundred servants or more were common.[77] Wealthy merchants employed similar numbers. Even families of modest means (artisans, traders, small landlords) kept a small staff of servants—from one or two to several. According to one contemporary observer:

> In Nanjing it is customary, in households of the middle rank or above, that the wife does not personally take charge of accounts, nor does she personally wait on her parents-in-law. Instead, for the food and drink that must be served, for travel abroad in comfort, and for sewing and mending garments, the wife depends on servants. She employs male and female servants, and also female slaves, for all these tasks. Even in families that are poor and simple, with modest clothing and coarse food, scarcely able to provide for themselves, the wife will insist on having a female servant (*beinü*).[78]

Among these dependent laborers, two categories of persons received special treatment under the Qing legal code: long-term hired laborers (*gugong ren*) and slaves.[79] In the six-tiered status ranking system employed for determining punishments according to the Qing statutes, hired laborers and slaves sat on opposite sides of the critical line dividing respectable commoners (*liangmin*) from pariahs (*jianmin*).[80] The category *jian* in Qing times referred to people registered as pariahs in the local population records. They included slaves, persons engaged in what were considered polluting or degrading occupations (butchers, yamen runners, actors), and certain local outcast groups. Though the criteria defining these groups varied, all were subject to the same constraints in the early Qing period under laws inherited from Ming times: first, no descendants in the male line could sit for the civil service examinations or purchase a degree; second, no pariah male could marry a "respectable" (*liang*) woman. Customarily pariah women were not supposed to bind their feet, though anecdotal evidence shows that pariahs throughout the late Ming and early Qing period found ways to do so, at least in the Lower Yangzi region. As Chapter 5 shows, in the Lower Yangzi region courtesans rarely came from registered pariah households, and all Lower Yangzi courtesans serving elite customers bound their feet.

Hired laborers were counted as the lowliest of commoners; slaves belonged to the pariah population. Above hired laborers, in ascending order, were the ordinary commoners, degree-holding scholars without official titles, titled officials, and finally the imperial family and the emperor.[81]

The Manchus, whose political system relied on a clear distinction between slaves and commoners,[82] tried to eliminate the ambiguous status group "hired laborer" entirely.[83] In a series of cases building on a Ming law of 1587, High Qing courts sought to clarify the precise distinction between *liangmin* and *jianmin*. A key ruling in 1727 specified the types of laborers who should be classified as slaves under the law. These included "house-born slaves" (*jiasheng nupu*) belonging to Han people, all persons sold into slavery with a government-certified "red" contract (*yinqi*), and, for the sake of consistency, all persons sold as slaves prior to 1727 with "white" contracts (those without an official seal). From that time on, the edict stated, any long-term laborer sold without an officially stamped red contract naming him a slave would be considered a hired laborer under the law.[84] Persons sold with white contracts naming a low wage and a short term of service were to retain the legal status of hired laborer.[85] Further rulings in 1742 reiterated these standards, stressing that they accorded with definitions of slavery among the Manchus found in Banner regulations.[86] By 1788, the category "hired laborer" had been eliminated from the statutes altogether, and even persons whose labor was under long-term contract were classified simply as respectable commoners under the law. This made the line separating pariahs from commoners sharper than ever.[87]

None of these changes in hired laborers' status affected women in indentured servitude. In fact, legal limits on the enslavement of males may have driven up the cost of male slave labor, making the purchase of female slaves more desirable.[88] Female slaves were generally sold with white, not red, contracts, which the government did not regulate; whenever a female slave came before a court of law, her case was judged as if she had been sold under white contract.[89] In the 1730's, the vice-minister of the Board of Punishments, Zhang Zhao (1691–1745), complained about the difference between male and female slaves. He noted that, like a male slave, a female sold on the market became the property of the buyer, who was then responsible for arranging her marriage. However, whereas male slaves were generally married to other slaves in their masters' employ, a female slave could be freed and sent out of the household to marry a nonslave.[90] Zhang Zhao argued that persons who purchased females as slaves should be required to use red contracts so that their ownership claims could be protected in a court of law and so that the legal status of slave women in marriage markets would be clear.[91]

Zhang Zhao's concerns about the ambiguous status of unmarried female slaves are illustrated in the great mid-century novel *Dream of the Red Chamber* (*Hong lou meng*). Xiren, Baoyu's chief maid in the novel, is a highly intelligent body servant.[92] Her status as a slave is contrasted explicitly with that of her mother's sister's daughter, a free commoner. In one scene Xiren, angry because a visit from her cousin has attracted her master's attention, exclaims bitterly, "Because I have the misfortune to be a slave . . . does that mean that all my relations ought to be slaves too? I suppose you think every pretty girl you see is just waiting to be bought so that she can be a servant in your household!" Her master Baoyu becomes distraught when Xiren alludes to her own pending departure for marriage: "Today I heard my mother discussing it with my elder brother. They want me to hold out this one year more, then next year they will see about buying me out of service." When Baoyu questions her, Xiren continues: "I'm not one of your house-born slaves, my family lives elsewhere.[93] I'm the only member of my family away from home. There's no future for me here. *Naturally* I want to rejoin them." Baoyu protests, but Xiren informs him that the law applies even inside his mansion: "A bond is a bond. When their term of service has ended, you *have* to let people go. You can't force them to stay in service for ever and ever—especially in a household like yours."[94] Although slaveholders expected to arrange marriages for "house-born" offspring of their own slaves, they might defer to the wishes of the family from whom a slave was purchased, if those wishes were known.

The novel also provides some insight into the emotional effects of slavery as Xiren reflects on her ambiguous plight. She hates her parents for selling her in the first place; to them she declares her refusal ever to return to her natal family and claims to enjoy her current status: "I'm not beaten and sworn at all day long and . . . I'm fed and clothed as well as the masters themselves." But this defiant statement is belied by a later outburst in which, after telling her mother not to bother to buy back her freedom, Xiren cries, "Why don't you just pretend that I'm dead, then you won't need to think about buying me out any more?"[95]

Xiren's ambivalence mirrors the ambiguity of her social status. As an inside maid who serves as personal attendant to members of the Jia family, she is part of the elite of the household servants, "a cut above the free daughters of poorer households outside."[96] The Jias' relationship to Xiren is likewise ambiguous, if hardly as wrenching. On the one hand, despite her claims, they have purchased her for life. They own her and could in theory (as Baoyu points out) refuse to permit her relatives to redeem her for any sum. On the other hand, Xiren is well aware that the Jias' high status and their reluctance to abuse their power mean that, in her words, they would "*never* be willing" to break up someone else's family; they could even be expected to give her back to her family without compensation of any kind.[97] Xiren's plight dramatizes the contradictions of female slavery in the best of circumstances. The Jias are fond of her. They feel a moral obligation to accede to her mother's wishes, and they would not deign to accept money from such a lowly family, even to buy out a lifetime contract. Xiren, for her part, is well aware of the Jias' position. She even taunts Baoyu with the paradoxical power her family holds over her fate. Yet she can hardly take comfort in leaving the opulent Jia household to become an ordinary commoner's wife. Her confused and bitter outcry underscores the ironic plight of female slaves in the best of families.

In the end, Xiren's fate rests not on a contract but on the Jias' sense of noblesse oblige. The government did not regulate slave women's contracts, as we have seen. State law nevertheless protected the coercive power of slave owners over slave women. Had the Jias chosen *not* to return her, Xiren would have been at great risk had she run away or been forcibly removed by her family. A female slave who ran away could be punished with a beating of 80 strokes, increased to 100 if she married secretly. The same punishment befell complicitous commoners, even if they were the girl's own parents.[98]

Other problems involving female slaves and their relationship to their owners drew the attention of High Qing lawmakers. Abuse of female slaves by women in elite families was a recurrent problem, the example of the Jias notwithstanding. A Kangxi regulation that allowed a mere fine as punishment if an official's wife caused the death of a slave was finally repealed in 1740 on the grounds that it abetted brutality by female slave owners toward their slaves.[99] Sexual abuse of female slaves and their daughters by male slaveholders was also recognized as a problem, even though an unmarried slave woman was considered the sexual property of a male master, who could not be punished for having sexual intercourse with her.[100] In theory a female slave could resist rape. In practice, however, if she injured her master while resisting, she was punishable under severe laws concerning slaves who struck and injured their owners.

Under High Qing law, commoner females were banned from the slave market. No female commoner could legally be sold into slavery, whether on contract or by verbal agreement. However, since the government permitted the buying and selling of women with white contracts (that is, without official supervision), it seems clear that young girls whose backgrounds were never checked could be rented or purchased by the lot. For example, in the novel *Dream of the Red Chamber* (*Hong lou meng*), a representative from the Jia household is sent out to Suzhou to hire twelve young girls to perform opera at the Jia home.[101] In the late seventeenth century the Suzhou scholar Tang Zhen (1630–1704) observed, "Many people in Wu sell their sons or daughters to distant places. Attractive boys are sold as actors, ugly ones as slaves. Beautiful girls are sold as concubines, ugly ones as slaves, in such numbers that they have flooded the realm."[102]

Individual sales of young girls are described in satiric poems like the following:

> The young female prostitute Jiang
> Was sold here from the Zhang River region.
> They stripped her to the waist
> To expose her lute-string fingers.*
> They opened her eyes and peered

*The sleeves of a young girl's gown covered her hands.

To make sure she had no disease.
She was bought like an animal for slaughter.
She was sold for a measure of corn.[103]

A secret memorial submitted to the Kangxi emperor in 1707 reported at length on the traffic in women in Suzhou, which involved officials and wealthy merchants. This coercive traffic, described as *chu piao qiang yao* ("issuing a receipt to force the sale of the one you want"), fetched adult commoner women for prices as high as 450 taels, commoner girls for 140 taels, and slave girls for 70 taels.[104] Although the court strongly condemned the practice of "forcible sale" (*qiang mai*), the large amounts of money changing hands made legal cases difficult to try. Parents who could show they had sold a daughter under financial duress were treated lightly in the Qing code, and even a husband who sold his wife (an act legally subject to a penalty of 100 strokes with a heavy bamboo rod) could be let off if his poverty was extreme.[105]

Anecdotal evidence shows that girls of all ages were susceptible to sale or forcible servitude. In 1744, during a spiral of rising grain prices, a report from the judicial commissioner of Jiangsu province lamented that famine was causing poor households and smallholders to "pawn their young sons to 'great houses' and sell their betrothed daughters to wealthy families." Parents who believed they had only pawned a son's labor were often dismayed to find that when their circumstances improved, they were unable to obtain the child's release.[106] Wu Enzhao, *juren* of 1752 serving as a Zhejiang circuit intendant in Jinhua, Quzhou, and Yanzhou prefectures, tried to ban female infanticide and also to rescue "forcibly detained maids" (*gubei*) in his area.[107] Specialists in human traffic, part of Suzhou's class of "monopolists" (*tun hu*), kept their eyes out for comely girls in poor households who could be purchased and reared in their own homes, then sold to a distant province as concubines or slaves.[108]

Elaborate kidnapping rings supplied the slave market. In some cases professional agents used drugs to subdue young victims before moving them quickly across provincial lines, according to a report filed from Suzhou by Chen Hongmou in 1758: "One type of kidnapper from outside this area uses drugs to subdue his victims. When he meets a child, he gives a dose of the drug, sometimes concealed inside a bun or cake, and when the child has fallen under its spell, he leads the child away and is never seen again."[109] Other kidnappers were rapists; still others were interested in collecting ransom for children from wealthy families.[110] Violent threats to vulnerable women were so pervasive that when the first social institutions to care for "chaste widows" were established, founders stated explicitly that they wished to protect widows from kidnapping and bullying.[111] Finally, although a commoner who was forcibly sold into slavery risked a permanent "fall" (*xian*) into the ranks of the pariah population,[112] families with wealth and influence could redeem a kinswoman through legal action,[113] or they could relinquish their own prerogatives as slaveholders, as the Jias were expected to do.

In sum, the law protected respectable female commoners from sale into slavery, but in practice wives and daughters could be sold as slaves by relatives or by kidnappers. Although new safety nets created by High Qing law prevented laboring men from being classified as slaves, the barrier protecting women of commoner status from slipping into the ranks of pariahs remained fragile and was easily overridden by the pressures of the market, poverty, violence, and coercion. As a result of the changes in Qing law, male hired laborers may have been able to compete more successfully on the commoner marriage market, but the marriage of females sold as slaves or servants remained subject to the whim of their employers.

Sale into slavery was a downward slide threatening even respectable women during the eighteenth century. Yet the High Qing was also an era when lowborn females could shed their pariah status and move upward, mainly by marrying a commoner as his concubine. In addition, the High Qing government instituted a procedure for manumission to enable persons born as pariahs to pass into commoner society. Both these High Qing avenues to upward mobility for women are significant because the only legal barrier in High Qing marriage markets was the line separating *liangmin* (respectable commoners) from *jianmin* (pariahs).[114]

In 1723 the Yongzheng emperor published his first edict "emancipating" the pariah *yuehu*, or music households, suppliers of female entertainment to the court and officials in local government.[115] In the series of emancipation proclamations that followed, he named eight additional pariah groups and specified the steps required for them to shed their pariah status and move into the commoner registers. The cumulative effect of these edicts and legal changes may have been less significant than the slow erasure of old status barriers by economic and social change. Blurred lines between servile persons and respectable persons are features of High Qing rule that scholars of the period have long recognized. Angela Leung (Liang Qizi) argues that the High Qing era marks a watershed in changing attitudes toward pariah groups, who no longer commanded sympathy as the "deserving poor." She attributes the success of charitable institutions to popular concerns about saving respectable commoners from falling into pariah status, not to empathy for those "below."[116]

This brief survey of demographic and social change in High Qing Jiangnan underscores three themes. First, the rapid growth of the economy, especially the handicraft sector, made efficient use of female labor a high priority for both statesmen and ordinary commoner families. Second, in a society where the few remaining class barriers were disappearing, the family was the basic unit of upward mobility. Third, though class structure posed no legal barrier to mobility up or down, women were more vulnerable than men to falling from commoner to pariah or slave status; similarly, women were more likely to move upward from pariah to commoner status, through marriage or concubinage. Finally, the blurring of status barriers destabilized comfortable assumptions, feeding the tensions and anxieties of this competitive age.

Exemplary Women as Emblems of High Qing Rule

Whether contemporaries recognized women's fluid status in High Qing culture or not, it probably contributed to the carefully constructed self-presentation of elite women as *guixiu*—ladies cultivated in the inner apartments—and to their celebration of themselves in poems and publications. Evidence for the central place of the *guixiu* in High Qing discourse comes from descriptions of exemplary women in official documents, the literary works of scholars, and the writings of women themselves. It is most striking beyond China's heartland, as Qing officials' policies and writings spread their message about womanly conduct to non-Han peoples in the borderlands. The chaste-widow campaign, for instance, became part of High Qing acculturation projects designed to bring autonomous tribes into the mainstream of provincial governance (*gaitu guiliu*). Chen Hongmou, that staunch promoter of Han family values, was especially inspired to proselytize in the borderlands. While serving as treasurer of Yunnan province in the 1730's, he printed more than ten thousand copies of a tract on household management for Han and non-Han households, and his dedication to spreading word of the chaste-widow cult on the frontier is especially noticeable.[117] In other words, High Qing writers were inclined to judge the civilizing process in minority areas by the conduct of the women there.

As the policies of the High Qing government's robust bureaucratic state reached women across social hierarchies and ethnic groups, and as the chaste-widow cult became an integral part of the Manchus' ambitious plan to build a unified empire out of diverse local cultures,[118] women writers themselves embraced imperial rhetoric. The woman anthologist and poet Wanyan Yun Zhu, whose work we shall read at length as we continue and whose honor is celebrated by Jin Wengying in the lines that opened this chapter, cast herself as both a symbol of the Manchu civilizing project in the borderlands and the guardian of Confucian morals in the culture of the heartland.

3 *The Life Course*

TURNING AWAY FROM THE hallmarks of the High Qing, we now begin to address the individual and family context in which gender relations were negotiated, beginning with the life course. Among elite families in High Qing Jiangnan, special markers of the female and male life courses guided parents as they brought up their children.[1] These same markers were used by individuals in memoirs to chart their lives and to position themselves in relation to others. During the eighteenth century, the intensifying struggle for security and success had different effects on the life courses of men and women. For elite men, the struggle turned each marker into another ominous sign of potential failure. For elite women, by contrast, the passage of life's markers held out a growing promise: the end of child-bearing, a retreat from household responsibilities, and spiritual renewal.

Life's markers flew by more rapidly for women than for men, at least before the age of 50, because by convention a girl's life was measured in units of 7 years, a boy's in units of 8.[2] Thus, boys were expected to lose their baby teeth at 8 *sui*,* girls at 7; boys reached puberty at 16, girls at 14; full sexual

*Age in Chinese reckoning was calculated by taking the lunar year of one's birth as year one and adding a year at each lunar New Year's Day. On average, therefore, a Chinese child is about a year older in *sui* than she would be if her birthdays were counted by

maturity was attained by males at 24, but by females at 21. Parents in Jiangnan's elite households expected that boys' bodies would mature more slowly than girls', while girls' young bodies were watched closely for signs of fecundity. All of this made sense of observable disparities between males and females as their bodies mature. *The Yellow Emperor's Classic of Internal Medicine* (*Huangdi neijing*), the standard reference for these notions of aging, was familiar to Jiangnan readers through the work of Xu Dachun, in High Qing times the region's most respected authority on traditional Chinese medicine.[3]

At the peak of her physical development at 28 *sui*, a woman was nearly at the midpoint of her childbearing years. By contrast, men did not reach their prime until 32. Thus by mid-life, these different ways of marking time had produced radically different conceptions of aging. Physical decay for women was thought to commence at 35 *sui*. When a woman reached 42, her hair began turning gray, and at 49 she ceased to menstruate. Men's bodies, by contrast, did not begin to deteriorate until 40. Not until 48 did a man's hair begin to gray, and only at 56 did his sexual energy start declining. At the age of 64, men were finally losing teeth and hair.[4] In an ironic contrast with contemporary Western medical practice, the Chinese physician took no interest in the female body after menopause, whereas Chinese medicine carefully charted the aging process for men over 40. During the nearly 25-year period after age 40, males enjoyed—or suffered—an extra decade or so of productive social and cultural life.

These different ways of marking age for men and women complicated gender relations in the elite family system, which in theory was designed so that married couples would go through life together in a partnership, like the mandarin ducks to whom they were always compared. The mean age difference between husbands and wives in elite families of this period was slight, perhaps three years: most girls in elite families were married out between the ages of 17 and 18 *sui*, with boys marrying slightly later, at 20 or 21.[5] Yet because husbands and wives marked the passage of time differently, they did not "go through life together" at all. A wife at menopause was likely to find her spouse, aged roughly 53, at the make-or-break point in his career, just when his aging parents needed the most care and when the couple's children were engaged in their own life-course passages: early education, marriage, childbearing, or examination taking. However, beliefs about the responsibilities and privileges associated with each stage of the male and female life courses

---

the Western pattern. A courtesan of thirteen *sui* is properly considered twelve "years old." The situation is more complicated when calculating age at marriage. A female born late in a lunar year who marries early in a lunar year is nearly two years younger, by Western reckoning, than her "age at marriage" measured in *sui*.

and the sheer number of persons linked into networks of shared responsibility by the grand-family system often made it possible for elite women to negotiate this final turning point in their lives with grace.

Biological or medical measures of the life course were proxies for moral development in both ritual and law, as Ann Waltner has shown. In ritual texts, males and females charted specific paths to moral and intellectual development, following the biological markers of each phase in the life course. In the criminal code, children (defined as prepubescent males and females) were subject to special consideration regardless of their sex. Thus, as Waltner astutely notes, "the generative powers of the universe [depended] on the maintenance of clear boundary lines between male and female. And those boundaries [were] established well before puberty."[6] At each stage of the life course, a child was expected to assume more of the responsibilities and roles of an adult, and those responsibilities and roles were always specific to gender.

The Life Course of Elite Men

The experience of the male life course is described in an elegant essay composed in 1793 by the Changzhou scholar Hong Liangji. Inviting his readers to compare the passing of a lifetime to the passing of a single day, Hong unfolds the metaphor by playing on the symbolic possibilities of yang and yin, signifying morning/sun and evening/moon, good/positive and evil/negative, strength/youth and weakness/old age. In this reading of the male life course, the day/life begins at dawn:

> The cock's first crow marks the awakening, the time of infancy, when a man's every thought is good. He is bursting with life, anticipating all the good things he wants to do, as if he were going to leap out of bed without stopping to put on his clothes.
>
> His youth is the morning. The sun has risen, and he is up and about. At this point in his life, even the very serious man will be less intense, the introspective man less withdrawn. The peasant leaves for his fields, the scholar sets off to school, the trader marks prices on his wares, all skipping and jumping as they go. Even the sickly man suffers less during these morning hours than he will later, when night falls.
>
> Noon is his prime of life. He finishes his meal and goes bustling in and out, tending to his business with gusto. But as noon approaches, yin and yang also come into balance. This is because at noon the spirit and life energy a man is born with must be sustained with food and drink from this world.[7] The spirit and life energy a man is born with are yang, and in a yang condition good thoughts prevail. That is why a person who has stored up anger in his stomach or concealed hatred deep in his heart may pass a night in sleep and arise

feeling some relief, his anger slightly abated, his hatred somewhat undone. After one night's sleep, a man may even leave these feelings entirely behind, not because he has consciously calmed his anger or dissolved his hatred, but because the good thoughts that follow the peaceful dawn overcome anger and hatred: yang overcomes yin. However, the things of this world, the food and drink on which we increasingly rely as the day wears on, are yin, and from yin noxious thoughts arise. Rowdy fights and wild brawls always break out after too much eating and drinking.

Next comes the stage of life that Confucius called the "robust years when our physical powers are at their peak, and we must guard against quarrelsomeness."[8] This is the point when yin overcomes yang. Just as one day's activities are settled in the afternoon, so the achievements of a lifetime are fixed in a man's robust years. Once those years are over, although a few individuals may rise during the waning period of their lives and some great deeds may be carried out as the sun begins to sink, such cases are exceptional and cannot be counted on.

At last evening falls. The waning portion of the day is like the years after 50 and 60, the final portion of our lives. Now the man who has been strong and vigorous grows weak; the man whose mind was sharp and keen becomes forgetful. He rests quietly in the women's apartments. These are the years of decline, when the man who once charged headlong into the fray suddenly stops to calculate his losses, and the person who used to proceed without a backward glance pauses to consider the past and future consequences of his deeds. Melancholy people become more obsessed with their worries; sickly people take a turn for the worse.

If we look back now at the man who began the day at sunrise, we seem to be observing an entirely different individual. Of course, this is not because one man can turn himself into two. It is because the changing balance of yin and yang, dawn and dusk, change us so.

This is how a passing day resembles a passing life. If we can accept with equanimity the events of a single day, the events of a lifetime will surely bring nothing to daunt us.[9]

Hong Liangji's idea that a man's life proceeds in stages echoes his studies in ritual and philosophy, especially passages from the *Book of Rites* (*Li ji*), the *Analects*, and *Mencius*. In his youth, under his mother's watchful eye, he learned by heart this text from the *Book of Rites*:

> When one is ten years old, we call him a boy; he goes out
> to school.
> When he is twenty, we call him a youth; he is capped.
> When he is thirty, we say "He is at his maturity"; he has a wife.
> When he is forty, we say, "He is in his vigor"; he is employed
> in office.

> When he is fifty, we say, "He is getting grey"; he can discharge all the duties of an officer.
> When he is sixty, we say, "He is getting old"; he gives directions and instructions.
> When he is seventy, we say, "He is old"; he delegates his duties to others.
> At eighty or ninety, we say of him, "He is very old"; . . .
> At a hundred, he is called a centenarian and has to be fed.[10]

In the *Analects* Hong encountered Confucius's own reflections on the male life course, which stopped short of the ominous years after 70 and focused instead on moral maturation:

> At fifteen, I had my mind bent on learning.
> At thirty, I stood firm.
> At forty, I had no doubts.
> At fifty, I knew the decrees of Heaven.
> At sixty, my ear was an obedient organ for the reception of truth.
> At seventy, I could follow what my heart desired, without transgressing what was right.[11]

At the start Hong's essay echoes Confucius's confidence. His use of the phrase "peaceful dawn," for instance, invokes a passage in *Mencius* celebrating the original goodness of human nature.[12] However, Hong's concerns in his essay were entirely contemporary, and they were not optimistic. He wrote the essay just a few years before committing an act of lèse-majesté that nearly cost him his life. In 1799 he sent a letter, addressed indirectly to the recently enthroned Jiaqing emperor, decrying the official corruption and material decadence in the society around him and suggesting that their causes be sought in the court itself. Thus Hong Liangji's account of the male life course, while couched in timeless classical metaphors, actually sketches the bleak career trajectory facing scholarly men in the mid-Qing period. He describes the erosion of youthful idealism by aggressive competition, overwhelming debt, and physical indulgence—all inescapable facts of life for elite men in eighteenth-century Jiangnan.

For Hong Liangji and many leading social critics of the time, the "women's chambers" (*guige*) were a haven in a complex, brutal world.[13] Elite men faced a daily confrontation with material corruption (the "dusty world," as they so often called it); elite women were protected from it. Instead, women occupied the still point around which men's active lives were constructed. The image of the women's apartments as a timeless realm shielded from the cares and evils of this world, a retreat to which overstressed men might escape or retire, is a powerful trope in writings by men about women during the eighteenth

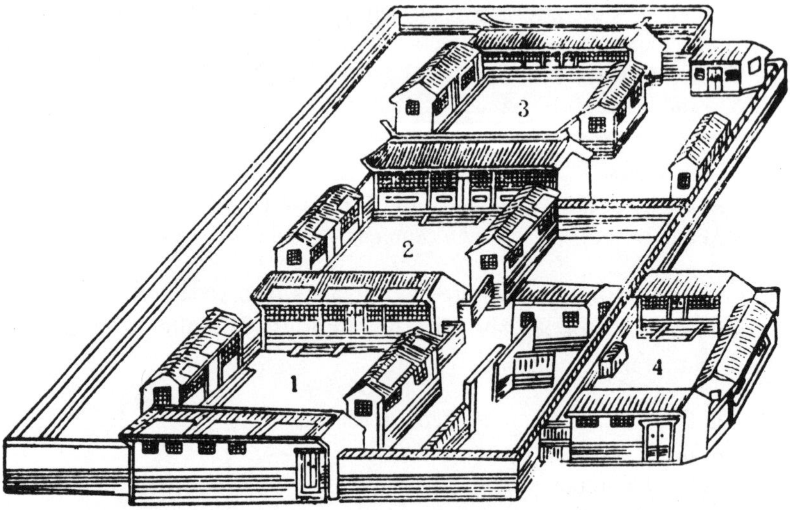

Fig. 3. Home of a *guixiu* family, showing (1) the outer courtyard, for receiving visitors; (2) the inner courtyard, where the daily activities of the household took place (study, record keeping, consultation, recreation); (3) the deeply recessed "inner apartments" reserved for women; and (4) the servants' quarters. From C. A. S. Williams 1976: 23.

century.[14] For many men resisting the pressures of scholarly careers, women appeared as guardians of stability, order, and purity. The women's quarters, secluded behind courtyards and doorways deep in the recesses of the house (Fig. 3), offered a refuge from a world of flux, chaos, and corruption. Women nurtured and tutored men when they were young, tended them when they became sick, and cared for them when they grew old. When a man holding office faced devastating financial losses or difficult political decisions, only his wife's disinterested advice and frugal savings could save his career. Although a man might often be called away to duty or might die prematurely, he could count on his wife or widow to care for his aging parents and his vulnerable children.

Men like Hong Liangji—reared by a widow himself—suffered unusual stress because they were expected both to strive for career success and to achieve moral self-realization at a time when both were increasingly elusive.[15] Autobiographical writings by men of the High Qing period suggest that they were giving up—abandoning the moral quest in favor of the practical career.[16] During the eighteenth century, learning was often seen as a pragmatic rather than a moral exercise whose primary goal was to win high office. Young men were told that their main responsibility was not seeking moral self-realization, but bringing prosperity to their descendants and honor to their ancestors. Doing so required first winning a civil service degree, then capturing an official post.

The sensitive Baoyu, hero of *Dream of the Red Chamber*, touches readers' hearts with his yearning for the aesthetic companionship and emotional comfort of the women's world inside his family's gardens, while his frustrated father torments him for his failure as a scholar. High Qing parents, identifying with Baoyu's father, started their sons up the ladder of success earlier and earlier as competition for examination degrees increased. By the eighteenth century, a boy's formal classical education began as early as the age of four *sui* (the equivalent of three years in Western parlance) under the tutelage of a family member, often his mother, especially if his father was away from home or deceased.[17] These little boys memorized simple rhymes and learned to recognize characters long before they were able to understand the meaning of any classical text. If parents themselves were not able to teach a son, a close relative began the tutoring process, and not until the age of seven or eight *sui* —or at the latest, ten—was a promising boy sent to school outside his home.

In school, removed from the womanly influence of mother, sisters, and aunts, a boy absorbed the manners proper to a future scholar-gentleman as he acquired manly social graces, interacting with peers who might become his future colleagues and with teachers who would surely become patrons. In school, boys from elite families cultivated networks of friendship and patronage that would form the fund of "connections" (*guanxi*) on which they could draw as they built their careers. In the classroom, and later in the examination hall, a young scholar might attract the eye of a powerful patron, while among his peers he had a chance to prove his worth vis-à-vis his brothers and cousins.[18]

Rituals of early childhood display the anxiety and uncertainty that attended a family's assessment of how far to push each son toward an official career. Most dramatic was the Twelve-Month Ceremony conducted on a child's first birthday. In this rite, a boy was handed a tray filled with various objects. Many were scholarly implements: brush, inkstone, paper. Others included an abacus and a carpenter's tool. At least one son in every family was expected to reach for the brush and inkstone, although the rest could and should have other aptitudes. First-born sons bore the brunt of parental pressure to succeed.[19]

Even the most promising young man, selected for grooming as a future scholar and official, was thought to remain vulnerable as he approached the age for marriage.* His physical body was understood to be lusty and still immature. Like Confucius and Hong Liangji, he could not be trusted to "stand

*For men, around 20 *sui*. It was certainly not as late as 30 *sui*, the year mentioned in the ritual texts, which commentators agree refers to the year by which a man should already be married.

firm" until at least the age of 30 *sui*. He was likely to fall in love, perhaps many times over, with beautiful young women to whom his wealth gave him access. He might be adventuresome, violent, and quarrelsome, chafing under the constraints of an academic career. He had to be allowed to give reign to these passions. In fact, he was expected to acquire sexual experience,[20] and he was schooled in hygiene and the healthy practice of sex.[21]

Elite parents simultaneously controlled and indulged young sons in their twenties and thirties. Access to women was included in stipends for study in the form of financial support for a wife and allowances for extramarital dalliance. Only after a wealthy young man had passed his lusty years was he expected to turn his back on his amorous or adventuresome life-style and attend to the serious business of taking over the family's financial affairs or taking up a government post, beginning only then to move into his father's shoes.[22] Biographies of men from upper-class families rarely provide details of dalliance, and men who wrote about courtesans usually did so under a pseudonym.[23] Where they refer to women at all, they stress the struggle against poverty and hardship that forced a son to study day and night under the watchful eye of his mother, who sat slaving at her spinning or weaving to keep him in school. Characters in plays and novels, however, display men's amorous weaknesses, represented in their most extreme and debilitating form in Jia Baoyu, the emotional protagonist of *Dream of the Red Chamber*. Literary accounts of elite men at mid-life show them traveling around the empire, passing through cities where pleasure quarters always featured female entertainment.[24]

Apart from these youthful experiences of sexuality, young men of elite families were expected to marry and father sons well before the classically sanctioned age of 30 *sui*. In the Chinese family system, each son lived to serve his descent line. Above all else, he was supposed to be filial, a devotion he demonstrated in the first instance by learning or laboring in obedience to his parents' instructions and later by success, preferably in the examinations and in office-holding. Wealth acquired through business or trade was an acceptable substitute for scholarly distinction so long as it provided for the scholarly success of descendants. The most unfilial act of all was not to produce a son to carry on the family line; hence the significance of marriage in the young man's life course, marked by his acquisition of a "marriage name," or *zi*, by which he would be known for most of his adult life.[25]

Ideally, then, a man began his life as a student, married while struggling to achieve office, balanced the demands of family life with office-holding (which meant long years on the road away from home, with intermittent returns to father children or mourn parents), and comingled all these experiences with sexual or social relationships with women outside his kin group and social class. This double sexual life continued for many men even after they retired from their official careers to become teachers and patriarchs, at which point a man often acquired one or more concubines, sometimes presented to him by his wife or even (in the case of widowers) by a daughter.

In sum, the elite male life course defined men's relationships to women in contradictory ways, and a scholarly career in mid-Qing Jiangnan introduced men to two women's worlds. One was the still point of the women's apartments, the *guige*, abode of the *guixiu*, or cultivated ladies. The other was the "floating" world of courtesan entertainers. The eighteenth-century ideal of the sequestered woman was vividly represented in didactic works and eulogies. It coexisted uncomfortably with a barrage of competing images of women outside the home. Plays and novels titillated readers with stories of cloistered young ladies seduced and betrayed by charlatans or foolish lovers. "Floating" images of accessible women filled records of the "painted boats" (*huafang*) that housed famous courtesans who worked in the towns along the Grand Canal from Yangzhou to Hangzhou and in the famous Banqiao section of the old Ming capital, Nanjing.

During the eighteenth century, it appears that women in the courtesans' quarters and those in the inner apartments occupied increasingly separate worlds. Unlike the late Ming period, when courtesans figured prominently in the lives of elite men and their families and when upper-class ladies consorted freely with their counterparts in the courtesans' quarters, the High Qing marked a strict divide between the courtesans' abode and the "inner quarters" where "cultivated ladies" (the *guixiu*) resided. Although High Qing courtesans, like their late Ming predecessors, still sometimes wrote fine classical poetry and conversed on topics from art to literature to history, we no longer find them at the center of literati culture. On the contrary, the brilliant women who occupy that center in High Qing times are *guixiu* themselves: the poets in Yuan Mei's circle, the prodigies in upper-class families, the contributors to literary anthologies.

Here we encounter a paradox, because men's writing about women during this period is full of confusion about where educated women belong, and their confusion stemmed partly from the knowledge that women writers in the late Ming were often courtesans or women who consorted with courtesans.[26] In High Qing times, with the boundary between courtesan culture and literati domesticity sharpened, the new position of upper-class women writers was still being defined, both by the women themselves and by the men in their lives. Conflicting definitions of women's roles troubled men who depended on women's support to meet the demands of their stressful lives. These debates are the subject of Chapter 4, "Writing."

The Life Course of Elite Women

If a son was reared to be filial by serving his natal family and its descent line through a successful career and progeny, a daughter was socialized to leave her natal family and supply the successful male progeny for another line. The gap separating little boys and little girls widened from the time of their birth, especially in elite families.

The Twelve-Month Ceremony described earlier, for example, acknowledged several ways for filial sons to serve the descent line; parents might choose to prepare each son for a different career—a strategy that compounded the family's chances of success by maximizing its range of claims to wealth and power. Filiality was not compromised as long as each son had offspring to carry on the line. By contrast, daughters in upper-class households were reared for a single future: marriage into another line.[27] There was no comfortable, legitimate place in an upper-class Chinese family for a daughter who had passed marriageable age. Not only was an unwed daughter a social anomaly; she was a ritual anomaly as well. Her tablet could not reside on her natal family's ancestral altar when she died; it could be installed only in the ancestral shrine of another descent line, following betrothal and marriage.

As we noted in Chapter 1, respectable alternatives to marriage did not exist for elite Chinese women in High Qing times. By contrast with early modern Western Europe, where a high proportion of women remained unwed and many entered religious orders,[28] eighteenth-century China offered women no haven; convents were considered a last resort for destitute girls. In rare cases among elite families, a young woman's acts of piety or faith forced her parents to give up their matchmaking plans and allow her to remain celibate. But these exceptions merely underscore the rule that virtually every young woman in the Qing upper classes expected to become someone's wife.

The highly charged process of grooming a daughter for marriage, including the preparation of her dowry, began when she was born. Even her birthdate was portentous, because her future husband would be selected through a process of matching the hour, day, and year of her birth with that of her prospective husband. Chastity was the focus of the grooming process. Keeping a daughter chaste and ensuring that not even a hint of rumor besmirched her reputation required vigilance on the same level accorded her brothers' classical training. Although elite women were not veiled, most of them spent their lives behind curtains, screens, gates, and doors that shielded them from view. Standards of propriety in elite families required a daughter once betrothed to remain faithful even if her intended spouse died before the wedding. So potent were the ritual bonds uniting a husband and wife that divorce among the elite was practically unheard of. The strains of enforced fidelity were resolved differently by men and women in elite families. Married men took concubines to produce more offspring and sought female companionship and sexual pleasure in courtesan houses or brothels. Married women wrote—of sexual privation, of loneliness, of boredom, of resentment, and of physical abuse. Somatic and psychological pain, sometimes defined as illness, drove many women to commit suicide.[29]

Perspectives on the Female Life Course

Autobiographical writing by women is rare before the twentieth century.[30] Accounts of the female life course in the eighteenth century must therefore be pieced together from men's biographical sketches of women they knew or loved and from women's poems, short prefaces, and editorial comments. These sources, explored in Chapter 4, "Writing," show that while the female life course in elite families resembled that of the classical model, women who experienced it gave the process its own meaning and even challenged the accepted meaning by their erudition and their eloquence as writers.

SHEDDING THE MILK TEETH

For a young girl in an elite family, the first recognition that she was different from her brothers came when she lost her milk teeth (*hui*) at the age of seven *sui*,[31] and her hair was tied up in tufts (*tiaoling*). Tying up the hair is a life-course marker commonly used by women writers to identify the earliest critical change in their lives. At that time if a girl was being tutored, she was separated from her brothers and schooled privately—by her father if he was at home or, if her father was absent, by her mother, an elder sister, an aunt, or a governess hired from a family of good reputation.

We know from other sources that at roughly the same time, a young girl's feet began to be tightly bound with strips of cloth to crush and reshape the bones, producing the tiny "lotuses" that would capture an appropriate marriage partner. Foot size was a vector of status for marriageable women; natural feet were regarded as the domain of the lowborn. In erotic discourse, bound feet signaled sexual desirability: the smaller the foot, the more alluring the woman. Elite families who would have scorned the erotic implications of their daughters' small feet seem to have regarded footbinding as a necessary, if discreet, part of female grooming. Elite mothers introduced footbinding at the youngest possible age, unlike laboring mothers in farm families, where footbinding did not begin until puberty and was often relaxed following marriage. Girls in upper-class families therefore stood to suffer the most rigorous and painful form of footbinding, and anecdotal evidence suggests that such families also commanded the best in medical care and remedies to mitigate the excruciating pain.[32]

The practice of footbinding was surrounded by such powerful taboos that few women refer to it in their writings.[33] Thus perhaps the terms *hui* and *tiaoling* should be read as euphemisms that shield this traumatic life crisis from the historian's view. It is unclear why women wrote so little about footbinding, especially during the late eighteenth century, when it was satirized and criticized in contemporary fiction and prose.[34] Perhaps it was not considered aesthetically or intellectually appropriate to mention footbinding in genteel company; perhaps the poetic vocabulary of elite women writers erased this form of bodily experience from their writing. There were, after all, no classical precedents for it.

Because of the exceptional dearth of information about footbinding in my sources, I treat it here as a taboo subject laden with symbolic meaning. Part of the meaning derives from the stark fact of excruciating pain, which young girls experienced as a condition of their lives. Another part of the meaning is the physical confinement of sexually active women by crippling. Dependency and class hierarchy figured in footbinding as well: the elite women whose feet were most tightly bound required maids to support them as they walked. Fashion and eroticism played a role, as women with bound feet walked with a gait that was considered graceful and pleasing. The foot coverings themselves were yet another sign of the cultivated status of the wearer, since marriageable women were expected to bind their feet in silk and embroider their own tiny shoes. Finally, we cannot dismiss the importance of footbinding as a cultural symbol during the Manchu conquest, a subject that is presently under study.[35] Bound feet thus were a bodily sign connoting wealth, leisure, beauty, vulnerability, dependency, respectability, and sensuality. No wonder they were powerful gender symbols.

The years within the "women's apartments" that followed footbinding and the cloistered lifestyle that accompanied it were often a luxurious setting for elite young women. They could study, read, write, paint, practice calligraphy and music,[36] sew, embroider, and exchange girlish intimacies. In many scholarly families a precocious daughter was the light of her father's life and an intellectual and emotional companion to her mother and siblings. Her erudition was nurtured and valued by family members and even flaunted by a father who could not resist showing her off to his friends.

Although girls were often close to their fathers and brothers, gender segregation for elite young women was strict where other male relatives were concerned. Within the household itself, the design of large family homes relegated women to the rear apartments where they could be shielded from the gaze of outsiders. Domestic seclusion was also considered important because the grand family compounds preferred by the upper classes necessarily threw large numbers of nubile young women together under the same roof with kinsmen from three or more generations. The "women's apartments" were the quarters where women cared for young children and, as Hong Liangji observed, elderly adults. Sexually active males were not to be seen there. In fact, if a wife appeared before her husband's friends at a banquet or party she had prepared for them in her own home, it was cause for comment.[37] In her handwork or literary pursuits, a young woman's closest companions were supposed to be kinswomen—sisters, aunts, cousins, mother, grandmothers, sisters-in-law. Concubines, maids, and the occasional governess extended the network beyond the inner kin circle.

If female seclusion within the home was strict, women's mobility beyond the gates of the family compound was even more tightly constrained. With bound feet and strict rules governing contact with outsiders and men, upper-class women had little opportunity for physical activity, let alone horseback riding, much favored by Chinese women as late as the Tang period. Dancing was considered lewd and was associated with courtesans, the theater, or peasant culture. When traveling abroad, except for short distances, upper-class women mounted sedan chairs carried by porters and sat behind drawn curtains so they could not be seen from the street. Travel on foot was discouraged, not only by pain and inconvenience, but by danger, since kidnapping was a constant threat. Reputations might suffer, too, if women were seen in public without proper chaperones.

Yet like their late Ming counterparts, young women in High Qing times did venture outside their homes, usually in groups chaperoned by maids and older women. A visit to a temple or shrine to burn incense was the most respectable reason to leave home (Fig. 4), but other occasions drew women out on a regular basis. A married woman, for example, was expected to visit her natal home periodically, especially at the lunar New Year. Visits with brothers and cousins were common. Fathers took daughters along on business trips. Brothers escorted sisters back home to see their mother. Sons squired their mother to scenic spots to benefit their health or for pleasure. Some mature married women even traveled alone and wrote about it, although we must consider such cases exceptional. Finally, anecdotal evidence tells us that groups of elite women still took occasional outings to the courtesan boats of Suzhou and Hangzhou, as they did during Ming times.[38]

Given the constraints on their own mobility and the regular sojourning of beloved male relatives—especially sons and brothers—young upper-class

Fig. 4. A religious procession of ladies to a temple. From G. Smith 1847: 169.

women were expected to feel bereft and bored. Cloistered in the women's apartments or, more happily, in expansive gardens such as those frequented by the Jia girls in *Dream of the Red Chamber*, they were urged to keep busy and work industriously. Handwork, especially embroidery, was considered the most appropriate womanly activity, being productive and practical as well as aesthetically pleasing. In addition, upper-class women in Qing times, even more than their counterparts in the late Ming, read and wrote. Most studied biographies of famous women, including long-suffering chaste widows and heroic martyrs who committed suicide to preserve their chastity. Elite women practiced the fine arts of painting, calligraphy, and music. They plucked classical stringed instruments. They wrote volumes of poetry. And in addition to learning the standard didactic texts for women, many studied the classics alongside their brothers.

The education of daughters seems to have become increasingly important in the High Qing period. In the marriage market, erudition marked a woman as a highly desirable marriage partner, one who could provide not only sons but also the very best in early childhood education for them.[39] Moreover, she was seen by her kinfolk and by society at large as the heir to her family's tradition of "house learning" or "family learning" (*jia xue*). A daughter's erudition embodied the scholarly history of her natal family and was a crucial mark of marriageability, as Chapter 4 will show.

Fig. 5. Delivery of the dowry chests to the groom's family residence. Before the bride arrived, her dowry was paraded through the streets for all to see and judge the honor of her natal family. From Nakagawa [1799] 1983: 350–51.

HAIRPINNING

The second great rite of passage in a girl's life marked her entry into puberty and signaled her readiness to marry. Once again, the visible sign of this transition was hairdressing. Her hair was pinned up in a coif as she entered her fifteenth year (fifteen *sui*), one year after she was expected to begin menstruation. Hairpinning was also the time when her family began assembling the dowry for her future marriage, if they had not done so already (Fig. 5).[40] Girls generally married within a few years of hairpinning, the mean age at marriage for elite women who became first wives in the eighteenth century being just under eighteen *sui* at the beginning of the century and falling nearly to seventeen by 1800.[41]

For young women the transition from puberty to sexual activity after marriage was abrupt. Whereas males from upper-class families were expected to indulge their youthful appetites for sex, females in the same families were reared to suppress or deny theirs. A soft, low voice, gentle submissive demeanor, charm, wit, and grace were the virtues of moderacy that elite girls were supposed to cultivate as they attained puberty. Nonetheless, respectable girls found ways to learn the arts of passion and to express their emotions. Hints about homosexual attraction among women, especially within the same family compound, suggest that it was not considered abnormal or unhealthy.[42] Young girls might have an opportunity to observe married women within the same household (wives or concubines) who were sexually attracted to one another; in fact, a wife might select a concubine for her spouse with her own sensibilities in mind.[43] Sexual intercourse was not necessarily private: erotic paintings and drawings commonly show one or two maids assisting or participating in a mistress's sexual intercourse with a male partner, supporting her or sharing her pleasure. While paintings may represent male fantasies rather than female experience, there is no reason to assume that women did not take pleasure in such sexual encounters, especially if they found one another's presence arousing. Between young girls and their maids, who were likely to have had their own or vicarious sexual experiences, gossip or conversation about sex seems likely.

Women's writing clearly shows that sexual passion figured in their fantasies and their dreams. Desire, however, focused on the distant lover, usually a man and usually inaccessible or accessible only for fleeting moments. The poetic occasions for exploring passion were carefully defined and attached to the seasons. The seventh day of the seventh month, discussed at length in Chapter 6, "Work," was the most elaborate of these, but nearly every season of the year offered topoi to the lovelorn poet. Spring flowers, summer butterflies, autumn winds—all gave the poet the language for conflating desire and pain, anticipating denial and loss even when desire was consummated.

Conflating sexual desire with pain and privation was an accurate writing of the fate of desire in the lives of most elite women. At marriage, a young bride would travel to her new husband's home in a curtained sedan chair (Fig. 6) to sleep for the first time with this man she had never seen and to live the rest of her life in his family, whom—often—she had never met. Even the best efforts of parents determined to place a beloved daughter in good hands were stymied by these odds against happiness. Unhappiness was usual, disaster unsurprising. Women's misery in arranged marriages was so commonplace in upper-class families that it pervades their memoirs. Brothers write sorrowfully about their married sisters; fathers lament the suffering of married daughters. The strictest childrearing could not prepare a young girl for the mental and psychological strain of a hostile or indifferent spouse or for the self-denial of widowhood in a society where remarriage was considered a disgrace for upper-class women.[44]

On the contrary, for newly married young women the very intimacy of natal family ties compounded the profound loneliness and alienation that

Fig. 6. New bride in her sedan chair en route to the groom's house. From Nakagawa [1799] 1983: 372–73.

followed her wedding. Even if she cared for her husband, a bride from an upper-class family had to spend most of her early married life in the company of her mother-in-law or the other women in her husband's family. Though many affectionate memoirs attest to the bonds between a kindly mother-in-law and her devoted daughter-in-law, mothers-in-law were demanding and sometimes cruel. A husband's sisters or his brothers' wives might be vindictive or spoiled, jealous of the attention a new bride received and anxious about their own future. In any case, since the average elite couple waited more than six years for a son,[45] a new bride could not expect comfort from children for several years after marriage.

It is no wonder, then, that married women developed close bonds with female servants. A young servant might accompany a bride from her natal household as part of her dowry; another might nurse her infants. Elite women spent much of their time in servants' company, and young married women especially relied on a servant's confidence to hear out their tales of pain, loneliness, and isolation.[46] The body servant who served her mistress before and after marriage was also counted on to convey candid information about a married woman's circumstances to her natal family when the need arose.

Married women themselves rarely complained, for girls were reared to understand that marriage was a lifelong commitment and that voicing grievances to parents would merely magnify the suffering born of an unhappy marriage.[47]

To some extent marriage between cousins of different surnames alleviated marital stress, especially for women. A daughter married to a cousin entered a family well known to her parents, who could also use their kin relations to monitor her fate and protect her interests. For the daughter's part, marriage with a cousin meant entering a network of women she knew, if only by reputation. Finally, cousin marriage broadened and deepened the scholarly and kinship networks joining elite families, serving to consolidate and sustain prestige and wealth otherwise threatened by competition. Anecdotal evidence cited suggests that some prominent families maintained marital ties over many generations.[48]

CHILDBIRTH AND EARLY CHILDREARING

An upper-class married woman in High Qing Jiangnan could expect to bear children throughout her fertile years. The risks and burdens of childbearing may have made the advent of a concubine a source of relief rather than jealousy or turned widowhood into a time of respite rather than loneliness. Infant mortality was high, and the births of children who died young went unrecorded. In addition, genealogists routinely omitted daughters from the records microdemographers use to reconstruct the population of China in times past. Therefore we cannot accurately measure the average fertility of upper-class women. Overall, it appears to have been surprisingly low, given the cultural pressures favoring sons, in part because of relatively high rates of widowhood. One analysis shows that from one-fourth to one-third of the married women in elite lineages of Zhejiang were widowed during their reproductive years. Those women taken as first wives in upper-class households whose childbearing years were not interrupted by death could expect to bear five children.[49]

Charlotte Furth has demonstrated that the *fu ke* (women's medicine) texts used by Ming and Qing physicians focused on maternal health and reproductive success.[50] Popular medical texts of Qing times, she notes, were "socially organized to support the forms of gender subordination required by Confucian familism and to reinforce its moral values."[51] Medical texts advised women about the proper way to practice "fetal education" (*tai jiao*) so that a woman's moral conduct and even her thoughts during pregnancy would help shape a worthy as well as a healthy child. Some texts suggest that women approaching childbirth practice meditation exercises to help them bear the pain,[52] a discipline that would prove useful for other purposes in later years.

An exceptional poem about childbirth shows how it magnified the spiritual crises of a young mother's life, calling up fears of death at the very moment of birth:

ON GIVING BIRTH TO ANOTHER GIRL JUST AS THE SOUL OF MY SECOND DAUGHTER, DEAD OF SMALLPOX, RETURNED

I summoned her soul and she happened to come
Just as my new daughter was born.
From this I know that life returns from the dead,
That reincarnation is possible.
She could see my old gold bracelets and recognize her
  mother.
As the jade swallow settled in my breast,*
I thought still more of my dead child.
Your coming again confirms the dream
That your former life seemed to be.
I called you back as if you were still
In that liminal state from which the dead may return.
I strained to hear the baby's cries,
And see the handkerchief hung to the right of the door,†
Half to console myself, half to cherish my grief.[53]

Domestic rituals helped young mothers cope with the threat of childhood disease and death. Variolation against smallpox was known in the eighteenth century, but it could fail or result in a secondary infection.[54] The Smallpox Goddess demanded twelve days of prayer for a child diagnosed with the pox. A room of the house was specially swept for the sick child's mother and other close female relatives to make their appeals to the goddess. They made a dress of dark red cloth for the sick child to wear. Parents abstained from sexual intercourse and kept a special diet; no one in the household prepared fried or sautéed food. In the homely rituals honoring the Smallpox Goddess, young mothers withdrew from the bedchamber and the kitchen to concentrate on saving a child's life.[55]

The traumas of early marriage were not always managed through ritual. Passionate outbursts erupt from records of young married women's lives, displaying the emotional costs of the female life course: reactions against footbinding and the painful end of childhood play, the wrenching departure from

*That is, as I became pregnant.

†A handkerchief was hung to the right of the door to announce the birth of a daughter; for a son, a bow and arrow were hung outside the door.

siblings and parents, the sudden onset of sexual intimacy with a stranger in a strange family and household, the pain of children's births and deaths.

Among mature women, illness itself often inspired confusion between spiritual turmoil and bodily malaise. "Rising from my sickbed" (*bing qi*), a trope in High Qing women's poetry, conveys the sense that women expected to fall ill often and that they experienced illness as an emotional and physical withdrawal from the world.[56] Here Hu Shenrong describes a fever:

WHILE ILL

My soul feels lost, uprooted.
I float, as in a dream.
When I walk, leaning for support, I fear the ground
will give way.
Lying back down, my head feels empty.
When I open my eyes, everything turns misty.
When I hear a noise, it sounds like wind rushing.
How can I bear the rain beneath my window?
Solitary and alone, a single red lamp glows.[57]

Even in this clear description of the flu, Hu manages to invoke not only solitude, but loneliness and sadness. Less symptomatic but more like others in the genre is this determined poem titled "Recovering":*

The new spring is just appearing, the moon slender and fine.
Because I dread the spring chill, I do not raise the screens.
Moved to seek out the clear night, I lean on my maid to rise.
I light the incense, sit straight upright, and read the "Zhou nan."[58]

Recovery from illness could signal the hopeful beginning of new love:

RISING FROM MY SICKBED

Still content and satisfied, I reluctantly descend from the tower.
Leaning on the ballustrade, I play idly with my jade hairpin.
This morning the wind of its own accord came from the northwest.
I can hook up the pearly screens facing east.[59]

Few of these illnesses seem life-threatening. They are poignant because they punctuate the seasons and because illness is an ephemeral state from which women recover and "arise." But early death from unspecified causes and abuse

* Stephen West (personal communication) notes that this poem is clearly about love lost, especially in the resolute determination to read morally uplifting poetry and the shutting out of "spring." The "Zhou nan" ode referred to here is the first in the classic *Shi jing*, discussed at greater length in Chap. 4, "Writing."

of wives by their husbands are matters of record.[60] Suicide—by hanging, starvation, or drowning—was also known in elite families, especially among young widows.[61] One young widow, who tried to kill herself ingesting lye, failed when relatives intervened, but succeeded in starving herself to death within two weeks, leaving a suicide poem addressed to her parents.[62]

Other strains produced by marriage were expressed in domestic violence among women. The mistresses of upper-class households were notorious for their abuse of servants, a practice male contemporaries ascribed to women's "jealous nature." Didactic handbooks written by men contain special sections on this problem. They advise women to "nurture" their servants, to be "generous, humane, kind, and gracious" (*kuan*, *ren*, *ci*, *hui*), noting that the strains of a cloistered life provoke outbursts of feeling that a young woman would refrain from venting on her own kin, but might unleash with full force on her servants.[63] Temper tantrums and sleeves wet with tears, conventional topoi in novels and poems by or about women, hint at the turbulent emotional lives concealed in the women's apartments.

RICE AND SALT

The tumultuous years of regular sexual relations, childbearing, and childrearing are glossed benignly in women's writings as the years of "rice and salt." During this time, elite women often had to set aside literary interests and aesthetic pursuits in favor of the material needs of family members and the practical demands of household management. Women who were not recovering from childbirth were busy handling account books and investments, supervising servants, organizing entertainment, caring for the sick and aged, and teaching their children reading, writing, and manners.[64]

Some of these occupations were more pleasant than others. Embroidery—considered work—might serve as well as an aesthetic pursuit, an occasion to socialize, or a welcome reprieve from hard or dirty physical labor. Women's allusions to embroidery show that some viewed it as a job to be got out of the way while others considered it a badge of duty performed; women's literary activity is often prefaced by phrases such as "when I had finished my embroidery," "when my embroidery was done," and "in my spare time, when I wasn't doing embroidery."[65]

Caring for an aging mother-in-law or covering up the foibles of an inept or ne'er-do-well spouse consumed emotional as well as physical energy. Zhang Xuecheng reverently recalled the devotion of one young matron to her invalid mother-in-law's care:

> In her final years, Lady Xun's mother-in-law was afflicted with an illness of the mouth and teeth that grew increasingly severe, so that whenever she ate,

> she would clench her teeth and press her lips together. Lady Xun would rise at dawn, kneel down and hold her and feed her, tilting the spoon between her lips. Each mouthful took a long time to swallow; every meal required plenty of steamed beans and grain. Only when her mother-in-law was satisfied could she unbend her knees. For half a year, thus, she was unfailingly respectful.[66]

AGING

Aging brought many elite women respite from the labor and emotional turmoil of marriage, childrearing, and caring for parents-in-law. The major turning point in the elite female life course arrived with the onset of menopause, the first of many markers. Another marker for elite women was leisure time. Menopause, coinciding as it often did with the marriage of a woman's eldest son, marked a shift from years of mothering to years of presiding as mother-in-law, from waiting on others to being waited on. Given that a mother's average age at the birth of her first male child was close to 24 in elite families, she would be 44 years old when her first-born son married at 20 and nearing menopause by the time he and his own wife had their first son.[67] Ideally, then, a married woman gained a daughter-in-law to wait on her precisely as she contemplated the end of her own childbearing years.

The formal turning point marking the end of childbearing was the age of 50 *sui*.[68] Whereas for men, as we noted earlier, the decade beginning at age 50 marked the peak of an official career, for women it signaled the start of the final stage in the life course. The significance of 50 *sui* for women is recognized, as we have seen, in imperial edicts honoring chaste widows, honors reserved for women widowed before the age of 30 *sui* who remained celibate and refused to remarry past the age of 50.[69] Qing official policy concerning widows, in other words, clearly brackets a woman's reproductive years as those between menarche and the fiftieth year.

A mother-in-law might signal this transition in her life by retreating into her private chambers to recite the rosary or read Buddhist sutras. Some women joined together to chant sutras or go on pilgrimage.[70] Some commenced a spiritual quest, Buddhist or Daoist, requiring close concentration (such as copying sutras) and disciplined meditation. Such a quest might also include embroidering sutras or images of the Bodhisattva Guanyin with silk thread or, in the case of some devotees, one's own hair.[71] Occasional accounts mention a male teacher or guru.[72]

Women's writing celebrates the turn to mid-life with reflective verses and assertions of spiritual and emotional autonomy.[73] A woman in her mid-fifties writes about "letting go" of her cares and worries (*fang huai*) as she contemplates the success of some offspring and resigns herself to the death of one. Another speaks of passing on her burdens to the next generation. Some women greet old age with a flourish. Zhang Shulian titles a long spirited poem "Congratulating Myself at Ninety" ("Jiushi zi shou"). Still writing in her nineties, Mai Yinggui takes a new literary name (*hao*) and styles herself *Youxing laoren*, "The Old Person Who's Still Lively [or, Still Alive]."[74]

The years after 50 *sui*, the final stage in the female life course, were cause for celebration among all women except widows. Stories and biographies of faithful widows remind us time and again that the learned woman who survived her husband must not celebrate her longevity. She knew from her classical studies that she was the *wei wang ren*, "the person who had not yet died."* Having survived her spouse, she was required to rear his sons and support his parents, but on no account could she revel in her passage to old age alone. The widow whose portrait appears in Fig. 7, Lady Han (1742–81), is the mother of Yuan Tingtao (1764–1810), a noted bibliophile. Widowed at the age of 25 *sui*, Lady Han remained faithful to her late husband for fifteen years before her own death at the age of 40 *sui*. On her fortieth birthday, according to her biographer Sun Xingyan, "her son and his wife wanted to give her a birthday banquet, after the custom of the time. But quoting ancient precedents, she demurred, saying 'This is not appropriate for one who has not yet died.'"[75] Lady Han's demeanor in the portrait conveys the female artist's appreciation of her austerity. At the same time, the painter—who styled herself *nü shi* (woman scholar)—displays her mastery of classical norms.

In contrast to the abstemious widow, a married woman whose husband was still alive was expected to host a major celebration on her fiftieth birthday. In the Lower Yangzi region, the celebrant planted a profusion of flowers in her garden as homage to Hua Shen, the Flower Goddess.[76] Birthday greetings portray the Daoist Flower Immortal, Hua Xian, accompanied by two atten-

*The phrase is from the *Zuo zhuan* commentary on the classic *Spring and Autumn Annals*, Chronicles of Duke Zhuang, 28th year. The commentary explains how Ziyuan, the chief minister of the state of Chu, attempts to seduce the widow of King Wen by entertaining her with troupes of dancers. However, his gesture sends an unintended double message: it is supposed to amuse and entrance her, but she interprets it as an affront to the honor of her deceased husband. Recalling how the king had used dancers to distract an enemy before an attack, the weeping widow shames Ziyuan with these words: "My deceased lord by means of these dances made preparations for war. But now the minister makes no use of them against our enemies, but exhibits them instead in front of this person who has not yet died (*wei wang ren*). Is this not strange?" (translation adapted from Legge 1991, 5: 115). This passage is also cited by Zhu Xi in his commentary on Mao Ode no. 47. Zhu Xi's commentary says, "A woman is born to serve a man with her person, so the wife draws out her life with her husband and should die with him. Hence when her husband dies, she calls herself 'the person not yet dead.' Henceforth she is simply waiting for death and ought not to have any desire of becoming the wife of another" (adapted from Legge 1991, 4: 76).

Fig. 7. Portrait of Lady Han (1742–1781), by Lu Danrong (Songling nüshi). This ancestral portrait depicts a widow of no more than 40 years of age. Reprinted from Zhou and Gao 1988: 130.

dants who carry baskets of flowers (*hua lan*).[77] Flower baskets are the emblem of Lan Caihe, one of the Daoist Eight Immortals, who commonly appears as a woman "dressed in a blue gown, with one foot shod and the other bare, waving a wand as she wanders begging through the streets."[78] Lan Caihe chants a doggerel verse denouncing this fleeting life and its deluding pleasures.[79]

After 50 *sui*, a woman was free to pursue her own spiritual quest. Anthropologists have sometimes interpreted the independent spiritual quest of women after menopause as a "ritual of post-parenthood" with the practical aim of easing a woman into a stage of life that might otherwise leave her feeling useless or marginalized. Scholars have also pointed out that Buddhist religious practice conferred merit on women who renounced the polluting activities of daily life, especially sexual intercourse.[80] Folktales from the Lower Yangzi region express women's wish to escape the polluting effects of childbearing and pursue their quest for immortality. After menopause, women addressed these Buddhist concerns with bodily disciplines learned from Daoist physical alchemy books. Powerful regimens purified the female body, purging contamination from menstrual blood and opening the way to a new level of spiritual development.[81]

DEATH

Funerals were more important than marriages in the Confucian rituals marking the life course. In fact, death rituals and ancestor worship were the focal point of the grand family system, continually redefining its boundaries and reconfirming the relationship among members of a common descent group.

However, for women approaching death, Confucian mourning rituals seem less important than other forms of piety, owing to the ambiguous role of women in the death rituals of the mid-Qing period. In Qing times, sons and unmarried daughters mourned for a full three years following the death of either parent.[82] But as soon as a daughter married, she transferred her parental mourning obligations to her husband's parents. A married woman was formally expected to mourn her own mother and father for only one year.[83] As a result married women, especially those who lost a parent in the years immediately following their entry into another household, had to steel themselves against the meaning of Confucian death rites, for as wives they could be denied the full expression of grief for their own parents and siblings.[84] At the funerals of commoner families, women sang laments to express their sorrow and bereavement over these losses. But women's laments belong to an oral tradition expressing alienation from, not affirmation of, the patrilineal kinship bonds sanctioned by Confucian ritual.[85]

THE QUEST FOR IMMORTALITY

In old age, women turned to religious disciplines that were solitary and inward looking. These disciplines invoked the bodhisattva Guanyin as protector (see Chapter 7, "Piety"), but they focused as well on Daoist goddesses, especially Xi Wang Mu, the Queen Mother of the West, goddess of immortality. Like Guanyin, female Daoist deities figured in women's religious imagination as emblems of eternal life.

The search for transcendence or immortality that underlay so much of women's religious and aesthetic imagining intensified with advancing age. At birthdays older women called on Daoist immortals to grant long life. Birthday wishes, written on elegant hanging scrolls, were accompanied, if possible, by a drawing or painting of a Daoist immortal. At fifty *sui* a woman would receive a painting of Ma Gu—Lady Hemp, goddess of the east (Fig. 8)—or Xi Wang Mu and would bow, burn incense, and pray before it for several days.[86] Her friends would greet her with the wish, "May you live as long as the immortal Ma Gu" (*Ma Gu xian shou*). Ma Gu recalls another immortal, He Xian Gu, one of two women among the Eight Immortals of Daoist legend and history. He Xian Gu, said to have lived during the reign of Empress Wu of the Tang dynasty, was once seen floating on a cloud of many colors before Ma Gu's temple, and so she appears on many birthday paintings.

As part of her practice of spiritual purification to promote long life, an

Fig. 8. "Ma Gu Offering Birthday Felicitations," by Gai Qi (1773–1829). A birthday painting suitable for presentation to a woman on her fiftieth birthday. Ma Gu is the Daoist immortal who, according to legend, saluted the Queen Mother of the West herself on her birthday. Ma Gu is shown here surrounded by other symbols of longevity and immortality, the deer and the pine. In her left hand she holds a basket of *lingzhi* (the fungus of immortality) and *xian cao* ("grasses of the immortals"). Her right hand grasps a whisk made from a yak's tail, used to keep herself free of dust and worldly contamination. A peony, the flower of prosperity, adorns her hair. The gold phoenixes on her robes are emblems of her literary talent. The deer, who returns her greeting, also carries peonies and magical fungi, symbols of prosperity and long life. Reprinted from Shen Yizheng 1984: 125.

older woman was particularly likely to abstain from polluting foods. Vegetarian diets were not limited to the elderly, however. Lay biographies of Buddhist female devotees praise them for "perpetual abstinence" (*chang zhai*) from meat, wine, garlic, and other strong foods proscribed by Buddhism. A mother and her married daughter from the Suzhou area abstained from such foods for more than 40 years. A husband, his wife, and his elder brother's wife all practiced abstinence and lived long lives. Husbands and wives might permanently abstain from polluting foods together. Elderly as well as middle-aged women "practiced purity" (*xiu jing ye*), that is, they practiced not only abstention but celibacy as well.[87]

Like the bodhisattva Guanyin, Daoist immortals are celibate. They abstain from polluting foods. They are also, like Guanyin, filial daughters: He Xian Gu fed her mother the fruits she gathered in the mountains; Ma Gu, according to one story that resembles the Miao Shan myth (recounted in Chapter 7, "Piety"), restored her cruel father's sight.[88] But where Guanyin promises release from suffering after death, the Daoist quest for immortality invites the living to prolong their lives by mastering the techniques of inner alchemy (*nei dan*). Inner alchemy manuals lead a woman through a rigorous process of bodily discipline and mental concentration that culminates in spiritual and bodily transformation.[89] In guiding women to sexual purity, these manuals invoke the powers of Guanyin and Xi Wang Mu and sometimes appeal to ideals of Confucian womanhood.[90] In this they recall women's religious practice in purification rites at funerals and beliefs about pollution associated with childbearing and the female body.[91]

The disciplines of inner alchemy enhance the effects of bodily massage with mental concentration. Written texts, invoking images of immortality and purity from Buddhist sutras and Daoist philosophy, reveal that practitioners of inner alchemy were not only literate but often highly educated. The woman who masters *nei dan* is told to expect a state of enlightenment like the one described in the *Surangama*, *Lotus*, or *Avatamsaka sutra*.[92] She is advised to recite the *Dao de jing* and passages from the *Zhuang zi* each day.[93] In Daoist religious practice, women's authority is both spiritual and philosophical, and it rests on women's visible role in the creation and transmission of the Daoist canon.[94]

High Qing readers were familiar with an inner alchemy manual titled *The Queen Mother of the West's Ten Precepts on the True Path of Women's Practice*, which claims to transmit the instructions of the Queen Mother herself.[95] The text begins with "nine disciplines" that reiterate Confucian and Daoist precepts familiar to any educated woman:

> Be filial, respectful, yielding, and gentle; be cautious in speech and avoid jealousy; be chaste and restrained; shun all wanton ways and love all living

> things; be compassionate and refrain from killing; recite with decorum and be diligent and careful; abstain from meat and wine; dress simply and without ornamentation; regulate the disposition; do not let yourself become troubled; do not go frequently to religious feasts; do not mistreat slaves and servants; do not conceal the virtues and expose the faults in others.[96]

Abruptly leaving the subject of social behavior, the manual next turns to the question of how to preserve and nurture an individual woman's life. The reader learns that she is at the apex of her yang state just before she begins menstruation, at about the age of 14 *sui*. After that, the text explains, her yang essence is steadily depleted, a process that can be slowed or reversed only through complex exercises. First, to restore the blood lost in menstruation, she must "cultivate the menses" by entering a state of "awareness within stillness." In that state of awareness, she will use a combination of massage and mental concentration to circulate *qi* (life force) through the body, to transform her bodily fluids into blood, and ultimately to transform her blood into *qi*.[97] If she is successful, she will have "slain the dragon."[98] She must beware the violent, sometimes highly erotic, sensations she will experience during these arduous exercises. She must subdue her emotions and distance herself from pleasure at all times. In other words, to slay the dragon—to become a successful practitioner of *nei dan*—the postmenopausal woman must first restore her lost blood, recover her former maidenhood, and return to the body of a child.[99]

Through inner alchemy, then, a woman learned discipline of the physical passions, transforming sexual desire into a quest for spiritual liberation. The victorious woman who slays the dragon and transforms her blood into *qi* reaches a state resembling that of the bodhisattva Guanyin during her enlightenment atop Mount Potalaka.[100] At the culmination of her efforts, she will feel an overwhelming sense of well-being as *qi* suffuses her body:

> When the *yang* spirit is able to come and go freely and easily, then the true self travels comfortably at will. Still living in the world of men, one establishes great merit. When one's merit is profound and the moment of destiny arrives, the true master appears with final salvation and brings [one] into the presence of the Lord on High. One next visits all the heavens and finally the "jade pool," where after an audience with the "Golden Mother," one receives appointment as an immortal. This is transcendence of the world.[101]

In inner alchemy, transcendence was understood as a state in which a woman achieved the yang position occupied by the great female deities of the Buddhist and Daoist traditions, Guanyin and Xi Wang Mu. She passed out of a state identified as yin by polluting *xue* (blood), and into a state identified as yang by purifying *qi*.

Poems about women's experiments with inner alchemy do not appear in standard Qing anthologies, though they certainly can be found in earlier periods.[102] The best evidence we have in the High Qing for women's practice of *nei dan* is the symbolic act of taking a Daoist name. Even here, taking a Daoist name could merely signify an identification with the practice of earlier female poets much admired in the High Qing period, such as Yu Xuanji and Xue Tao.[103] But casual references in women's writing, such as Yun Zhu's remarks about her own "quiet sitting," suggest that spiritual disciplines of this sort were considered a healthy part of the life course.

By contrast with references to *nei dan*, Buddhist and Confucian reflections on entering old age are common. In the following poem, the widow Wang Feiqiong describes meditation and a kind of transcendence:

SITTING IN SILENCE

Sitting in silence, idly humming, I smile to myself.
Reaching the age of 69, I live in poverty.
From my tapestry loom pour elaborate new patterns,
From my giant inkstone roam tiny silverfish.
My family now has grandsons whom I teach to read.
Our house, though lacking food, still keeps a library.
To satisfy one's wishes in a lifetime is a beautiful thing.
The vain world around me is mere emptiness.[104]

This mood of self-absorbed contentment is at once transcendent and grounded in virtuous worldly concerns: work, grandsons, and the future success promised the line as a result of the poet's hard labor. It echoes the sentiments in poems that "lay cares to rest" (*fang huai*), which were commonly composed by women in their late years.[105]

Another poem about spirituality describes a talented woman's transition from study of the classics to mastery of the Buddhist canon, though the age of the poet is unclear. The image inspiring the poem is a painting of the Dragon Girl (Long Nü), also called the Jade Maiden, an attendant and pupil of Guanyin. The Dragon Girl's legend portrays her as the daughter of the third son of the Dragon King, whom Miao Shan rescued when the king was trapped in a fisherman's net and about to be sold as a fish. After her father's rescue, the Dragon Girl received his permission to study with Miao Shan and became her attendant when Miao Shan later became the bodhisattva Guanyin.[106] The poet Zhang Yin, writing a colophon on Jiang Biqin's painting of the Dragon Girl holding a sutra, laments that the girl's talent was "envied even by Heaven" and invokes her gaze:

> Having returned to the Pure Land and joined the souls in Paradise,
> She turns once more toward the dusty world to gaze on unusual talent.
> Having read to the end all the Confucian texts in thousands and
> thousands of scrolls,
> She now follows the Buddha and sits to receive instruction in the
> sutras.[107]

Zhang Yin's allusion to envious heavenly spirits refers to the widespread belief that talented women were fated to sicken and die young. The poet here remarks hopefully that she, as one whose talent Heaven may envy, will find refuge in Buddhist learning, where her "unusual gifts" will attract only the benign gaze of the bodhisattva who will guide her to the Pure Land. Religious studies, in other words, especially in the later years of a woman's life, provided a safe haven for intellectual endeavors that scholars and family members might envy or marginalize because they found them too threatening.

As women aged, many withdrew from the family altogether, seeking a private meditative space or turning to Buddhist texts for respite from their wifely and maternal responsibilities.[108] Lady Zhang, the mother of the eminent Qing official Tian Wen (1635–1704), widowed in 1654 when her husband died while serving as a magistrate, saw one son take the *jinshi* degree ten years later. Before she died, two of her three boys had won high office at court. In a memoir, her sons recalled her years of widowhood, reeling thread in her chambers while tutoring them in the classics. On her seventieth birthday, friends and relatives decided to throw a party in her honor. When news of their plans reached her, however, Lady Zhang composed a scathing rebuke a thousand characters long, quoting the classics and the histories on proper behavior for widows and reminding her admirers that she was a "person who had not yet died." The party was summarily canceled. The following poem, one of Lady Zhang's few extant writings, may have been composed at about the same time:

SHOWN TO MY CHILDREN

> A copy of the *Surangama sutra*; my door is barred by day.
> The wooden fish, the bamboo staff* lean against the folding screen.
> This old person† decides for herself to keep a vegetarian diet.
> I don't recite Buddhist sutras for your benefit.[109]

*The pilgrim's companions.

†She uses the term *laoren* ("old person"), not *laofu* ("old woman"), invoking her authority as the surrogate patriarch.

Tracing the trajectory of the life course for men and for women shows that the women's apartments were far from the comforting still point men imagined—indeed willed—them to be. Instead, they were sites of rupture and conflict where women, having no still point of their own to rely on and forced instead to create one for men, developed the skills that would steel them against a lifetime of emotional turmoil and prepare them for the respite and the disciplines of old age. The difference between male and female perspectives on the life course emerges clearly from the evidence about gender and culture in the Lower Yangzi during the High Qing era. Let us turn now to that evidence.

4 *Writing*

OF ALL THE HALLMARKS OF High Qing rule, the classical revival reveals the most about gender relations by bringing to life conflicting ideals of erudition for women in scholarly families, ideals that scholars vigorously debated. These debates swirl around two powerful images: the stern female instructress, represented by the historian Ban Zhao, and the graceful willow catkin, whose symbol was the female poet Xie Daoyun. (Both women are discussed at length in the next section.) These images invoked in the Chinese literary imagination ancient myths of a powerful goddess who holds out the promise of passion and transcendence, at once seductive and morally pure, "the perfect mother, perfect lover, and perfect teacher."[1] The potent image of a divinely inspiring woman helps explain the powerful emotions aroused in men who were attracted by women writers during the High Qing period. A woman capable of expressing her emotions in pure and evocative language, a woman who truly "knows me" (*zhi ji*), a woman who had mastered classical learning called from men a response that was more than intellectual or aesthetic. Was she alluring? Did she threaten? The debates surrounding her suggest something of both.[2]

Qing writers, both male and female, domesticated the powerful image of the divine woman and brought her under control. Men did so by relegating the seductive power of the female literary voice—its passion and vulnerability—to daughters or mothers or to courtesans whose lowly status made them less threatening. Women did so by taming passion with domestic metaphors of loneliness, illness, and longing and by developing an authoritative moral and spiritual voice that transcended passion. We could read the metaphors in women's poetry as conventions or comfortable tropes. But this chapter reveals women's poetic tropes as creative, personal, individualized, and highly expressive. The writings of Jiangnan's elite women were like the poems sung by Bedouin women and analyzed by Lila Abu-Lughod.[3] In a patriarchal culture, they created a women's discourse that upheld Confucian honor while voicing the passions and sentiments that threatened to violate it. Their poetic voices carried them beyond their place in the family and the household and into the public discourse of the imperium itself.

Learned Women in Men's Eyes

Elite fathers held strong views on the proper rearing of their daughters. In High Qing Jiangnan, most elite fathers appear to have wanted their daughters educated. But educating daughters raised questions. If men studied the classics and learned to write fine ancient-style prose and poetry to become sage officials, what of the women who were born with the same potential, received the same training, and acquired the same literary skills? Why did they learn to write, and what should be their relationship to men?

One strategy elite families used to assuage their concern about their writing daughters was to teach them to work first and write later. For women, writing was a pastime reserved for moments when their work was done. To put work first was one comforting solution to the problems posed by women writers because, as we shall see in Chapter 6, womanly work was the quintessential sign of virtue in the eyes of eighteenth-century officials and scholars. Male writers applauded "women's work" (*nü gong*)—especially weaving—as a sign of a woman's character and as a measure of their own moral worth.* Forced to reconcile the competing demands of wifely roles and artistic talents, educated women always understood which came first. A female writer makes a bow in this direction in the preface to her poem when she assures her reader that she wrote it "after finishing [her] embroidery."[4] To some extent the life cycle itself took care of the conflicts between the demands of work and writing. In Jiangnan's elite families during the High Qing period, young girls were educated and encouraged to write poetry (and to paint and practice calligra-

*Mencius's mother, toiling at her loom, slashed her cloth to chastise her son for neglecting his lessons, an incident discussed in Chap. 6, "Work."

phy as well, if they showed the talent) until they married. At marriage, these same young women were expected to set aside brush and inkstone to manage the "rice and salt." Finally, as mothers-in-law or widows, many women were able to resume their writing, turning over family responsibilities to the next generation of women.

Always, however, the larger question of the purpose of women's learning remained. For men, the practical purpose of learning was clear: learning was the path to upward mobility through examinations and office. Moreover, study of the classics was a kind of moral practice that led men, through self-cultivation, to a full realization of their human potential as cultured beings. But did learning mean the same thing to women? The answer to this question was partly no, because women could not sit for the examinations, and they had no opportunity to serve in office. At the same time, many statesmen believed that women should be educated for the practical reason that they had to prepare their sons for the exams as well as for the moral reason that they were responsible for the rearing of future generations. Women also required moral authority as wives and household managers.

The classical revival confirmed these convictions. The intensive scrutiny of classical texts confronted High Qing writers with a history of erudite women in a variety of roles. Significantly, in seeking models and explanations for women's learning, Qing scholars almost completely ignored the brilliant culture of elite women writers and readers in the Ming dynasty's Lower Yangzi cities.[5] Instead of harking back to a Ming tradition of women's learning associated with scholars like Lü Kun, Li Zhi, and Chen Zilong, they reconstructed the classical tradition of women's learning and gave it contemporary significance.

The classics and histories featured learned heroines who emerged to special prominence in periods of cultural and literary creativity. In contrast to the dominant female role models enshrined in Liu Xiang's classic biographical collection *Biographies of Exemplary Women* (*Lienü zhuan*), who sacrifice their own bodies and interests for a higher moral good, women celebrated in the classical revival were heroines of civilization who possessed and expressed *wen*, the cultural refinement displayed in writing. The first of these heroines was a scholar in her own right, the Han historian Ban Zhao (Fig. 9).

Ban Zhao (c. 48–c. 120) was descended from a long line of court scholars. Her paternal aunt, Ban Jieyu, is featured as one of the moral exemplars in Liu Xiang's collection of biographies of exemplary women. As concubine to the emperor Cheng, Ban Jieyu won fame when she refused to ride with the emperor in his palanquin lest she distract his mind from affairs of state. A well-known painting attributed to the artist Gu Kaizhi depicts her at that powerful

Fig. 9. "Cao Dagu [Ban Zhao] Teaching Calligraphy," by Jin Tingbiao (fl. 1760–64). Here the Qianlong emperor's favorite court painter portrays Ban Zhao in her study. Her one intent pupil, the little boy before her, is none other than the precocious Qianlong emperor himself—his demeanor a pointed contrast to the other little boys playfully tumbling about. The painter has transformed his subject from a representation of women's learning (women teaching women) into a metaphor for motherly instruction. Courtesy of the National Palace Museum, Taipei, Taiwan, Republic of China.

moment, symbolically walking behind the emperor's litter. Ban Zhao's elder brother, Ban Gu, was an acclaimed poet and historian of the Han dynasty; her second brother served as a general in the central Asian frontier. Married at the age of 14 *sui*, in accordance with the custom of elite families at that time, Ban Zhao was widowed at an early age and declined to remarry (inadvertently making herself a role model for the late imperial chaste-widow cult). Instead, on her elder brother's death, she completed his unfinished work on the official history of the former Han dynasty (*Han shu*), including portions of the "Treatise on Astronomy." The classical record makes it clear that Ban Zhao's reputation as a scholar, and her unique position as a *female* scholar, made her a logical choice as the women's instructor in the palace.[6]

From her experience in the Han court, Ban Zhao wrote a text titled *Instructions for Women* (*Nüjie*) in which she outlined four essential female "attributes": virtue (*de*), speech (*yan*), comportment (*rong*), and work (*gong*). The same text was later adopted by scholar families outside the court for use in their own households. By the Qing period, it had become a classic in its own right, one of the Four Books for Women that constituted required reading for the daughters of all upper-class families.[7] Although this text has remained the most important legacy of Ban Zhao's scholarship, her complete works—now mostly lost—filled sixteen volumes and included narrative poetry, commemorative essays, inscriptions, eulogies, expository essays, elegies, treatises, and even memorials.

Ban Zhao herself grew up in the company of educated women and seems to have taken some of them as role models. Her works were collected and edited by her daughter-in-law, who honored her memory just as Ban Zhao had honored the memory of her own female relatives. One of her pupils became the empress Deng, who studied classics, history, astronomy, and mathematics under Ban Zhao's tutelage. When the empress later became regent on the death of her husband (whom Ban Zhao had instructed in painting and calligraphy), she is said to have conferred with Ban Zhao on affairs of state.

Ban Zhao's role in the writing of the Han history and her prominence as a learned stateswoman were almost completely ignored in the centuries after the fall of the Han. Even though her contributions included some of the Han history's most difficult technical materials, the work is conventionally attributed entirely to her elder brother. Most of her collected works disappeared in the political turmoil of the Six Dynasties period. Only the *Instructions for Women* survived, along with a few memorials and poems. In the imagination of the eighteenth-century elite, however, all of Ban Zhao's many roles defined her place in history, not merely her famous advice book. To her contemporaries she represented all that an educated woman should be: She was a powerful moral instructor. She inherited and displayed the learning of her family. And she was capable of taking a man's place when he was unable to complete his own scholarly responsibilities.

For scholars in the classical revival, the Tang period offered a second example of female erudition recognized by the imperial court: the five learned Song sisters. Invited to positions at the court by the emperor Dezong (r. 780–804), each received the title "scholar" (*xueshi*). The two most erudite, Song Ruohua and Song Ruozhao, were appointed palace instructors in classics and history, serving as personal consultants to the throne. Although, like Ban Zhao, the Song sisters were said to be the authors of a didactic text—a women's version of the *Analects*, the *Nü lunyu*—it was their scholarly distinction in classical learning and their display of "family learning" (*jia xue*) that caught the eye of High Qing classicists.[8]

Other historical records show that at crucial points in the transmission of the classical canon—namely, during periods of disorder—women were responsible for preserving bodies of family learning threatened with extinction. The daughter (some accounts say granddaughter) of the Erudite Fu Sheng (Fig. 10) translated her father's recitations of the ancient *Book of History* (*Shang shu*), lost in the Qin burning of the books in 213 B.C.E. The daughter's role was crucial because Fu Sheng spoke only the dialect of the ancient state of Qi, an idiom incomprehensible to the official charged with transcribing the text.

In a similar vein, Zhang Xuecheng's essay on women's learning (discussed later in this chapter) tells the story of Lady Song, another woman carrying on the tradition of learning from her family:

> When the Fu Qin[9] rulers first established their educational system and assembled a broad array of erudites and teachers of the classics, they discovered that all the classics were roughly in hand except for the *Zhou li* [Rites of Zhou], which had been lost. The erudites submitted a memorial stating that one Lady Song, the mother of the chamberlain of ceremonials, Wei Cheng, came from a family where the *Zhou li* had been transmitted from generation to generation. The emperor issued an edict declaring her home a lecture hall and establishing 120 scholarships. The scholars came and sat on the other side of a curtain to receive instruction from Lady Song, who was ennobled with the honorary title "Master of Illustrious Culture."[10]

Still other erudite women much admired by Qing scholars wrote nothing but dazzling poetry. Yet they—like Ban Zhao, the Song sisters, Fu Sheng's daughter, and Lady Song—were all exponents of the expressive possibilities of *wen*, written culture, and they too acquired their learning through their fami-

lies. Among these brilliant poets, the memory of Xie Daoyun is the one most often invoked by High Qing writers, male and female alike. Xie Daoyun's emblem was not the historian's brush, but the willow catkin (*xu*). The catkin motif first appears in a story describing a grand-family gathering presided over by Xie Daoyun's famous uncle, Xie An. The uncle challenges his sons, daughters, nephews, and nieces to a poetry contest. Pointing to the snow that has just begun falling outside, he asks them to compose a couplet describing it. His eldest son confidently writes, "Could it be salt shaking down through the air?" (*san yan kong zhong cha ke ni*). But he is quickly demolished by his younger cousin, Xie Daoyun, who wins the day with a tour de force: "More like willow catkins tossed up by the wind" (*wei ruo liu xu yin feng qi*).[11]

Xie An's dazzling young niece Daoyun contrasts with Ban Zhao in several important respects. She is young, precocious, even naughty. She can easily outdo her male relatives. She delights the senior men in her family; she is her uncle's pride and joy. Like other women in the society of philosophes that dominated intellectual discourse in the Six Dynasties era, she even takes pleasure in insulting men. In that sense, she is fearsome, unfathomable, unpredictable, and threatening. But she is only a child.

For some High Qing scholars these two classical models—the moral instructor and the brilliant prodigy—represented competing ideals of erudite womanhood that were impossible to reconcile. They became symbols in a debate about the nature and purpose of women's erudition that erupted at the close of the eighteenth century, a *querelle des femmes* led by two outspoken scholarly opponents, Yuan Mei and Zhang Xuecheng.

Classical Revival and the 'Querelle des femmes'

The *Book of Odes* (*Shi jing*), the *Book of Rites* (*Li ji*), and the various commentaries on the *Spring and Autumn Annals* (*Chun qiu*) all revealed to classical scholars of the High Qing how the ancients had lived their lives and conducted their rituals. These scholars were struck by the prominence of learned women in the classical age, by their high rank and visibility, and by the ways in which they called attention to certain violations of the classical norm in High Qing society.[12]

Fig. 10 (opposite). "The Scholar Fu Sheng in a Garden," by Du Jin. His daughter—or possibly granddaughter—is seated next to him, translating the ancient Qi dialect in which he is reciting the text of the classic *Book of History* (*Shang shu*). This painting may date from the late fifteenth century. Hanging scroll, ink and color on silk. Courtesy of the Metropolitan Museum of Art, Gift of Douglas Dillon, 1991.

The erudite Wang Zhong took detailed notes on his classical studies, which he collected and published under the title *An Account of Learning* (*Shu xue*). In his collection are two essays noting discrepancies between the position of women past and present. One, titled "Answers to Questions About Whether Wives Should Have Ancestral Tablets" ("Fu ren wu zhu da wen"), was considered important enough to be reprinted in the standard collection of classic essays on state policy, the *Huangchao jingshi wenbian*, under the category "family instructions."[13] Taking issue with the noted authority on Confucian ritual Fang Bao, Wang argued from classical evidence, that wives as well as husbands must have ancestral tablets for funeral rituals and for installation on the altars of ancestral shrines. As his authority he cited chapters on funeral rituals in the *Book of Rites* and in the *Gongyang* commentary on the *Spring and Autumn Annals*, both of which made clear that the tablets of deceased married couples should be installed together to be worshiped by their descendants.

Although Wang Zhong's essay does not explain why the subject of enshrining wives properly was so important, it reminds us that the High Qing classical revival posed wide-ranging questions about the proper place of women in elite families. Wang expresses concern with ritual propriety and women's dignity in another essay titled "A Critical Opinion on Female Suicide Following the Death of a Fiancé and on Widow Chastity" ("Nüzi xu jia er xu si congsi ji shouzhi yi").[14] Here Wang criticizes the principle of wifely fidelity (*jie*) canonized in the Qing chastity cult, especially the increasingly common practice in which a young woman affianced to a man who died before they married would either kill herself or swear fidelity to her dead fiancé to preserve her honor. Wang argues in disgust that this kind of blind obedience to an abstract norm, encouraged by the state and honored in contemporary society, was actually based on a misreading of classical texts. By a careful investigation of the *Book of Rites*, he demonstrates that a wife's lifelong obligation to her husband does not begin until the marriage ceremony itself, and that betrothal is not to be regarded as a lifelong commitment if extraordinary circumstances intervene:[15]

> Marriage rites are completed with the ceremony of *qinying*, during which the bride is received by her new husband's parents. In later times people have not understood this, and so they have stressed instead the importance of the ceremony *shoupin*, during which the bride's family receives betrothal gifts. I have in mind certain cases, such as the case of Yuan Mei's younger sister, who was betrothed as a child to a man named Gao, and the maid of Zheng Huwen, who was betrothed as a girl to a man named Guo. In both cases, not long after the betrothal the young men to whom they were engaged fell

into bad company and went off on their own for nearly ten years, so the parents on both sides agreed to call off the engagement and make other plans. In each case, however, the young girls themselves resolved to remain faithful to their original marital agreement and could not be persuaded to change their minds. For years Yuan Mei's sister was brutally beaten by her husband, who finally sold her. Only after her elder brother brought a lawsuit was she returned to her natal family, where she died. The Zheng maid's husband insulted her so grievously [*jiong*] that she swallowed poison and died. In the *Analects* it says: "To love benevolence without loving learning is liable to lead to foolishness [*qi bi ye yu*]."[16] We may call such women as these foolish. They knew nothing of the rites, yet they believed themselves to be preserving the rites to the point where they lost their lives [*yun qi sheng*]—how pitiful! Tradition teaches that "a woman who is wife to one person should take no other for the rest of her life." This is not the same as saying once you have received betrothal gifts you may take no others for the rest of your life. Tradition also holds that "a virtuous woman does not serve two husbands." But this is not to say that one cannot receive betrothal gifts from two persons![17]

Wang Zhong presents several arguments about women in the classical revival: Educated women must study rituals and understand them correctly, according to their original meaning. Popular or vulgar contemporary practice cannot be allowed to demean or subvert the true teachings of the classics. Women are likely to be victims of this subversion unless they are truly learned. And a truly learned woman must be dignified with a ritually correct marriage.

Classical research lent itself readily to empathy for women's learning because the sources were so rich. Zhang Xuecheng found the *Book of Odes* and the *Book of Rites* full of evidence about women and their activities. The *Book of Rites*, of course, was the source of reference for scholars like Wang Zhong who were questioning women's roles in rituals such as marriage and funerals. The rich evidence on women in the *Book of Odes* was more complex. Most of the poems about women writers that interested High Qing scholars are found in the "songs of the states," the *guo feng*. These songs are full of contradictory notions of womanhood and of the female poetic voice. High Qing scholars were of two minds about them. In Zhang Xuecheng's reading of the *Odes*, the moral instructress looms as the dominant female figure, especially in the two opening chapters of the *guo feng*, which portray a moral royal wife admonishing her wayward kingly husband. Poems in these chapters, titled "Zhou nan" and "Shao nan"—sometimes referred to as the "Two South" poems ("Er nan")—celebrate the virtues of the wife of King Wen during the golden age honored by Confucius. Zhang also favored other songs of the states, including the first of the Odes of Yong, titled "Cedar Boat," which was read as an allegory for the determined suffering of a faithful widow, and the first Ode of Qi, "The Cock Crows," in which a wife admonishes her husband to attend to his duties instead of lingering abed with her in the morning. In all these poems, the subject is the virtuous wife, not simply a virtuous woman, and the theme is her moral influence over her husband and, through him, over society at large. Thus the *Odes* could easily be read as an injunction to women to speak through poetry in ways that would provide moral guidance and display the Dao.

Zhang embraced the voice of the moral instructress in the *Book of Odes*, but he adamantly rejected the other womanly voice in that classic, the passionate lover. He thought it absurd to imagine that ordinary women could just "open their mouths and pour out verse." He criticized the licentious poems of Zheng as aberrations that obscured the true meaning of women's roles. Those licentious poems, he insisted, were political allegories that had nothing to do with passion or women. They were written by men for another purpose.

The true record of women's learning in the classics was the theme of Zhang Xuecheng's essay on women's learning ("Fu xue").[18] The essay, written in 1797, remained for many years his most famous work. It is a long, vitriolic tract presenting a meticulously documented critical history of erudite women in the Confucian tradition. All evidence, drawn from the classics and the standard dynastic histories, is carefully reviewed, and it rarely refers to poetry.

In the golden age of Zhou rule, Zhang shows, women served as instructors with titles at court. With the decline of the Zhou, learning separated from government and passed into the hands of families and various ruling houses. At that point women became custodians and transmitters of family learning (*jia xue*), which they could convey from one patriline to another by personal instruction or through their children.[19] Such learned women played a crucial role during periods of political upheaval, when family libraries and family teachings were the only safe haven for the preservation and transmission of the Dao. When men perished or were incapacitated, women transmitted precious knowledge to future generations.

Zhang observes, however, that during the Six Dynasties, Tang, and Song periods, from the second through the thirteenth centuries, these scholarly functions were gradually displaced, and learned women came to be known as poets rather than as classical scholars or historians. As a result, the Zhou and Han tradition of women's learning was lost. Although women's learning in the classical tradition survived among a small number of women in exceptional circumstances, these few were unaware of women's scholarship in earlier times. Therefore, although exceptional women sometimes transmitted the Dao, they did so inadvertently, unable to see their knowledge as part of a tradition of women's learning. Among these exceptional women, Zhang includes

Fig. 11. "The Han Scholar Cai Yan [Cai Wenji]," by Jin Tingbiao (fl. 1760–64). Here the controversial scholar-heroine of Han myth and history, taken captive by the Xiongnu and later ransomed by Cao Cao, is shown in a court painting wearing Qing period attire, including hairpins decorated with painted enamel. She plays her song of loneliness on an erhu in the company of the two sons she bore while in captivity. Reprinted from Shen Yizheng 1984: 114.

Cai Yan and Yu Xuanji (Figs. 11 and 12),* erudite writers whose personal lives he found problematic, but whose fame was restored by the classical revival.

So complete was the loss of classical women's learning from historical memory, Zhang argued, that learned women after the Tang mistakenly embraced men's learning as the appropriate standard for their own. Special versions of classics written by and for men, including the *Analects* and the *Classic of Filial Piety*, were rewritten for women. The *Analects for Women* (*Nü lunyu*) and the *Classic of Filial Piety for Women* (*Nü xiaojing*) were, in Zhang's view, unworthy of women's learning in the classical tradition. At best pale imita-

*Cai Yan, married at fifteen, was abducted and forced to remarry a Xiongnu leader, to whom she bore two children. Three poems attributed to her describe her years in exile and her return to China, when she endured a painful separation from her children. This story from the second century plays on powerful themes of forced remarriage, foreign invasion, and maternal sorrow. See Nienhauser 1986: 786–87. Zhang was bothered by Cai Yan's twice-married status, but he admired her central role in history.

Yu Xuanji was a talented courtesan and concubine to the Tang Remonstrating Official Li Yi. After Li rejected her, she became a Daoist nun. As a nun, she received male visitors in the convent where she lived in the ninth-century capital, Chang'an. She was killed in the aftermath of a murder charge against her. In all her roles, she moved in the central political circles, and her poems reflect her understanding of and participation in the major events of her time—hence Zhang's mixed evaluation. See Nienhauser 1986: 944.

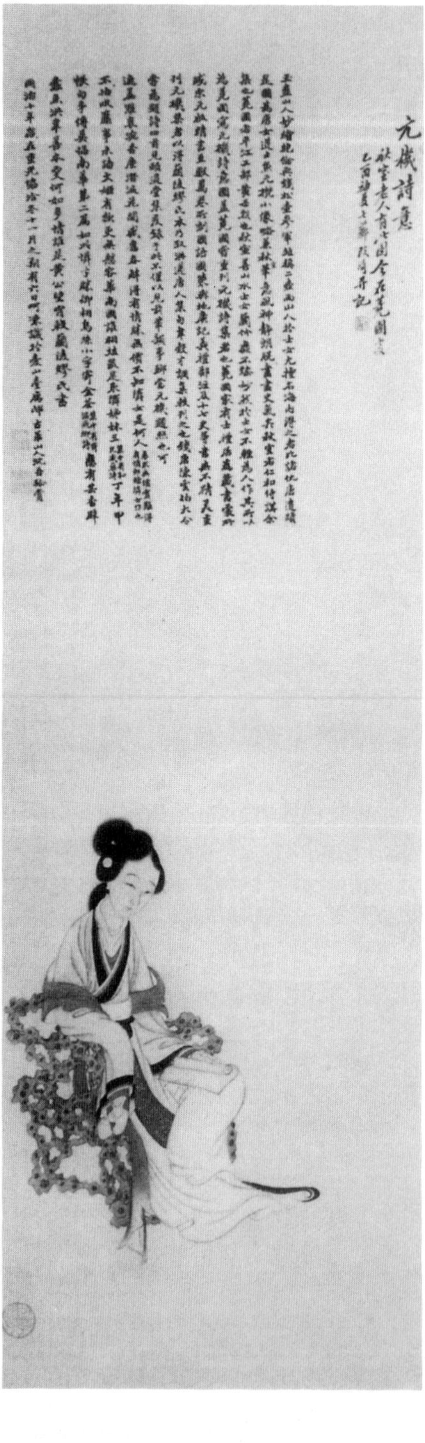

Fig. 12. "Yu Xuanji Reflecting on a Poem," by Gai Qi (1773–1829). This is a copy of an earlier painting of the controversial Tang poet. Reprinted from Shen Yizheng 1984: 124.

tions of the original classics, these works for women only served to confirm women's loss of their own heritage.

Zhang focused on a paradox: whereas "speech" (*yan*) was one of the four classical womanly attributes named in the *Rites of Zhou*, Confucian teachings elsewhere in the same text insisted that women's speech not be heard outside the women's quarters (*nei yan buchu men wai*). After an exhaustive search of the classical evidence, he concluded that it was improper for women to speak publicly as poets. Women's poetic voice, for him, smacked of lewdness: it was the voice of the courtesan. In the same vein, Zhang insisted that poems written in a woman's voice in the *Book of Odes* must actually have been written by male poets using a woman's voice for dramatic and emotional effect:

> The words of men and women in the "songs of the states" are all imitations invented by poets. If we examine the evidence for this in the writings of Han, Wei, and Six Dynasties poets, it is beyond doubt.

In a note, he added:

> The past and the present are governed by the same principles. We cannot claim that in ancient times children and young girls could spontaneously make up verses that later scholars struggled all their lives to produce, but failed.

To drive his point home to the reader, Zhang chose an analogy from the stage:

> We could compare these men's poetic imitations to those of a male actor who impersonates a young virgin in a play: the actor cannot quite pull it off, and he fails to capture perfectly the elegant simplicity of the inner chamber. Yet ignorant people who do not understand these principles of imitation insist that among the ancients even children and women could spontaneously make up verses. On that basis, they claim that women were well suited to writing airs and hymns. To argue this way is just the same as seeing a leading actor mount the stage and enact a historical event from ancient times, and then to imagine that every time one of the ancients moved, they sang a song first.

Amplifying this point in a further note, he wrote:

> When an actor impersonates a person in an event from the ancient past, the words of his songs are just like the commentaries and opinions inserted by historians into historical texts. Thus they are words full of meaning, but they absolutely do not come out of the person's mouth. In the same way, an observer's views will never come out of the person being observed. But the libretto of the opera pays no heed to these distinctions. Thus [on the stage] the gentleman will sometimes step out of line and praise himself, or the petty

> man may even humiliate himself. The audience, like the person who reads a history book, will hear both the praise and the blame [i.e., the audience will appreciate what is not said as well as what is said]. Drama is supposed to be this way, and there is nothing wrong with it. However, if one were to cause these same words to come out of an actual person's mouth, they would not make any sense. The words of men and women in the "songs of the states" and the ancients' imitations of their words ought to be viewed in precisely this light. If we were to say that these words truly came out of the mouths of these men and women, [we would be wrong, because] the promiscuous among them would never expose themselves in this way, and the chaste among them would never be so open.[20]

In this way, Zhang's search of the classics for examples of the proper use of the female voice led him first to the instructresses at the Zhou court and ultimately to a complex understanding of the ways in which proper female speech, confined to the women's quarters, could inform public discourse.[21] Zhang found other evidence of women's education in the classics in accounts of the activities of women who did not necessarily hold formal positions at the court:

> The imperial consorts and the wives of highly ranked officials and their female attendants were all charged, as women, with greeting guests, making ancestral offerings, observing mourning, and performing sacrifice. All these duties required a mastery of rituals that could not be achieved without learning.[22]

Zhang admired not only the learning of these women, but also the vivid records preserved in their own writings. He praised not only Ban Zhao's *Instructions for Women* (*Nü jie*), but also her contribution to the history of the former Han dynasty. And he admired early poems by the imperial consorts Ban Jieyu ("Fu on Unwavering Trust") and the Lady of Tangshan ("Songs of the Inner Chamber") because, "written in the inner chambers of the palace, they nonetheless refer to events in the past history of the country, events described in our historical records."[23] Like all classical texts, he argued, these writings by women were actually history: they had enduring value because they illustrated the Dao of ancient society.[24]

Although Zhang lamented the disappearance of classical women's learning, he was convinced that it could once again be revived. He was personally acquainted with women who had pursued classical studies as part of a tradition of family learning (*jia xue*); in fact, his mother came from such a background.[25] More important, Zhang believed that the time had come for women to recover their heritage of classical learning. This was possible, he wrote, because of the extraordinary age in which he lived.

Zhang's research on women's learning thus influenced his historiography, especially his treatment of women's voice and women's speech. His biographical sketches of contemporary women, for example, dramatize his conviction that learned women could serve as transmitters of the Dao in the present. And he took pains to interview family members and maids so that he could bring his female characters to life through quotations and letters.[26]

Zhang's understanding of the relationship between women's private and public speech is illustrated in an epitaph he composed for his friend Shao Jinhan's mother, Lady Yuan. He began by describing her ancestry, which was crucial to his point that she, like Ban Zhao and others before her, used "family learning" in the home to transmit the Dao of history. He explained that Lady Yuan was descended on her mother's side from the Lüs of Yuyao county, east of Shaoxing. Her ancestor Lü Zhangcheng had served at the exiled Ming court in Guiji, fraternizing as a young man with illustrious Ming loyalists like Gu Yanwu. Her own father, Yuan Susheng, had compiled Lü Zhangcheng's collected works. After celebrating the match between this learned woman and the learned Shao Jiayun, Shao Jinhan's father, Zhang was then able to illustrate how Lady Yuan's learning affected her role as a mother. He painted the Shao children gathered at their mother's knees while she kept her husband company reading late into the night. He noted that although Lady Yuan professed not to understand the great books, deferring to her spouse as the children's teacher, after a drink or two she could rise to the intellectual occasion, retelling tales of Ming history she had learned sitting at her own mother's feet. Then he concluded, in a pointed reference to Lü Zhangcheng and to Lady Yuan's role as a transmitter of history, "Although her stories were 'family tales' (*jia yu*), all had a basis in fact; they were far from hearsay."[27]

For Zhang, the authentic woman's voice was a moral voice, the product of classical learning. Moreover, even when a woman's voice was confined to the women's apartments, even when she spoke properly from behind the screen, she was capable—in his view—of "public" speech. The learned woman could transmit the Dao; her words could be "everyone's" (*gong*).[28]

During the classical revival other models for a legitimate female poetic voice were unearthed from pre-Song texts, and in many circles the talents of female poets were much admired. Eighteenth-century writers especially praised the female poets of the Six Dynasties period, and they often cited stories from the literary lives of characters in *A New Account of Tales of the World* (*Shishuo xinyu*). These Six Dynasties poets supplied a contrapuntal textual voice that spoke directly to women, for female poets and conversationalists in the *Shishuo xinyu*—especially Xie Daoyun of willow catkin fame—were renowned for upstaging their male friends and relatives in verbal combat and poetry contests.

Even Zhang Xuecheng acknowledged the compelling voice of Xie Daoyun when he allowed that the women writers of the Six Dynasties period might still be considered merely errant, not utterly fallen, from a state of moral rectitude:

> The women of the great families of Wang Dao and Xie An of the Jin period transgressed the laws of ritual, but in their pure conversation and their logical reasoning, they showed great intuitive understanding. Thus they mastered Confucian manners and also displayed a thorough understanding of Daoist teachings. If we were to measure them by scholarly standards, they would be merely what Confucius once called "those who strayed from the middle path" on the "ardent" side.[29]

But Zhang Xuecheng was no friend to women poets. On the contrary, his essay on women's learning was written to attack the High Qing era's greatest connoisseur of women's poetry, Yuan Mei. Yuan Mei's unabashed ideal for women was the catkin image. He fancied himself at the center of an entourage of female poets, whose work was collected and published under his literary name as *Collected Poems by Yuan Mei's Female Pupils* (*Suiyuan nüdizi shixuan*). In addition, Yuan's many stories of women writers, scattered throughout his two-volume collection of *Poetry Talks* (*Shi hua*), tell us clearly that in his view a learned woman's highest achievement was to write poetry. His readers too looked to the classics for models, as the preface to the collected works of his so-called female pupils suggests: "In our illustrious dynasty, literary instruction illuminates the realm, womanly virtue is correspondingly felicitous, and the women of the empire's great families have all been transformed by the teachings of the 'Er nan' " (the first two chapters of the *Book of Odes*).[30]

Although the preface to his collection of women's poetry invokes the classical image of the moral wife, Yuan Mei's recollections of the women poets he knew are full of catkin images, especially stories of child prodigies who were brilliant poets. One was Sun Yunfeng, who later became part of Yuan Mei's entourage. At the age of eight *sui* a precocious reader "of great critical intelligence," Yunfeng was presented to a guest visiting her father. The guest, thinking to test her prowess, challenged her with the first line of the *Book of Odes*: "Guan guan ju jiu" (Guan guan! cries the osprey).[31] No doubt he expected to hear the second line in return. Instead, little Yunfeng shot back: "Yong yong ming yan" (Honk honk! cries the goose).[32] This line is not the second line in the *Book of Odes*, but a parallel phrase from a different poem in the collection. Yunfeng signaled her precocity not simply by choosing a parallel line, but by selecting a line in which the bird-call metaphor was identical—both *guan guan* and *yong yong* symbolize the husband calling to his wife—and where *guan* and *yong* are harmonic (*he*) rhymes. Her reply created perfect linguistic, aesthetic, and moral symmetry.[33]

Young prodigies corresponded with one another, as Yuan Mei's story of Yan Jing of Wuxing shows. A skilled calligrapher and bamboo painter at the age of barely nine *sui*, Yan received this colophon on one of her paintings from a fourteen-year-old girl admirer from Putian: "Who would know that the one in the golden carriage [the poet] is not yet ten years old?"[34] Narratives describing young prodigies pointedly contrast their psychological and physical fragility with their robust creativity. Zhang Lunying's younger brother Yuesun recalled his sister, a brilliant calligrapher, as a person with a "soft, mild disposition" and "so slight that she barely filled her clothes." Yet when she applied her brush, he wrote, she was "strong and robust, weighty and bold, uncontrollable."[35] Yuan Mei found young female poets appealing because the child's mind represented spontaneity, simple diction, and pure emotion: "The poet is one who has not lost her* childlike mind" (*shirenzhe bushi qi chizi zhi xinzhe ye*).[36]

Yuan Mei's sentiments sometimes suggest the interactions between talented young female poets and mesmerized aging men that are analyzed in Chapter 5, "Entertainment," which examines the lives of young courtesans and their patrons. Here suffice it to stress once again that women's learning invoked sharply different reactions from learned men. At one extreme was Zhang Xuecheng's ideal, a moral instructress whose family roles (whether maternal, wifely, or daughterly) at once desexed her and endowed her with power and autonomy. The other extreme was Yuan Mei's ideal, a young passionate aesthete whose frail body and sexual naiveté signaled her vulnerability and dependency.[37]

Of course, men encountered both these ideals in the scholarly households of High Qing Jiangnan in the company of their daughters, sisters, and mothers. Young girls who wrote fine poetry could speak to their fathers and brothers in powerful ways that deepened their mutual affection. A father confronting his daughter's unhappy marriage had a profound sense of its cost when her misery was conveyed in poetry. Yuan Mei, whose sisters' suffering provoked cries from his heart, captured a father's anguish over his poet daughter's unhappy marriage by depicting the moment when the father reads one of his daughter's poems and exclaims: "This child is pure and fine; how tragic that fortune has cheated her!"[38] Mothers, the moral instructresses to whom every scholar owed his success, loom in the background, overshadowing everything else. In these ways, women writers young and old touched elite men of all ages, causing controversy in their scholarly work and turmoil

* The Chinese does not specify gender.

in their emotional lives. To illustrate further, we shall explore the High Qing era's great anthology of women's poetry, *Correct Beginnings*, which shows how women writers presented themselves to men.

Wanyan Yun Zhu and 'Correct Beginnings'

The editor of *Correct Beginnings*, Wanyan Yun Zhu (1771–1833), was a native of Yanghu, part of Changzhou prefecture. She was a descendant of the painter Yun Shouping (1633–90), who had been adopted as a youth into the family of a Han Chinese Banner general during the Manchu conquest of the Lower Yangzi region.[39] Her father held an inconsequential post (jail warden) in a county yamen. Her husband, a Manchu aristocrat of the Wanyan clan named Tinglu, died in 1820 while holding office as a prefect in Tai'an, Shandong. Yun Zhu was 49 at the time.[40] After her husband's death, as she entered her fiftieth year, she signaled the new stage in her life by taking a Daoist literary name, Adept of the Lotus Lake.*

Yun Zhu reared three sons, each of whom won an official post. Her favorite, and the most successful among them, was the writer and hydraulics expert Linqing (1791–1846). Linqing's remarkable aesthetic and administrative talents owed much to his mother's company, a debt he took pains to acknowledge in his published writing. His most famous work is a three-volume illustrated autobiography recounting his travels. In it we find glimpses of his companionship with his mother. One entry describes seeing her home after a party he gave on the banks of Daming Lake in Jinan city, in the eighth month of 1816.[41] In another scene, a few years after his father's death in 1824, we see Linqing preparing to transfer from a post in Huizhou prefecture to Yingzhou prefecture, both in Anhui province. Yun Zhu loved the scenery in the Xin'an area surrounding Huizhou. Since she was living with her son at the time, she ordered him to travel through the hazardous Dahong mountain passes to reach his new job so that she could admire the views. Linqing commissioned a drawing of the trip, showing his 53-year-old mother ensconced in a sedan chair (Fig. 13). As bearers struggle to maneuver the chair along the steep mountain road, Linqing leads the way on horseback, calling back to Yun Zhu the names of the famous scenic spots as they pass.[42]

To her devoted son, Yun Zhu owed the inspiration for her monumental anthology. It was Linqing who unearthed the more than three thousand women's poems his mother had collected since her childhood, he who urged

* *Zi* Zhenpu, also Xinglian; *hao* Ronghu daoren. Chap. 3, "The Life Course," explains the significance for women of the fiftieth birthday and explores the implications of Yun Zhu's literary name.

Fig. 13. "Bearing the Palanquin Through Peach Gorge," by Wang Yingfu. This drawing depicts Wanyan Yun Zhu traveling through the Dahong Mountains, guided by her son Linqing. Reprinted from Linqing [1897] n.d., vol. 3, collection 1 *xia*.

her to publish them, and he who arranged to print the final work (Fig. 14). As Yun Zhu recalls affectionately in the preface to her anthology:

> One winter day in the year 1827, my eldest son, Linqing, while on leave from his duties on the Yellow River conservancy, was searching through my old portfolios and found all those poems that ladies had written for one another and presented to one another as gifts, along with many collections of poetry in manuscript. Altogether there were more than three thousand poems. He asked my permission to give them to a woodblock carver so that they could be printed and distributed to a wide audience.[43]

Yun Zhu was inspired, but not ready to give her son permission without reviewing the entire corpus first:

> I resumed my customary practice of years past and read them all through again. Concerned that there were too many poems and undaunted by my

Fig. 14. "Bringing Still More for Consideration and Selection," by Hu Junsheng. Here Yun Zhu is at work in her studio, examining manuscripts offered for consideration by her son Linqing. Two granddaughters are copy editing. Reprinted from Linqing [1897] n.d., vol. 3, collection 2 *shang.*

> own limitations, I reread each one carefully, rejecting any poems that did not conform to refined standards, including all poems depicting sensual images such as rosy clouds and all poems that conveyed emotion through erotic images, regardless of their beauty. The poems retained in the present volume are barely one-half of the original collection. This final edited version I have titled *Correct Beginnings.* The genres and their contents vary, but the sentiment and tone of each is correct. Pure beauty, chaste emotion, conjugal harmony, limpid verse—none would shame Ban Zhao's admonitions,* and all conform to the standards required of a poet.[44]

Correct Beginnings was published in 1831, copyedited by three of Yun Zhu's granddaughters in rotating sequence.[45] One of the three, Miaolianbao, continued the anthology after her grandmother's death, in accordance with Yun

* I.e., *Instructions for Women.*

Zhu's dying wishes. Jin Wengying's preface to the continued edition records the events as follows:

> After *Correct Beginnings* was published, people continued to send poems as before. The Grand Lady [Yun Zhu] selected all the most superior and unusual poems and gathered them in her dowry chest, unable to cast them aside. Whenever she had time, she would read them through and edit them. As her health deteriorated, she gave them all to her granddaughter, saying: "These are the illustrious works presented to me by women scholars throughout the realm who heard about my project, and here also are poems from literati collections. I fear that I will not recover and that I will fail the people who have sent poems to me. You must carry on the project and publish a sequel to the first anthology to fulfill my dream.' O woe! How those words made my heart ache! All the talented women under heaven should weep together for the Grand Lady. As I write these words, I cannot keep the tears from pouring down my face onto my clothes!
>
> Her granddaughter is extremely intelligent, and she took her grandmother's words to heart. Practiced in ritual and honoring poetry, she also paints in the style of Baiyun waishi [Yun Shouping]* when she is able to set aside her embroidery. She continued the project begun by her grandmother to fulfill her grandmother's dream. She gave it all of her attention. When it was finally completed, it included ten *juan* of poems, together with an addendum, a supplement, and an elegy, each in one *juan*—in all more than twelve hundred verses, which she titled *Correct Beginnings, Continued*.[46]

Yun Zhu intended her anthology as a summation of the great literary achievements of women in the first half of the Qing period. Unlike Zhang Xuecheng, who was waiting for women to abandon poetry in order to recover their classical scholarly authority, she believed that women's scholarly authority rested in their poetry. As her editorial decisions show, Yun Zhu was more interested in women's talent than Zhang Xuecheng was, and she was more insistent on women's moral authority than Yuan Mei was. In fact, like most women of her class—the *guixiu*—Yun Zhu believed that in the female poetic voice, talent and virtue were joined. Moreover, she was convinced that women's learning should be put to the broadest possible use, a conviction she illustrated in her own life. Whereas Zhang Xuecheng dismissed women's poetry as a diversion from learned women's true calling and Yuan Mei celebrated women's poetry as a manifestation of their sensual beauty and emotional spontaneity, Yun Zhu believed that women's poetry gave the truest and fullest expression of their moral authority.

* Miaolianbao's ancestor on her grandmother's side—more evidence that *jia xue* was inherited matrilineally as well as patrilineally.

Yun Zhu claimed still more for women's writing voice than that, however. It is plain from her own writing and from the comments of admirers who wrote prefaces to her work that she regarded women's learning as both hallmark and product of the High Qing era.[47] She exclaims with amazement when women living at the edges of the empire—on the Miao borderlands of Hunan, in the malarial swamps of Guangxi on the Vietnam frontier, in the Muslim regions of Hami—all contribute poems to her anthology,[48] and she includes in her appendix women poets from Korea.[49]

Zhang Xuecheng would have had no quarrel with Yun Zhu's poetic standards. She demanded moral rectitude and eloquence of expression; she expected classical erudition and mastery of allusions. With a few notable exceptions, she adamantly refused to print poems by courtesans in her anthology. She was not charmed by romantic subjects. Her "Editorial Principles" ("Li yan"), outlining the premises that shaped her decisions, stand as a classic statement of the consciousness of the *guixiu* in mid-Qing Jiangnan:

> In compiling this anthology, I have attached the greatest importance to purity of emotional expression and to the harmony and elegance of the rhymes; style has been a secondary matter. As for female adepts and Buddhist nuns, among whom are many able poets, they are not fit to appear in the ranks of respectable ladies, and accordingly I have not included them. However, I have devoted a special section to Xia Longyin and Zhou Yubu, who in fact had hidden reasons for avoiding fame and preserving their chastity in order to display their concealed virtues.
>
> Poems about sexual love and romance by courtesans, those fallen women of the green chambers,* whom earlier compilers anthologized profusely and rhapsodized over, are not included here. However, women like Liu Shi, Wei Rongxiang, Xiang Yun, and Cai Run were in fact able to live a pure life in their advanced years. Accordingly, out of respect for our empire's practice of honoring such persons, I have included them in a separate chapter in order to display their quest for purity.[50]

Despite all the commonalities with Zhang Xuecheng's views, Yun Zhu's editorial principles invite us into the womanly side of the classical revival. They show us how women appropriated the terms of the debates of the day and used them to empower themselves as literary critics, as publishers and anthologists, and as writers. Yun Zhu simultaneously claims for herself the authority of the classics, distances herself from the women's writing culture of the late Ming, and establishes her own voice as a High Qing writer.

It is now time to turn to the poets themselves, to see how the female poetic

* "Green chambers" (*qing lou*) is a euphemism for a brothel.

voice expresses these unique values of the High Qing era: concern for moral authority, especially wifely authority, and the celebration of the female writing voice. Their poems make plain the similarity between this female literary realm and the late Ming literary culture so elegantly documented by Dorothy Ko. But in the context of the High Qing era, women's poetic voice had new meaning. It was more audible, it was more controversial, and it engaged directly with men in discussion about women as writers.

The female writers whose work Yun Zhu admired had usually studied the classics at home, often in tutorials with their brothers, sometimes under the guidance of a female teacher.[51] They did not attempt the kinds of public writing that absorbed the men's Han learning movement; few women, for example, published philological research during the classical revival.[52] Instead virtually all women writers wrote poetry, either classical (*shi*) or lyric (*ci*).[53] Their intended audience was usually friends and family. However, since family members would commonly compile, print, or copy a woman's collected poetry, many women writers expected their work to reach a broader audience at some future time.

Women writers often locate themselves with respect to the life course—or they are so located by Yun Zhu in her prefaces. Like Zhang Xuecheng and Yuan Mei, Yun Zhu appreciated the gifted poet who was precocious. She uses the term *zao hui*, "brilliant at an early age," to refer to a poet who produced a memorable line of poetry between the ages of seven and fourteen *sui*, that is, during the interval between losing the milk teeth and the hairpinning ceremony conventionally known as *wei ji*, "before hairpinning."[54] Precocity is sometimes captured in dazzling erudition and cleverness, as in the case of Sun Yunfeng (see p. 92) or Wang Fen, who at seven *sui* composed a poem she modestly titled "Dashed Off While Sitting at Night" (*Ye zuo ou cheng*), which includes this brilliant description of a moonrise: "Above the moon, a thousand peaks are still" (*yueshang qian feng jing*).[55]

Precocity was also signaled by a sense of dark foreboding and melancholia that made a young poet seem old beyond her years. At the age of seven *sui*, Hou Cheng'en wrote:

> I live in sadness on this moonlit night,
> My body thin, like a flower dropped from heaven.[56]

Other dimensions of precocity are more conventional: Liu Ruzhu memorized all 1,000 poems in the comprehensive anthology of Tang poetry (*Quan Tang shi*) by the age of ten *sui*. At the same age, Cao Xishu mastered the entire *Book of Odes* and was able to expound the meaning of its poems. To celebrate the hairpinning of the precocious (*zao hui*) Tan Guangyao, her elder brother printed her collected poems and placed the woodblocks in storage for her dowry.[57]

Most educated girls began learning to read and write with family members. The father of the female anthologist Wang Duanshu was heard to remark one day after their lessons that he would trade eight sons for one daughter.[58] The distinguished Qian Weicheng, like many fathers, "personally instructed" (*jing kou shou*) his daughter Mengdian.[59] Sonless fathers especially doted on their gifted daughters.[60] Yun Zhu's remarks about the poet Wen Pu hint at the conflicting emotions such fathers experienced:

> Wen Pu's father, lacking a son, had her dress as a boy and hired a tutor to instruct her in the classics. When she reached the age of fourteen *sui*, she had mastered the current examination-style prose,* and her father wanted her to sit for the exams. But someone challenged her father with these words: "Wouldn't it be better for her to be a Cao Dagu than a Huang Chonggu?"† Eventually her father desisted, but from that time on, Wen Pu declined to receive visitors and donned the garments of a man, caring for her parents to the end of her life and never marrying.[61]

The only insight Yun Zhu provides into this gifted daughter's reaction to her father's attention appears in Wen Pu's own poem, "Writing My Feelings":

> Fitful and falling, autumn moonlight fills clumps of chrysanthemums.
> Lonely and desolate, the circling wall endures the west wind.
> Night lengthens, the lamp oil runs out: I am blocked from my studies.
> My malaise lifts, the window is still: I set aside my needlework.
> Stirred by the wind, chilled crows flock and scatter.‡
> Shriveled by the frost, worm-eaten leaves are half transparent.
> Slanting sunlight is chill and cold—evening in the deserted village.
> I stand in the quiet courtyard and count the wild geese who've lost
> their flocks.[62]

How can we decipher the reactions of a young girl to the intense combination of affection and interest that older men lavish on her in the name of poetry? For Wen Pu, her father's mixed messages make it impossible for her to succeed as a scholar, but she cannot face marriage either. The psychology at

*That is, she could write "eight-legged" essays, the rigid formal style required for the civil service examinations.

†That is, your daughter should remain true to her nature as a woman and emulate Ban Zhao instead of trying to pass as a man like Huang Chonggu (see n. 61).

‡The phrase "jackdaws [or crows] passing" was a conventional way to mark the hours just before daybreak during the winter months. The crow here signifies winter and the predawn darkness.

work here is complex. She fears and dreads marriage as the end of childhood; she sees the end of childhood as the end of her intellectual life. Interactions between father and daughter here, focused as they are on sonlike achievements, deeply conceal the erotic or titillating nuances so evident in many of Yuan Mei's descriptions of very young female poets. Harold Kahn proposes that connoisseurs like Yuan Mei might be called "literary pedophiles."[63] But what can we say of a father's desire to make his daughter a son?

Perhaps most learned men facing learned women were simply scared: threatened by the power of mature women's writing, they could still be attracted to the harmless delights of young girls' work. Literary relationships between fathers and daughters were far more complex. A father could disguise his deep attraction to a daughter's beauty and talent by treating her like a son, but this created profound confusion—for him and for her—about the role each should play in the family.[64]

Women, like men, used the willow catkin symbol of the innocent poet-genius to describe the work of women dear to them. The catkin recurs in Yun Zhu's anthology and elsewhere during the High Qing era,[65] as in the following poem by Zhang Wanying, written in memory of her elder sister:

ON READING DRAFTS OF MY SISTER'S WORK

Ephemeral life is like water flowing:
Suddenly we have been separated by death all these years.
Tears well up as an early autumn begins.
A distant ghost dreams and draws me in,
A crane flies, set off against the moon,
A flower falls, suffused with golden sunlight.
On this day under the western window
In a quiet moment I recite your catkin verses.[66]

A daughter who carried on her father's teachings by instructing her sons was said to "pass on" (*chuan*) or "inherit" (*cheng*) the "family learning" (*jia xue*) of her natal line.[67] This is how, we are told, brilliant daughters who dazzled their families with catkin poems became moral instructresses exhorting their sons with classical learning. One example is the poet Cao Xishu (1709–43), credited with "stern mentoring" of her son, the official Lu Xixiong. Her biography in the Shanghai county history records that she exhorted him to study with the following phrase: "The spirit of the Han and Six Dynasties is not far removed from antiquity; do not let yourself sink into wild Chan Buddhism!"[68] Lu Xixiong, who was eventually appointed co-editor-in-chief of the *Imperial Four Treasuries of Extant Works* (*Qinding siku quanshu*), may himself have approved the decision to include a notice of his mother's collected works in the imperially authorized catalog (*Siku quanshu qinding tiyao*), where she is eulogized for "carrying on the learning of her house" (*cheng qi jia xue*).[69]

It is noteworthy that Cao Xishu was known for being "strict," for the mother-as-teacher is most often marked by the adjective *ci*, "kindly" or "nurturant." For example, describing a son and daughter studying at their mother's feet, Yun Zhu chooses the phrase *tong cheng ci xun* ("together they received the maternal instructions"), using the word *ci*, "nurturant," as a synecdoche for mother.[70] This term is often contrasted with its paternal counterpart, *yan*, meaning "strict," "stern," or "severe." The phrase *yan fu ci mu* ("stern father and indulgent mother") appears in very early texts,[71] and in High Qing times it forms an axis around which parent-child relationships were negotiated. In fact, Louise Edwards describes *Dream of the Red Chamber* as a chronicle documenting the displacement of the stern father by the kindly mother whose nurturance becomes monstrous indulgence and ruins the son.[72] Significantly, Yun Zhu sees only the positive effects of maternal care and instruction. Her anthology denies and erases the destructive possibilities so clear in *Red Chamber*'s indulgent and ineffectual maternal figures.

Zhang Zao (d. 1780), the mother of the scholar-official Bi Yuan and herself the daughter of an accomplished poet-mother, is a fine example of the exemplary kindly mother. Zhang Zao's first reward for her devotion to her son's training came when the emperor singled him out for special first-place honors in the palace examination of 1760.[73] Later in life, Bi Yuan's praise for his mother came to the attention of the Qianlong emperor during his southern tour of 1780. While Bi was mourning his mother at the ancestral home in Zhenyang, Jiangsu, the emperor presented him with a scroll on which appeared, in the emperor's own hand, these words: "Her classical instruction sustained the family" (*Jing xun ke jia*).[74] Bi Yuan subsequently served with distinction as governor and later governor-general in two troubled provinces. However, he was posthumously disgraced and his family's property confiscated when evidence linked him to a corruption scandal in the purges that followed the Qianlong emperor's death.

In a cautionary ode composed in 1773 as her son departed for his first governorship, in Shaanxi province, his mother appears to foresee Bi Yuan's future disgrace. The poet begins by reminding her son that she prays for him day and night. Then she warns him in metaphor of the dangers awaiting him ("a cornice, cut too small, may be worthless; a laden carriage, without a driver, may stumble to a halt"). No matter how high he climbs, or how great his talent, he is constantly at risk: "Discipline yourself and strive for purity and integrity; temper your virtues to influence those below you," intones the poet. Then, in a stanza that won praise in the local history honoring her memory,

Zhang Zao adds a historical note on the moral economy of Shaanxi's people, to emphasize the weight of her son's responsibility as their governor:

> The people of the west are pure by nature;
> Their character is simple and few are given to extravagance.
> The sounds of the ancient Zhou capitals still echo;*
> Arts and learning flourish there and thrive.

In the closing lines of the poem, she regrets that Bi Yuan's father died when his son was still so young, comforts herself that "the instructions he bequeathed to us did not die with him," and reflects sadly on her own declining years.[75]

Like many famous mothers, Zhang Zao was a widow who assumed responsibility for her son's support and education after her husband died. By including this poem in her anthology, Yun Zhu might be stressing that Bi Yuan's mother, had she lived, could have saved her son from the missteps that blighted his record and disgraced his family.[76] Yun Zhu's anthology contains countless admiring records of other wives who, though not widowed, took charge while a husband traveled to sit for the exams or to take office at a distant post.

In the following description of the poet Kong Jiying of Tongxiang, Zhejiang, Yun Zhu conflates the image of Mencius's mother slaving at the loom with the ideal of the mother instructing her sons (work complementing her other virtues):

> She was a gifted calligrapher and painter. Because her husband traveled abroad, each night she would teach her son his lessons and instruct the maid in weaving the whole night through. She once wrote the following line: "Inside the study, I watch my son discussing the *Analects* of Confucius; by the light of the lamp, I teach my maid to cull the Wu cotton."[77]

A poem by Jiang Lan, who was honored for her devotion to her husband's parents, plays self-consciously and even sarcastically on the same theme. The poet exhorts her spouse to study as he departs to sit for the examinations:

> I have heard it said that the Dao of learning
> And spinning and weaving are the same kind of occupation.
> You spin floss to make an inch of thread;
> You accumulate inches of thread to make a foot.
> Now that you have dropped the curtain of Dong,†

*Here she alludes to Feng and Hao, the capitals, respectively, of the Zhou kings Wen and Wu; both are in Shaanxi.

†When the great Han philosopher and scholar Dong Zhongshu studied, he pulled down the curtain and did not gaze at his own garden for three years.

How can I find words to express my delight?
I'll not say that you have learned well,
For the classics and the histories are truly worth endless contemplation.
I'll not say that your years are tender,
For one must make every second count.
I'll not say that your talent has reached a peak,
Because only when you focus your energy will you achieve your heart's ambition.
Here at home, your father and mother are still living,
But let them not disturb your thoughts.
Though family problems are overwhelming,
I'll not burden you with the plans for solving them.
You read your ten thousand books,*
I'll weave my finest silk of the seventh.†
If I fulfill my wifely duties in every way,
You should make your parents happy.
Let us both look forward to your return with autumn winds,
Certain to pluck the branch of the cassia tree‡ this time.
The Moon Goddess has beguiling eyes,
Don't let her laugh at this woman.
Exert yourself, my husband!
Do not be burdened by your wife's complaints![78]

The sharp edge of a virtuous wife's poem makes public the faults of a wayward, lazy husband.[79]

Of course, a son could be corrected by his mother without suffering embarrassment. In fact, sons endured motherly criticism openly—even sentimentally—and turned it into a record of their own filiality. Here is a memorial to a mother's overbearing tutelage by Xie Daocheng,[80] an early Kangxi official, in a poem titled "Remembering My Mother Urging Me to Study":

"Son, come here. How many years has it been since Yao?
Son, you must remember. From Yao to the present, how many emperors have reigned?"
As a boy, whenever I showed the slightest hesitation in my reply,

*An allusion to a poem in which the Tang poet Du Fu exhorts a friend: "Read your books 'til you wear out ten thousand volumes! Apply your brush as if you were a god!" (*du shu po wan juan, xia bi ru you shen*), a euphemism for broad learning and consummate erudition.

†The phrase *qi xiang* here refers to the seven daytime positions of the star Vega, the symbol of the Weaving Maid honored in the Festival of Double Seven that celebrates women's work. See Chap. 6, "Work."

‡That is, win the *juren* degree.

My mother's face changed color and flared up in anger:
"To spread out a book with a humble heart, this is a student's
responsibility;
In studying the ancient ways, are you no better than a woman?"
Alas!
My mother's words are still in my ear,
My face still gleams with perspiration—
Would that she could ever be angry, and I ever anxious!
Now I hear no one urging me to study.[81]

The fraught relationship between sons and their learned mothers was a favorite subject of painters who decorated the enameled porcelain wares popular in the Qianlong era. Chinese ceramic artists learned the technique of enamel decoration from the Jesuits, who showed them European porcelains adorned with pictures of mothers and sons, including Mary and the boy Jesus. Chinese artists transformed the theme by adding the more familiar books, paper, and brushes they associated with mother-son intimacy. At the same time, by reducing the boy to a child and his mother to a charming young woman, the artist disarms the threat of the powerful learned mother (Figs. 15 and 16).

For a daughter, mother's effort and example lay at the heart of emotional bonds so powerful that we must imagine many found them impossible to write about, especially because daughters left their mothers so early in life for marriage. Yun Zhu stressed the intellectual ties between mother and daughter, commenting frequently on how a daughter might "inherit her mother's teachings" (*cheng mu jiao*). Zhang Zao, the mother whose influence followed her son Bi Yuan into high office, learned to write poetry from her own mother, the poet Gu Ruoxian. The poet Yu Xiefan "received instruction from her mother" (*bin xun ci wei*), the *nü shi* Liu Wanhuai.[82] For some women, instructing a daughter was an act of love and joy that produced in time a female companion with whom one could exchange poems and, through them, feelings and thoughts. For others, teaching a daughter only served to recall bitter memories of youthful talents and hopes that were never realized, as Liang Lan'e wrote in the following poem:

TEACHING MY DAUGHTER

My trifling, lowly little girl,
Reciting your lessons by the window.
Now warbling like an oriole,
Now mumbling like a parrot.
Copying calligraphy, your brush is still rough.

Seeing someone, you're too embarrassed to speak.
Your mother's fate in life has been cruel.
I appreciate fully the bitterness in history and poetry.*
The four attributes and the three followings†
I have taught you with scrupulous care.
Meekly obey and practice wifely conduct—
As for everything else—it's beyond your reach.[83]

Liang Lan'e's last stanza sums up the legacy of many creative daughters who "inherited mother's teaching." Dai Yunyu of Gui'an, Zhejiang, whose mother named her for a dream about the poet Xie An, reared two talented daughters despite her extreme suffering as she followed her unsuccessful spouse from exam to exam and, later, on an arduous journey through the coastal mountains of the southeast as he sought to escape his failures. After a miscarriage and the loss of another young son, reduced to direst poverty and forced constantly to travel, she poured her anguish into verse. She died at the age of 30 *sui*—just before her husband passed his first examination.[84]

But pitiful stories like Liang's and Dai's were not for everyone. Yun Zhu

*This double-entendre expresses the mother's sympathy both for the difficulty her daughter experiences trying to learn these ancient texts and for the hollowness of her efforts, which will in the end lead her nowhere.

†The four attributes for women, encoded in didactic texts after Ban Zhao, are "womanly virtue" (referring to moral virtue), womanly speech, womanly comportment, and womanly work. The three followings refer to the family system, in which formal authority belongs to males; therefore the daughter defers to her father, the wife to her husband, and the widow to her son.

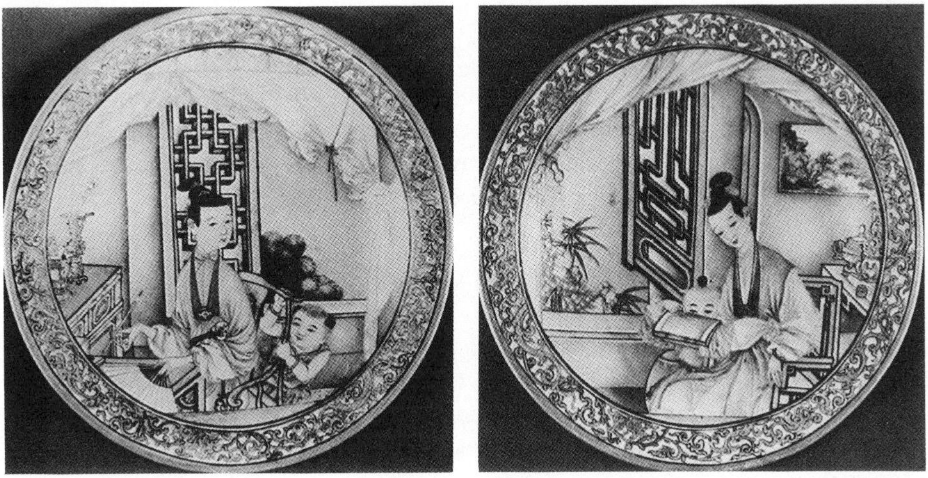

Fig. 15 (facing pages). Saucers and teapot with painted enamel showing mothers educating their sons, Qianlong period. Courtesy of the National Palace Museum, Taipei, Taiwan, Republic of China.

Fig. 16. Pair of painted enamel saucers, Qianlong reign, showing a mother instructing her son in the inner chambers. Courtesy of the National Palace Museum, Taipei, Taiwan, Republic of China.

also introduces us to Zhang Shulian, of Shangyu, the daughter of a *jinshi* degree holder and the mother of successful officials. We see Zhang, at the age of 90 *sui*, energetically "passing on the teachings of her natal home" (*cheng ting xun*) to her granddaughters. In a poem titled "For My Granddaughters Studying Poetry and Calligraphy," Zhang Shulian shows what a nurturant environment could do for a female intellectual's self-confidence:

> Long ago when I dwelt in the women's chambers,
> My father loved to recite poetry.
>
> . . .
>
> Understanding that I was quite intelligent,
> He taught his daughters as he taught his sons.
> Brothers and sisters, elders and juniors, we all
> recited for each other.
>
> . . .
>
> "Even if you girls are not sons
> Who must aim to make their name known [he would say],
> You should preserve a pure and simple style,
> Make fine poetry and calligraphy your calling,
> Strive to make talent and virtue
> Develop together, support and do not impede each other."[85]

The contrasting fate of Dai Yunyu and Zhang Shulian, conveyors of women's learning in the family, is reproduced in their offspring. Dai Yunyu's younger daughter, Chen Qiongpu, the more accomplished of her two talented girls, committed suicide at the age of 29 *sui* following her husband's death. By contrast, like Yun Zhu herself, Zhang Shulian was an inspiration to her granddaughters, sustaining them with a family tradition that nurtured women's talent and providing a living example of a productive and satisfying womanly life as an artist and intellectual.

Erudite sisters in fortunate families also served as literary confidantes and emotional companions to their brothers. Liu Wanhuai of Yanghu, Jiangsu, tutored together with her younger brother by their mother, the *nü shi* Yu Youlan, became his close intellectual partner. In his company she developed her aesthetic sensibilities and her ideas about how to write, as she reveals in a poem she addressed to him:

> SITTING AT NIGHT DISCUSSING
> POETRY WITH MY BROTHER
>
> Writing a poem is like making a friend.
> You want to see inside to the true liver and gall.
> Why enlist ornament or decoration
> When art and feeling will pour out spontaneously together?

A spiritual energy charges my brush;
An enlightened mind shuts out worldly cares.
Compare it to a silkworm spinning thread;
Liken it to a stone holding gems in a matrix.[86]

After marriage, ties between brothers and their learned sisters remained strong. A brother's visit to his married sister brought painful memories of the home where she grew up, sometimes compounded with concern about aging parents.[87] A brother's death, described here, unleashed feelings the poet Dai Lanying tried to capture:

WEEPING FOR MY ELDER BROTHER

A death notice comes; sudden shock.
I fight to hold back the flood of tears.
What use is it to take up official seals
If in the end you will leave this ephemeral life?
News from afar might be mistaken—
I still remember your face so clearly—
But now comes a letter from Dalei.
As I reach into the bamboo satchel, the sharp pain doubles.[88]

Gifted sisters even used poetry to create ties with their brothers' wives. Yao Yundi of Jinshan, Jiangsu, studied poetry and read the *Book of Changes* (*Yi jing*) with her elder brother's wife, Zhang Foxiu. The formidable Qian Mengdian, daughter of Qian Weicheng, wrote 30 rhymes for her younger brother's wife and sent them to her so that she could use them as models.[89]

Poet sisters found special ways to express their mutual feeling in poetry. Parting from her fourth elder sister, Hu Shenrong declared:

We have depended on each other for so long,
Our emotional bonds are stronger than brothers'.[90]

Zhang Qi's four daughters wrote countless poems to one another during the years when they were separated by marriage.[91] The Xu sisters both married into the Li family, where they happily continued exchanging poems every day.[92] A younger sister might take charge of a deceased sibling's child, as Zhu Wenyu records painfully in the poem "Looking After My Orphaned Nephew":

Your mother is dead, and who will care for you?
As I lead you by the hand, my heart aches even more.
Sobbing, sobbing, your cries never cease,
As if they were my own elder sister's sounds.[93]

In another poem, Fang Jing of Tongcheng recalls her childhood with her sisters:

TO MY SISTERS, IN MEMORY OF TIMES PAST

As little girls, we matched shoulders to line up according to height,
How hard to forget those splendid days of our childhood!
By a window draped in blue gauze were crammed a thousand books,
Incense of aloeswood encaged a whole bed's quilt.
When spring reached the loft of our house, we embroidered there together.
We made linked verse beneath the flowers, our lines spreading fragrance of their own.
Laughing and chattering freely at our parents's side,
How could we know that the poem "Tao yao" threatened eternal sorrow?*
The glow of companionship had not lasted long, when suddenly autumn grew dark,
Frosts and snows came out of season and took our father's life.†
Like ranks of snowgeese disturbed by the wind, we grieved to lose our orderly formation,
Like swallows with mud in our beaks‡ after the rain, we lamented the dying spring.
Once we enjoyed a happy meeting, but each of us had grown old.
Even if we could return to the old days, the path back is all worn away.
This white head cannot bear to dwell on what happened long ago,
My poem takes shape, each word a taste of bitter sorrow.[94]

Dread of marriage and the end of childhood led some young girls to rebel. A few managed to convince their parents of their religious beliefs and seceded from the family altogether, in the manner of the young Ming mystic Tanyangzi.[95] Yuan Mei recorded the tale of a child who "liked to dress in Buddhist robes and recite rosaries and pray six times a day." Her parents observed this behavior with growing resignation as she matured and eventually built a convent to house her when, still unwed, she turned 30 *sui*.[96] But most young girls who vowed celibacy and embraced a religious life did so only after

*The poet refers to their studies of the classic *Book of Odes* (*Shi jing*). The sixth ode, titled "Graceful Is the Peach," celebrates the joys of a newly married woman, who is likened in the poem to a graceful peach tree, fecund and comely (Fig. 17). In other words, Fang Jing and her sisters did not realize at the time that marriage would mean permanent separation and sadness.

†Lit., "snapped the mighty cedar."

‡That is, trying vainly to build a nest.

Fig. 17. "Illustrated Appreciation of the Poem 'Graceful Is the Peach' ['Tao yao tu zan']." The drawing depicts a new bride demurely concealed by the draperies in her carriage. Reprinted from Wang Chun [1816], in Zhou Wu 1988, vol. 1: 179.

the death of a fiancé or husband. At that point, Confucian morality defended their piety, making it seem not rebellious but virtuous.[97]

Anecdotes from the lives of "famous" women writers provide rare examples of gifted young women who nurtured their talent right through the transition to wifehood. A bride might bring her writing directly into the nuptial bedchamber, as did Bao Zhihui, of whom Yuan Mei wrote: "If she didn't have a pen and inkstone in her boudoir for even a single day, she was disconsolate."[98] The poet Jin Yi brought her inkstone and brushes into her marriage as part of her dowry and "within a few days turned the bedroom into a study."[99] Husbands and wives shared literary and scholarly pursuits: Jin Yi's spouse exchanged poetry with her,[100] and a friend of Yun Zhu's son enjoyed collating texts with his wife "on fine days in the spring and autumn."[101]

Yuan Mei liked to joke that in such companionate marriages, the wife was usually the better writer.[102] His best example is the story of Wu Ruoyun of Jiading. Reading her husband's poetry one day, Wu sees the following line: "Before the mirror stand, I bow to my female pupils [*nü mensheng*]." "You need to change one character," she says to her husband. "Which one?" he asks. She smiles. "*Men* should be *xian*,"* she says sweetly.[103]

During the years of "rice and salt," these enterprising married women continued to find time to write. Zhang Yuesun, in a biographical sketch of his elder sister Lunying, recalled: "In her home the account books, abacus, scissors and rule, and rice and salt were all mixed up with her books and manuscripts." Lest this remark cast aspersions on his sister, he hastened to add: "It was not that she neglected her womanly work for her writing. . . . In fact, most of her poems were about family and kin relationships."[104] For obvious reasons reflected in Zhang Yuesun's comments, wifely poems tended to focus not on art, but on spouses or sons, especially on their trials in the examinations. Zhang Yin wrote this poem for her husband as she saw him off to sit for the exams:

> Fallen leaves fill stone stairs,
> West wind rattles paper windows.
> I rose early to urge you on your journey;
> We were both disoriented, lost.
> Although we shall not be parted long,
> My heart feels pain I cannot help.
> Shall I be like the wife of Baili Xi,
> So poor I must burn the doorbar to cook the rice?†
> The morning meal is not yet ready;
> You sail away on an empty stomach.
> Fine rain wets your travel clothes,
> Cold gusts blow your short jacket.
>
> . . .
>
> Your travel bags are too thin,
> How will they withstand the harsh frost?

*In other words, the compound *mensheng* (pupils) should be changed to *xiansheng* (teachers); the line would then read, "Before the mirror stand, I bow to my female teachers."

†This line may be not a complaint but, in Stephen West's preferred reading, an expression of confidence: "Do I compare with the wife of Baili Xi, who survived poverty in her husband's absence and shared in his glory when he returned?" (personal communication, October 1994).

Grasping your hand, here I must stand;
I have tears, but my eyes are already full.
My husband, you are rich in classical skills,
You have endured distress day after day.
Go, and do not look back;
Give all your strength to success.
May your worn brush exude rare talent,
May your old ink give forth new fragrance.
Don't depend on those study guides for answers;
Rely on the learning stored in your mind.
If you are fortunate enough to encounter ice, make
  it a mirror for your virtue,
And pray don't slight the art of writing.[105]

In the tense economy of her poem, Zhang Yin captures every emotion of the wife left alone: sadness, resentment, guilt, fear, and moral authority. It could not be an accident that she arrayed her feelings in this order.

Mothers too, guiding their sons through the grueling competition for degrees and office, wrote poems to express their anguish. Few experienced the heady fame that accrued to a son who placed first in the exams. Failure of the sort reflected in the following poem was far more common:

TO MY SON YONGJI ON HIS JOURNEY FAR AWAY

My son, the grandson of a man honored by the emperor as
  a "pure official,"*
Was very studious, but unable to support himself.
At the age of 30, fame still eluding him,
He returned to his old home, empty-handed.
Threats from the outside returned,
Distress within the land continued;†
Suddenly he set off to join the army,
He threw on his clothes and rose at night.
The bright stars shone in the sky,
The river flowed to the top of its banks.
The moving clouds will always return,

*The phrase "pure official" (*lian li*) refers here to the poet's own father, a holder of the *juren* (provincial civil service examination) degree. Such degree holders were given the literary designation "filial and pure" (*xiao lian*).

†The poet uses "external" (*wai*) and "internal" (*nei*) in reference to the empire and military unrest, but she may also be using the terms to criticize the humiliation from outside the home (*wai*) and distress within the family (*nei*) that her son suffered because of his failures in scholarship. Thus these two lines could also be read: "Humiliation from the outside world followed him back; / Distress within his family gave him no reprieve."

But my traveling son stops for nothing.
Grasping at his streaming face,
He left his parents' home.
His long journey began here.[106]

Here we see the poet once again leaning over her balcony, looking off into the distance for a loved one—this time a son. Hard as it was to face the enormous odds, it was a mother's challenge to keep her son from giving up the struggle for a degree. Li Hanzhang of Yunnan, the daughter of a *jin shi* degree holder and the mother of two eventually successful sons, sent this poem of encouragement when both failed the examinations at the capital:

Success and failure pass like dew and lightning;
This old person* has paced the floor many times for you.
Do not shrink if your wings are clipped in this once-in-three-years' flight;
You may yet shed light to illumine ten carriages.
Within these four seas, how can any man climb the road to a high position?
Most, like fish, lie hidden at the muddy bottom.
Years ago, with the bow and arrow hung outside my door,†
Was it for fame in the examinations that you first began to read?[107]

This motherly admonition and exhortation sums up a double message: try your hardest; your mother loves you no matter what happens. Motherly and wifely poetic voices use the authoritative cadence of classical verse to pass judgment on their society, criticizing its harsh competitive examinations and speaking out for the suffering of their menfolk. At the same time, they echo society's larger messages, reminding sons and husbands of the great deeds they must accomplish and the daunting obstacles that lie ahead.

Not all women struggled successfully against the pressures and sorrows of married life. Melancholia, illness, despair, and death dominate the stories of countless young wives. Men found these poems exceptionally moving; Yuan Mei recorded them in profusion. One of his tales of a pathetic young poet reads in part: "When Miss Lu married Cao Huangmen at the age of seventeen, she had already styled herself with a literary name [The Person from Elegantly Wooded Hills]. Her dowry was full of books on literature and history. She was especially fond of the *Chu ci* [Elegies of Chu],[108] and when she was not doing her embroidery, she would always recite them." Miss Lu was so

* See second footnote to p. 74.

† She alludes here to the arrow made of *peng* rushes and the bow made of mulberry wood that were hung outside the door of the birthing room to announce a son.

fond of these tragic poems that her maids gossiped about her. Alarmed, her husband warned her not to read them. But Miss Lu died very soon after her marriage, overcome by melancholy.[109]

On another occasion, Yuan Mei wrote, apropos of no one in particular, "These days respectable women with a talent for poetry never find a perfect match."[110] A scrap of poetry left by one unhappy daughter who burned her work before she died, unwed, at a young age attests to the girl's dark view of a married future she did not live to experience:

PALACE SONG

The eunuchs proclaim the imperial will that the new woman play on
the *zheng*.
Her jade-white fingers lightly pluck sounds of sorrowful separation.
Just then the sounds scatter on a breath of spring wind.
The lords and princes outside, suddenly hearing, don't understand.[111]

Another poem, this one recorded by Yun Zhu, reveals the agony of one young person whose very mastery of the moral lessons in her classical studies drove her to kill herself:

FAREWELL, MOTHER

Though your daughter's body is very weak,
Her spirit is strong as iron.
Though the books she has read are few,
She grasps their meaning with clarity and determination.
Before a woman is betrothed,
Her body is pure like snow.
After she is betrothed, her commitment cannot be scorned.
If she is lucky, she will sleep with her husband all her life,
In keeping with the proper roles for husband and wife.
If she is unlucky, her husband will die when he is young,
And she will vow to keep her chastity forever.
Sadder yet am I, who never saw her future husband!
His fate grieves me each time I see the waning moon.
I am still called "the person who has not yet died,"*
But now I am as good as buried with him.
I do not die from the pain of grief;
For three years I have waited to lay aside mourning.
Once I stopped, I began to fast,
But emotions are strong and the rites are hard to violate.
To destroy my life will violate my mother's heart,

*See footnote to p. 67.

My heart too is pained beyond measure.
As I follow my betrothed to the Yellow Springs,
Human bonds, moral bonds, none will split apart.[112]

For the woman who survived young wifehood to enter middle age, advancing years proved no bar to learning. We know of a few women (Zhang Lunying was one) who actually began their literary careers in what was regarded as old age, as in this story recounted in Yun Zhu's anthology:

> Zuo Muguang was in her fiftieth year before she began the studies that placed her in the ranks of accomplished woman poets (*shinüzhong zhi gaoda fu*). When her husband died, she took her two sons with her and left Tongcheng, Anhui, to stay in Jizhou (Jining prefecture, Shandong). There she wrote an entire manuscript every day, and from that time her progress was rapid and her poetry increasingly accomplished. She kept company with two other women writers (*nü shi*): the sisters Shi Qianxian and Xiangxia, with whom she exchanged poems. She had a maid carry their poems back and forth.[113]

Yun Zhu's own life course shows how the precocious poetess becomes the upright wife, then greets old age with a fresh burst of creativity. Her experience is captured in the allusion she chose for the title of her anthology: the notion of "correct beginnings" (*zheng shi*), which first appears in the "songs of the states" (*guo feng*) in the *Book of Odes*. "Correct beginnings" refers to the women's apartments (i.e., the domestic realm, women's realm) as the starting point for the process of kingly transformation that ordered the imperium. Notice how Yun Zhu appropriates this classical trope and makes it her own authority for writing. In the autobiographical preface to her anthology, she describes the path of maturation that leads a gifted young female writer to the powerful moral center described in the *Odes*:

> Of old, when Confucius edited the *Odes* [*Shi jing*], he did not eliminate writings from the women's apartments. In later times, parochial scholars always say that the task of wives and daughters should be limited to taking charge of making wine and drawing water, sewing clothes and embroidering. They are not aware of prescriptions for women's learning presided over by Palace Women [the so-called Nine Concubines], which are described in the *Book of Rites* [*Li ji*]. These prescriptions begin with "womanly virtue," followed by "womanly speech." Now speech [*yan*] does not refer to written words, but surely it is nearly the same as writing. So if in recent times, women have been studying poetry, what could be the harm in it? Only when the study of poetry neglects the Greater Odes ["Da ya"] does the teaching of the *Book of Odes* degenerate. Only then will the poet compete to compose the most seductive or sensual song or lapse into artful or frivolous phrases. At worst, her head

> may be turned by sexual attraction and carefree dalliance, and she will utterly neglect the dictates of modesty and gentility. But this does not result from studying poetry; it is the result of studying the wrong poetry.
>
> From the time I lost my milk teeth [i.e., from the age of seven *sui*], my father believed that I ought to read books to comprehend their underlying principles, and so he commanded me to study in our family school alongside my two elder brothers. I was tutored in the Four Books, the *Classic of Filial Piety* [*Xiao jing*], the *Odes* [*Shi jing*], the *Classified Lexicon* [*Er ya*]. When I grew a little older, my father personally instructed me in poetry in the ancient and modern styles, repeatedly stressing the idea of "correct beginnings" [*zheng shi*]. At that point, for the first time, I began to learn how to compose a poem. Since relatively few works from the women's quarters are passed along, when I was finished with my embroidery and came on the collected works of some famous woman poet, I would copy one or two by hand to express my admiration for them. After I married I had to manage the rice and salt, so I set aside my brush and inkstone. As the years passed, I grew absorbed in looking after my health and doing "quiet sitting."* The only books left on my desk were a few volumes of Song philosophy and the single chapter that makes up the *Leng yan jing* [*Surangama sutra*].[114]

She then goes on to talk about the turning point that came when her exuberant son burst into her study clutching her portfolios of collected women's writing. As we know, she spent the remaining years of her life absorbed in that enterprise.

High Qing Models of Learned Womanhood

Images of the brilliant young female poet and the upright, morally transformative wife could, of course, be compatible. Though Yuan Mei admired Sun Yunfeng for her poetic precocity, his story about her also reveals that a young woman schooled in the *Book of Odes* learned carefully the moral significance of the wife's role in a marital relationship. As a young girl, Sun Yunfeng already knew that a wife served as the moral preceptor of her spouse, and she was able to demonstrate her knowledge by comparing two lines from disparate poems with the same wifely image. Moreover, the images that Yuan Mei used to embellish sketches of the more flamboyant female poets in his circle—conflating physical beauty and poetic talent—recur even in staid biographies of upright women. Zhu Yun made the same point in his epitaph for Zhang Xuecheng's mother when he mentioned that as a young girl "she was likened to the women in Xie An's family because her poetry was as beautiful

*The phrase she uses here is *jing yang*, a cryptic reference to the spiritual disciplines of the years after childbearing.

as her person." Zhu Yun's biography goes on to say that as an adult, Zhang's mother forsook writing, put on practical short-sleeved clothes, and went to work, serving her mother-in-law and managing the household.[115]

Zhang Xuecheng's mother renounced her role as brilliant poetess to become a transformative wife in the best tradition of the *Odes*, as her epitaph tells us. When Zhang's father's career was ruined by a false accusation of impropriety, Zhang's mother—who had always "stayed at home, tending her proper sphere, and counseling him to follow a middle course"—produced a thousand taels saved out of her household accounts, enabling him "to pay off his debts and clear his name."[116] Zhang Xuecheng's mother's girlish voice spoke through the willow catkin, but her wifely voice was the moral voice of the *Odes*: counseling her husband during his term in office, supporting him at the nadir of his career, and—thanks to her frugal investment of the household budget surplus—sparing him further public humiliation when he lost his post. If a brilliant female poet did not marry unhappily and die of illness or heartbreak or both, she might voluntarily decide to stop writing to fulfill her duties as daughter-in-law, mother, and family manager. When she did, her poetic voice would be heard as a moral voice. Both drew inspiration from the *Book of Odes*.

The two High Qing models of learned womanhood—the image of the willow catkin and the instructress who represents correct beginnings—can be reconciled in this way. But their power derives from the contradictions they represent. Both suggest that women are men's betters. Both convey a powerful aesthetic authority, one sensual, the other moral. The divine woman writer, whether catkin poet or potent moral force, is contained by these images and transformed into someone a man can understand. For women writers themselves, however, brilliant precocity and wifely wisdom meant something entirely different. Young prodigies used their poems to create lasting bonds with the natal kin they were about to lose, in the process making themselves still dearer to their doting readers. Mature wives used their brushes to criticize their world: competitive examinations, cruel disease and capricious death, heartless husbands, lazy maids. But as Lila Abu-Lughod reminds us, poetry is not pure commentary. A poem is created; its writer is an artist. The women poets in Yun Zhu's anthology and Yuan Mei's poetry talks, and the wives and prodigies whose poems fill the pages of High Qing collections, were creative artists for whom the very act of writing was a powerful gesture. Their poems shaped their age, drawing on the *Odes* to weight their voices with the authority of Confucius himself.

Before we turn in Chapter 6 to the practical work that occupied the time of even the most gifted women poets, we must reconsider some of the questions the present chapter raises about gender relations in the High Qing era. The most important question involves the extraordinary power of the written word in the hands of learned women. Why did men find it so controversial and compelling? I think the answer lies in the juxtaposition of two profound cultural sentiments, lodged in the person of the female figure in literature. One demands total separation (*bie*) between well-bred men and women, even in the same family and even in the realm of language (*yan*). As Zhang Xuecheng argues repeatedly in his essay on women's learning, men and women each have their proper sphere, and women's words must never pass beyond the inner apartments. His commitment to absolute separation of the two sexes is one reason why Zhang had so much difficulty imagining what women were supposed to write. For the learned woman, in the act of writing, enters at once the domain of *wen*, literary high culture. Since the time of Confucius, that domain had been the unmarked sphere of men, into which women might enter, as Zhang also notes, only under the most extraordinary historical circumstances. As a master of *wen* entering this domain, a woman communicates directly with a man. She becomes, at that moment, someone capable of "knowing him"—the goddess on the mountain, the divine woman by the turquoise pond, offering both passion and transcendent wisdom, consummating his worldly existence and promising immortality. Few men could contemplate this powerful encounter with the divine woman as writer. Instead they tried to reduce her to recognizable domestic shapes: mother, wife, daughter.

For women, entering the domain of *wen* could be equally overpowering. But women did not seek union with a divine man. Instead, they yearned—like men—for transcendence. This they achieved in two ways: through sentiment, relived in memory and revitalized in poetry, and through pious disciplines that transformed body, mind, and spirit. Pious disciplines lay beyond language. But preparation for pious disciplines depended on brush and inkstone, on creating an autonomous spiritual identity lodged in poetry.

These meanings of women's writing, for men and for women, may have persisted in various forms throughout Chinese history. But in High Qing times, they posed existential and philosophical problems that both men and women tried to solve. Men found two ways to preserve separation from women writers while admiring and supporting their work. Yet even in their carefully defined roles, women writers remained threatening. Women writers as prodigies and women writers as moral instructresses both represent particular kinds of social pressure afflicting elite men in High Qing times. Daughters brought respite and comfort from the stressful competition of official life, but they must marry and leave. Wives could be counted on for economic security and sound advice, but they were too often critical. Mothers, with their powerful moral authority, fused discipline with indulgence, punishment with maternal love: discipline and punishment promised future success; indulgence and maternal love foreshadowed ultimate failure.[117]

For their part, women as matrons used the power of their writing voice to assert and extend their authority in the family and to reach beyond the domestic realm to criticize the commercial sex markets of their time. They became like "Republican mothers,"[118] rearing the future subjects of the realm and celebrating the triumphs of the imperium while pointing to themselves as hallmarks of their glorious age.

5 Entertainment

THE WOMEN YUN ZHU CHOSE to exclude from her anthology, the so-called famous courtesans (*ming ji*), were actually young girls, usually in their late teens. A *ming ji* attracted clients to her "painted boat" (*hua fang*) by making a reputation for herself in one of the great cities that lined the waterways of the Lower Yangzi—especially Suzhou, Yangzhou, and Nanjing. In men's eyes, the High Qing courtesan was a living tragedy: a woman of talent who had lost her virtue. For women in elite households, the courtesan defined an "other"—though learned, she did not participate in the rituals that marked a respectable wife and mother. Moreover, as Chapter 6 will stress, the courtesan's work marked her twice over as a polluted woman, because as an entertainer she neither spun nor wove.

For reasons we have been exploring, the status of even high-ranked courtesans appears lower in the High Qing period than it was in late Ming times. Kang-i Sun Chang and Dorothy Ko have shown that during the late Ming, learned courtesans like Liu Rushi could command the devotion of the most distinguished literati.[1] Courtesans were the emblem, Chang suggests, of late Ming culture: their aestheticism, their talent, their beauty, their suffering, their suicides—all capture the tragic fate of the dynasty itself. Moreover, as both Ko and Chang have emphasized, in late Ming times courtesans could expect to move with ease in the social circles of elite women as well as men, especially in Banqiao, the riverbank area of Nanjing that was the focal point of late Ming courtesan culture.

The High Qing era represents a striking contrast, almost certainly because of the classical revival. As we saw in Chapter 4, the classical revival placed daughters, wives, and mothers at the center of a debate about women's learning. In the course of this debate, courtesans became increasingly marginalized in the aesthetic lives of elite men. Meanwhile, the daughters, wives, and mothers at the center of the High Qing debates used their power as writers to trivialize or even silence (as did Yun Zhu) the voice of the courtesan in the historical record.

By studying courtesans, therefore, we reach a better understanding of notions of womanhood shared by elite men and women in the High Qing period. But we learn of the courtesans themselves only with difficulty and by inference. A courtesan's fame, which defined her as a professional and sustained her as a worker, spread through gossip, rumor, stories, and copies of her writings. These were passed by word of mouth and recorded in notebooks by male patrons who fancied themselves both friends and confidants. Seven such notebooks, published between 1784 and 1841, reveal a world where the boundaries of class and kinship were frayed by the market for commercial sex.[2] To convey a sense of that world, we must distinguish between the conventional language used to describe it ("pleasure quarters," "courtesans") and the economic and social hierarchies that language masks ("sex market," "sex workers"). This chapter moves back and forth between the mystifying speech of male writers and the harsh, often coercive, conditions of sex work for women that blur, but are nonetheless visible, even when seen through a man's gaze.

Class and Kinship: 'Guixiu' and Courtesan

In theory, the gap separating elite women from courtesans was vast. Elite women in High Qing times, as Chapter 4 shows, were reared to consider themselves in a special class: child prodigies destined for a wifely moral future. The High Qing *guixiu*—women "cultivated in the inner apartments"—self-consciously distinguished their own learning from the learning of courtesans. Part of their self-consciousness, as we have seen, derived from the classical revival, which stressed the moral authority of married women. The *guixiu*'s recognition of "talent" in a woman was contingent on the use to which that talent was put.

Yun Zhu's pointed decision to omit writings by courtesans from her anthology was part of her wifely disdain for all women's writing in a sexual or romantic vein. Courtesans wrote for a particular audience interested in love poetry—at least, their writings were preserved by clients for whom this poetry was written, and perhaps in fact they wrote little else. Even if they did write other things, mid-Qing courtesans—unlike the *guixiu*—had no kinsmen who were able or willing to preserve and publish their work. Therefore the few extant poems and letters attributed to courtesans of the mid-Qing era were written down by their admirers, and these writings speak with only one voice. They were easily eliminated from Yun Zhu's collection, given her criteria.

In denying the courtesan poet a place in her anthology, Yun Zhu was not merely voicing a personal opinion. Her views were widely shared in the High Qing era. Unlike the late Ming period, when courtesans still set the standard for "talented women,"[3] Yun Zhu's time reserved "talent" for gentry women as the domain of wifely respectability. The true *cainü* ("talented woman") was a *guixiu*.[4] To be sure, not all elite women in the mid-Qing period distanced themselves socially or intellectually from courtesans. Some even sought out their company for entertainment and companionship, following the custom of the late Ming,[5] as we shall see. But by contrast with customs in late Ming times, the social interaction between courtesans and *guixiu* in the High Qing was secretive, even surreptitious.

The apparent gap separating courtesan and *guixiu* in High Qing times may reflect elite sensitivity to friable class boundaries in the mobile urban economy of the Lower Yangzi region. The men on whom we must rely for evidence—those who wrote descriptions of courtesans—were attentive to the differences in class and kinship roles that distinguished their subjects from *guixiu*. The language they used to describe *guixiu* differed sharply from that reserved for courtesans, as two examples, each from a biographical sketch of a woman written by a man and each rendering a woman's voice by quoting from one of her letters, dramatize. The first is a letter written by the *guixiu* Jiang Lan to her husband at the capital, just after she learned that he had once again failed the examinations. The second letter was sent by a famous Suzhou courtesan, Cui Xiuying, to a patron three times her age who had just declared his love for her. Of course, these two letters merely *represent* a woman's voice. But the tone and language of each reveals the difference between *guixiu* and courtesan in the eyes of an eighteenth-century upper-class man.

Jiang Lan's sarcastic letter to her husband, quoted approvingly in her biography in a local gazetteer (written by Zhang Xuecheng and included in Zhang's collected works), reads in part as follows:

> When a man leaves home and goes into the outside world, he should not be distracted by concerns about his domestic affairs. So if you run short of money, my two elder brothers holding office in the capital will be glad to help

> you out. If you grow depressed staying alone in your lodgings, by all means get out and enjoy yourself with the beautiful women in the pleasure quarters! My brothers won't begrudge you their money! For myself, I long ago cast aside any dream of "growing old together," that old mandarin duck fantasy. As for you, concentrate on this: Serve wise men; befriend humane persons; succeed in your studies; conduct yourself in accordance with the Dao; spread your fame; bring glory to your ancestors! These are your responsibilities. I cannot take them on for you. You are the one who must strive with all your might.[6]

Jiang Lan's wifely voice, dripping with moral authority, is a far cry from the voice we hear in the letter that follows, written by the youthful courtesan Cui Xiuying to her aging patron:

> Your servant Xiuying offers this missive to her master. I am a frail body facing the wind, scattered branches reflected in the water. Although I broke off the branch at Micheng,* my heart remains alone here at Hufu. Year after year I play my flute for the evening moon; but how dare I long for the call of the imperial bird? Each day I cover my mirror as the autumn insects sing, the better to suppress my earthly passions. I live alone, in isolation, aloof. I long for a pure life. I abhor lewd behavior. My heart is like tender grass ruined by cold frost and withering dew. When by some good fortune I met you, I snatched at happiness, riding on the clouds and gazing up at the sun. You scorn the sea of men, you look with contempt on this earthly world. You wrote of encounters with courtesans, but you never chose a favorite. For 30 years you never pledged your love. On the day we met, I asked myself: Who am I that I should receive your special invitation? How dared I not, from such a lowly position, turn with my full trust to you, as a mallow turns toward the sun? I vowed to return your kindness. Since that moment twenty days ago when I bowed before you, I have loved you constantly. If I could study with you for three years, I would be as good a poet as the courtesan Bei. . . . Because of this, I have painted you this lowly portrait. My only wish is to gaze forever at your face and never be cast aside. Your heart is strong like bronze and stone. I cling to you as mistletoe clings to a tree. Pointing to the cave in the moon, I pledge our happiness. Facing the deep blue heavens and the jade ocean, may we rise up among the clouds and join our thoughts. My soul climbs the jade mountain peaks and the cinnabar steps, humbly hoping that you will look with favor on our union. I pray for our earliest fortunate meeting. Pen in my mouth, I weep. I cannot put all my feelings into words.[7]

In these contrasting letters, the courtesan's admiring dependence on her patron is a code revealing her learning, just as the moral autonomy of the wife

* Perhaps she refers to the place where she first began her life as a courtesan.

as her spouse's critic is clear in the framing of her speech. The voice of the *guixiu* gives her power over men; the voice of the learned courtesan dramatizes her dependency.

To understand this representation of the courtesan, we must explore the culture in which courtesans lived and its relationship to the respectable world that surrounded the pleasure quarters. This requires, first, a review of the conditions that produced the opulent pleasure quarters of the High Qing era; second, an appreciation of the ambience the pleasure quarters offered to patrons and clients; and third, some grasp of the economic conditions of the sex market.

The Revival of Courtesan Entertainments

The High Qing pleasure quarters flourished during a brief interval between the fall of the Ming and the outbreak of the Opium War. Their revival followed years of depression after the Manchu invasion, which devastated Yangzhou and other southern cities. By the late eighteenth century, the Lower Yangzi's thriving pleasure quarters invited a return to the halcyon days of the late Ming, when courtesans' clients could indulge their tastes to the limit. The moment was short-lived, however. At the end of the High Qing era in the 1830's, recession and the arrival of armies to defend the coast against foreign invasion began to alter the clientele and even the location of the pleasure quarters, transforming the ambience of courtesan culture and reducing the pleasure quarters to a nostalgic remnant of late-Ming Banqiao.[8]

The High Qing pleasure quarters, even at their height, differed in important ways from late-Ming Banqiao. Economic recovery after the Qing conquest revitalized the urban consumer culture of the Ming on a grander scale. In descriptions of this urban world, the rhetoric of pleasure seekers seems virtually unchanged and the plight of the women who entertained them as poignant as ever. But two distinctive features of High Qing society set the courtesan culture of the High Qing apart from its Ming precursors. The first was the demographic transition, which made courtesans an unprecedented demographic luxury. The marriage crunch centered on young women of childbearing age, precisely the same young women in demand in the entertainment industry. The purchase and sale of female slaves and servants, the kidnapping and abduction of young women of all classes—all are signs of this relentless demographic pressure. We see it in records of the courtesan quarters, which portray a constant stream of nubile young women sold into them as entertainers and of fecund young women bought out as concubines.

The second distinctive characteristic of eighteenth-century courtesan culture was a new legal regime created by Qing state policies that altered the market for women's bodies. Three specific policies directly affected the pleasure quarters. The first was the emancipation of pariahs, which offered female entertainers the opportunity to shed the stigma of pariah status. The second was the series of Qing decrees banning female entertainers from official functions of state. Finally, the Qing government tried to curb the private (i.e., for commoners, not officials) market for female entertainment in the Jiangnan pleasure quarters themselves. Although Chapter 2 reviewed these state policies, aspects that most directly affected courtesans require further explanation here.

QING STATE POLICY

Almost immediately after the conquest, and long before pacification was complete, early Manchu rulers issued important edicts affecting the status of female entertainers. Qing policy had its first impact in the Forbidden City, where the new Manchu leadership immediately began to remove indentured female entertainers from the palace precincts as the first step in an effort to abolish an institution with a long courtly history. Troupes of court-sponsored "singing girls" (*nüyue*) had performed in the courts of Chinese emperors since the Tang period. Singing girls held formal appointments in an office called the Office of [Music] Instruction (Jiaofang si), first created in 714 under the jurisdiction of the Court of Imperial Sacrifices (Taichang si). Its director was a eunuch, and its charge was the general training of court entertainers, including clowns, jugglers, female musicians and dancers, and so forth. Beginning in the Yuan dynasty, the Office of Instruction was transferred to the jurisdiction of the Ministry of Rites. Ming rulers downgraded the office, giving its director a more modest title and reducing his rank from 4a to 9a.[9] But the Manchus did not stop there.

Secure in their knowledge that there was no precedent for the Office of Instruction in classical Chinese institutions before the Tang, the Manchus issued a series of imperial edicts designed first to remove women from the Office of Instruction and then to eliminate the office altogether. The first decree, in 1651, commanded that all singing girls in the Office of Instruction be replaced by eunuchs. Though the order was temporarily rescinded four years later, doubtless in response to bitter complaints, another edict dated 1659 succeeded in ending court patronage of singing girls at the palace.

The Manchus found it more difficult, however, to extend these bans beyond the palace precincts. Local officials widely ignored an edict issued in 1673 forbidding provincial and local officials to hire female musicians to perform at the spring rites celebrating the new agricultural season, when custom called for troupes of female dancers and singers to welcome a procession led by "Mang shen" (the clay driver) and his clay oxen—and also to keep presiding officials company at the banquets and parties that followed.[10] At length this imperial order may have had its effect, according to a comment from a gazetteer in Yangzhou:

> Since the Tang we have had "official courtesans" (*guanji*) here. Early in the present dynasty, they were called "musicians" (*yuehu*). By local custom, on the day before the first day of spring the prefect would welcome spring. . . . He would order the *guanji* to dress up for the "lighting of the community fires" (*she huo*). One would dress as the Spring Dream, two as the Spring Sisters, one as the Spring Clerk, two as the Spring Runners, another as the Spring Official. The next day the Spring Official would give each of the others 27 copper coins. The Spring Official herself received 10 almanacs (*tongshu*). Then during the Kangxi reign, the *yuehu* were eliminated and suddenly there were no more *guanji*. So they replaced them with people who light the lanterns and play the flower drums at festival time. All are men; none are women. This was the origin of the local saying that "a good woman does not go out to look at spring, and a good man does not go out to see the lanterns."[11]

In any case, the Yongzheng emperor, in the process of reorganizing all the music personnel at court, reissued the order banning female musicians during his reign. In 1729 he abolished the Office of Instruction (Jiaofang si) altogether, replacing it with the new Music Ministry (Yue bu) comprising two newly created offices: an Office of Harmonious Sounds (Hesheng shu) and an Imperial Music Office (Shenyue shu).[12]

Precisely how these bureaucratic changes affected female entertainers at the court or in the provinces is unclear. Scholars have suggested that the abolition of the Office of Instruction and the court bans on female entertainment helped stimulate the commercial market for female entertainers for two reasons. First, *yuehu* forced out of jobs in the court or in official bureaucratic posts elsewhere would have entered private commercial entertainment markets to support themselves. Second, officials denied the pleasure of female entertainment at state functions would have turned instead to the private market. The present-day scholar Yan Ming, a proponent of this view, also points out that depriving female entertainers of state support dealt a blow to the quality of courtesan arts and to the security of the courtesan's status from which they never recovered, while giving new license to pornographic commercial sex markets.[13] In sum, it appears that Qing government policy interacted with social and economic changes already in progress to change attitudes toward female entertainers in the High Qing era. Among these changes we must remember the important role of talented, respectable women, who appropriated many of the old courtesan roles—entertaining and delighting men—while arrogating to themselves the power to marginalize courtesans. Here, the power of the state inadvertently heightened the wifely moral authority of educated elite women by delegitimizing the role of courtesans in elite government circles.

For courtesans themselves, the prestige and security of work were vital issues. As we saw in Chapter 2, and as the stories of courtesans in this chapter will show, although High Qing law gave respectable commoners legal protection designed to keep them out of the slave market, in practice wives, children, and kidnap victims were regularly bought and sold. Since legal protection from the slave market extended to concubines as well as wives, it offered some hope even to courtesans, provided they entered respectable families as concubines. In a court of law, they became persons who "follow the spouse into respectability" (*cong liang*), entitled to the same protections available to respectable women. But the law itself was full of loopholes. For instance, it forbade officials—but not commoners—to take courtesans as concubines. This restriction meant that courtesans often became concubines to wealthy men who lacked the connections to protect them in a court of law. We shall examine these and other tensions that accompanied mobility across class boundaries after viewing the courtesan's workplace, a site designed to attract customers of varying tastes and means.

THE PLEASURE QUARTERS IN MEN'S EYES

The Chinese phrase *hua fang* means literally "brightly painted boat." A euphemism for the entertainment district in the cities of the Lower Yangzi, the term reminds us that courtesans often entertained on boats anchored along riverbanks or near bridges. The phrase invoked a pastiche of images in the minds of travelers and clients. Most of those images mystified or otherwise disguised from consumers the fact that the courtesan's world was a labor market in which sex was exchanged for money. Indeed, as appreciations of courtesans show, sex was considered the least of their services. The focus of the connoisseur was on the courtesan's talent and aesthetic tastes. Connoisseur texts, in fact, contrast sharply with pornographic descriptions of sex found in work by the High Qing fiction writer Li Yu and other masters of realistic prose. Instead, they present an idealized world that is part nostalgia and memory, part myth and fantasy. They describe the feelings of a sensual man in the presence of a beautiful young girl; they speak of nostalgia for youth and its fleeting passage; they express distress at the frailty and vulnerability of beautiful women unprotected by respectable wifehood or manly patronage. They convey their delight in the palpable luxury of scented rooms, fine music, and intimate, refined conversation. They relish the escape, even the purification, afforded by a pristine moment in a courtesan's boudoir, far from the cares and the "dust" of this world. A few, in their detailed descriptions of a meeting with a beautiful woman, even invoke the sequence of the mythic encounter with a divine woman: passion, then transcendence.

Books describing the centers of courtesan culture during High Qing times self-consciously copied *Banqiao za ji*, the classic notes on Nanjing courtesans by the late-Ming connoisseur Yu Huai (1616–96).[14] Because of Yu Huai's work and other memoirs of late Ming aesthetes, the manners of Ming courtesan life were well known and appreciated among mid-Qing literati and merchants, who seemed to enjoy the pleasure boats in self-conscious imitation of Yu Huai himself.[15] So in a sense, the courtesan culture of the eighteenth century revived the world of late-Ming Banqiao on a broader scale. The city of Suzhou took Nanjing's place as the center of imperial taste and fashion, displaying the affluence that accompanied the economic recovery of the southland; Yangzhou's courtesans competed with Nanjing's as well. Affluence fed by the growing market economy encouraged materialism, creating a rowdy consumer culture in which courtesans' clients could indulge their senses to the hilt. Against this backdrop, aesthetes criticized materialism and sought ironic refuge from it, protesting their revulsion at gambling and sensual indulgence and their distaste for superficial beauty and material things. Over this discord the courtesan presided.

For the crude and rude, the courtesan's quarters directed sensual appeals straight to physical appetites, featuring not merely sex but a profusion of noise and visual display. For the rich, the grosser forms of entertainment invited clients to stuff themselves at catered gourmet picnics on the river and spend their remaining waking hours at round-the-clock gaming tables, surrounded by troupes of actors and female musicians.[16] By contrast, the fastidious, reclusive man who fancied refined entertainment to feed the soul might seek instead a breathless encounter with one particular woman. All of these experiences, from the breathless encounter to the boisterous blow-out, have been preserved in delicate metaphors and deadpan slapstick on the pages of High Qing records of the courtesan quarters. This remarkable language invites us to enter their world.

For the loud crowd, the pleasure quarters meant drums, gongs, songs, shouts, red rouge, and green robes. Red and green were the dominant colors in the pleasure quarters, as in the phrase "she was like a kingfisher pheasant beside a cinnabar phoenix," or, more wantonly, "drunk on red and clasping the green." Dominoes, cards, chess, water pipes, and lots of food and liquor came with the package, as the following description shows:

> A group of eight or ten boors will come along the river beating gongs and drums, and they'll act out a song or play some medley of tunes. In opera, this is called an "impromptu strike"; it started out in the military. Old reprobates bring these kinds of people along to amuse their guests. They all go off on grand boats with everyone squatting on deck. They sound just like a bunch of chickens squawking—*ya ya*—what a racket! You can never understand a word they're saying. A day's worth of this stuff costs between 1,000 and 2,000 cash.[17]

The tinny effect of this cacophony cannot be lost even in translation. Note also that the cheapest entertainments on the river involve men, not scarce and expensive women.[18]

Here is another example:

> Just at the end of the year 1804, I was out in a craft with a lot of young, strong oarsmen. While the evening sun was still glowing red, they strung together about ten [boats] in a row and started off down the river. At first they rowed slowly as they churned along, but gradually they picked up speed, and we got going faster and faster, so the boats were cutting through the waves leaving a great wake and the sharp slap of the water sounded "*pengpai*" against the sides. None of the guests on board could make them stop, and they ignored the people shouting at them from the bank. Just when our hearts were beating wildly and our eyes were glazed with fear, they all reversed their oars and came to a stop, as if someone had given an order. They all kept looking at each other without saying a word, and they avoided looking at our clothes, which by then were soaked with water. They call this "fighting the current" (*qiang shui*) or "reining in the river" (*fang shui pei tou*). People brag about how many times they've done it.
>
> If you've never done it, you're really behind the times. People who make a habit of it end up with a heart attack.[19]

The pay-by-the-day, loud-and-gross revels of this river crowd contrast pointedly with the priceless moment when an individual man and woman shared wine and music alone. For this, a client had to search out a shy young girl. He left the river and walked deep into winding lanes or willow groves, finding at last an intimate companion with whom to sit quietly, perhaps writing letters or chanting poetry. In her room he admired a luminous face free of makeup, a fine-boned form floating in gauzy robes. The most prized courtesans were especially admired for guarding their solitude, for their continual retreat from "city dust," for their refusal to open their doors to any man—except those few judged sufficiently pure of heart (*su xin*) to tolerate for the pleasure of their company. Such a man longed for "a beauty who understands me" (*hong fen zhi ji*); someone who would "sit alone" (*gu zuo*) until he came, perhaps receiving even him with evident reluctance.

Here is a description of one man's encounter with the young courtesan Cui Xiuying, whose face, free of makeup, belied her profession:

> Her dwelling was known as the "Hall of Green Clouds." The curtain weights were of silver, curved like garlic cloves. From the duck-shaped brazier crept a warm fragrance. A bronze dragon water clock dripped slowly. Her parrot* chattered as if joining our tea party. In this setting she welcomed two or three intimates (*zhijizhe*). She rinsed red conch shells, decanted rare wines. Half drunk on her beauty—those golden hairpins—we were lost in emotion. When it pleased her to pluck the strings of a song, the words came like pearls from her throat.[20]

In this short passage we see a young girl presenting an older man with a moment so vivid that he can recall it precisely. Such moments are recorded again and again in remembered encounters with courtesans. Pure, chaste moments of this sort enhanced the reputation and the allure, along with the price, of the youngest and loveliest—and least accessible—of these beauties. Since many of the most desirable girls were barely twelve or thirteen *sui* when they entertained discerning clients with their poetry and song—prodigies like their *guixiu* counterparts—it is possible that such early encounters did not involve sex. Perhaps it was only after such a girl reached puberty—after her reputation and her allure had been mystified a hundred times over—that she became available for sexual relations at an appropriately inflated price. A story about the courtesan Jiang Yuzhen explains that she was seduced by a merchant "just at the age when she was to have sex for the first time" (*nian fu po gua*, lit., "when she had just reached the age for breaking the gourd").[21]

The connoisseur describing Cui Xiuying in her boudoir manipulates images to heighten the power of his narrative. The things he sketches here belong exclusively to a woman's room. This knowledge alone heightens the reader's appreciation for the sensuality of his experience. In fact, we might say that the courtesan here is appreciated as an object in the context of other objects; each enhances the others. Of course, many descriptions of intimate encounters between female entertainers and male clients contain bolder state-

*Parrots are "all categorically things of the women's quarters" (Clunas 1991: 42). See also n. 24.

Fig. 18. A *guixiu* boudoir and bedchamber. Reprinted from Nakagawa [1799] 1983: 114–15.

ments of sexual pleasure. A Nanjing visitor describes how to make his favorite erotic paraphernalia:

> Break a walnut in half. Discard the meat and hollow out the shells. Fasten them together with fine copper wire, so they open and close. In the middle, use five-colored rice powder to mold a "secret pleasures picture" (*mi xi tu*). Hang it from the bed curtains or on your kerchief or your shoes. I saw these once in a certain courtesan's home. It was a tiny space, but she had row after row of them. The spirit and feeling of the pictures inside was graphically realistic, evidence of her surpassing skill.[22]

Some of these erotic miniature tableaux had moving body parts that could be manipulated using threads pulled from outside the shell.

Such gross titillation was not necessary or even appreciated by many clients. For the connoisseur, simply entering a female space (Fig. 18) was a sensual experience heightened by a sense of mystery and violated taboos. In the homes of wealthy families, sharp divisions separated the part of the house at the front dominated by men and their activities from the inner quarters at the rear, reserved for women. To cross the boundaries from front to rear was to anticipate a mingling of male yang and female yin, sexual intercourse, in the bedroom.[23] Women's rooms were decorated and appointed with things that men were not supposed to use or have in their own quarters. *Bo* silk, for instance, could properly be used to make a woman's bed curtains, never a man's; a parrot adorned the suite of a woman, but had no place in a man's room.[24]

Meanwhile, the company of courtesans entertained elite women as well as men. To maintain the illusion of cloistering, the *guixiu* traveled to the riverbank in a closed sedan chair. Approaching the river, a *guixiu* needed temporary accommodations for changing her clothes and relieving herself. For this she would choose a "river kiosk" (*shui xie*)—a scenic pavilion overlooking the river—operated by a proprietor she knew. As the *guixiu* party embarked, the screens on all sides of the courtesan's boat would be lowered and female attendants posted to ward off unwanted spectators or other clients. Yangzhou pleasure boats accommodating a *guixiu* clientele had square corners to accommodate their bulky sedan chairs on board. Once aboard, each party was shown discreetly into a private chamber. Men found ways to enjoy this as well. Watching such a party disappear was titillating enough for one voyeur, who recalled that he could "smell the fragrance of their clothes and see their shadows, and hear them speaking softly to each other" behind the screens.[25]

Language conveys the breathless sense of an otherworldly, ephemeral encounter when a man entered a courtesan's boudoir and later recalls that she looked as if she might disappear at any moment. The Nanjing courtesan Huang Cui'er, age nineteen *sui*, had "bones like melted butter" and "flesh shaped from powder." She was a creature so luminous that a "flower of purest jade" could not compare with her.[26] Describing Wang Long's entrance after rising from a nap, wearing a gauze headscarf and free of makeup and perfumes, her admirer wrote: "She floated before us, a vision of culture and taste."[27] In other, cruder, rhetoric, girls in the pleasure quarters appear as commodities, flowers to be graded, or talents to be judged in competition.[28] The brothels were "thickets of flowers" (*hua cong*) awaiting the connoisseur's discriminating judgment;[29] courtesans, like flowers, were ranked in 26 grades (*pin*), each with its distinctive combination of qualities.[30]

A writer created his illusions of the floating world, or stripped it of illusion, by selecting his rhetoric carefully from the repertoire used to describe women in the High Qing era. Unlike *guixiu* biographies, which are filled with stories of suicide and death, courtesan tales seldom mention morbidity or mortality. Where death and suffering appear, they are mere hints or innuendo, not the detailed descriptions reserved for the bodily sufferings of respectable women martyrs. Thus, in one of the rare cases where a courtesan's death is recorded, we learn only that Zhou Cuiling died of depression at the age of 21.[31] Venereal disease is never mentioned.[32] Pregnancy is rare; the occasional pregnant courtesan is portrayed as a romantic figure whose child is a sign of

Fig. 19. "The Money Tree." Reprinted from C. A. S. Williams 1976: 214.

love.[33] Finally, in stories about courtesans, money never changes hands. Cost accounting is reserved, as we have seen, for lewd or crude entertainments. It is the courtesan's cruel oppressors, her relatives, who "shake her like a money tree" (Fig. 19); her patrons are blameless, her employers invisible.

Courtesans' refined patrons were not oblivious to the misery of these women's lives. However, when their stories turn to misery they follow similar plot lines: the young courtesan is vulnerable and weak, her infatuated client a confidant and protector. Storytellers imagined young girls in the brothels as victims repulsed by the noisesome pollution into which they had haplessly fallen. The writers positioned themselves as outsiders—at best rescuers; at worst, voyeurs. In these tales, pure young girls are constantly pursued by lecherous, wealthy reprobates (*zangfu*). Rarely, a brilliant young scholar (*wen xing*) comes to the rescue, meeting any price and using all his influence to save the innocent victim for himself.

A biography of the courtesan Fang Xuan, written by the Recluse of the Pearl Spring, describes one young girl's rise and disappearance in a sketch that reveals complex relationships:

> Born in Jiangyin, her original surname was Shui, her milk name A'quan. She was the adopted daughter of Fang Yunu. As a child she was a musician in Jinling. During that early autumn stay in Jinling, I had met her once at the Wang River Pavilion. She was both talented and beautiful, already far surpassing her peers. Because her name was not elegant, she changed it to Xuan, and took the *zi* Xianlai. When our paths crossed again after three years, she looked to me like mist floating, like a thin moon. She was pure and delicate like the snow, captivating like a flower. By then she was nearly sixteen. She was by nature modest, pure, and elegant, deep and quiet, a woman of few words. When she was young, she lived south of Nanjing, but to escape the dust and clamor there, she moved her abode to an old pavilion on a crooked lane, tucked away in a remote place. There she allowed no one to pay her calls except those with "simple hearts" [*su xin*]. Her adoptive mother also acceded to her wishes. She was precious like a pearl in a shell.
>
> The former official Luping, a relative of mine on my mother's side from the same native place, was an otherworldly man who loved gardens and was also a brilliant scholar. After he retired, he moved to Zhuxi, where he fell completely in love with her. Just at that time, however, an old reprobate came around cursing her over his drink, meaning to slander her. Luping pleaded with me to intercede on her behalf, and I was able to put an end to the matter.
>
> Every time I had a spare moment, I would go by to see her. We would talk freely about this and that, heedless of the passing hours. Once I watched her fix her hair and wrap her feet in silk bindings, laughing so sweetly; her every motion was beautiful; truly it appeased my hunger to watch her. I had no need for "drinking with rouged faces" or "touching the flesh of green-garbed women." I composed a prose-poem titled "Jade Plums" in two verses and presented it to her. It included the following lines: "Against the spring tunes of the flautist, the first branch appears" and "Brighter than the new moon, paler than the clouds." She was quite pleased with those rhymes, and asked me to write them for her on a scented fan; she would always sing them to herself, and kept the fan inside her sleeve. Then at the end of that summer her adoptive mother Yunu became involved in a lawsuit and on the spur of the moment took her back to their old neighborhood.
>
> I recall this as if recalling a lovely flower in the moonlight, with unbearable nostalgia.[34]

Sex Work

The appointments in the chambers of the courtesan Cui Xiuying, described in such loving detail earlier, are part of the language that masks the reality of the courtesan's working life. A mesmerizing visit may follow a sleepy awakening in which the courtesan is forced to rise reluctantly from her bed after a long night's work singing and dancing for the guests at a banquet.[35] This structure of the courtesan's labor—her long hours and the bribery, coercion, or brutality that enforced them—is only obliquely and momentarily visible in otherwise romantic accounts of trysting in the pleasure quarters. Romantic as they are, the records of the High Qing pleasure quarters cannot be read as if one were reading Yu Huai's *Banqiao za ji*. The unique politics, culture, and economy of the eighteenth century gave courtesan culture a different social meaning and altered the status of courtesans in Lower Yangzi society during the High Qing era.

Changes in the status of courtesans are reflected in two bodies of evidence that we have already examined. The first change stemmed from new state policies toward female entertainers and sex workers. By the end of the eighteenth century, the pleasure quarters of Nanjing, Yangzhou, and Suzhou flourished as never before, but in a political and cultural context where the social relation of the sexes had dramatically altered. The second change, reflecting this new social and political climate, is evident in the elite discourse that trivialized the talents of courtesans and valorized the erudition of the morally upright, classically educated *guixiu*. Prominent women writers like Yun Zhu, who sought to contain the emotional power of women's poetic voice within the confines of marital and kin relationships, led this discourse, echoing scholars and officials like Zhang Xuecheng and Chen Hongmou who insisted that women's learning and education should flourish only within the family.

Beyond sentiment and fantasy, the seven notebooks open a narrow window from which it is possible to see through the mystification and criticism of courtesan culture to the working lives of the women who entertained men in the brothels. According to the 277 biographical sketches in the notebooks, only frayed lines separated the marriage market from the courtesan market. Competition for scarce women pulled courtesans out of the pleasure quarters and into binding family relationships, mainly as concubines, even as economic pressures thrust wives and daughters out of the family and into the brothel.

The path to courtesan status was one-way; once "fallen" (*duo*), a girl could not hope to become a respectable commoner's wife. If she "rose" again, it would be through the process called "following the respectable partner" (*cong liang*) by becoming a concubine in a "marriage" recognized and protected by the law. Such an outcome was more commonly thwarted than not, judging from the sad stories told by these anonymous writers. An example is the tale of the two Tang sisters who "fell into harlotry while they were young" (*zao duo feng chen*) and, "failing to make a respectable match" (*cong liang wei sui*), were left with an "entire household of many persons" (*hehu shu shizhi*) "relying on two girls for financial support" (*lai erji zuo sheng ya*).[36] Many sketches aver that a particular courtesan was "originally from a respectable family" (*ben liangjia nü*).[37]

A girl might be forced into the brothel when she became a burden to her brothers after their parents' death, as in the story of one courtesan who took the oft-used name Zhang Baoling, whose elder brother had no way to support her.[38] The courtesan Shao Suyun worked in the same brothel with her brother's daughter.[39] The courtesan Dan Fanglan used the surname of her husband's family.[40] The courtesan Gao Guizi's sister-in-law, Gao Shunlin, the primary wife of her elder brother, later became a courtesan as well.[41] Blood sisters might enter a brothel together.[42] Women from ordinary commoner families who worked as courtesans included a concubine (*qie*), a sister-in-law (that is, a woman living with a married brother), a successor wife (*ji fu*), and a daughter-in-law (*xifu*).

In the Lower Yangzi region only blurred and sometimes imperceptible lines separated respectable commoners from courtesans, though legally courtesans were classified as pariahs. Lower Yangzi writers certainly did not regard the courtesans they admired as pariahs. However, Jiangnan intellectuals were quick to ridicule the pariah status of courtesans in brothels outside of Jiangnan. Yuan Mei, well-known as an admirer and patron of Suzhou courtesans, had this to say about Guangzhou courtesans in his *Poetry Talks*:

> I have long heard of the beauty of the "pearl maidens" of Guangdong. When I went to Guangzhou, various friends and relatives invited me to the pleasure boats for refreshment and entertainment. There I saw not one single person that I would call beautiful or talented [*suo jian jue wu jia zhe*]. Someone once described one of them as follows: "Dark lips breathing fire, her slippers sticking out, she's hard to approach—enticing like a ghost." I hear that in Chaozhou magnificent courtesans are especially numerous, but I have a hard time believing it.[43]

Zhao Yi, perhaps a more evenhanded source, was no kinder. He wrote:

> In Guangzhou no less than seven or eight thousand boat people (*danhu*) make their living from prostitution. Their daughters go with older prostitutes who sell their services as if they were their own children. At the age of thirteen or

> fourteen they are ordered to serve guests. Few, in fact, are beautiful. When they rise in the morning, their complexions are yellow, though after a day of rouge and drink, they turn red. They may serve seven or eight boats with guests every day. . . . The boat people have no permanent abode on land, and those who earn a living from prostitution also make the boats their home.[44]

By contrast, Jiangnan writers describing courtesans of their own region allude frequently and with empathy to a courtesan's "fall" (*xian*) and to the "respectable" (*liang*) origins from which she came.[45] Indeed, not a single source alleges that Lower Yangzi courtesans hailed from the pariah groups common in the Jiangnan area (*gaihu, duomin, jiuyü*), although no attempt is made to conceal that some came from families who were engaged in pariah occupations, such as musicians, actors, and scavengers. For example, the courtesan Wang Xiaoheng had been betrothed to an actor at the age of seventeen.[46] Courtesan Zhang Xiuqin's mother's sister (*a'yi*) was the courtesan Zhang Xinglin, who was an apricot picker when she was small.[47] The courtesan known only as Guizhi (Cassia Branch) was the adopted daughter-in-law (*tongyangxi*) of an actor named Zhu Lanyun.[48] The father of the courtesan Lu Qiqin was an actor; she and her younger sister were both sold into a brothel.[49] The mother of the courtesan Hu Baozhu was a singing instructor in the brothels who had many adopted daughters.[50] Courtesan Zhu Yunguan's father was a singer, and her background was one of the factors that explained her success as a performer.[51]

When apprised of the polluted origins of a refined and talented young courtesan, Jiangnan connoisseurs expressed amazement. In fact, Jiangnan writers savored stories of a "fallen" woman, such as the tale of the Nanjing courtesan from a respectable family who was formally betrothed and lost her fiancé, forcing her to join a brothel. The power in the tale derives precisely from the description of her as "upright and beautiful like a respectable matron" (*duan yan ru liangjia fu*).[52] Another Nanjing courtesan, Yu Yuzi, is described sympathetically as a child abandoned by her mother and reared by her mother's commoner family, which owned a kiosk on the river where travelers and revelers could rest.[53]

Clients wanted to know a courtesan's background: not only her family history, but also her birthplace. Lower Yangzi connoisseurs judged that the best courtesans were born and reared in Jiangnan itself, and only rarely did a famous Jiangnan courtesan hail from outside the region. Place of origin, especially in the few cases where courtesans were not local people, invariably drew comment. Thus everyone knew that Liu Fulin came from the northern Grand Canal port city of Linqing in Shandong,[54] and people gossiped that the scavenger's daughter Zhao Fu was originally from Jiangbei.[55] In fact, so unusual were these cases that a reference to a courtesan from "up north" usually meant simply that she had moved from Yangzhou to Suzhou.

Whatever her background, a courtesan could not be certain of moving out of the brothel as a concubine. Perhaps, given the marriage prospects of most courtesans, few wished to become concubines anyway. In any event, those who lacked family ties invented them. Courtesans sustained themselves and provided for their future by adopting younger women to serve and care for them as they aged. Networks in the brothel were formed by adoptive mothers (*yang mu*) and adopted daughters (*yi nü*), and these filiations became part of the courtesan's record.[56] Thus the courtesan Yang Zhi was the adopted elder sister (*yi jie*) of Yang Zhaoling.[57] "False" (*jia*) bonds joined an elder with a "false younger sister" (*jia mei*)[58] or a junior with a "false mother" (*jia mu*).[59] Some courtesans referred to an adopted daughter using the legal term for stepdaughter (*ji nü*).[60] A courtesan might also bear and rear her own daughter to succeed her, as in the case of the *ming ji* Xu Suqin, whose only daughter, Xu Xiao'e, later became famous in her own right.[61]

Surrogate and blood kin groups in the courtesan quarters were matrilineal: whether a courtesan was born to or adopted by another courtesan, she took her mother's surname. The courtesan Yang Youhuan had a daughter named Yuxiang and later adopted for her a younger sister (*yi mei*) surnamed Wang. As the courtesan Yang Baoqin, the child took the surname of her adoptive mother and elder sister.[62] Courtesans who were sisters either by blood or by adoption were said to have the "same mother" (*tongmu*). Tokens of matrilineal descent hint at the ways in which the courtesans' all-female communities mimicked even while they subverted the kinship structure of respectable families.[63] Some courtesans brought with them and kept the surname of their natal family. In one striking example of mimesis, a courtesan took another courtesan as her concubine (*qie*).[64] A very few courtesans, it seems, had no surname at all. Guizhi (Cassia Branch) was the *tongyangxi* (adopted daughter-in-law) of an actor and perhaps did not know her own surname.[65] Wenxin, the daughter of a respectable commoner family, was perhaps ashamed to make her surname known.[66]

If shared surnames represented an invented matrilineal kinship system in the courtesan quarters, each courtesan's given name was artfully chosen to suggest her individual distinctive qualities. Gems (jade, pearls), musical instruments (the *qin*), flowers (hibiscus, lotus, cassia, apricot), and sensations (notably fragrance) were especially favored. A name bestowed by a famous patron became part of a courtesan's legend. Everyone knew, for example, that Yuan Mei had selected the given name Rulan, "Iris," for the girl known only as Courtesan Ma (Ma Ji).[67]

In adoptive kin networks, courtesans commonly acquired a rank (*hang*) that placed them in a hierarchy. Thus, a young girl might be identified as *hang san* (number three), *hang da* (eldest), or *hang yi* (number one). Less distinguished courtesans were known only by rank and surname, hence Wang Si (Wang number four) or Tang Xiao (Tang the younger).[68] Such ranking systems, which mimic the practice in patrilineal descent lines, usually identified seniority in the brothel rather than actual age. Thus, a girl identified as *hang san* would be the third daughter adopted into a group centered on a "mother."[69] Mothers might be of lower rank than their daughters in this fictive kinship system. Thus Mi Manyun, who was rank one, was the adoptive daughter of a woman whose rank was three.[70] Among girls working for the same mother, rank was a proxy for sibling position, though whether the relationship between sisters was biological or adoptive was not considered important enough to mention. Wang Suzhen, rank three, had an elder sister Su'e, rank two;[71] Kong Qinxiang, first rank (*da*), had a younger sister Rongxian, rank two.[72] In one case, a rank three courtesan was said to be the "elder sister by the same mother" (*tongmu jie*) to a rank four courtesan with the same surname.[73] Similarly, whether or not the mother is adoptive or biological is not clear from the language.

Rank orders suggest that elite courtesans lived in small, intimate surrogate kin groups.[74] In the seven records I have analyzed, the largest adoptive sibling set mentioned was ten, and more than 75 percent of cases were sets of three or fewer, with many courtesans listed as living together in pairs with an adoptive mother. Some courtesans cohabited (*tongju*) a house, sharing quarters without establishing a hierarchical relationship.[75] A very popular courtesan might have her own "house" (*jia*). The residence of such a courtesan would then become associated with her name and occupied subsequently by a younger woman when the elder retired. A few such cases suggest an arrangement in which a courtesan owned her establishment independently, although clear evidence on this point is lacking.[76] A courtesan who occupied the residence of a former *ming ji* appointed herself the heir to her predecessor's legacy, creating other lines of affiliation within the courtesan culture. Again, these successions probably involved the payment of substantial sums of money, but that is never mentioned in the sources. In rare cases, an order of succession was established by talent and reputation rather than by adoption, rank affiliation, or residence. Thus Du Ningfu, regarded in her day as the best *pipa* player in Suzhou,[77] was succeeded by Yi Jingzhu, whose talent on the *pipa* was likened to hers.[78]

Courtesans, especially those who maintained their own residence, often appeared to be autonomous women empowered by their beauty to dominate men while remaining free of the oppressive bonds of patriarchal families. Anecdotes describe courtesans who cast off or rejected powerful patrons out of boredom, antipathy, preference for a rival suitor, or even a taste for solitude. Independent or not, however, the courtesan had to work a grueling schedule to maintain her reputation as a *ming ji*. Even romantic admirers noticed that courtesans worked themselves to exhaustion performing late into the night and entertaining early the next day. Letters from suitors caution courtesans against overwork, prescribe healthy diets, and suggest ways to relieve stress.[79]

Whether or not a courtesan worked for someone else or owed money to a procuress or a go-between, she was enmeshed in ties that drained her financial resources. Her position made her or her adoptive mother vulnerable to lawsuits. Attractor of the rich and powerful, target of jealousy or rivalry, protector of girls in her employ or under her patronage, she herself had no sure protection nor could she count on special connections (even support from kin) if she faced legal action. An adoptive mother might be sued by a disgruntled client. A seller might have second thoughts and take the buyer to court. A "sister" might be implicated in a scandal requiring expensive bribes and appeals to settle.[80]

Financial obligations of other kinds burdened working courtesans in the best of times. Unscrupulous kinfolk, whether adoptive or not, shook their valuable young girls as "money trees" for all they were worth. One "mother," who was originally a scavenger in Jiangbei, set up a stall where she sold clothing and jewelry and "shamelessly assumed an air of respectability" on acquiring the courtesan Zhao Fu (by what means is not clear from the record).[81] The "false" mother (*jia mu*) of the Nanjing courtesan Hou Shuangling "treated her like a money tree" (*yi ji wei qian shuzi*).[82] Kinfolk who retained the power to collect or dun a courtesan's earnings could also turn away any client who wanted to buy her as a concubine.[83] Under those circumstances, a courtesan had little choice but to continue working until she could no longer attract customers.

Courtesans past their twenties disappear from the historical record. An occasional comment alludes to the continued beauty of an "old" courtesan just entering her thirties. Some courtesans at that age were doubtless married off by families who could no longer shake the money tree. Others who could no longer work as entertainers or madams were probably cared for by adoptive daughters. We have no way of knowing how many died from complications of pregnancy or childbirth or as victims of disease, neglect, imprisonment, or penury.

Conclusion

All the evidence suggests that in the Lower Yangzi region during High Qing times, the lines between courtesans and respectable commoners were permeable and shifting. According to the law, courtesans were not legally permitted to become first wives. In that sense they were relegated to a position permanently outside the ritually constituted kinship unit. However, since courtesans were publicly linked to legitimate families through blood, legal adoption, or concubinage, the line dividing so-called mean people (*jianmin*) from "respectable commoners" (*liangmin*) was not drawn—in Jiangnan at least—as rigidly as Qing legal codes would suggest. With or without the manumission edicts, the pleasure quarters displayed, for all to see, the social flux that made women central figures in the High Qing era.

At the same time, the gulf separating courtesans from women in respectable society widened, as *guixiu* claimed the aesthetic and political space courtesans had formerly occupied. The courtesan Liu Rushi—described by Chang and Ko as the famed companion to the late Ming's most distinguished gentlemen and herself a formidable published poet and anthologist—has no counterpart in the High Qing era. The scholar Yan Ming attributes much of this shift in the courtesan's status to the withdrawal of government support for their arts and to the increasingly repressive moralism of High Qing rulers, especially the Qianlong emperor.[84] But evidence from the women's quarters of *guixiu* families shows that the impetus for change came from within the homes of the elite as well, especially from the writings and teachings of married and marriageable women who reclaimed women's literary arts as the exclusive domain of their own moral authority.

6 *Work*

THE CRUCIAL LINE DIVIDING courtesans from respectable women was not literary art, but work. In the rhetoric of the High Qing era, the courtesan's work marked her as a polluted person, inferior to even the lowliest peasant woman who labored honestly at her spindle and loom. Qing statesmen argued that women's labor was the fulcrum of Jiangnan's agrarian economy. Essays on statecraft published and circulated in High Qing times reiterate the practical and moral significance of womanly work (*nü gong*). The woman who was industrious (*qin*) was also frugal (*jian*). She created the surpluses and hoarded the savings that enabled her family to survive or, with luck, move ahead. The industrious, frugal woman must be resourceful as well (a quality dubbed *xian*, or "practical wisdom"), capable of wresting advantage from the most forbidding situation. Above all, women as "wise mothers" (*xian mu*) labored and sacrificed to ensure the success of their sons. Playing on but also subverting the symbolic meaning of women's work in official rhetoric was women's own celebration of the Double Seven Festival, which conflated women's work with sensual desire and skilled handwork with marital success.

Together, rhetoric and festival tell us that in High Qing times a woman's worth—her value to the household and government fisc and her worthiness

Fig. 20. Reeling thread. Reprinted from Nakagawa [1799] 1983: 198.

as a human being—was measured in productive labor and in her skill with shuttle and needle. But studies of the High Qing economy show that the rapid development of the Lower Yangzi economy was marginalizing women's handicraft production during the eighteenth century, creating a dual economy in which women's work supplied subsistence needs while skilled artisans in the towns catered to the tastes of wealthier consumers. This contrast between rhetorical ideal and economic reality reveals that Qing officials' interest in promoting women's work was more than economic. Women's work represented a way of life that Qing statecraft writers were eager to preserve and promote in the face of economic change.

Class differences divided women with respect to manual labor, as we shall see. But all women, regardless of class, were expected to work with their hands. Mindful of the last of Ban Zhao's "four attributes," "women's work" (*nü gong*), elite women sewed and embroidered and also learned how to rear silkworms, reel thread, spin yarn, and weave cloth (Figs. 20 and 21)—if not for their own use, then to instruct and supervise servants. An allegori-

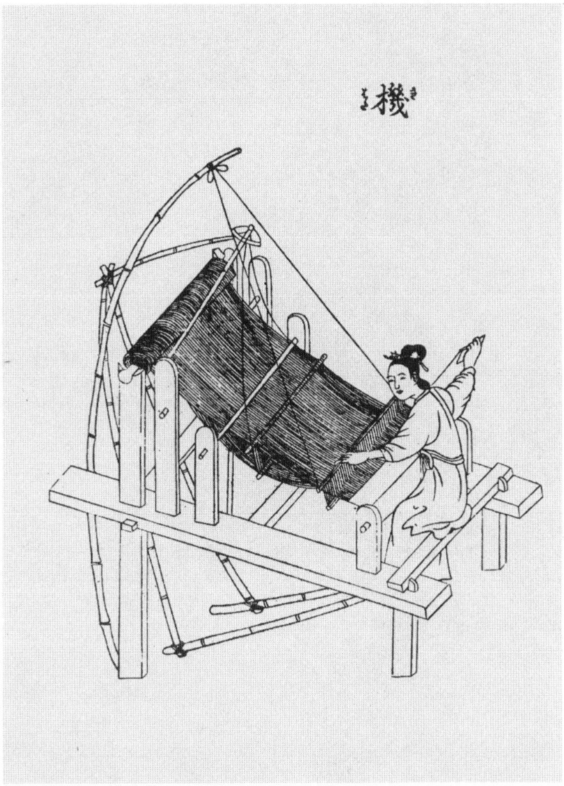

Fig. 21. Loom. Reprinted from Nakagawa [1799] 1983: 197.

cal painting by the Qianlong emperor's leading court painter illustrates in a charming scene the moral and economic significance of women's labor in the eighteenth century (Fig. 22), and a portrait of an imperial consort dramatizes the relationship between a woman's needlework and her virtue (Fig. 23).

There are practical reasons why this rhetorical emphasis on women's work made sense to ordinary people during the High Qing era. As the mobile society around them attested and stories in didactic texts confirmed, the family that was affluent today might face penury tomorrow. If that happened, especially if it happened during widowhood, women were expected to support themselves—and their in-laws and offspring, if necessary—by their labor. Biographies of exemplary widows routinely allude to their excellence in spinning or weaving, invoking the powerful image of the mother of the philosopher Mencius.* Not surprisingly, the poems of elite women imply

* Mencius's mother, a widow, sold her weaving to support her son's studies. Distraught over his conduct (the young Mencius fell in with a bad crowd and neglected his schooling), one day she dramatically slashed the cloth on which she was working and declared to

Fig. 22. "Adding Thread at the Winter Solstice," by Jin Tingbiao (fl. 1760–64). This court painting puns on the relationship between women's work and the changing seasons. Two maids are shown measuring their mistress's shadow with a thread. The shadow is longest at the winter solstice, when the midday sun is at its lowest position in the sky. "Adding thread" has a double meaning, because as the sun rises higher again, the hours of daylight will increase, permitting women to "add more thread" to their looms because they can work longer. Courtesy of the National Palace Museum, Taipei, Taiwan, Republic of China.

their familiarity with the manual arts of spinning and weaving and their self-conscious relationship to the peasant women and servant women who per-

her shocked son that his neglect of his studies was just as destructive: "If you do not study now, you will surely end up as a menial servant and will never be free from troubles. The same thing would happen to a woman who supports herself by weaving if she were to give it up" (translated in Ebrey 1981: 33–34, translation slightly adapted). Of course the young Mencius, stricken by his mother's words, became the greatest of the early Confucian philosophers.

Fig. 23. "The Consort Yinzhen Sewing." In this court painting, one of a series of a favorite consort of the Yongzheng emperor, she is shown sewing a garment by candlelight, an obvious tribute to her virtue. Reprinted from Shen Yizheng 1984: 111.

formed those tasks for a living. Elite women's skill with embroidery, a more frivolous and problematic form of handwork, they left to others to praise.

Yet even our knowledge of the practical use of women's manual labor conveys little about the actual impact of rhetoric about women's work on the lives of laboring women, who made up the majority of the female population in Jiangnan. Writings by scholars and officials, poems by elite men and women, and observations in local gazetteers, pieced together, yield only a limited picture. Sometimes they describe an observer's feelings or perceptions or beliefs; sometimes they explain the kinds of work women did and why it was valued. At best, these sources reveal elite attitudes toward women's work, and toward woman as workers, that underscore tensions and anxieties in the growing High Qing economy. Let us begin with "statecraft" writings—essays on women's work by scholars and local officials concerned above all with maintaining a stable agrarian economy.

Statecraft Writings on Women's Work

High Qing officials produced a stream of documents discussing the importance of the gender division of labor in peasant household economies. Their recommendations about female labor (*nü gong*) outline two major goals. The first was to raise the productivity of peasant households. The second was to buffer the impact of seasonal shortfalls, drought, flood, and pests by providing nonfarm sources of household income. Both goals reflect the state's consuming interest in the land tax, which was based on individual household registers and therefore on the productivity of peasant family units. Therefore policies on women's labor focused on promoting home spinning and weaving. In the process, officials hoped to achieve a third and fourth goal as well: to shape the values, along with the production strategies, of families in local communities while securing and expanding the government's tax base.[1]

In Qing times, these concerns came into focus during the reign of the Yongzheng emperor (1723–36), when the minister of the Board of Public Works submitted a long memorial on agricultural development in Yunnan province. The memorial uses the Jiangnan region as a model of economic development, stressing the unique local conditions in Yunnan and proposing adaptations of the Jiangnan model appropriate to a developing region. One of the memorialist's three major recommendations is that "women workers must be industrious" (*nü gong zhi yi qin ye*).[2] He carefully describes ways to manufacture and distribute looms to peasant households and explains the advantages of promoting cotton rather than silk weaving in this frontier society, appealing to the emperor's wish to "exhort and instruct" his people for their benefit.

The memorialist writes as if responding to the emperor's concerns. In fact, however, High Qing officials' writings on women's work appear to represent their own deep personal convictions about the relationship between womanly virtue, status, and work. These convictions, as we have seen, had diverse roots. One was research in Confucian classical texts, where women's handwork was a normative value. Even apocryphal classical models such as Mencius's mother bent over her loom dramatized working mothers as providers of the material support as well as the moral example that made sons great scholars. Another source of officials' feelings about women's work was their sensitivity to issues of status and propriety where women were concerned, a product of elite men's complex interactions with proper and improper women. Womanly work, in these men's eyes, was an emblem of woman-as-wife-and-mother, the anchor of the household and the moral center of the family. These are some of the motives that led local officials to drum out to farm families a singular message about women: economic success and social respectability depended on women's work in the household economy.

The proper division of labor in farm families was summed up in a four-character phrase taken from the classics: "Men plow, women weave" (*nan geng nü zhi*). This ideal had been a staple of imperial government policy at least since the Song. It was widely promoted during the first great economic revolution in the Song period as output from women's spinning and weaving increased with the introduction of cotton ginning.[3] However, evidence suggests that by the Ming dynasty, skilled male weavers and so-called weaver households (*ji hu*) had come to dominate the production of fine cloth for luxury markets, even as cotton spinning and weaving continued to spread through the peasant household economy. The early Ming government registered skilled weavers as a hereditary artisanal class that catered primarily to the pockets and tastes of the court and the wealthiest members of the elite.[4]

During the sixteenth and seventeenth centuries, as the farm economy commercialized and monetized, consumer markets in the countryside created new demands for the products of loom and spindle. These new markets, competing with the old luxury trade, drove hereditary artisans out of business and eroded the line between hereditary artisans and newcomers until, by the middle of the seventeenth century, the hereditary artisanal class was a class in name only. The Jiangnan region led the transition to commercial handicraft production in the Ming-Qing transition. During the last century of Ming rule, state-sponsored artisanal enterprises collapsed as the Ming consumer economy expanded. The rapidly increasing population in the sixteenth century fueled specialization and commercialization in the peasant economy. Major centers for silk weaving and textile marketing sprang up at Shengze, Zhenze, Huangqi, Puyuan, Wangjiangjing, and Shuanglin,[5] while Lower Yangzi cotton-weaving centers developed in Songjiang, Jiading, and Changshu.[6] Under pressure from this competition, registered artisans absconded, disregarding the severe punishments that threatened those who were caught.[7] At the same time, the registered-artisan system was invaded from without by commoners who attached themselves to registered artisans as adopted sons or sons-in-law and then opened shops using the name of their in-laws or adoptive parents.[8] Meanwhile, increased commercial production drew prices down, bringing silk and cotton textiles within the means of ordinary commoners.[9] As a result of these changes, by the end of the Ming dynasty the moribund registered-artisan system had been entirely displaced by commercial labor markets. In the process, the peasant household emerged as a primary production and consumption unit for the commercial spinning and weaving of cotton and silk in the Lower Yangzi region.[10]

Under these circumstances, the new Qing government abandoned all pretense of maintaining weavers in hereditary-artisan status. An edict of 1645 announced the formal emancipation of all registered artisans, opening the market for artisanal labor to every commoner.[11] Yet like their Ming predecessors, Qing statesmen wanted to limit the number of artisans in the economy. They feared labor unrest,[12] and they believed that grain production would decline if artisanal pursuits became too lucrative. These concerns are clearly stated in a Yongzheng edict dated June 22, 1727:

> Among the four classes of people, next to the scholars, farmers are the most valuable. All scholars, artisans, and merchants rely for their food on farming, which is why farming is the basic pursuit (*ben wu*) throughout our realm, while crafts and trade are merely secondary (*mo*). With the rising demand today for ever more elaborate and finely crafted implements, clothing, and amusements, we are surely going to be needing more artisans. One more artisan in the marketplace, however, means one less farmer in the fields. Moreover, when the simple people see how much more artisans make than farmers do, they are sure to stampede to learn a craft. A sudden increase in the number of artisans will mean a glut of manufactured goods on the market, which will make it harder to sell things, so prices will fall. Thus not only will an increase in people pursuing secondary occupations harm agriculture, but it will also have a harmful effect on the artisans themselves.[13]

Imperial sentiments stressing agriculture as the "base" of the polity hark back to ancient concerns about the moral dangers of commercialization, summed up in a rhyme from a Han dynasty text:

> For the poor to seek riches,
> Farming is not as satisfactory as crafts,
> Crafts are not as good as trading.
> To prick embroidery does not pay
> As much as leaning on a market door.[14]

Commercial wealth, in this logic, is a temptation to corruption; profit is the goal of the "petty man." As one High Qing writer remarked loftily but without originality: "The common man thinks only of profit" (*xiaomin wei li shi tu*).[15] Writings by other High Qing officials show that they viewed farm policy as a moral and economic program to keep peasants from leaving the land and becoming wholly dependent on the market for survival.[16] Statecraft writers discussing agricultural policy presented spectres of a population living at the margins, incapable of feeding and clothing itself. Their solution was to go back to the basics through policies promoting household self-sufficiency. The ensuing campaigns featured two classical phrases as watchwords: *zu shi* ("enough to eat") and *heng chan* ("stable income"—i.e., property). The ideal was a society where every peasant household produced all of the food and clothing it needed.

This focus on stable farm families comforted local officials, whose nightmares called up visions of refugee mobs or starving townspeople beseiging yamen gates.[17] They envisioned firmly anchored married men whose parents, wives, and offspring would help them weather periodic shortfalls and whose land would provide insurance against impoverishment. Moreover, peasant families were not the only target of official concern. Writers painted idyllic pictures of the scholar's life on his country estate, reminding genteel readers of the joys of "farming and studying":

> If you live in the countryside, you can personally oversee the tilling and keep count of your acreage and earn rents that will double your income so that you can feed eight mouths. You'll raise chickens and pigs in pens, grow vegetables in your garden, cultivate fish and shrimp in your pond, and gather fuel on the hillsides. For months at a time you'll need hardly any cash at all. Besides, when you live in the country you'll have few relatives to entertain and little hospitality to repay, and if company comes, you need only serve chicken and millet. If the women and children work hard, they can manage the spinning and wear plain cotton clothes.[18]

The self-sufficient rural household, poor or genteel, was an idyll based on a division of labor between men and women, and it depended for its success on women's handwork in the home.

The imperial court, to reinforce its message to the scholar elite, revived ancient rituals honoring the goddess of sericulture, pairing them with the emperor's annual ritual ploughing of the fields. These rituals, first described in the *Guliang* commentary on the *Spring and Autumn Annals,* stress the importance of farming to the moral health of the empire by appealing to the image of the emperor and empress as filial spouses serving their ancestors:

> The emperor himself plows to supply millet for the sacrificial vessels; the empress herself tends the silkworms to supply robes for the sacrificial rites. This

> does not mean that the realm lacks good farmers and woman workers, but rather that it is not as desirable to serve your ancestors with what others have produced as it is to serve them with what you have produced yourself.[19]

The imperial ritual display of *nong* and *sang* (agriculture and sericulture) makes emperor and empress archetypal father and mother of the realm who serve as examples for the people.

Lei Zu, the patron goddess of sericulture, was honored in elaborate ceremonies reinstituted by the High Qing court.[20] The Lei Zu rites were the only public function at which women presided as imperial officials during the Qing dynasty. Beginning in 1742, the ritual was conducted at a new shrine complex specially constructed for that purpose by the Qianlong emperor. Located about one-half mile north and slightly west of the rear gate of the Forbidden City, the shrine included dressing rooms, an altar, a terrace from which the audience could observe the gathering of mulberry leaves, and an enclosed courtyard with a large pool and rooms for the hatching of the silk worms and for weaving silk. Sluices carried water from a stream for washing the silk. A separate sanctuary housed the tablet of the deity herself.

The annual Lei Zu rites commenced on a propitious spring day selected by court astronomers, with the empress herself presiding. Preparations for the ritual began with two days of fasting to purify sacrificers and their attendants. The participants then presented cooked food and wine to delight the spirit of the goddess and made additional offerings of incense, candles, and silk. On the day after the sacrifice, the empress led two imperial concubines, along with princesses and other noble ladies, in the ceremony of gathering mulberry leaves. Ideally this took place on a day when the silkworms at the shrine complex had hatched; the leaves gathered by Her Majesty were then scattered over frames for the worms to feed on. Another delay followed while the worms matured and spun their cocoons, after which an auspicious day was selected and the empress returned to Lei Zu's altar to offer silk personally reeled for the goddess by the empress's own hands. The empress was required to supply three basins of silk in all—dyed vermilion, green, and deep yellow—to be set aside for use in embroidering garments for ritual sacrifice. The scale of this great rite may be gauged by the 117 persons who participated in the first sacrifice, including 56 women and 34 eunuchs. Those who took part in the initial sacrifice were then admitted to the subsequent rites of gathering mulberry leaves, feeding silkworms, and reeling silk.

The cult of Lei Zu was part of a wider Qing government agenda for the "moral education" of the populace, starting with the rural scholar-elite and moving outward to ordinary commoners.[21] Lei Zu, in other words, was the symbolic pinnacle of a government program to promote sericulture throughout the empire's farm households. This plan was implemented through county agricultural extension bureaus where county and provincial officials sponsored programs to teach local farmers how to grow mulberry, rear silkworms, and reel and weave silk.[22] At court, the ideals behind these statecraft programs were celebrated in specially commissioned handbooks like the *Imperially Commissioned Illustrations of Farming and Weaving* (*Yuzhi gengzhi tu*). These works depict in woodblock prints the proper gender division of labor in sericulture households: men and young boys plucking the leaves; women tending and feeding the worms, sorting the cocoons, reeling the silk, and weaving the silk thread into cloth. Other illustrations dramatize the saying "Men plow, women weave" (Fig. 24).[23]

In the writings of Qing scholars, silk, not cotton, was viewed as the preferred material for household weaving, and sericulture was primarily women's work. Statecraft writers used the phrase "farming and mulberry" (*nong sang*) to describe the ideal gender division of labor. The *Collected Essays on Statecraft* name sericulture a pillar of state agricultural policy.[24] In Huang Liuhong's "Four Policies to Nurture the People" ("Yangmin sizheng"), mulberry trees are identified as one of the state's four crucial concerns.[25] A lengthy report on problems in the agricultural economy of Shaanxi province by Chen Hongmou, who was familiar with sericulture from his years of service in the Lower Yangzi, recommended six remedial measures, of which the first was "broad promulgation of sericulture."[26]

These writers may have taken their cue from the late Ming statesman Gu Yanwu, himself a native of the Lower Yangzi, whose statecraft essay "The Profitability of Weaving" ("Fangzhi zhi li") was given pride of place by the High Qing editors of the *Collected Essays on Statecraft*. Gu proposed that the state promote silk weaving in households in border areas by bringing in master weavers from China's heartland to teach them. His practical argument was that silk weaving would bring down the cost of living by making households more self-sufficient. In the process, Gu suggested, peasants would produce new surpluses that could be taxed by the government.[27]

A similar model for propagating women's work appears in a later proposal by Tang Zhen (1630–1704), who spent much of his life in the Lower Yangzi region:

> Wu silk clothes the world. It is collected in Shuanglin, and people from the Lower Yangzi and the southeast coast and even from the islands in the sea flock there to buy it. In the fifth month they descend on the markets with silver piled up in their boats like bricks. So all the rural areas in Wu and south-

Fig. 24 (facing pages). "Men Plow, Women Weave." Reprinted from the *Yuzhi gengzhi tu* [1696], in Zhou Wu 1988: 276–77.

ward [i.e., the Lower Yangzi] make more than ten million in profits every year. That is why, although the tax burden is heavy in that area, even poor people are not driven to destitution. Indeed, their ordinary dwellings and vessels surpass those of other places. Such is the wealth to be gained from sericulture![28]

Tang, like Gu, proposed that local officials import teachers from sericulture areas to instruct women living in regions where silk was not produced. He predicted that with the right official leadership—"reward those who produce a lot, warn those who produce little, punish those who don't produce any" (*duozhe, jiang zhi; shaozhe, jie zhi; feizhe, cheng zhi*)—sericulture would spread to every part of China within ten years.[29]

Poems by elite women included in Yun Zhu's anthology echo the conviction of statecraft writers that farm families relied on women's silk weaving to

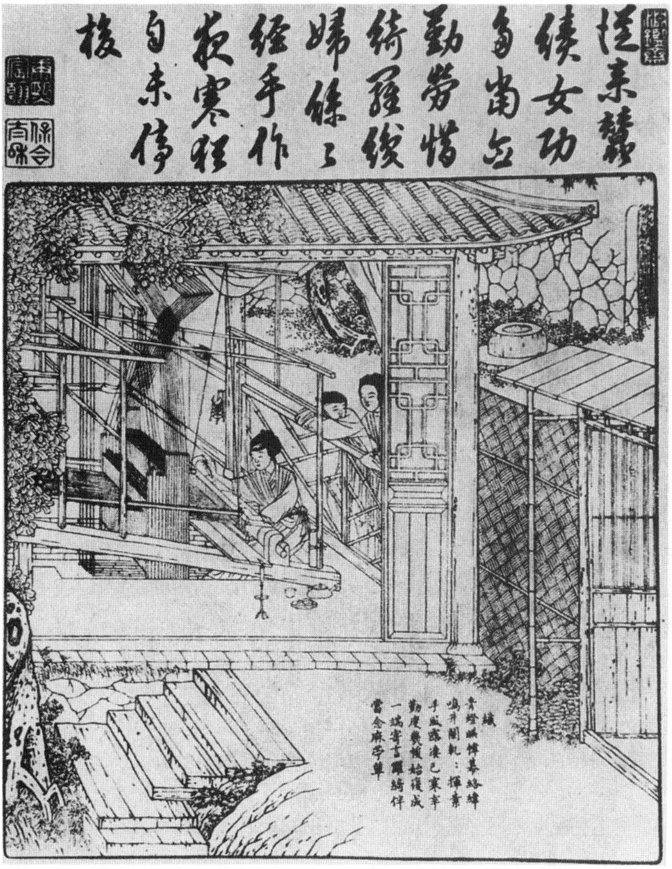

pay their taxes, as in this stanza from "Song of a Farm Family," by an Anhui poet known only by her surname, Liu:

> On the loom there's silken thread,
> In the garden edible ferns.
> With taxes on the paddy land covered,
> We need not exert ourselves further.[30]

Tang Chao's poem "The Wife Who Tends the Cocoons" reflects on the pressures of poverty that drove women to work long hours:

> The feathered bird flies low and the willow floss disappears;
> As the worms molt and grow, my anxiety increases.
> Our dikes have no *zhe* trees, our orchards no mulberry;

To buy mulberry leaves I have pawned every last bit of clothing.
From neighbors around us the sound of silk reeling presses in on me;
The hungry silkworms, growing older, lift their heads in vain.[31]

The poet Fang Yao of Tongcheng, Anhui, addressed this whimsical poem to the worms she tended:

Dawn and dusk, arranging the food, I begin to acquire some skill,
Busier than the spring winds on the third day of the third month.
Your silken threads are all spun out, now turn into a butterfly,
In another life I want to be a rosy silkworm.[32]

Cotton joined silk in this late-imperial system of household handicraft production. Prior Ming efforts to promote cotton cultivation and the production of cotton yarn and cloth were repeated in the High Qing era, which saw a stabilization of the technologies that were fully developed by the end of the Ming period.[33] An authoritative estimate suggests that in late Ming and Qing times, between three-fifths and four-fifths of all Chinese counties were manufacturing some cotton cloth.[34] In recognition of the importance of cotton to the farm economy, the High Qing court endorsed the publication of an annotated collection of illustrations titled *An Illustrated Guide to Cotton* (*Mianhua tu*), by Fang Guancheng (1698–1768), an official from Tongcheng, Anhui. This text was presented to the throne with an accompanying memorial in the spring of 1765 and inscribed in the emperor's own hand three months later. Eventually it was even carved in stone and embellished with poems written by both the Kangxi and the Qianlong emperors. In 1808 the Jiaqing emperor commissioned a special reprint, titled *Imperially Commissioned Edition of Wide-Ranging Instructions on the Provisioning of Clothing* (*Qinding shouyi guangxun*), which was published the following year.

The preface to the imperial edition of Fang Guancheng's work declares emphatically that the ordinary clothing produced by the people for their daily use should be honored alongside farming and sericulture as a "basic occupation" (*ben ye*).[35] It presents idealized drawings of large happy families engaged in cotton cultivation and manufacturing. Unlike the *Illustrations of Farming and Weaving* (*Yuzhi gengzhi tu*), this text shows women and children working outside the home (Fig. 25). Illustrations of cotton production—beginning with the sowing of seeds and ending with the final bolts of cloth—portray the appropriate gender division of labor.[36] Initial preparation of the soil—hoeing, irrigating, sowing, and weeding—was all done by men. Women took charge of the cotton plants, pinching back the shoots and then plucking the mature cotton. Plucked cotton fibers had to be ginned to remove seeds, then "bowed" to fluff them out and remove remaining debris; these tasks could

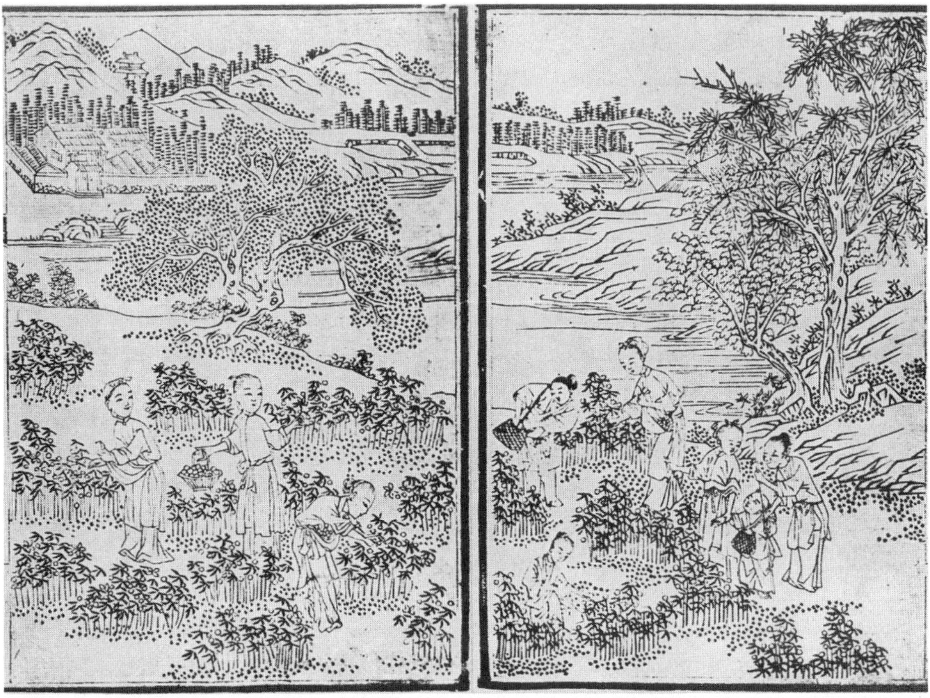

Fig. 25. "Plucking Cotton." Reprinted from Fang Guancheng [1809], in Zhou Wu 1988: 270.

be done by men or women, depending on the equipment. Bowed cotton in rovings went to women for spinning and weaving; dyeing and calendering to finish the cloth was men's work.

Descriptions of cotton production in contemporary documents belie Fang's idealized portrait of cotton as the industry of self-sufficient peasant households. These descriptions show that wholesale brokers often purchased raw cotton from peasant households and ginned and bowed it before reselling it to other households or businesses for spinning, weaving, and finishing. Similarly, dyeing and calendering were often the domain of master artisans whose family secrets ensured a monopoly on their sector of the cotton market.[37] Craig Dietrich, in his definitive study of Qing cotton textile production, concludes that "family production for family needs was the dominant pattern in the Ch'ing cotton industry."[38] But, Dietrich observes, in the highly commercialized Lower Yangzi region, specialization was well developed, resulting in a two-tiered system in which farm families made "woman-loom cloth" for their own use and for sale in local markets and skilled artisans manufactured "waist-loom cloth" for more discerning clients.[39]

Like the cotton industry, the Qing silk industry had two tiers. Silk was highly profitable, and its classical symbolism made it the material of choice for most statecraft writers. Women's role in silk production, however, was a lowly one, confined mainly to the labor-intensive, low-paying, but respectable work of rearing silkworms, tending cocoons, and reeling silk thread. "Sericulture households" that produced cocoons or thread sold their output to brokers or middlemen, who in turn supplied merchant "account houses" (*zhangfang*). Account houses in Suzhou and other Lower Yangzi cities controlled as many as a hundred or more looms by subcontracting to "weaver households" (*ji hu*) where two, three, or more looms were operated by men.[40] Although male weavers in this system were said to be exploited by their employers, they belonged to guilds and even conducted occasional strikes over wages and working conditions,[41] enjoying an artisanal status denied to women, who remained dispersed in farm households where they could neither organize nor negotiate for pay. The much-vaunted "sericulture" work of women, then, had less to do with weaving or even with spinning—the tasks vaunted by statecraft writers—than with the menial tasks of feeding worms and reeling cocoons.

Officials ignored the low returns to female household labor in sericulture. But they sometimes complained about the cotton industry. A few criticized policies promoting cotton production on the grounds that women had to work too hard for too little when they wove cotton. One official pointed out: "The value of one length of cotton cloth is less than one-tenth that of a comparable roll of silk. The labor is great, the profit small—not enough to feed even one individual. A young girl [trying to support herself by weaving cotton] would find it difficult to avoid starvation." His real purpose seems to have been the promotion of sericulture instead, for he went on to add that "only the profits from sericulture are a worthy complement to farming."[42] Another source of opposition to cotton growing in the Lower Yangzi was concern about the food supply. The governor-general Gao Jin, writing in 1776, argued that peasants should return to rice cultivation 30 percent of the 70 percent of Lower Yangzi paddy land that had been planted with cotton.[43] To induce peasants to restore half their landholdings to paddy, Gao suggested state subsidies for irrigation designed to lower the labor costs of planting rice.[44] That official concerns about cotton and silk production focused on the peasant household underscores the general consensus among scholars that the household remained a basic unit of production and consumption in the textile industry throughout this period.[45]

In all these discussions about specialization and commercialization, interregional trade, and work and leisure, officials remained united in their conviction that womanly work was important and its moral significance absolute.[46] As in ancient Greece and Rome,[47] "women's work" in High Qing China referred not only to the physical production of cloth, but also to the moral attributes associated with women's cloth making: industry, frugality, and dedicated service to the patriline. In the statecraft rhetoric celebrating women's work appear other hierarchies of value joining work and gender. As a commodity, silk was more valuable than cotton. But the value of silk was also symbolic. Unlike cotton—crude, rough, fit for commoners—silk was the imperial fabric, the clothing of the rich. It was the thread used in embroidery, the cleanest, purest, most refined of the womanly arts.[48] Silk and cotton technologies mimicked this hierarchy of value. Rearing silkworms and reeling silk required purity and cleanliness: not only the symbolic purification represented by taboos barring menstruating females, but also meticulous material cleansing—clean hands, disease-free air.[49] Compared with silk reeling, cotton spinning was a craft that young girls of barely seven or eight *sui* could learn. Cotton weaving required more strength and maturity, but a twelve-year-old daughter was thought capable of it, and the equipment was cheap and simple.[50] Both profitability and purity measured the value of work in silk and cotton—work that a daughter could do "before hairpinning."

Even though women of all classes were expected to be skilled handworkers, women's work itself defined a hierarchy of value and status. The poorest farm women engaged in the home handicrafts of hat weaving and mat weaving, working with harsh, rough materials in cramped, dim quarters. Cotton spinners did gentler work and came from a gentler class, albeit from households with neither income nor space for a loom and without the capital for sericulture. Weavers were another cut above; like those who reared silkworms and reeled thread, they lived in households with space and labor to spare. At the pinnacle of this hierarchy stood silk embroidery, the labor of the *guixiu*, the cultivated lady of the inner apartments. Silk embroiderers needed light to work, a clean spacious room for the frame, and servants to fan their delicate hands and foreheads in the summer heat to prevent perspiration from marring their needlework. The fine needles and delicate smooth hands of the *guixiu*, fit for embroidery, marked her as a woman secluded from harsh manual labor inside or outside the home. Embroidery was an emblem of purity associated with moral refinement.[51] Embroidery was also an emblem of industry, the task to which elite women constantly repaired when other more pressing jobs were done. So great was the demand for embroidered garments in the upper classes that much of it had to be either purchased or supplied by servants' labor at home.[52] Embroidery, finally, was charged with sexual meanings. The young woman embroidering appeared fecund and sensual, her needlework a symbol of her sexual allure. These erotic signs are

Fig. 26. "Ladies Embroidering." Courtesy of the National Palace Museum, Taipei, Taiwan, Republic of China.

especially clear in paintings and illustrations depicting women embroidering (Figs. 26–28).[53] Because the word *xiu*, "to embroider," was a homophone for a term used to describe a woman engaging in sexual intercourse, the phrase "to love embroidery" (*ai xiu*) was a pun suggesting a lustful woman.[54]

The myths of origin and patronage for silk and cotton echo hierarchies of purity and class. The patroness of silk, Lei Zu, was an empress,[55] but the patroness of cotton, Huang Daopo, was a lowly commoner born to a poor family who made her way as a Daoist nun. Lei Zu was a heavenly spirit, the incarnation of a stellar constellation. Huang Daopo, according to local legends, was a *tongyangxi*—a little daughter-in-law—adopted as a child to become a bride of her "brother" because her family was too poor to arrange a proper wedding.[56] In this way, even the patrons of silk and cotton reflect their relative value in the rhetorical discussions of women's work during the High Qing period.

Qing statecraft programs promoting women's household handicrafts asserted a hierarchy of place as well as a hierarchy of value and class. The Lower Yangzi region served as a model for the realm. Fine cotton weaving from the Jiangnan core was held up as a model for the poor areas of Subei, in the Huai

Fig. 27. "Weary from Embroidering." Qing dynasty painting from a collection illustrating the embroidery styles of Jiangnan. Reprinted in *Chūgoku rekidai josei zōten* 1987: 103. The title of the painting alludes to a poem by Bo Juyi about a girl waiting for her lover who "leans wearily on her embroidery frame, sad and still." See comments on a Ming painting with the same title, in Lawton 1973: 215.

region to the north.[57] Hardworking Jiangnan women weavers put women workers to shame in peripheral areas like Yan'an, where, an entry in the *Gujin tushu jicheng* proclaimed, women were barely able to weave enough cloth to cover their bodies.[58] Statecraft writers worried that women outside the Lower Yangzi region relied on the products of Lower Yangzi female labor instead of producing for themselves. Li Ba, a prefect in Fuzhou, complained that none of the peasants in his jurisdiction planted cotton, preferring instead to purchase it from Jiangsu and Zhejiang, and that local women had no idea how to weave.[59] Jiangnan cotton culture was the pacesetter for the Fujianese, just as Shandong sericulture was the inspiration for Guizhou's new protoindus-

Fig. 28. Ladies embroidering. Reprinted from Nakagawa [1799] 1983: 339.

try. Compilers of the local history of Lai'an, a county in Anhui province not far from Nanjing, derided local people who refused to learn sericulture, complaining that "the women here don't know how to spin or weave."[60]

Plainly, to Qing statecraft writers, those regions in China where women wove were culturally and even morally superior to areas where women had no specialized home handicrafts. Officials carried home handicraft models from the Lower Yangzi to the southeast coast and from the North China plain to the Upper Yangzi; they used their knowledge of sericulture from areas where they had lived to promote it when they held office elsewhere.[61] In every case, officials introducing handicraft industries into new areas viewed them as an antidote for women's indolence and a tonic for female morality. As one county magistrate put it:

> The customs of Xinghua favor indolence (*tou'an*). . . . Poor women here do not do their work diligently, but let their hands and feet rest idle, as a result of which their whole manner appears loose and profligate. . . . Our county yamen has been extremely concerned to remedy this situation, and I have already contributed a modest sum from my own salary to establish a weaving bureau (*fangju*). Any young woman from a poor commoner family between the ages of eleven and thirteen *sui* can come here to learn.[62]

Sericulture was especially touted as a check on female promiscuity.[63] A striking essay by Zhou Kai (1779–1837), written while he was holding office in Xiangyang, Hubei, joins classical models and contemporary policies in a program of moral transformation.[64] The essay begins with an oft-quoted classical injunction about agricultural policy: "If one man does not plough, then the people will starve; if one woman does not weave, then the people will freeze"[65] (in other words, no one's labor is expendable; everyone must work as hard as possible). Next it invokes the reader's awareness of the value of silk as a commodity, quoting from Mencius and also from the *Records of the Grand Historian* (Sima Qian's *Shi ji*) to emphasize the importance of mulberry in the imperial economy. Moving to more practical concerns, the essay notes that whereas field crops are vulnerable to flood and drought, silkworms can be tended by women in the home regardless of the weather, and that the trees are completely profitable: the leaves feed silkworms; the fruit can be made into liquor; the wood can be used for kindling, the bark for paper.

Then Zhou Kai specifies the connection between a sharp gender division of labor in peasant households and sexuality, between women's work and wifely fidelity:

> I especially pity the women of Xiang[yang]. They have no way to develop specialized work of their own and thereby affirm their commitment as faithful wives [*wu yi zhuan qi zhiye er yi qi xin zhi*]. The woman who has no work of her own should take up sericulture. Whether she comes from a gentry family or a commoner household, a wife can personally tend silkworms to clothe her husband. When she sees that her own strength is sufficient to provide for her family's subsistence, her heart will be pure.[66]
>
> Once when I was out walking in the country, I saw some poor women. They were at work breaking up clods of earth with a hoe, and they were even ploughing in pairs alongside their husbands with other couples who were doing the same thing [*za geng'ou*]. I concealed my shock at observing this, for when the *Odes* refer to women in the fields, they speak only of women who bring food to their husbands while their husbands do the ploughing.

["The husband ploughs, the wife brings him food."] In fact, these were the same couples who had been suing one another in court not long before. (Note: I refer here to the court cases in the Xiang region involving the many women who are kidnapped, flee, or are seized and forced into another marriage as well as those who buy and sell their way in and out of marriages.) These wives no longer observe deep mourning for their husbands. To be sure, there are those women in Xiang who "warn their husbands about the crowing of the cock" [*jie jiming*; i.e., are goodwives] and who "swear to be a cedar vessel" [*shi bozhou*, i.e., vow to preserve their chastity].[67] But most women do not stop at even one remarriage; they simply take their cue from everyone around them: families seeking a bride see nothing wrong with a twice-married woman, and families marrying off a daughter do not think it shameful if she marries more than once.

All human beings have "feelings of shame and dislike" [*xiuwu zhi xin*].[68] Can it be that these women's hearts are different from other people's? Truly the cause of their behavior is that they have no specialized work of their own to do, and they have no commitment to wifely fidelity—as a result, their labor is not sufficient to provide for themselves. All of this is because they grow no mulberry.[69]

A less emotional statement about the link between stable farm families and women's work appears in an earlier essay, "Treatise on Farming" ("Nong shu"), by Zhang Lüxiang (1611–74), a one-time magistrate of Tongxiang county, Zhejiang province:

In the western districts [of my county], women's work may consist of weaving silk or twisting hemp and straw to make cloth. In the eastern districts, women's work may be a mixture of farming and sericulture, or it may be spinning. As for my district, here women's work is mainly cotton spinning and weaving, or rearing silkworms for floss. Though the source varies with the locality and the product, each woman earns income to help support her husband. Where a woman works diligently, her family will surely rise; where a woman is lazy, her family is certain to fall. What a woman works at may be nothing more than hemp and silk, and whether she is industrious or lazy may appear to have a minor impact on her family. But in fact if she is hardworking, all the family's undertakings will prosper; if she is lazy, everything the family tries will fail. Thus it is said: "The family that is poor longs for a good wife; the country that is in chaos longs for a good minister" [*jia pin si xianqi; guo luan si liangxiang*]. In each case one relies on their assistance, and the results are the same [in other words, the family is a microcosm of the state, with the wife the key advisor to the head of the household]. Take an ordinary married couple. The man can till perhaps ten mu of land. The woman can rear perhaps ten baskets of silkworms and weave two rolls of cloth a day or spin eight liang of thread. Would they need to worry about hunger and cold?[70]

As these writings show, government officials in High Qing times assiduously promoted programs to employ women as household handicraft workers. These officials spoke with horror of households where looms were not clacking away. They associated women's idle hands with dependency, sloth, and promiscuity.[71] But their rhetoric masks a growing gap between skilled urban weavers, mainly men who produced for urban markets, and women working at home in peasant households. Because the system of production was stratified by gender, especially in the Lower Yangzi region, we must carefully consider the relationship between rhetoric and reality during High Qing times. Although women's work opportunities may have been increasing in the border provinces where High Qing officials were promoting home weaving and spinning, in Jiangnan the picture was different. Despite the growth of the High Qing economy, women's work opportunities in the Lower Yangzi economy appeared frozen in an anachronistic mode that suited the interests of both High Qing statecraft writers and heads of peasant households. The conclusion to this chapter returns to this problem.

Women's Work in Elite and Popular Culture

A repertoire of signs and symbols and a family system structured around values of work and frugality created a receptive audience for statecraft appeals in the households of commoner families and in the imagination of the privileged elite. The Lei Zu rituals of the eighteenth century, for example, invoked a complex of symbols and stories celebrating the supervision of women's work by mythical founders and elite patronesses. Drawings depicting scenes from the daily lives of the Qing empresses frequently portray them inspecting the silkworms raised by their court ladies,[72] just as Ming biographies praise elite women for working alongside their servants.[73] On a practical level, marriageable women even from elite families were trained for manual labor for two reasons: to meet the exigencies of widowhood or poverty and to set an example of industry in the home for children and servants. The widowed mother replaced the father as the sole support of the family, and income from her work paid for her sons' education. At the same time, the image of the laboring mother became a powerful sign of maternal devotion and filial debt.

In High Qing times, the ideal of elite women as models for the labor of the lower classes was joined by a model of women as partners in a household economy where they worked at handicrafts alongside their farmer husbands. Qing policy presented the working goodwife as the key to both household self-sufficiency and family honor.[74] The early Confucian texts invoked by Qing policy makers stressed the moral values embedded in this ideal gender division of labor: "womanly work" was one of the "four attributes" (*si de*) that every young girl must cultivate. Women's work (*nü gong*, often written *nü hong** to suggest thread and fine embroidery) was glossed in Han sources as a reference to "hemp and silk"—in other words, work with needle, spindle, and loom.[75]

In High Qing Jiangnan, when it came to womanly work, upper-class and commoner women were held to the same moral standard. Confucian gentlemen (*junzi*) were supposed to eschew manual labor, but Confucian gentle*women* were expected to work with their hands alongside their servants and tenants. The ability to do womanly work was a sign that a woman possessed the three attributes most essential to her family's future success: thrift, frugality, and diligence. Among poor families, these womanly qualities were the key to survival. For women of the upper classes, the same attributes were essential to the proper discipline and management of domestic help—the mistress set the standards for her servants' work by her own example. For a woman, in other words, manual labor suited to her station was never demeaning.

At the same time, laboring women in peasant households were sometimes viewed as victims of a system that coerced their labor and assigned them unfair burdens. A poem of the early Qing period shows how working women could be used as symbols of state oppression and class hierarchy:

> Peasant families in the fourth month, mulberry leaves sparse.
> Wood dove coos in the rain, young swallows fly.
> Mountains of Wu caterpillars with their snowlike cocoons,
> The silk-spinning wheel rumbles behind the brushwood door.
> The young wife at the wheel, her dishevelled hair flying,
> For two months she toils, her elbows bare.
> Mornings forgetting to wash and comb, nights without sleep.
> Where can she find the helping hand of a sewing woman?
> Soon, the prefect's order comes to the village;
> In rushes the village head, knocking at the door.
> She has not suffered enough just paying off the taxes;
> She must also run to the kitchen to search for wine and meat.
> Don't you see:
> The daughters of wealthy families are lovely in their resplendent
> silk garments,
> The silk gauze of Wu, the thin pongee of Yueh—who will want to
> carry these to market?[76]

* The character *hong*, written with a silk radical, could be used in place of *gong* in this phrase to connote silk reeling and weaving.

Here, as in earlier times,[77] the bodily image of women's work in sericulture was a metaphor for the suffering of overburdened taxpayers and an emblem of class difference. In a similar poem by Wu Lan, titled "Picking Tea," the image recurs:

> The daughter of a hill family, her hair dressed in coils,
> Before the rain, and after the rain, is picking new tea.
> Backwater eddies of a mountain torrent are almost like a mirror,
> Across the ripples she sees her reflection, her face like a flower.
> The plucked leaves don't fill her basket, and she breathes a long sigh.
> After three spring seasons of endless bitter suffering,
> The tiny load she carries to a rich family has no value.
> In a single cup of spring snow, a thousand mountain tea leaves.[78]

Poems idealizing the happy lives of simple rural folk were written by many High Qing woman poets.[79] But they were equally likely to write poems reflecting their awareness of class difference and even empathy with the suffering of the unfortunate.[80]

FOOTBINDING AND WORK

Nowhere were the marks of class distinguishing women more clearly displayed than in the practice of footbinding. As we saw in Chapter 3 (pp. 55–56), unbound feet marked the lowborn pariah woman and set her apart. High Qing officials avoided the delicate subject of bound feet in their writings, but they wrote volumes about the kinds of womanly work that signified respectability. The link between the unspoken and the spoken here seems patently clear. If officials like Zhou Kai had had their way, women working as field laborers would all have been moved indoors to reel thread or weave cloth. And once there, they could bind their feet.

There is every reason to expect that a peasant couple given an economic incentive to move a daughter out of field labor would do so promptly. Not only did a sequestered daughter bring a higher brideprice, but her seclusion also enhanced her natal family's status, improving the marriage prospects for her brothers as well as herself. Again, the link with footbinding seems inescapable. But did the spread of home handicraft industries in the eighteenth century—a phenomenon consciously associated with female cloistering—encourage farm families to bind their daughters' feet? We have no evidence to prove this. We know that women working outside the home performed all kinds of heavy labor. For instance, the brutal task of hauling mud up from river bottoms and depositing it by the basketful on the waiting rice fields as fertilizer was performed by men with the help of their wives and daughters. According to a mid-nineteenth century Western traveler who observed a couple beside a canal in Huzhou, "the women in China do not scruple to engage in any, even the most dirty, occupation, if it have but a reference to the multiplying of the means of subsistence."[81]

Many women performed heavy labor even with bound feet. Robert Fortune, traveling through the rice fields near Suzhou and Jiading between 1843 and 1845, observed:

> Many females are employed in driving the water-wheels, generally three or four to each wheel: these ladies have large feet, or rather their feet are of the natural size; indeed, if they were cramped in the usual way it would be impossible for them to work on the water-wheel. Small feet, however, are general amongst the lower classes who work in the fields, for of the hundreds whom I observed hoeing the cotton, or engaged in other agricultural operations, but a small proportion had feet of the natural size.[82]

Bound feet did not, in other words, ensure that a woman would be spared heavy labor, much less that she would live in seclusion.[83]

So it cannot be proved that the expansion of women's home handicrafts accompanied the spread of footbinding down the status hierarchy. What is certain, however, is that secluded women's work in the home signaled respectability. Hence farm families where women spun and wove instead of working in the fields would find footbinding a desirable practice, one that would raise the family's status without compromising the productivity of female family members. Since the spread of cotton cultivation went hand in hand with the development of home spinning and weaving,[84] we can plausibly assume that the desirability of footbinding and the spread of women's home handicrafts in peasant households were systematically related.

MOTHERHOOD AND WORK

The connection between a hard-working mother and a successful son, in myth at least, begins with Mencius. Specific debts to laboring mothers were widely celebrated in Qing poetry and imperial government policy. The chaste widows (*jie fu*) honored by imperial commendations were commonly young women who not only refused to remarry, but also dedicated their labor—in the prime of their youth—to their in-laws and to the rearing of a successful son. Individual statesmen in turn honored the memory of dedicated, laboring mothers in poetry, prose, and paintings.

In a poignant verse inscribed on a painting titled "The Sound of the Loom and the Glow of the Lamp," the poet Huang Jingren recalled his earliest memories of his childhood friend, the essayist Hong Liangji:

You told me you were orphaned* while you were young
And so you had come with your family to live in your mother's
 old home,
A three-room house heaped with dust and spiderwebs
Where the sad and lonely mother taught her son his lessons.
When he read eagerly, her face showed her delight.
When he read lazily, she was sick at heart.[85]

Huang's poem invokes the image of Mencius's mother weaving to provide for her son's education. Other accounts of laboring mothers show them weaving and teaching at the same time. An entry in Yuan Mei's *Poetry Talks* notes: "Since ancient times, many literary men have acquired their virtuosity through a mother's instruction" (*cong gu wenren de gong yu mujiaozhe duo*). He cites the two most famous historical examples (Ouyang Xiu and Su Shi), mentions a well-known contemporary (Yin Huiyi), and then records a colophon by Qian Chenqun (1686–1774) on a painting that, like the painting of Hong Liangji and his mother, depicts Qian's mother spinning at night while teaching him the classics:

Hard at work by the latticed flame, the night lamp glowing bright,
From the child by her knee, the sound of reading echoes the sound
 of her wheel
While her hands are busy with the needle, her ears hear his recitations.
You know my kindly mother is my teacher too.[86]

These poems about the relationship between mothers' work and sons' success remind us of the fraught relationship between a mother's love and a mother's instruction: a "kindly mother" is a "teacher too." A son learned quickly that his mother worked for her family's future and that her labor was a sacrifice for his leisure. Other normative texts, such as the imperial commendations (*jing biao*) honoring faithful widows, likewise stress a woman's duty to work for the family by serving her in-laws as well as laboring for her sons' benefit. But did working women view their work the same way?

The answer to this question is not easy to find. Most working women were illiterate, and whereas elite women sometimes expressed in poetry pride or regret over their sons' achievements or failures, no woman's poem or memoir links her own work with her son's success. The large body of women's poetry —and men's too—celebrating the Double Seven Festival deeply romanticizes women's work, but never mentions sons, and rarely alludes even to marriage. Instead, Double Seven was the occasion to write about passionate lovers and

*That is, your father died.

lonely mates. Moreover, most Double Seven poems depict women in pensive repose, gazing at the moon and thinking of a lover or a spouse far away. The occasional flying shuttle does little to dispel the languorous mood of these poems, to which we now turn.

Double Seven

Rituals of the Double Seven Festival dramatize the identification between ordinary women's work and women's labor in the high culture of the elite. These rituals, performed on the seventh day of the seventh lunar month, marked the celestial unification of the star Vega (the Weaving Maid) with three stars of the constellation Aquila known as the Cowherd. Double Seven and its rituals—performed throughout the Lower Yangzi region where women writers were active in High Qing times—dramatized the basic division of labor in peasant society: men plough, women weave. Their meanings played on notions of work and rest, denial and desire, separation and reunion. The lore of Double Seven told of the Cowherd (Niulang) and the Weaving Maid (Zhinü) who were separated in the heavens by an angry deity because whenever they were together they lost themselves in lovemaking and neglected the work assigned to them. In the original story, the amorous pair were young lovers, but centuries of retelling reinvented them as a devoted husband and wife. Whatever their human relationship, this couple's tryst in the heavens on the one night alloted them each year marked the beginning of autumn (*li qiu*) in the seventh month, when they crossed a magpie bridge.

The ambiguous imagery of Double Seven rites stems from the liminal character of the seventh lunar month whose advent Double Seven marks. The seventh month is when humans must propitiate hungry, dangerous ghosts; it is also the start of the sewing season, when winter garments must be fashioned or mended before cold weather sets in.[87] Celebrations of Double Seven play on both these themes, promising eternal bliss and immortality and threatening eternal pain and death. These ambiguous meanings are explored further in Chapter 7. Here we shall focus on the practical and romantic aspects of Double Seven personified by the Weaving Maid, patron goddess of women's handwork and ruler of the fecund female world of seedy melons and fruits, sericulture, and the gathering and storing of precious things.[88]

A description of Double Seven in Ningbo (Yin) county, Zhejiang, says: "On the seventh day of the seventh month, women wash their hair in water made from soaking hibiscus leaves. On the evening of the same day, they spread out melons and fruits and 'test for skill' [*qi qiao*]. In the light of the moon they try to thread a needle, and if the thread goes through, they will be skillful [*de qiao*]."[89] A more elaborate version of the Ningbo myth explains that on the night of Double Seven, women arranged basins on the ground lined with hibiscus leaves, orange leaves, and leaves from other plants, including walnut and a purple-leaved plant called perilla. Next morning, when the leaves were soaked with dew—the Weaving Maid's tears—women ground the wet leaves into a fragrant paste used to wash their hair. Meanwhile, before the moon set, younger girls plucked red balsam flowers and mixed them with the alum used to purify rainwater for drinking. These too they ground into a paste, which they wrapped around their fingertips with a cloth at night. When the cloth was removed the next day, the nails first appeared yellow, but then as time passed they gradually grew red and beautiful. This was done not to all the fingers, but only to the fourth and fifth, so that when embroidering or plucking flowers, the hands would look especially lovely.[90] In nearby Dinghai county, women pounded juice from the leaves of a small chestnutlike tree, then left the liquid standing overnight so that the tears of the Weaving Maid would fall on it, using the aromatic water to wash their hair the next day. The most lively event of Double Seven was the "test for skill," or "quest for skill" (*qi qiao*). Spreading melon and fruit seeds as an offering for the Weaving Maid to "beg her for skill" (*qi qiao*), women and young girls threaded fine needles by the light of the slender moon (Fig. 29). The successful among them claimed to have "won skill" (*de qiao*).[91]

The meaning of the Double Seven Festival for Jiangnan women can be found in records like these and also in the thousands of poems women wrote for the occasion. Double Seven—with its literary tropes of the lonely Weaving Maid and the eager Cowherd, their eternal separation in the heavens and their single yearly tryst on the seventh night of the seventh lunar month, the earthly casting of needles to test for the embroidery skills that foretell a woman's marriageability—gave writers a vocabulary for writing about loss, loneliness, and desire that proved irresistible to generations of poets, especially women.[92] The following poems suggest the range of aesthetic and emotional expression the night of Double Seven inspired in talented women writers.

SEVENTH NIGHT

The autumn night obscures the misty shore.
The crane carriage waits by the Heavenly River.
The bridge complete, let us thank the magpies.
But rising delight brings an overwhelming sadness.
You girls who now can test for skill—
Don't dwell on the songs among the clouds,
Think instead about the nights that will follow the songs,
When your lonely shadow will lift the golden shuttle.[93]

Fig. 29. "Begging for skill" at Double Seven. Reprinted from Nakagawa [1799] 1983: 42–43.

SEVENTH NIGHT

On the green gleaming mossy steps the rain has spun silk,
Insects cry "*jiji*" announcing the approach of autumn.
We humans are the ones burdened by the passions and feelings
   of the sensual world;
How could heavenly creatures be moved by the sorrow of parting?
In my empty pavilion I roll up the blinds; the moon is like a fishhook.
On the flowery wall pure fragrance; the dark of the night is deep;
A new poem wants to sing forth.
But my husband's younger sister calls me upstairs to my needlework.[94]

A RECORD OF LIGHT REFRESHMENT TAKEN
IN THE MOON TOWER ON SEVENTH NIGHT

The tower is high, the shadows of the trees are deep green.
The bamboo leaves unroll as the heat of the day recedes.
The moon also envies the peace of this quiet night,
As a faint trace of movement reflects across jade-screened windows.[95]

SEVENTH NIGHT

Vast, boundless thin clouds send off the setting sun.
People say that on this night she will meet the Cowherd.

The first rays of moonlight glow, a reflection in the river;
The magpie carriage hastens anew, a jewel on the water.
Now that she has reached this happy state, does she yet feel resentment?
At once she will be told to leave again, her passions stirred even more.
How many humans are fated to pass long years apart!
Do not despise the star raft for being ephemeral.[96]

SEVENTH NIGHT

Heaven has sent down its instructions; thoughts of separation flood
over them.
They face each other, east to west—what can they be thinking?
She must regret that she is the Cowherd's lady,
Alone waiting every year for one river crossing.[97]

As these poets tell us, Seventh Night celebrated passion, and yet the poets linger over the pain of separation and disappointment as if in preparation for the privation that marriage would bring. A long year of labor could not be offset by a single night of bliss.

Women's Double Seven poems sometimes play ironically with the image of the Weaving Maid, thus:

The Weaving Maid wants to talk with the Cowherd about the year they
have spent apart.
Where will she find the time to send me skill?[98]

The poet may invoke the dark side of the festival, as here:

Humans have a worse separation in death,
The magpies flown, the bridge empty, and nothing else.[99]

Or she may play with two goddess images at once to resolve the tension between death and longing:

On this night we should beg for the techniques of immortality,
Clawing away some of Ma Gu's medicine to cure the Lady in the
Moon.[100] *

Death, the dark side lurking behind the levity of Double Seven rites, is part of the liminal seventh-month rites discussed in Chapter 7.

* The image of the claw is from the iconography of the immortal Ma Gu, who has not hands, but claws. The Lady in the Moon, Chang'e, stole the elixir of immortality from her husband and then escaped to the moon, where she remained forever separated from him.

Conclusion

Surveying the flourishing economy of mid-Qing Jiangnan, scholars trying to explain the pervasive commercialization of the countryside have stressed that China's decentralized production processes centered on household handicrafts. This decentralized economic organization, they argue, diffused risk and lowered the costs of entering competitive markets, which in turn accelerated the process of economic transformation and broadened access to its opportunities. What has not been sufficiently stressed is that women's work was at the core of this unique production system. The state, with its concern for stable revenues and self-sufficient households, recognized the central importance of women's work, and so did farm families. They acknowledged it in a number of ways: by declaring that married women ought to remain inside the home; by insisting that households produce to pay taxes as well as feed family members; by continually saving for weddings and funerals, on which the cycle of the family's reproduction depended. Silk, cotton, rice, and tea production in the Lower Yangzi region all assigned crucial roles to female labor, some of it (as in the case of feeding and rearing silkworms and reeling the silk thread) highly skilled, some of it (hauling manure, peddling waterwheels) exhausting but unskilled. In every case, the household relied on female family members to achieve its objectives.

Recent scholarship by Li Bozhong[101] and others tracing the rising productivity of the agricultural economy during the seventeenth and eighteenth centuries shows that productivity rose for many reasons, including increased input to irrigation and waterworks and rising supplies of labor thanks to immigration and population growth (enabling double cropping of rice, for example, and the growth of labor-intensive industries such as sericulture). No attempt has yet been made to quantify the share of female labor in this economic upswing. But without doubt, the increasingly efficient use of female labor in the household economy was crucial. As this chapter has demonstrated, women became more productive members of the rural workforce for many reasons: official programs, the quest for upward mobility, the drive to raise household income, the struggle to pay taxes. As employment for female workers in the household opened up, a daughter became valuable for her own labor and for the price she could bring in the labor or marriage market; wives became more important co-workers on whose skills and abilities the slim profit margins of the household depended.

Did women themselves benefit from their crucial role in the High Qing economy? It is possible, I have argued, that these circumstances reduced the incidence of female infanticide in poor families, so that more girls lived to adulthood. Even in families who could not afford to raise girls, potential workers may have been adopted out or sold rather than killed. At the more lucrative end of the scale, attractive young girls could be reared for outside employment in the entertainment districts or sold into brothels. There is no direct evidence to show how changing labor markets may have affected female life chances or childrearing practices or attitudes toward daughters and wives in peasant households. No officials remarked on it, and peasants kept no written records of this sort. Yet spinning and rearing silkworms were both described in proverbs as "money trees,"[102] pointing to female labor as a key to the viability of farm households in the present and to the mobility of its younger members in the future. Beyond these strictly economic considerations, women's seclusion in the home was a powerful symbol of respectability for peasant families. Finally, women's needlework provided the trope around which communities of women constructed rituals and poetry, reinventing the meaning of "womanly work" (*nü gong*) in their own terms. In all these ways, women's labor was the key to mid-Qing Jiangnan's economic transformation, and, we could argue, women's own interests were served as well.

Valorizing women's work in the household economy sounds good in a history of Chinese women. But it also raises important historical questions about the pace and direction of economic change. Many scholars have wondered about the stability—one even calls it a "trap"—[103] of the cotton industry in the Qing period. Why, in particular, did labor-saving innovations that were obviously compatible with traditional textile technology not emerge?[104] In one dramatic case, in fact—a water-powered loom invented in China in the fourteenth century—innovative technologies previously in use were abandoned or apparently forgotten by Qing times.[105] The extreme lack of interest of the Chinese government and the Chinese elite in promoting technological innovations in industrial production has been attributed to many factors. Mark Elvin has argued that population growth in late imperial times produced labor surpluses that discouraged the invention of labor-saving technologies and led to the abandonment of old technologies using inanimate sources of power.[106] More important, he points out that where production is centered in households, incentives to produce labor-saving machinery are reduced because households are flexible in their use of labor, absorbing underemployment in periods when demand is slack and increasing labor hours when demand returns. With the production of cotton cloth and yarn centered in the household where labor was cheap, wholesalers who owned dyeing and calendering shops—now removed from the actual production process—relied on contractors and brokers to supply them with cloth. The organization of production, Elvin concludes, combined with other disincentives such as the Confucian education system, which scorned technological expertise and applied knowledge, ensured that a technological breakthrough in the cotton industry would not occur.[107]

A similar argument about "commercialization without industrialization" in late imperial China appears in Philip C. C. Huang's study of economic change in the Lower Yangzi region after the fourteenth century. Comparing the peasant economies of the Yangzi delta and the North China plain, Huang adds an additional factor to the analysis when he observes that the "most important" feature of the delta's rural labor market was that "a substantial part of the productive labor force—especially women—remained outside of it." The primary factors restricting the market for women's labor, he suggests, were "cultural constraints against women venturing outside the home, plus the logistical difficulties of managing female labor that came with those constraints."[108] This crucial shortage of female labor for light industry, he ventures, was one reason for the slow pace of industrialization in early-twentieth-century China.

Returning to the High Qing era with these questions in mind, we can view in a new light the statecraft writings and normative campaigns valorizing women's labor in household industries. On the one hand, High Qing officials failed to prevent the rise of a class of skilled artisans in the towns, even if that was their goal. Shops where skilled weavers, dyers, and calenderers finished cotton cloth for wholesale markets were prominent in the Lower Yangzi region, as were brokers' account houses to manage the silk textile industry. As Francesca Bray points out, the prominence of these skilled artisans makes the High Qing call for the spread of women's home industry ring hollow.[109] But China's so-called failure to industrialize may dramatize the great success of this nostalgic, conservative move on the part of High Qing officials, which served government interests as well as their own as heads of joint families. The obligation of every Chinese bride to serve her husband's parents cohered nicely with the priorities of the Qing state to anchor male and female labor in the countryside. As a result, the senior couple in every Chinese farm family remained a staunch ally of Qing officials who promoted women's work in the home long after the growth of protoindustry and the development of a flourishing system of trade and craft guilds had altered the political economy of the late empire. Together, High Qing officials and heads of peasant households produced "cultural constraints" that reduced the number of women available to work in China's factories on the eve of industrialization.

If this was the result for the country, what did it mean for women? Bray proposes that Chinese women in Ming and Qing times lost the economic power that classical discourse had earlier given to women by dividing household labor between male farmers and female weavers. The phrase "men plow, women weave," she argues, was a mere homily in High Qing times, when skilled male weavers dominated the high-paying end of the weaving industry, leaving the cheaper, low-paying unskilled tasks to women. If more women were learning to weave, she suggests, that means simply that economic opportunities for women, as opposed to men, were not improving and perhaps were worsening in late imperial times.[110] Of course, rhetorical evidence alone cannot answer these important historical questions about women's economic roles. Yet the evidence forces us to recognize that High Qing rhetoric about women's work did have some measurable effect on the labor force and that the impact of this rhetoric—and of the family system and the values that supported it—must be acknowledged by historians trying to make sense of China's unique path to modern economic development.

7 *Piety*

THE DOUBLE SEVEN FESTIVAL described in Chapter 6 displays a small part of women's ritual lives in the High Qing era. A broader picture of women's ritual practice and female piety appears in women's poetry, in folklore, and in evidence from diverse government records of imperial tours and statecraft policy. This evidence enables us to examine women's religious practice in many arenas and to see how piety expanded the scope of women's spiritual authority as it developed through poetry. On a personal level, as we have seen, religious words, beliefs, images, and practices defined the female life course. But women's spirituality also had a seasonal rhythm, culminating each year in the community rites of the liminal seventh month. In many other ways, women's piety and spiritual devotions reached beyond the individual to the household and the community. Women's lay piety was honored in High Qing elite circles, where female erudition enhanced and dignified religious practice. In other words, although female religious experience was intensely personal, it was also highly visible. In the home, a woman might make a simple gesture such as refusing meat or retiring to pray. A young girl embroidering might choose a religious subject. A pupil learning to paint might try her hand at Guanyin.[1] Laywomen copied sutras by hand or paid a calligrapher to do so or invited family members to make copies for a special devotional project. Among the upper classes, erudite women composed poems on religious subjects. Many such poems were self-consciously "shown" (*shi*) to children or to the maidservants for whom they were written; others were carefully preserved for literary collections. Piety may have been personal, in other words, but it was by no means private or secret, even within the household.

Female spirituality was likewise visible outside the home when groups of women traveled to neighborhood shrines to attend funerals and to make offerings or set off into the mountains to visit Buddhist shrines and monasteries. Here women's piety became more transgressive and controversial, threatening to violate the familial roles and responsibilities that elite officials and scholars were comfortable with.

Women used the language, gestures, and signs of Buddhism to communicate the intimate meanings of piety to others. Their Buddhist vocabulary, learned from a monastic establishment subsidized by the High Qing imperial government, reveals the historical specificity of their religious experience. The eighteenth-century poet who dreams of Guanyin sees an icon conjured in eighteenth-century Jiangnan, the Nanhai Guanyin familiar to female devotees of this region, whose cult center was restored by Manchu imperial patronage in High Qing times. Official tracts attacking women's religious practice reveal historical links of another sort. Local officials in eighteenth-century Jiangnan were bent on eradicating the female religious rituals associated with pilgrimage and temple worship, and their writings enable us to view women's piety from a different perspective. In other words, women's religious practice, a personal experience, was both facilitated and attacked by state policy, once again placing women at the center of the High Qing era.

To examine women's religious practice, this chapter begins with the icons whose images filled women's devotions during the life course and then shows how they figured in the yearly rites of the seventh month and in the quest for long life and immortality. The second part of the chapter examines piety in the home and situates women's personal rituals in the larger context of community and state during the High Qing period.

Bodhisattvas as Protectors and Teachers

At each stage of the life course, women turned to particular deities and texts for guidance and comfort. The bodhisattva Guanyin was important at every stage, and her presence dominates women's rituals.

Children first became acquainted with Guanyin at the festivities surrounding her birthdays, which drew immense crowds. On the day before her most important birthday, the nineteenth day of the sixth lunar month, people gathered in raucous groups all night long. By morning, the entire road leading to her shrine would be lined with tiny huts, decorated with lanterns and colorful banners, where pilgrims could rest, wash their hands, sip tea, and recite sutras. Some groups of pilgrims included mothers and their children; others were flocks of young unmarried women, as in this account from early nineteenth-century Nanjing:

> All the young ladies who have a mind to marry come along, fasting and wearing plain clothes and chanting their sacred books in low tones. Like lotus blossoms they blend together, stopping their fragrant carriages briefly to admire the lakes and hills. A poem by Master Yuan Mei says: "Guanyin has no other happiness but receiving all these lovely ladies' bows." When you see this spectacle, you certainly believe it.[2]

Near the city of Yangzhou during the eighteenth century, all three of Guanyin's birthdays[3] were the occasion for massive pilgrimages up the hillsides, making for lively business in all the city's shops and restaurants. The day before the pilgrimage, each "incense organization" (*xiang hui*) prepared a sedan chair to carry the deity. Members fasted, abstained from polluting acts, and offered sacrifice. On the day itself, sandalwood and other fragrant wood was stored in a cloth sack on which was written "paying respects to the mountain and presenting incense" (*chao shan jin xiang*). Each group carried banners, umbrellas and parasols, lanterns, an identifying flag, and, in the lead, a giant torch to ward off demons: "Local people with flowing hair and bare feet, garbed in black, come carrying small wooden benches. On every bench, incense burns. Each time they take a step, they bow in prayer. Chanting the Song of Pilgrimage, their voices rise, at once mournful and joyful. They are the pilgrims (*xiang ke*)." Along the road, beggars pleaded for alms and water vendors offered basins where pilgrims could wash their hands.[4]

To the young unmarried girl, Guanyin appeared as a daughter who refused to marry yet remained filial to her parents. This miraculous resolution of moral conflict was part of Guanyin's legend, a version of which was allegedly recorded as early as the thirteenth century by the female scholar Guan Daosheng, herself much admired in High Qing times.[5] The legend dramatizes the filial devotion of the resolutely unmarried princess Miao Shan, who cuts out her eyes and removes her arms to save her dying father. When her father belatedly acknowledges her devotion, her missing eyes and limbs are replaced a thousandfold, producing the thousand-eyed, thousand-armed deity—who "hears all the sounds of the world"—familiar to devotees of the Guanyin cult in the eighteenth century.

A High Qing version of the Guanyin legend, emphasizing marriage resistance and the conflict between parental demands and young women's spiritual autonomy, appears in a "precious scripture" (*baojuan*) titled the *Xiangshan baojuan*, for which the earliest known extant edition is dated 1773.[6] This scripture too tells the story of Miao Shan, a young girl who refuses her father's orders to marry. Her defiance so enrages her father that he first commits her to a monastery and then tries to destroy her by burning the monastery down. Miao Shan is saved by a mountain spirit who carries her off to the Forest of Corpses. From there she is taken as a spirit by the bodhisattva Dizang Wang, who conducts her through the various levels of hell. She preaches a sermon to suffering beings and releases them, which causes Lord Yama to permit her to return to the world of the living lest she release all his captives.

In these accounts, legends of a Chinese princess from Miao Shan who was later deified are interwoven with stories of the bodhisattva Guanyin, originally a male deity. Glen Dudbridge points out that these Chinese Guanyin legends describe a profound rite of passage leading from earthly existence to divine transfiguration.[7] The stories appeal to women oppressed by married life, emphasizing the pollution of intercourse and childbirth and the purity of chaste women who resist parental pressure to marry. At the same time, they stress the repayment of the debt all children have to their parents from birth. Miao Shan, though defying her father's dearest wish, returns to save him from disease by replacing his withering, putrified limbs with her own healthy ones and giving him her eyes as medicine. When Miao Shan leads her father to spiritual salvation by revealing to him the true doctrine, we find a theme common to other myths about female goddesses in China: an encounter between the divine and human worlds.[8] In this encounter, a visit to hell by Miao Shan results in her transfiguration as the bodhisattva Guanyin,[9] and Miao Shan teaches all children how to perform the ultimate filial act: serving the ritual needs of their departed parents' souls.

In this ultimate reading of the story, Miao Shan first separates herself from her worldly role as a daughter by dying and entering a liminal state as she travels through the underworld. There she witnesses the sufferings of souls at various stages in their progress through the nine compartments of hell, and in compassion she performs acts of deliverance for each. These acts in turn transform her and prepare her to leave her liminal state and assume a new status in the world of the living as a manifest deity, no longer human.

In this way, apocryphal stories of Guanyin spoke to women at every stage in the life course. Guanyin as a young daughter, with her independent quest and her obsessive devotion to her spiritual beliefs, appealed to younger laywomen like Tao Shan, whose unique life circumstances gave her the leisure to study, write, pray, and meditate, despite her marital obligations.[10] The promise of transfiguration and immortality offered older widows new visions of life after the death of a spouse. Even the chaste fiancée who insisted on entering the household of her deceased future husband as a daughter-in-law, claiming Confucian virtues, sought comfort in Buddhist piety.

Stories in a collection of lay biographies provide examples of piety's comforts as well as its opportunities. A woman known only as Pure Daughter Xie, whose fiancé died when she was eighteen *sui*, enters the household of her late betrothed, carries out all the funeral rites, and then begins a life of abstinence, humbly performing the daily tasks of the household. Declining her mother-in-law's offers of financial support, she asks her instead to set aside land in trust. The accumulated income, she notes, could provide for the burial of her late husband and, when the time comes, her parents-in-law, and it would support the son of her late husband's younger brother, whom she treats as her own. Testifying to her piety, Pure Daughter Xie foretells her own death and requests that those around her burn incense and chant the name of the Buddha of the Western Paradise as she draws her last breath.[11] In a similar story, another devout widow takes advantage of her station in life to embrace a life of piety and philanthropy. As she enters middle age, the devotee turns the management of the household over to her son's wife, retreats to her own domicile, and prepares her own vegetarian meals. Meanwhile, she carefully sets aside income-producing property to support charitable causes.[12]

Buddhist beliefs and practical management supported one another, as women overwhelmed by their responsibilities used meditation and devotions to center their minds and escape from pressure. A telling Ming memoir from the late-seventeenth-century writings of Yuan Biao (1533–1606) and his brothers records with awe their mother's entrepreneurial skills, including her ability to wring savings out of the family's spartan budget and keep the patriline out of debt. When they asked her how she managed everything so ably, she told them that she kept her mind clear with Buddhist meditation.[13] During the busiest years of Yun Zhu's married life, as we saw, even she turned to quiet sitting and the slim *Surangama sutra* (*Leng yan jing*).[14]

Guanyin's complex iconography, vivid in women's minds, fills dreams, portraits, and embroidered designs. The poet Qian Hui once embroidered the bodhisattva's image using her own hair instead of silk thread, in a style "not inferior to the inkline style of the Song painter Li Gonglin."[15] At the age of 53, the artist Chen Shu painted a portrait of Guanyin emerging from the sea.[16] Zhang Youxiang, widowed young, tried to commit suicide but then "devoted the rest of her life" to rearing her son and embroidering images of the Buddha. In a poem of renunciation, she turns her back on her youthful marriage:

Not dying, my sincere heart has turned at last to stone;
Still living, the black hair at my temples has all become frost.[17]

Bi Yuan's younger sister Fen, from a family of accomplished women writers, took as her literary name The Female Scribe Who Embroiders the Buddha (Xiu Fo Nü Shi).[18]

Embroidering Guanyin was an act of spiritual devotion, to be sure. But it was also a creative work of art, a sign of sexual purity and fidelity, and a discipline of self-cultivation. In this Buddhist project we see the complex of meanings embodied in women's religious devotions. Confucian values, Buddhist piety, and individual talent and creativity all joined in the act of lifting a needle to embroider an icon.

Rites of the Seventh Month

The Guanyin legend promised that a young girl facing marriage might endure suffering and even death, but that she would eventually attain spiritual transfiguration and immortality. Stories of young girls' lives reveal that the legend did not exaggerate the fearsome prospect of marriage for many daughters. As a daughter considered her parents' plans for her marriage, she simultaneously confronted the possibility of her own death, for as a bride her life would often pass into the hands of persons unknown.

Women's rituals of the seventh lunar month focused on these womanly concerns about life and death, marriage, birth, and transcendence. The rituals made it possible to confront life and death as intelligible phenomena that could be imagined and controlled. We have already seen that the seventh month began with the Double Seven Festival celebrating women's work, skill, marriage, and fecundity. The history of that festival shows that it began as part of the rites called the Feeding of Hungry Ghosts, which in the eighteenth century took place at the midpoint of the seventh month.[19]

In the Lower Yangzi region, the hot humid summers brought noxious disease, especially malaria, that filled the seventh month with sickness and death. Double Seven marked a mere diversion in the ominous "ghost month" (*gui yue*), when women shivered as cool winds blew over land that was still hot and humid.[20] To protect themselves, for several days before and after the midpoint of the month (*qiyue ban*), groups of local residents invited Buddhist monks and Daoist priests to conduct sacrifices feeding and propitiating solitary souls and "unruly ghosts" (*ye gui*) who were released through the ghost gates of the underworld to roam among the living in search of food.

The mid-month ceremonies were part of a cycle of death rites performed throughout the southeast coast. Held when the moon was full, they were festivals of light. Lanterns, perhaps made of lotus leaves, held a candle to guide lost souls on their way. On All Souls Day, at the ceremony called Yu Lan Hui, groups of devotees at every Buddhist temple lit lanterns and recited sutras to lead the suffering souls in the underworld across the sea to the Pure Land.[21]

The Feeding of Hungry Ghosts during the seventh month provided especially for the "orphaned souls" (*gu hun*) of those who had no ancestral altar or of persons who had not been buried properly, whose ghosts were thought to wander abroad seeking revenge on the world of the living. Worshipers who fed them and helped them achieve a higher existence in the next life accumulated merit that could then be transferred to the accounts of other dead souls. Such worshipers appealed in particular to Guanyin as the patroness of the "structurally anomalous dead," women polluted by childbirth whose souls needed special help to endure suffering in purgatory.[22] In this manner, the seventh-month festivals displayed and assuaged anxieties surrounding the transition from life to death.

Echoing themes of Double Seven, funeral rites and mid-month rituals enabled people separated by death to communicate,[23] thanks to the mediation of the bodhisattva Guanyin and of another bodhisattva who figures in the Miao Shan legends, Dizang Wang (Ksitigarbha).[24] The *Lotus sutra*, a favorite of female devotees, promised the believer that Guanyin or Dizang Wang would intervene in her behalf when she faced death. As long as she meditated on the power of the bodhisattva, she would be delivered from "all the evil states of existence, hells, ghosts and animals."[25] The bodhisattvas' help was crucial at the liminal point when the souls of newly departed persons passed through the underworld. There they endured critical trials in the courts of hell, which culminated 49 days after death in rebirth in a new existence. Throughout those 49 days and on the anniversary of every death, as well as during the Feeding of Hungry Ghosts, mourners performed rituals calling on Guanyin and Dizang Wang. The rituals fed their relatives' stores of merit and helped protect them from suffering as they passed through purgatory. Dizang Wang acted in their behalf from his home in the underworld, where he challenged Lord Yama, the King of Hell, confounded the laws of karmic retribution, and saved the souls of the damned.[26]

Dizang Wang's birthday, on the last day of the seventh month, marked the moment when the ghost gate of the underworld finally closed once again. On this day children from every household placed rows of incense sticks in the ground ("lining up the incense"). One account of these "last-day" rites says that the presiding priest donned a five-pointed crown, symbol of the Vairocana Buddha. The priest chanted prayers and mudras while mixing water and rice, creating a cosmos in which he played the central role. At the climax of the ceremony, he uttered lines celebrating Guanyin's saving power, made with his fingers the mudra "entering the Guanyin mediation," and concentrated his mind on the bodhisattva herself. When he emerged from the meditation, he pronounced himself one with Guanyin. This signaled his readiness to perform the mudra "breaking open hell," which caused shafts of light to burst open the gates of hell. He then repeated the bodhisattva vow: "I vow not to attain buddhahood until hell is empty." Then he was ready to summon Dizang Wang and all the compassionate deities to meet all the orphaned souls. He pronounced absolution, distributed sacred food, and directed the souls toward rebirth in Paradise. He became, in other words, Guanyin, and he relived her experience.[27]

While the priest celebrated the closing rites of the month, laywomen recalled the story of Mulian and his quest to release his mother from the polluting consequences of childbearing. On Dizang Wang's birthday, every woman who had given birth ceremoniously removed a red skirt she had specially dyed for the occasion, once for each child she had borne. This disrobing would protect her from danger in future births.[28] Children who observed these rites, lit the lanterns, and watched operas and acrobatic shows learned about the boy Mulian's descent into the underworld to rescue his mother.[29] They came to understand that communication between the dead and the living might depend on a child, and that a child—especially a son—should act on his mother's behalf to save her from death or suffering. In funeral services, a child's agency was sometimes expressed in his ritual smashing or drinking of a bowl of symbolic menstrual blood, an act that purified his dead mother and released her from purgatory.[30] But children could invoke the bodhisattvas' aid in other ways; for example, in one lay biography a son prays to the White-Robed Guanyin by calling out her name 12,000 times. He entreats her to reduce his life span by twelve years (one *ji*, or cycle), one year for every 1,000 names, in exchange for prolonging his dying mother's life.[31]

Ceremonies of the liminal seventh month were more than rituals of life and death. For female celebrants, the ceremonies produced both filial children and protective deities who could purify and immortalize them. These collective rites, shared by parents with their children and engaging entire communities, contrast with older women's religious disciplines which tended to be solitary and inward-looking. They also differ from the homely household rites that set women's domestic rituals apart from men's, while at the same time integrating women's religious practice with that of their male kin.

Household Rites

Pollution, illness, and death were the everyday concerns of women in the household as well as the focal points of their spiritual and ritual lives. Within their apartments, they worshiped the deities who oversaw these homely concerns. The goddesses of the household were territorial deities who shared the domain of the Stove God, worshiped by men.[32]

The most important household deity for women was the Purple Goddess, or Privy Goddess, so named because the word for purple (*zi*) serves as a genteel homonym for latrine (*ce*). Her cult was the exclusive domain of women in the home; no temples honored her, and no men participated in her rites. Like He Xian Gu, she is said to have lived during the reign of the empress Wu (684–705) of the Tang dynasty. The Purple Goddess embodied multiple meanings for women. By one account she was the spirit of a concubine murdered in a privy by a jealous wife and later canonized by the empress Wu. Her history in this story is a record of sexual rivalry and domestic strife. Another origin myth names her the Third Daughter of the Privy (San Gu, or Keng San Guniang), after a female immortal who was canonized following her defeat in a mythic battle pitting the ancient Shang rulers against their enemies in the Zhou kingdom. The goddess called San Gu was associated with magical charms suggesting female fecundity and productivity: a golden bushel and golden dragon scissors. The term for privy that appears in one version of her name, *keng*, is the word for a red lacquer chamber pot, also used as a birthing pot, that was the centerpiece of every bride's dowry at marriage.

Whatever the origin myth of the Privy Goddess, her domain was the domestic space associated with pollution and human waste, from which men kept their distance. Like the Weaving Maid, the Privy Goddess granted favors to her supplicants, and like Double Seven rituals honoring the Weaving Maid, the rites for the Privy Goddess celebrated fecundity and plenty. In some local traditions she was guardian of sericulture and forecaster of the harvest. Her annual ceremony, conducted on the evening of the twenty-ninth day of the twelfth lunar month, called for young girls on the verge of puberty to offer her a nightsoil basket covered with decorations (earrings, flowers, hairpins). At the time of the offering, the girls spread pounded rice on an altar table set with candles and burning incense. In the rice they traced the outlines of women's sewing and cooking implements or decorative motifs such as flowers while asking the goddess leading questions about the bounty of the next year's harvest or about more personal matters, such as wishes for a husband. The basket moved in response to their questions, signaling replies and gaining weight as the questions continued until the girls could no longer lift it.

Rites honoring the Privy Goddess were linked to the rites of the men's world, which focused on the Stove God. On the eve of the Stove God's return from his weeklong trip reporting on the household's doings to the Supreme Ruler in heaven, women honored the Privy Goddess. Men alone reported to the Stove God at the annual New Year accounting, but in Jiangnan lore, the Stove God was genealogically related both to the Weaving Maid and to the Privy Goddess. According to a Suzhou legend, he was the father of the Weaving Maid, who was allegedly his seventh daughter.[33] In other Jiangnan legends (in Jiading, for instance), the Privy Goddess is said to be one of the Stove God's seven daughters. By filiation, then, the Privy Goddess joined women's domestic rituals to other rituals, honoring territorial gods, that were dominated by men.[34]

The visions, rituals, and spiritual exercises of individual women and of women together in the home reached beyond the practitioner to connect her with larger structures of spirituality, religious imagination, and monasticism. Within these structures, as women positioned themselves to face marriage, motherhood, illness, aging, and death, they relied on texts and teachers whose messages crossed the boundaries between the inner quarters and the outside world.

Teachers and Devotions

The inner quarters was a territorial site in which women worshiped the Privy Goddess, whose domain was the household. But women also left their homes to worship publicly at temples (see Fig. 4), and they traveled to sacred sites on pilgrimage. Moreover, in reading sacred texts they often sought the advice and instruction of teachers from outside the home. In other words, religious practice was a vehicle that moved women and their ideas across the household boundaries designed to sequester them. Women came into close contact with religious specialists both inside their homes and in temples and monasteries. Piety cut through the walls of the inner quarters and challenged Confucian norms that celebrated cloistering women.

The sutras favored by the most highly educated women were sufficiently difficult to require studying with a teacher. They belong to the Huayan tradition that originated during the Sui and Tang dynasties as a distinctly Chinese form of Buddhism. Within that tradition, one apocryphal text was a favorite of well-educated women in the mid-Qing era, including Yun Zhu. This text, originally written in Chinese and titled *Lengyan jing*, is better known by its spurious Sanskrit title, *Surangama sutra*.[35] The *Surangama sutra* is part of a body of Huayan texts expounding the *tathagatagarbha* (in Chinese, *rulaizang*), a state of tranquil awareness. The sutra teaches that all sentient beings originally possess an empty, tranquil, true mind. This mind, which exists through time without beginning, is intrinsically pure, effulgent, unobscured, and clear. It is described as a bright, ever-present awareness (*changzhi*) that abides forever and will never perish. It is sometimes called Buddha-nature; it is also termed *tathagatagarbha*, or "mind ground."[36] Huayan texts espouse the Chan (Zen) belief that a devotee can be "suddenly awakened" to this state of awareness, after which she may "gradually begin to eliminate the residual effects of [her] past conditioning."[37]

This difficult, intellectualized Huayan text contrasts with the popularized "precious scriptures" (*baojuan*) favored by devotees with little formal education. For scholarly, erudite women, the study of abstruse sutras offered intellectual as well as spiritual satisfaction. An analysis of the content of the *Surangama sutra*, known in High Qing times as a "message of ultimate liberation,"[38] will show why.

The sutra tells the story of the Buddha's disciple Ananda, who must overcome his obsession with sensual delights. The text begins by locating each of the six senses, by turns identifying the distorting sensations that are conveyed through the eye, ear, nose, and other tactile organs. It then tells the devotee how to pass beyond those sensations into the state of pure awareness.[39] The story in the sutra depicts the Buddha asking each of his disciples how they became enlightened to determine the most suitable form of enlightenment for Ananda. At length it is time for Avalokitesvara Bodhisattva (the male deity later known as Guanyin) to speak. He names "thirty-two transformation-bodies" or shapes in which he might appear in response to human needs and makes it clear that some of his forms are especially accessible to women:

> If there are women who are eager to study and learn and leave home to observe the precepts, I will appear as a bhiksuni to teach them the Dharma so that they reach their goals.
>
> If there are women who observe the five precepts, I will appear as a upasika to teach them the Dharma so that they reach their goals.
>
> If there are women who are keen to fulfil their home duties thereby setting a good example to other families and the whole country, I will appear as a queen, a princess or a noble lady to teach them the Dharma so that they reach their goals.
>
> If there are young women who are keen to avoid carnality in order to preserve their virginity, I will appear as a maiden to teach them the Dharma so that they reach their goals.

Asked specifically to explain his method of achieving perfection, Avalokitesvara Bodhisattva reports, "My method . . . consists in regulating the organ of hearing so as to quiet the mind for its entry into the stream of meditation leading to the state of Samadhi and attainment of Enlightenment."[40]

After listening to all the bodhisattvas, the Buddha asks Manjusri to choose the method most suitable to Ananda—in other words, the method easiest to achieve. Manjusri replies that Avalokitesvara's method of using hearing is the best: "The five other organs are not perfect [that is, they are contingent on interaction or contact with specific objects, or they are defined by finite movements—as speech, for instance, or smell or taste or bodily movement or mental discipline], but hearing really is pervasive [that is, it continues even in silence]." He advises Ananda to "inward turn your faculty of hearing to hear your own nature which alone achieves Supreme Bodhi."[41] Ananda finally sees that the Bodhisattva Avalokitesvara is the most enlightened of all, because the Bodhisattva's enlightenment came through his/her ears, which, alone of all the organs, receive sensory perception continually and without conscious effort. The text explains that this is why Avalokitesvara is called Guanyin, the bodhisattva who, constantly and without effort, heeds all the sounds of the world (*guan shi yin*).

Perhaps this story was compelling to elite women like Yun Zhu because they had to rely so much on hearing to make their way in the difficult family transitions they were forced to negotiate. Exhorted to be cautious in speech, deportment, and sexual expression, they would have needed to hone the skill of listening and rise, like the bodhisattva, above the emotional and sensory chaos around them.

The complex language of the *Surangama sutra* was intelligible only to the most erudite women, but this audience surely included some learned courtesans, for its main theme is the renunciation of the courtesan's passion. In the conclusion, the female protagonist, who works as a prostitute, uses the *Surangama* mantra to "extinguish the fire of lust completely."[42] Since we know courtesans mainly through the notebooks composed by their admirers, we rarely encounter descriptions of courtesans' devotions. However, the Ming record of Nanjing's courtesan district includes an account of a courtesan who retired from her work with the support of a patron who was a physician: "She fasted prolongedly before an embroidered Buddha and was extremely strict in holding to the precepts and commandments." To repay her patron's kindness, she reportedly "cut her tongue and wrote out in blood the Dharma-Resplendent Classic." When she died, she was buried on the grounds of a convent.[43]

Women who studied sutras, like the courtesan who recited the mantra, memorized them and copied them as acts of devotion, spiritual discipline, and gratitude. In their devotions some pious women recited the *Huayan sutra* twice or three times daily,[44] and we know that at least a few male family members took surprising pains to accommodate the spiritual lives of women dear to them. One married woman née Ling made obeisances to Guanyin six times daily, rising at the fifth watch to visit a Buddhist temple. Her husband prepared the broth on which she subsisted.[45]

Copying a sutra was a special act of devotion, sometimes performed at the request of a patron or kinswoman. In *Dream of the Red Chamber*, Grandmother Jia's eighty-first birthday is marked by a nine-day mass requiring a full year of preparation. During that year, Grandmother Jia asks all the women in her household who can write (including servants) to make 3,651 copies of the *Heart sutra* to accompany the 3,651 copies of the *Diamond sutra* that she has commissioned for the occasion. She supplies each person with a special roll of plain paper and asks that while copying, each woman light a Tibetan incense stick.[46] The poet Tao Shan, who by the age of fourteen *sui* had created her own collection of 100 poems, copied by hand both the *Diamond sutra* and the *Amidha sutra*.[47]

Copying was not simply a devotional exercise or an obligation. The act of copying itself inspired new insights and is perhaps best regarded as a particular way of studying a text. Chen Anzi, the mother of two successful officials who reared them alone as a widow, wrote this poem:

AFTER COPYING THE *DIAMOND SUTRA*

The substance of the *Diamond sutra* is without dust.
The piles of silk are fragrant without heat.
If one asks, "How does Nirvana look?"
One answers, "It is the heart-mind, without a place, without
extinction."[48]

The poem suggests how the full meaning of a difficult sutra became clear as a pious woman recited or copied it.

On a more mundane level, other texts offered practical guides to salvation that were immediately accessible. The widely reprinted morality book known as the *Tract of Taishang on Action and Response* (*Taishang ganying pian*) was one of a genre of "ledgers of merit and demerit" that provided checklists and guidelines for accumulating merit by doing good deeds and for calculating the demerits accrued through wrongdoing.[49] Another work in the same genre explicitly addressed women as a status group, along with other groups such as soldiers, physicians, merchants, and monks. This book, titled *Meritorious Deeds at No Cost* (*Bufeiqian gongde li*), was reprinted approvingly by Chen Hongmou in his compendium of didactic instruction books.[50]

Merit ledger books upheld the family values that were of special concern to the elite of the eighteenth century. For instance, a text by Chen Xigu written in 1680 stipulates that masters must arrange for the timely marriage of bondservants and that officials ought to teach women productive employments like weaving so that they would have no time for immoral pursuits.[51] But they hardly addressed the spiritual needs that women sought to fulfill in precious scriptures or sutras. The merit ledgers have more in common with didactic instruction books than with religious texts.[52]

Texts such as the merit ledgers could be read without coaching. But for assistance in understanding and applying the instructions in more difficult texts, like the *Surangama sutra*, we know that many women relied on teachers. These teachers included Buddhist priests and nuns as well as Daoist female adepts. Flouting the instructions in Confucian didactic handbooks, which warned against the chicanery of "dames" who transgressed the boundary between the corrupt world outside and the pristine domestic realm of women at home, respectable laywomen invited religious teachers into their homes.

Sutras and "precious scriptures" meant that women confined to the home had access to a rich religious life independent of pilgrimage or visits to temples. In some families, reading Buddhist scripture together was a form of "house learning" like Confucianism. A "literati Buddhist" and lay devotee from Changzhou, Peng Shaosheng, nightly retired after dinner to the inner apartments, where he instructed the women in his family in Buddhist teachings. Peng's two daughters, his only children, regularly recited portions of the *Lotus sutra* for him, after which he would drink a cup of Dragon Well tea prior to retiring. Peng built this tradition on a sound Confucian foundation: he was the youngest son of a learned woman, née Song, who had taught him the *Book of Odes*.[53]

Other teachers came from outside the home. Religious texts were distributed by itinerant female preachers who visited women in their homes, sometimes conducting readings or spiritual meetings. The male elite viewed such women as a source of disorder and danger. As the well-known local official Huang Liuhong complained:

> Female intermediaries, such as marriage brokers, procuresses, female quacks, midwives, sorceresses, or Buddhist or Taoist nuns,[54] often act as go-betweens for people indulging in sensual debauchery. Many innocent women from good families are enticed by these female ruffians to engage in licentious acts. The magistrate should also post notices to the effect that Buddhist and Taoist nuns should remain in their monasteries performing their religious services, and are not permitted to visit any household.[55]

Huang's fear that innocent women might be beguiled into leaving home and lured into a sexual encounter in a Buddhist temple is difficult to confirm with evidence. The evidence we do have shows women leaving home for religious purposes in decorous and proper fashion.

In the novel *Dream of the Red Chamber*, the women of the Jia family visit Daoist temples close to home, within the city walls or just outside the city gates, always in the company of chaperones and careful to preserve a modest bearing.[56] In the novel, the Daoist temple endowed by the Jia family provides facilities for the grand funeral masses that follow every death. These masses, celebrated simultaneously by Buddhist monks and Daoist priests, last 49 days. Rites in the temple outside the home complement small household ceremonies.[57] In the Ningguo mansion, paper offerings were burnt every night at seven during the 49 days of Qinshi's funeral.[58] On the day of the burial, "Qinshi's daughter, acting in the capacity of unmarried daughter of the deceased, smashed a rice bowl on the floor at the foot of [her mother's] coffin."[59]

With respect to religious matters, then, the boundaries of the Jia compound were continually crossed by Jia women going outside as well as by religious women coming in. This permeability existed despite the class barriers that, as the novel makes clear, divided most nuns from their patrons. Even the head prioress at the Water-Moon Priory, which the Jia family generously endowed with a substantial monthly stipend, is referred to by a servant's wife as a "bald-headed old mischief."[60] The novel depicts young nuns as sexually promiscuous girls who cannot be counted on to take their vows seriously. The nubile young religious named Sapientia, who comes often from the priory to play with the girls,[61] eventually moves into the Jia compound, where she falls in love with the hero's close friend. They finally succeed in having sex one night during the funeral observances for his sister.[62] Later in the novel, Sapientia absconds from the priory to search for her lover.[63] The narrator implies that nuns and lowly actresses come from the same background, as evidenced by the three young actresses engaged to perform for the family who leave their employ for a priory. Nuns, like actresses, are engaged (rented, so to speak) for special occasions. When the Jias construct a garden to welcome the daughter who has become an imperial concubine, they decide that they must have nuns to perform appropriate liturgies as well as actresses to put on plays, so they send out the wife of one of the stewards to acquire 24 nuns (12 Daoist and 12 Buddhist).[64]

Nevertheless, *Dream of the Red Chamber* includes one exceptional nun whom the family treats with respect: the erudite and devout Miaoyu, who is engaged to keep the hero Baoyu company while pursuing her religious devotions under the shelter of the Jia roof. Unlike Sapientia, Miaoyu is not from the priory. Instead, we are told, she was born into a highly educated official family from Suzhou. Her parents, judging her too sickly to marry off, encouraged her to enter a convent as a lay sister without shaving her hair. When her parents died while she was still young, leaving two aged nurses and a maid to care for their talented daughter, Miaoyu attempted to pursue her religious quest on her own. The Jias in conversation describe her as follows: "She's said to be well read and knows all the classics by heart. What's more, she is a very handsome young woman. She moved into this area with her teacher a year ago because of some relic of Kwanyin she had heard about and because there are some old Sanskrit texts here that she wanted to look at."[65]

A nun of Miaoyu's class cannot be purchased. She must be persuaded to live with the Jias. This she at first refuses to do, even after her teacher dies and she is temporarily waiting for "a call." She complains that "noble households are given to trampling on other people's feelings" and remarks that she is "not disposed to be trampled on."[66] So the Jias, recognizing that she must be "a proud young woman, coming from a family of officials," arrange to send her a formal written invitation, and she is brought to the mansion "in a style befitting a young gentlewoman of tender susceptibilities."[67] Yet even Miaoyu is portrayed in the novel as a young woman with suppressed sexual desires. We are led to believe that she secretly longs for a passionate relationship, starting with her evident attraction to Baoyu and continuing through trances when she has fantasies about men vying for her hand in marriage and kidnappers carrying her off and raping her. A dramatic abduction scene makes this her ironic fate.[68]

By contrast with the novel's frivolous treatment of young women in religious orders, the faith of the lay Buddhists in the Jia family is portrayed with great seriousness. The young intellectuals Baoyu, Daiyu, and Baochai are all devotees of Chan Buddhism. Significantly, Baoyu's grasp of its abstruse teachings is said to be inferior to the girls'.[69] The younger sister of the head of the Ningguo Jias, Xichun, even vows to enter a monastery herself, causing great consternation.[70] Unlike Miaoyu, Xichun is portrayed as a devotee truly committed to chastity. Dismayed by her marriage prospects, she resolves to escape from sexual relations at any cost, insisting to her family that "Sutra-copying is the one thing I can do with conviction."[71]

In a similarly serious vein, the collection of biographies of lay devotees compiled by Peng Shaosheng describes priests and monks entering women's domestic space to guide their spiritual practice.[72] A mother and her married daughter each take as a teacher a monk known as the Monk of the Ancient Pool (Gutan heshang),[73] and a son calls a monk to offer spiritual guidance to his ailing mother. This interaction between men and women in private and public spaces provoked special ire from government officials in the High Qing period, the subject to which we now turn.

Imperial Patronage and Official Opposition

The Qing state's view of female spirituality was mixed. On the one hand, the mid-Qing emperors—devout Buddhists themselves and the filial sons of pious mothers—were lavish patrons of Buddhist shrines. Imperial patronage of Buddhist shrines enhanced their attractiveness to lay devotees, who came by the thousands to visit the temples frequented by the empress dowager and her filial son. Imperial visits encouraged local officials and lay donors to invest in the restoration and maintenance of favorite pilgrimage sites. In addition, the southern tours of the Kangxi and Qianlong emperors stimulated household handicraft industries employing women who manufactured religious artifacts in the neighborhood of the shrines and along pilgrimage routes.

This lavish imperial patronage contrasts ironically with the outlook of local officials representing the throne in provincial and county politics. In High Qing times, leading local officials condemned women for worshiping at the very shrines emperors patronized. Their agitated memorials and pronouncements on the subject reveal their contradictory views of women who traveled abroad on pilgrimage: they were promiscuous and in need of control, and they were vulnerable and in need of protection. Either way, eighteenth-century provincial and county officials saw women on pilgrimage as one of the most troubling signs of disorder and declining moral standards. They dismissed women's "spring outings"—those languid picnics and sorties to view (significantly) the plum blossoms—as so many perverse opportunities for dalliance. But they reserved their most voluble complaints for the rites of pilgrimage ("burning incense and bowing before the Buddha") to which Jiangnan women were especially devoted.

Official documents criticizing women's religious practices conflated Buddhist piety, sexual libido, and social disorder, including criminal activity—echoing the ambivalent attitudes in *Dream of the Red Chamber*.[74] Local officials, on the lookout for the "marginal clergy" in the troublesome underclass of vagrants and single men,[75] accused monks of using their temples as a cover for illicit sex rackets. Racketeering monks, they charged, seduced devout and innocent women while giving opportunistic wayward wives a chance to indulge their passions. Here is one such allegation:

> The Zhiping Temple in Suzhou has 22 chambers. Like bottomless sacks in plentiful supply, they become havens for intimate encounters where women can indulge their licentious passions without restraint. In 1759 the governor Chen Hongmou devised a scheme for discovering the facts about these rooms. He made secret arrests, searching for and seizing four women together with

clothing, jewelry, and dowry objects beyond reckoning. He then sent officers to conduct a judicial investigation of all 22 chambers. They found illicit sexual activity in 14 of them and accused 16 monks of fornication, in addition to identifying 25 women as victims of rape. Chen then memorialized the throne, reporting that he had the offending monks in fetters and was remanding the case to the capital for sentencing by the Board of Punishment. He requested that the prisoners be beaten to death. In reply he received an imperial order that the monks be sent to Heilongjiang and given to the soldiers there as slaves.[76]

The experienced magistrate Huang Liuhong, in his standard guidebook for local officials, finds four separate occasions to remind readers that women should be forbidden to visit temples and devotes a special section entirely to the subject.[77] Prohibiting women from visiting temples, in Huang's view, was a cornerstone of order in local government, together with policies prohibiting infanticide and preventing masters from beating their servants and slavegirls.[78] Visiting a temple could supply the pretext for adultery under the guise of offering incense, he writes.[79] Huang paints lurid pictures of the atmosphere at temples during pilgrimages when, he warns, "women go to temples or shrines in droves and, on the pretext of burning incense and worshiping idols, they actually participate in orgies on the premises."[80]

Huang's manifold concerns about women and temples pale beside the problems that worried the provincial governor and prominent advocate of women's education, Chen Hongmou:

> A woman's proper ritual place is to be sequestered in the inner apartments. When at rest, she should let the screen fall [in front of her]; when abroad, she must cover her face to distance herself from any suspicion or doubt and prevent herself from coming under observation.* But instead we find young women accustomed to wandering about, all made up, heads bare and faces exposed, and not a care in the world! Some climb into their palanquins and go traveling in the mountains. Some ascend to pavilions and gaze at the evening moon. In the most extreme cases, we find them traveling around visiting temples and monasteries, burning incense and forming societies for prayer and meditation, kneeling to listen, chanting the sutras. In the temple courtyards and in the precincts of the monasteries, they chat and laugh freely. The worst times are in the last ten days of the third lunar month, when they form sisterhoods and spend the night in local temples; on the sixth day of the sixth month, when they believe that if they turn over the pages of the sutras ten times they will be transformed into men in a future life; and on the last

*The phrase *kuisi* used here, conventionally means "to keep a household under surveillance to rob it"; in other words, "to case."

> days of the seventh month, when they light lanterns and suspend them from their bodies in hopes of gaining good fortune.[81] They may spend the night in a mountain temple to fulfill a vow made to ensure the birth of a son. Or they may renounce the world and shut themselves up in a cloistered chamber, performing menial services on the first and fifteenth days of each lunar month. The monks and priests entertain them cordially; evil youths encircle the place. And their husbands and relatives think nothing of it! This is really a blight on the reputation of the local community!
>
> I herewith announce to all nunneries and monasteries, Daoist and Buddhist: if it becomes known that young women have entered their grounds, local officials will put the monks or priests there in a wooden cage in front of the temple as a warning; and they will take their menfolk into custody and punish them as an example.[82]

Chen's comment on Jiangnan customs, singling out pious women as a central problem in local culture, was probably based on observations during his tenure as a provincial official in Jiangsu, where he served first as judicial commissioner in 1740 and then (with one interruption) as governor from 1758 until 1762.[83]

His descriptions of the wide range of women's religious experience outside the home remind us of the pious acts women performed at every stage of the life course. The young formed sisterhoods, pledging mutual support as they offered incense. Young wives prayed for sons. Older women recited sutras. Religious experience could be intensely communal, as when crowds of all ages gathered at temples to celebrate Guanyin's three birthdays. And within the household, the pilgrim's staff and wooden fish by the door signaled a woman's religious conviction and quest for solitude.[84]

Official critics may have been correct about the vulnerability of female pilgrims. The worst threat they faced was from kidnappers and highwaymen, the least from rumormongers. These threats were hardly sufficient, however, to deter respectable women from going on pilgrimage. For protection they traveled in groups, and the wealthy took dozens of servants.[85] Charges that monks and nuns themselves posed a threat to women's security and that temples provided a haven for women's sexual experimentation with lecherous priests are impossible to confirm. We do know that the "orgies" involving women did not always involve men, let alone priests. Paroxysms of religious ecstasy were common among Guanyin devotees on pilgrimage who, at the peak of their devotions, made "flesh lanterns" of their fingers or other parts of the body.[86] Chen Hongmou was revolted by a scene, perhaps recounted from hearsay, in which female pilgrims attached burning lanterns to their breasts; he describes acts of self-mortification in which devotees demonstrate their freedom from bodily pain, as we see from one of the few eye-witness descriptions of pilgrimage that survive, written by the Ming scholar and loyalist Zhang Dai (1597–1684?). After a trip to a temple to observe the customary *sushan* ("overnight on the mountain") at the Guanyin shrines on Putuo Island, Zhang recorded this in his notes:

> When we arrived at the great hall, the smoke from incense had risen in a fog stretching for five *li*. A thousand men and women were seated close together like fish scales. From the throne of the Buddha down to the verandas of the hall, there was not even room to stand. On this particular night, a number of nuns were lighting fire to the top of their heads or their arms or their fingers, and even some of the respectable women from lay families were following their example. In the fierce heat of burning flesh, they recited their sutras in clear voices, believing that if they did not suffer or feel pain or wince, that would be a sign of a believing heart or of meritorious virtue.[87]

The concerns of officials like Chen Hongmou were overshadowed, however, by the patronage of the Kangxi and Qianlong emperors, who made the restoration of Buddhist shrines part of their record of imperial munificence. In the High Qing period, at precisely the moment when local officials were vehemently criticizing pilgrimage and temple worship by women in their jurisdiction, the emperors were actively supporting the very temples that were most attractive to female devotees. As local officials condemned women's pious excursions, emperors poured money into the restoration of pilgrimage sites that drew still larger crowds.

Of course, it is likely that the High Qing rulers never saw popular displays of religious ecstasy on the carefully scripted southern tours that brought them to Jiangnan. Their pet projects were concentrated in the Hangzhou area as part of imperial plans to revive West Lake's historic beauty. In the course of their southern tours these two rulers paid six visits each to the lake, beginning in 1684. They commissioned the construction of new pavilions and even, in 1780, a special palace to house copies of the imperial encyclopedia and the Siku collections.[88]

This extravagant imperial investment in the aesthetic and cultural life of the Lower Yangzi region came about partly because both emperors were exemplary filial sons and their mothers were intensely interested in the temples of the Hangzhou region. Perhaps, too, the High Qing rulers were self-consciously reviving a precedent set in the late Ming period. In 1586, on the eve of the Double Seven Festival, the mother of the Wanli emperor dreamed of nine lotuses blooming on Putuo. In her honor, her son donated a thousand taels to restore the shrines there. Gazetteers recording the history of the shrine mark this date in Wanli as the turning point in imperial patronage of the shrines.[89] When the mothers of the Kangxi and Qianlong emperors accompanied their sons on southern tours devoted to temple restoration, their delight was well publicized.[90] The Kangxi emperor traveled six times to the south, in 1684, 1689, 1699, 1703, 1705, and 1707.[91] On his third southern tour, when he spent a week in Hangzhou, the empress dowager went along.[92] The Qianlong emperor arranged the first of his southern tours to coincide with his mother's sixtieth birthday in 1751.[93] She later accompanied him on three other tours, in 1757, 1762, and 1765, and when she grew too old to make the journey, the emperor postponed his final tours until after her death.[94] Like the Kangxi emperor's mother and the Wanli emperor's before her, the Qianlong emperor's mother took a special interest in restoring "lesser temples fallen into ruin."[95] That is one reason why, in the words of one writer, imperial tours inspired "a lively activity in the field of restoration" as "all the imperial palaces, mountain monasteries, historical sites, and famous gardens visited by the emperor were refurbished and in some cases extended."[96]

Imperial investment in the Tian Zhu ("Indian") shrines at Hangzhou began in the early Kangxi reign with the restoration of the Upper Temple in 1666. When the Kangxi emperor himself visited the shrine in 1699, he gave the abbot 500 taels to expand the halls of worship; on subsequent visits to the shrine, he gave additional money and in 1705 presented the temple with a prayerbook copied in his own hand.[97] The crowning achievement of the imperial patronage of Buddhist shrines in eighteenth-century Jiangnan was the restoration of the Putuo Island shrine complex. By the end of the eighteenth century, Putuo was well established as the Chinese Potalaka, the abode of Guanyin, by the vigorous patronage of emperors beginning with the Wanli reign.[98] Iconographically, Guanyin's representation during this period changed to incorporate elements that came to be associated with the Nanhai (South Seas) cult. In this icon, the subject of eighteenth-century women's dreams, Guanyin appears on the island of Putuo in the middle of the "South Seas." She is bathed in golden light. She wears a white robe and holds a willow branch and a vase of sweet dew—just as she appears in the poem by Li Dayi.[99] Pilgrims could reach Putuo Island, located off the shore of the Zhejiang coast, only by sailing three and one-half hours from the nearest coastal port at Zhenhai. Comments recorded by a Christian missionary who visited Putuo in 1845 indicate that at its peak in the High Qing era, the island may have been home to 1,200 monks.[100] The shrine lands were a tax-exempt sanctuary presided over by an abbot whose only responsibility to the central government was the remanding of penal cases to the Dinghai county magistrate.[101] Three hundred commoner laborers of various occupations made up the lay population; all were male, no women being permitted to reside in the sanctuary itself.[102] Only on pilgrimage, when hundreds and thousands of women gathered to burn incense, chant songs, and experience the orgiastic communal rites of worship before Guanyin and her attendants, did the population swell to numbers that entranced travelers like Zhang Dai and repelled officials like Chen Hongmou.[103]

Renovated temples and shrines in the Lower Yangzi region must have stimulated new businesses and revived old ones catering to temple visitors and pilgrims. Inns, restaurants, and vendors offered lodging, food, and water to pilgrims. Cottage industries in the region produced amulets, banners, pilgrim satchels, wooden fish, and other artifacts required by devotees, making nearby Shaoxing one of the empire's leading producers of the "spirit money" or "joss paper" burned in offerings to Guanyin. Women and children working at home folded bamboo paper into the shape of silver or gold nuggets, then pasted over them a thin layer of tinfoil.[104] By applying yellow paint or pigment to the finished ingots, they could increase the ingots' value as "gold" rather than "silver" currency. In this manner, we may surmise, imperial investment in pilgrimage sites contributed not only to women's spiritual lives, but to the value of women's labor as well.

Conclusion

Pious women's language, rituals, and beliefs were part of structures of meaning reaching from the imperial throne through local communities into the intimate relationships of household and family. Often, women's religious practices were the subject of critical official discourse, yet the temples they visited were endowed by government funds. Even so, women's religious lives seem remarkably free of state hegemony or official control. The politics of temple endowment and restoration was almost completely separate, socially and culturally, from the pious world of the female devotee, even though female devotion inspired it. Pilgrimage to Putuo Island, where no woman lived, was a focal event in the lives of many pious women. The peer groups who accompanied them in their devotions and the children who attended them as they passed through the life course were part of a devotional world that state funding encouraged and official proscription barely touched. Instead, this world existed apart from, and almost as an alternative to, the structures of family obligation to which most women were bound.

If female devotees and the imperial throne and its officials had a common ground, it was in the relationship between filial sons and their mothers and, to a lesser degree, between husbands and their wives. Even here, however, the reach of the state was limited, because the government manipulated and shaped family relationships mainly through Confucian learning. Buddhism and Daoism, as we have seen, repositioned Confucian family values for women, enriching the spiritual and emotional experience of motherhood, widowhood, and old age and even creating a tiny space where filial daughters could refuse marriage entirely.

As for the clear conflict between local officials seeking to eliminate Buddhist influence in their districts and the devout women whose spiritual ground they threatened, there can be no question which side prevailed. Pious women were not the target of officials' campaigns in any case; officials attacked the pervasive influence and religious authority of the Buddhist priesthood. The literacy and erudition of Buddhist priests, combined with the patronage they enjoyed under Manchu rule, doubtless made them doubly threatening to the Confucian scholar-elite in the Qing period.[105] Officials feared and despised the Buddhist priests, not the women who took them as spiritual guides and teachers. But officials who converted Buddhist monasteries into Confucian schools could not purge Guanyin's image from the female religious imagination. Their anger at Buddhist priests took aim at the wrong target. It was women's faith that empowered the priesthood, and women's faith continued to do so because it was impervious to official proscriptions.

The importance of women to the power of Buddhism in Chinese history is a challenge to contemporary historians, as it was to High Qing officials. Historians know well that Buddhism has been marginalized in studies of the history of Chinese thought and culture.[106] But we have long failed to see that this marginalization derives from our reliance on the perspectives and writings of the male Confucian scholar-elite. Studying Chinese women immediately illuminates the central importance of Buddhism in the community life and domestic regime of every mid-Qing householder.[107] Once again, gender as a category of analysis breaks down invisible barriers to scholarly inquiry, exposing those barriers to scrutiny when they would otherwise escape our attention.

8 *Conclusion*

GENDER RELATIONS THROUGH SPACE AND TIME

RETURNING NOW TO PROBLEMS IN historiography, let us review several questions that have arisen in the course of this book—questions about women's geographical and literary space and about women's place in the historical record.

Regional and Literary Space

There can be no doubt that Jiangnan was the heartland of women's literary production in Qing times. But why, in a region where elite women were generally educated, were they so much more visible in some localities than in others? As Map 2 (p. 6) and the data in the Appendix show, the core counties where 70 percent of Qing women writers flourished were surrounded by five microregions that appear like satellite zones, areas where women writers were important but not so highly visible. Why? Hu Shi was among the first to call attention to the regional concentration of educated women in premodern China. In an essay on women's place in history written in 1931, Hu noted that the regional concentration of women writers in Qing times seemed to reflect the distribution of "male authors and of historical personages" during the same period.[1] But this is not quite the case.

There are good reasons to expect that women writers would be concentrated in the core region centered on Changzhou and Hangzhou: namely, the exceptional correlation between investment in education for the civil service (for men) and the prominence of female poets (see the Appendix). But other reasons may account for the intraregional variation displayed in Map 2. For instance, Yangzhou and Nanjing—the great centers of late Ming courtesan culture—were eclipsed in Qing times by Suzhou. Moreover, since mid-Qing writers were less inclined to preserve the writings of courtesans than their Ming predecessors had been, the combination of these historical changes may have skewed the sample of surviving women's writing even further in favor of Suzhou and against Yangzhou and Nanjing. Tongcheng, another satellite region, was home to a school of Zhu Xi Confucianism that paid especially close attention to family rituals. The school's major spokesman, Fang Bao, was known for his conservative views on women.[2] Perhaps the conservatism of Tongcheng's leading lineage limited publishing opportunities for women who wanted to write. And in Xin'an, the native place of Jiangnan's great salt merchant families, the landscape was peppered with grand stone arches celebrating the death of female martyrs and the lives of long-suffering faithful widows. Such a region seems unlikely to nurture the showy female literary talent prized by High Qing connoisseurs.

In Shaoxing, the center of a prestigious literary culture, we would expect women writers to emerge in great numbers, especially given the strong correlation between men's intellectual attainments and women's learning in Qing times. Yet only a few of the most famous women writers of the Qing period hail from Shaoxing.[3] In fact, Shaoxing falls near the bottom of the list of leading homes to Qing women writers, producing female literati at rates far below those predicted by its famed tradition of classical learning and its dense population.[4] Zhang Xuecheng viewed the Shaoxing area as a culturally distinct region, which he referred to as the area "East of the Zhe" (Zhedong). In a much-debated essay, Zhang argued that Shaoxing's local culture differed sharply from its counterpart "West of the Zhe" (Zhexi) in tastes and traditions,[5] even suggesting that the two regions constituted two distinct local cultures.[6]

The region Zhang defined as "West of the Zhe" is precisely the area where women writers were most active. Contemporary descriptions of Shaoxing's local cultural style, some of which are reminiscent of Zhang Xuecheng's own comments, show that Zhedong culture was imagined as "pure," "simple," and "unadorned," by contrast with the other imagined community:[7] the "frivolous" and "overrefined" intellectual climate of regions west of the Zhe River, especially Hangzhou and Suzhou.[8] These imagined Zhedong values accord well with notions about women's roles that would limit their prominence as poets and support the views of scholars who, like Zhang himself, frowned on women's poetry writing.

By the same token, aesthetic or literary theories associated with particular local schools may further explain the unusual prominence of Zhexi women writers. Changzhou—one of the two most important centers of women's writing in Qing times—was the home of the Yanghu school of ancient-style prose (*guwen*) and the Changzhou school of lyric (*ci*) poetry. Both ancient-style prose and lyric poetry were considered specialties of writers from Changzhou throughout the eighteenth and nineteenth centuries.[9] Changzhou's special claim on elegant poetry may have provided an opening for educated women writers. Benjamin Elman's research has dramatized the crucial role of women's learning in the distinguished families of Changzhou. He shows how the Zhuang lineage, one of Changzhou's most eminent descent groups, sustained a long tradition of intermarriage with another Changzhou lineage, the Tang. Erudite Tang mothers schooled Zhuang heirs in the orthodox teachings of Zhu Xi, ensuring their continued scholarly success.[10] Women in Changzhou's elite scholarly circles were expected to be well educated, both for socializing with peers and for rearing children.[11] Well-educated Changzhou women moved back and forth between natal and marital families in their role as mothers, sometimes bringing a son back to his maternal grandfather for tutoring.[12] But here's the crucial point: Changzhou's male scholars favored prose writing, dismissing poetry as "ornamentation."[13] Men's disdain of the art left well-educated Changzhou women free to pursue poetry as their own metier. They were not only expected to write poetry; they excelled as poets.[14] In other words, Changzhou's local culture—its scholarly high culture—nurtured and promoted women's erudition in the High Qing period.

It is easy for us to see how the glittering poets of the Zhexi region made a public reputation for themselves. For one thing, they took pride in their literary names. The four nieces of Zhang Huiyan, for example, each sported at least one elaborate literary name along with a generation name bestowed by doting parents (their mother was also a poet),[15] and each left a collection of works, including calligraphy, that was carefully preserved and published—with prefaces and memoirs—by their father and their younger brother.[16] Yuan Mei's accounts of the brilliant women and girls he knew in Hangzhou perhaps drew unwanted attention to the women who belonged to his so-called female entourage, because his intimate anecdotes invited vicious attacks on the personal moral character and literary talent of both Yuan and the women in his circle, attacks led by that guardian of Zhedong moral standards, Zhang Xuecheng. All the same, there can be no doubt of the high visibility of Zhexi women writers.

In that sense, these women writers had a role in public life. But they were not so different from other women in that regard. Even the woman who remained nameless was eulogized publicly in High Qing times, and the most intimate details of her family life might be revealed. She saved the family from bankruptcy through her skillful, secretive maneuverings with the household accounts. She preserved family rituals at a time when no one else knew or cared enough to carry them on. She sold her dowry jewelry to purchase delicacies for an ailing mother-in-law or to buy rare books for her studious spouse. She treasured the children of concubines as her own. Her husband's career was saved by her strategic advice, delivered in the nick of time. She comforted disappointed nephews and cousins as they coped with examination failures, bore patiently the profligacy of a derelict husband, and saw her own sons on the road to official careers, without—or even in spite of—their father.

Women philosophized about their influence in the public sphere during the eighteenth century, achieving a sophisticated understanding of the relationship between their domestic roles and the social order beyond the inner apartments. This understanding is summed up in the words of a highly educated woman we have met before, Jiang Lan. In her biography, Zhang Xuecheng quotes with admiration one of her famous remarks:

> In those days the ladies from the great families, like the Lius, the Wus, the Jis, and the Wangs, all moved in the same circle and would visit back and forth, exchanging poems and matching rhymes. They had quite a reputation. Among them, Lan stood apart in her goodness and purity. When her female companions complained, for example, that they resented being shut up in the women's apartments where they knew nothing of government policy making, she would reply at once: "In fact, women are by no means absent from court policy making [a sarcastic reference to the influence of court ladies]. But when we [i.e., we *guixiu*] refer to 'the women's quarters,' we are talking about the place where filial respect and collegial relations begin, extending outward through those who rule. Since that is the case, what place would you say that women do *not* govern?"[17]

Jiang Lan did not reach this understanding by accident. She was a product of her time, influenced by the classical revival begun in the late seventeenth century. She had studied the *Odes*, where the goodwife who keeps her wayward husband on his true course lives side by side with the impassioned poet who pours her feelings into verse. She knew the story of Ban Zhao, the woman historian who wrote part of the official history of the Han dynasty while composing texts on women's moral conduct. Jiang Lan understood her place to be at the center of political discourse and at the heart of aesthetic expression. Moreover, she understood that her power derived precisely from her cloistered position in the home. This sense of empowerment came from Jiang Lan's unique historical consciousness, which was itself a product of the eighteenth-century classical revival.

Women in China's Historical Record

In the High Qing era, women began to write their own history, inspired by the histories of women created by men in the classical age. The Chinese historical record assigns women a clear and distinctive place of their own. Gerda Lerner has argued that women in Western Europe and North America had constantly to reinvent their own history because no systematic record of women's past achievements was preserved and taught to them.[18] But nothing of the sort could ever be said of China.[19] The record of Chinese women's history starts with Liu Xiang and continues through the great historians of every dynasty, who compiled women's biographies as part of the standard record of every ruling house. In this way, Chinese historians created a female sphere of historical memory. Liu Xiang's *Biographies of Exemplary Women* (*Lienü zhuan*), compiled in the Han dynasty, was the template for later dynastic biographies of women. Unlike biographies of men, which were classified under such headings as "officials," "scholars," "paragons of virtue," "healers," "monks and priests," and so forth, female life histories were classified by attributes or moral qualities, illustrating timeless paradigms of womanly behavior.

The paradigms for histories of women were all didactic. The original *Biographies of Exemplary Women* included one chapter of negative examples among its seven models of womanhood, but its successors featured only admirable female subjects. Exemplary women's lives chronicled such virtues as filial duty, intelligent judgment, tender nurturance, strict honor, wise instruction, and cultivated talent. All but one of these exemplary qualities required that a woman display her virtue in the context of the joint family. Thus filial responsibility referred to a daughter-in-law's devotion to her husband's parents. Intelligent judgment was the quintessential quality of the devoted wife. Tender nurturance characterized the loving mother's relationship with her sons. Strict honor ensured the sexual purity of all fecund females, protecting the legitimacy of male descent lines. Wise instruction in the women's quarters enabled young boys to get an early start in their studies for the examinations.

But one category stands out from the rest of these familial virtues in the historical record on women: talent. Whereas other women's virtues were displayed in relation to kinsmen or kinswomen, the womanly attribute "talent" named an aesthetic sensibility that was individualized. For that reason, a talented woman in the historical record helps us see the strains and contradictions underlying the position of learned women in High Qing times. Perhaps for the same reason, few official histories of women bother with the category at all.

In High Qing times, as we have seen, Jiangnan families incorporated talented women into their midst with relative ease. Such women were a necessary part of the symbolic capital of elite families, and their presence enhanced the stature of the family. Before and after marriage, in fact, talented women formed part of a genealogy of learning ("family learning," or *jia xue*) that visibly displayed the erudition of their parents and invoked the honor of their ancestors. But this very quality of the talented woman gave her a divided allegiance, strengthening her ties to her natal family while enhancing her value to her marital one. Parents invested heavily in the education of their daughters, a material sign of their commitment and concern. An educated daughter, through her writing, became a source of intense personal delight to parents and siblings alike, as memoirs attest. This made planning for marriage and a daughter's departure after marriage matters of enormous stress for her entire family. At the same time, a daughter's ability to write enabled her to maintain intimate and continuous communication with her parents and siblings, no matter how far away she moved and regardless of the outcome of her marriage. Talented daughters therefore remained subjects of deep sentimental attachment after marriage, when their letters and poems kept them in touch with the family members they had left behind. Not surprisingly, anguish over an ill-fated marriage was one of the most painful emotions known to eighteenth-century writers, both to parents who believed they had chosen wrongly in their daughter's behalf and to young brides who struggled to swallow their misery. This anguish was heightened by the expressive talent of educated daughters who wrote.

Beyond sustaining close bonds with natal kin, the education required to produce female talent strained womanly Confucian obligations in other ways. Education gave women a voice with enviable aesthetic autonomy in late imperial society. Free of the compulsion to study for examinations, the woman writer in High Qing China (who, incidentally, sometimes had a room of her own—see the illustration of Yun Zhu's studio in Fig. 14) used her erudition to develop her own subjective reading of her place in family and society as well as her views on life and art. As a talented woman, she both claimed her own identity and stood for a tradition of family learning.

Female talent was only one of the contradictory virtues displayed in the history of women told through biography. Other tropes of female virtue, accessible to women as readers and writers, included the legendary woman warrior Hua Mulan, who carried the exemplary qualities of the Confucian heroine to a glorious extreme.* Full of stubborn conviction, ready to sacrifice herself in the name of family honor, undaunted by suffering and death, the woman warrior's virtues echoed those of the chaste widow. But her moral and ethical autonomy touched a central theme of the most powerful female biographies, even those of women who martyred themselves. These powerful female life histories, told in a vivid classical style replete with direct quotations and larded with dramatic expletives, caught the imagination of young female readers. We know that many unhappy young women were attracted to images of female martyrdom in the histories, perhaps drawing on those images for the strength to take their own lives. Other women imagined different heroines and fancied themselves riding off to war in battle dress. Still others identified with the aesthetic sensibilities of female writers, painters, and calligraphers and copied their work. Literary critics are now exploring forms of High Qing drama, fiction, and lyric poetry set to musical tunes (*ci*) that show women acting in men's roles, sometimes deliberately provoking a confusion of gender for comic or satiric purposes. The dreams of Wang Yun and the extraordinary ballad (*tanci*) composed by Chen Duansheng show that women imagined themselves in their writings not only as woman warriors, but as male scholars—taking the examinations, winning high office, and issuing government decrees.[20] In all these ways, women's awareness of their history sharpened their sense of exclusion from the practical management of government affairs and political power. At the same time, the historical record gave them models for imagining and claiming other kinds of power, especially power as writers. This is doubtless why, as Louise Edwards has pointed out, the woman warrior in Chinese literature does not represent a desire for male privilege or a longing to escape female powerlessness. Instead, she inspires female readers to serve a "high purpose," especially in response to a parent's call or a dire social emergency.[21] Moreover, like Ban Zhao and other exemplary women who cross over and take on men's roles, she does so only because a unique historical circumstance has singled her out.[22] She does not foreshadow a revolution in gender roles.

*The story of Hua Mulan appears first in a poem written in the sixth century. The poem tells the story of a young girl who, as the eldest child whose brothers are "not grown men," leaves her loom to take her father's place in the army. After fighting for twelve years disguised as a man, she refuses the honors offered by the emperor for her distinction in battle, requesting only that she be permitted to return home to her parents. The poem is translated in Waley 1961: 99–101.

Books offering these complex but inspiring female role models, abundant in the High Qing period, included reprints of Ming editions of *Biography of Exemplary Women* (*Lienü zhuan*) with illustrations. One popular version, dated 1779, appeared in an edition of *Never-Enough-Knowledge Studio Collectaneum* (*Zhi buzu zhai cong shu*), the complete library for families trying to build respectable collections from scratch.[23] Another kind of women's history is the illustrated "one hundred beauties" genre—a series of books filled with hagiographic woodblock prints of famous women and their attributes. The drawings make their subjects look more like goddesses than paragons of virtue. One High Qing edition appears in Yan Xiyuan's *Combined Edition of the Illustrated Register of One Hundred Beauties with New Verses* (*Huapu baimeitu bing xinyong hebian*), with prefaces (including one by Yuan Mei) dated 1787, 1790, 1792, and 1804. Portraits in this edition include the famous women poets and calligraphers Su Hui, Guan Daosheng, Xue Tao, and Zhu Shuzhen, each with her emblematic attribute: needle, brush, paper, and book. "Hundred beauties" books present historical personages from literature and the arts alongside women from myth and legend, such as the warrior Hua Mulan and the Weaving Maid, blurring the boundaries between earthly and transcendent women and their spiritual and intellectual gifts (Figs. 30 and 31). The focus of the life stories shifts from dramatic, titillating narrative to idealized portraits of individual talents and essential qualities.

These histories of women, from the various editions of the *Biographies of Exemplary Women* to the "hundred beauties" anthologies, were all compiled by men. In the case of the latter, an appreciative male audience looms especially large, or so we can gather from the laudatory prefaces and beauteous illustrations. Even so, the texts were accessible to women readers as a source for their own history and as an inspiration for their historical consciousness. Reading the records of women in times past gave female readers the power to imagine themselves in other roles and to interpolate their experiences with the dramatic moments in other women's lives.

Women Writing Women's History

In High Qing times, women moved beyond reading to writing their own history. One of the first histories of women by a woman was—once again—by Wanyan Yun Zhu. In her *Precious Record from the Maidens' Chambers* (*Langui baolu*), printed in 1831,[24] we can see how one woman's reading of women's history departs, in content and format, from classical and contemporary genres compiled by male writers. We are warned that we may be confronting a different genre when Yun Zhu explains in the preface to her collection that she

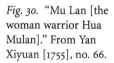

Fig. 30. "Mu Lan [the woman warrior Hua Mulan]." From Yan Xiyuan [1755], no. 66.

will tell tales not of beauties nor of ordinary moral exemplars, but of "women of high purpose" (*zhinü*). The title alludes to the cloistered women's quarters, echoing the sentiments of Yun Zhu's poetry anthology: the moral foundation of the realm lies in the authority of wives and mothers.

Her editorial principles set out the criteria that guided her work. First, she tells us, she has excluded women who already appear in Liu Xiang's collection and its successors. Second, she has arranged her chapters so that they begin with the "three routes" that guide women's actions, namely, filial service to parents, wise counsel for spouses, and tender guidance for children. These are followed, in order, by a chapter on heroic martyrdom illustrating women who steadfastly defended their sexual honor, and then—signifi-

蘇蕙

朱淑眞

織女

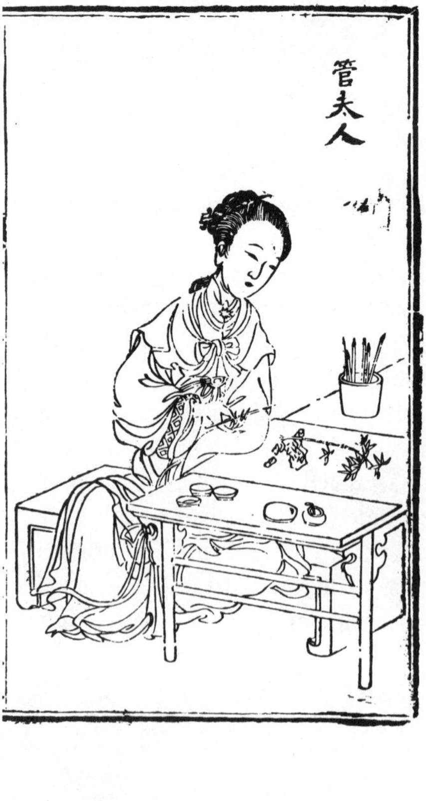
管夫人

cantly—by two chapters on talent, one on broad mastery of knowledge and the other on flowering talent. These two chapters display other dimensions of the "golden chambers" where women dwell. Third, she writes, within each chapter women are presented in chronological order, and for each dynasty from Han through Ming the stories of palace women precede those of commoners. (With characteristic discretion, she observes that for her own dynasty she has respectfully refrained from intruding into the august, confidential records of palace women, turning instead to biographies of Manchu and Han women drawn directly from published gazetteers for the eight Manchu banners as well as imperial and local gazetteers.) Finally, she explains that she has chosen only the most extraordinary examples, leaving commonplace stories for readers of the original sources to seek out on their own.[25]

If Yun Zhu self-consciously set her anthology apart from Liu Xiang's, let us see how her arrangement differs. Liu Xiang divided his biographies into seven sections, titled as follows: the correct deportment of mothers, virtue and wisdom, the benign and wise, the chaste and obedient, the chaste and righteous, those able in reasoning and understanding, and the pernicious and depraved.[26] Notice that Yun Zhu's categories differ in significant ways. There is nothing remarkable in her decision to drop the seventh category: like all of Liu Xiang's successors, she chose to omit pernicious and depraved women from her anthology. However, her choice of examples for the sequence of six chapters that make up the book is instructive. First, she allows the female life course to dictate the order of virtues. Thus, she begins with daughters, followed by wives and then mothers. If we focus on examples from the Qing period alone, we find that of nine examples of filial conduct, four are stories of unwed daughters' filiality toward their parents.[27] In the next chapter, on seven resourceful women of Qing times, four are wives, one is a concubine, and two are body servants who become the sole support of their owners' families. Chapter 3, on tender nurturance, contains six biographies of Qing mothers. Chapter 4, on martyrs, presents nothing unusual: these 30 full biographies of Qing women—five times the number of cases represented in other categories—reflect the inordinate interest in heroic martyrs that was characteristic of women's history in mid-Qing times. In a telling selection celebrating the virtue of the lower classes, Yun Zhu recounts the ironic tale of a serving woman who listened attentively whenever her mistress read and lectured on stories from Liu Xiang's *Biographies*. When her husband died, she

Fig. 31 (opposite). Other portraits of historical and mythical figures in the "One Hundred Beauties" genre: the poet Zhu Shuzhen reading by candlelight, the sojourner's wife Su Hui embroidering her palindrome, the calligrapher Guan Daosheng painting bamboo, the Weaving Maid at her loom. Reprinted from Yan Xiyuan [1755], nos. 73, 61, 64, 100.

committed suicide like the heroines in the stories, despite her mistress's objections.[28] Chapter 5, on practical knowledge, illustrates the qualities of the spouse-as-strategist. In the first of four tales, the wife of a Manchu official organizes the servants in her husband's yamen to carry stores of ammunition to government troops defending the city against overwhelming odds during a rebel attack; thanks to her, they hold out until reinforcements arrive.[29] The other three stories relate similar victories by courageous women literally under fire. Their clever stratagems and moral conviction pacify restive tribes and defeat villainous rebels.[30]

Notable in these tales are scattered accounts of women from minority areas. In one of the three last tales mentioned, the mother of a tribal chieftain is responsible for convincing her people to comply with the new Yongzheng regulations converting the autonomous chieftains into regular provincial officials. In Yun Zhu's recounting of Lady Lu's story, the matron "flies" from stockade to stockade proselytizing for the government's new policy and for the new title her son, the former chieftain, will bear. Awakened by her pleas, the tribesmen abandon their resistance and join together in support of imperial troops guarding the administrative centers in their Yunnan border region.[31] Yun Zhu's first chapter, on filiality, tells of the daughter of a tribal chieftain who gives up her precious silver jewelry, a talisman from tribal rites celebrating her first birthday, to provide her ailing mother-in-law with medicine.[32] These tales from the margins of the empire reiterate Yun Zhu's conviction that her flourishing age had brought the civilizing process to tribal peoples in the border regions. Because the same stories celebrate the women in chieftains' families, they also confirm the wisdom of High Qing policy aimed at bringing autonomous tribal administrations under the purview of the regular provincial bureaucracy.

Most interesting of all are Yun Zhu's stories of cultivated female talent, a category with no counterpart in Liu Xiang's biographies or in the biographical collections of Liu Xiang's various imitators. Many of these talented women were famous in Qing times, as we know from Zhang Xuecheng's writing. The chapter begins with the daughter of the Qin erudite Fu Sheng, whose specialty was the *Book of History* (*Shang shu*). The *Book of History* was destroyed in the Burning of the Books in 213 B.C.E., and the early Han court under the emperor Wen sought to restore a complete, correct text. By that time Fu Sheng was more than 90 years old and was no longer able to offer instruction himself, so he commanded his daughter to recite the text orally. The version transmitted and preserved thanks to her efforts was precisely the "modern text" version, in 28 chapters, treasured by eighteenth- and nineteenth-century scholars[33]—hence her special place in the consciousness of High Qing writers.

Other talented women honored by Yun Zhu include the most famous among them: Ban Zhao;[34] Xie Daoyun;[35] Lady Wei, the calligraphy instructor of Wang Xizhi;[36] Su Hui, who embroidered the famous palindrome on the handkerchief for her distant husband;[37] the mother of Wei Cheng, Lady Song, who preserved her father's house tradition of oral transmission of the *Book of Rites* and who made possible the recovery of that classic under the reign of the Former Qin dynasty;[38] numerous empresses and palace ladies who admonished rulers and instructed other women; three of the five Song sisters, the eldest of whom wrote a version of the *Analects* for women, which she used to instruct her younger siblings;[39] and mothers of famous Song dynasty statesmen and philosophers (the mother of Su Shi, the mother of Ouyang Xiu, the mother of the Cheng brothers, and so on).

The stories sound familiar themes: talented women carry on and transmit the family's tradition of learning; they are taught by fathers; they come from families where sons are absent, few, or disabled; they are child prodigies. For example, Yun Zhu concludes her biography of the Song sisters with the following remark: "Their father had an only son who was dull-witted and could not be taught. He remained a commoner to the end of his days."[40] Her tale of the nameless seven-*sui*-old daughter from Nanhai reproduces the following famous lines from the poem the child composed for her elder brother as he took his leave for the distant capital:

> Clouds gather over the receding road
> Just as leaves fly from the pavilion where we part.
> They grieve that humans are not wild geese;
> We do not go and return together.[41]

Yun Zhu's records of talented women focus on the Six Dynasties and the Tang (the source of the poem above). In fact, her records from this era contrast markedly with her account of the Song-Yuan period, when biographies of talented women were relatively rare. For the Song, in fact, Yun Zhu provides only four examples of talented women, echoing Patricia Ebrey's observation that literary talent was not a distinguishing class marker for women of that dynasty.[42]

Pursuing Yun Zhu's editorial strategies one step further by viewing her work as a whole, we can read the *Precious Record* for the womanly tropes that served as emblems of a particular dynasty, at least in Yun Zhu's mind (see Table 1). Whereas exemplary figures display the full range of womanly virtues in Han through Tang times, for example, during the Song they are heavily concentrated in familial roles, especially those of the nurturant mother. Ming women appear mainly as martyrs, with a good sprinkling of resourceful wives.

TABLE 1
Yun Zhu's Exemplary Women, from Her 'Precious Record'

Dynasty	Types of Exemplary Women: Filial	Wise	Nurturing	Chaste	Strategic	Talented	TOTAL
Qin	0	0	0	0	1	0	1
Han	7	7	6	7	2	6	35
Six Dynasties	10	15	7	11	30	13	86
Sui	3	1	3	1	1	2	11
Tang	15	13	10	10	8	11	67
Five Dynasties	1	4	0	3	1	1	10
Song	11	12	19	13	2	4	61
Liao/Jin	4	5	2	4	5	2	22
Yuan	11	8	3	6	1	1	30
Ming	15	27	4	53	10	3	112
Qing	9	7	6	30	4	5	61
TOTAL	86	99	60	138	65	48	496

SOURCE: Compiled from *LGBL*.

In fact, women martyrs fill Yun Zhu's records for both the Ming and the Qing periods, their large numbers overwhelming the accounts of all other exemplary women. In sum, if we take Yun Zhu at her word, we must conclude that the Six Dynasties era was the most interesting and lively period in the history of Chinese women. Here, ironically, she appears to share Zhang Xuecheng's assessment of that era: the time when the instructress and the catkin poet thrived together and when women took a lively and active part in the public lives of men.

Women's Poetry as Women's History

Rich as Yun Zhu's history of women is, it conveys only fragments of the grand picture of women in Qing times presented in her anthology of women's poetry, *Correct Beginnings*. In that anthology, which supplies much of the evidence for this book, carefully selected women's voices tell us the story of the age. Like texts by Zhang Xuecheng and Yuan Mei, it presents a simplified view of a complex world. But because it is told through women's voices, it defamiliarizes well-known scenes and always places women at the center.

Of special interest in Yun Zhu's organization and presentation of the poems in her anthology is her use of women's poetry to celebrate the "flourishing age" in which she lived. She marks the achievements of learned women as a hallmark of High Qing rule, an emblem of peace and prosperity, and a measure of the civilizing process that was extending the influence of Manchu imperial culture outward into the borderlands of the realm and downward into the ranks of commoners and servants.

Although Yun Zhu discreetly declined to include members of the imperial family in her anthology, she selected poems by a dozen Manchu women, from chaste widows to erudite painters to Buddhist devotees who declined marriage.[43] These poems may have come from an anthology of poetry by women in the Eight Banners compiled by the Manchu poetess Ruiyun under the title *Poetry Manuscripts from White Mountain* (*Baishan shi chao*).[44] White Mountain was a metonym for the Manchu homeland, the same area—in present-day Jilin province—from which Yun Zhu's marital family came. From White Mountain, Yun Zhu self-consciously ranged over the Chinese landscape as she chose the poems to round out her anthology. Women poets from Shunde in the Canton delta, from the minority regions where tribal chieftains ruled, from the Guangxi border with Vietnam, the Yunnan frontier, the Muslim communities of Hami in Gansu, and the Miao region of Hunan—all found a place in her work.[45] This landscape of women's poetry, as we have seen, provoked her amazement and delight. Of the poet from the Yunnan border, Yun Zhu exclaimed: "This place is very remote, separated from the barbarian regions by only a river. Yet to have this kind of excellent talent there—it is miraculous, otherworldly!"[46] Of the poet from Guangxi who preserved her chastity as a widow for 75 years while living amidst the "noxious vapors" of her "malaria-infested" homeland, Yun Zhu asked: "Without the sagely influence of our ruling dynasty, how could such a woman be found here?"[47] Yun Zhu's comments sometimes read as a panegyric for the great Qing military campaigns. She notes that the Muslim regions of the Gansu corridor had only been pacified under Kangxi's reign, remarking in wonder that eighteen days' journey beyond the passes one might now find a great woman poet—a true measure of the expansive "civilizing influence" (*wenjiao hua*) of the ruling dynasty.[48] Her preface to the work of a poet from the Hunan border adjacent to Miao territory observes that this region had been incorporated into the imperial educational and examination system barely twenty years before.[49] Yun Zhu's most explicit statement about the territorial and cultural scope of women's poetry and its meaning in the culture of High Qing times appears in her "Editorial Principles" ("Li yan"). Noting that less than half the poems in her anthology were drawn from the standard Qing collections of women's poetry, she explains how she broadened her horizons:

> As time went on, my own collection grew larger, including some writers from Yunnan, Guizhou, Sichuan, and Guangdong, extending to wives of former Mongol officials and a talented princess from Hami, female scholars from native chieftains' families, a fisherwoman from the seacoast. The appendix that makes up the concluding chapter even includes poems by four Korean

> women writers. All of this is more than sufficient evidence that there is no limit to the enlightening effects of our civilization and the achievements of the rulers of our august dynasty. Among the regions just mentioned, the tribal areas and Hami belong to the registered population; thus I have merged poems from those regions with the other entries in the various chapters. As for Korea, although that country has acknowledged our suzerainty since the year 1627 [the first year of the reign of the founding Manchu emperor], it still belongs properly to the tribute states. Therefore I have appended all the Korean poems in a supplementary chapter. The point here is that there are so many extraordinary women's poems, all from rare and valuable sources and all extremely difficult to trace and locate. For each one I have recorded, there must be ten thousand I have omitted.[50]

Yun Zhu may have been unusually self-conscious about the civilizing process in the borderlands for two reasons: her marital family's position in the Manchu elite and her own extensive travels in remote regions in the company of her son, Linqing. But Yun Zhu's individual proclivities cannot explain away the importance of the broad landscape of women's poetry in her collection. Clearly, the reading and writing audience of mid-Qing women poets crossed the boundaries of dialect, ethnicity, region, and empire in mid-Qing times, drawing women writers toward a deeper awareness of their place in the realm's elite and making them still more receptive to the classical ideals touted in imperial government policy and Han family practice.

In contrast to Yun Zhu's cosmopolitan view of women's writing is her attention to the domestic site of women's education. Like her contemporaries, she was keenly aware of the importance of "family learning" (*jia xue*) and of the central role women played in its transmission. A woman "transmitted the learning of her family" (*cheng qi jia xue*),[51] sometimes to her sons, sometimes to her daughters. The phrases *cheng mu jiao* and *cheng ci xun* ("receiving and transmitting mother's instruction") were used when speaking of daughters as well as sons.[52]

Close natal family bonds were expressed and affirmed in poetry. Girls exchanged poetry with their mothers, with elder and younger brothers, with sisters, and even with their brothers' wives, women from whom they would almost certainly be separated by marriage.[53] Happiest of all were sisters who married brothers from another descent line, for they could exchange poems as sisters-in-law within the same domicile.[54] Women's learning created bonds that marriage could not sever. Poems sent to loved ones voiced sentiments and affection across the distance imposed by patrilocal residence and the constant mobility of husbands, brothers, and fathers who held office. The songs and oral laments of brides in the Canton delta have been one of our few sources of insight into these enduring family bonds.[55] Poignant as they are, laments could be voiced only at certain ritual occasions. By contrast, we may imagine poetry as a constant personal resource available to learned women whenever they were moved to use it. Poems on silk or paper may not have strengthened affective bonds, but, unlike laments, they entered the arena of literati discourse where the sentiments they celebrated were dignified, appreciated, and accepted as normative by elite men and women alike.

The women anthologized in Yun Zhu's collection wrote for all kinds of audiences. Some poems were written in response to a text, like Qian Mengdian's "Written While Reading the Histories" ("Du shi ou cheng").[56] Some were written for "poet friends" (*shi you*).[57] Some were meditations on how to write. A poet might ask how she could make her poem represent her true feelings,[58] or she might reflect on her relationship to a reader: "Writing a poem is like making a connection, like a silkworm spinning thread . . ."[59] Poems carefully preserved and ultimately published, usually by kinsmen, became a form of symbolic capital that could be spent in the marriage market.[60] Parents of a prospective groom could bask in the talents of an in-marrying daughter-in-law, collecting the compliments of friends when they announced the match. "*Jia ou!*" they would shout—"a perfect match!" The felicitous union of a brilliant scholar and a learned woman might even capture in real life the romance of the scholar-beauty novella[61]—or so fond parents liked to think.

Published women writers were doubtless outnumbered by those whose work was lost or consciously destroyed by the writer herself.[62] Somehow, though, even poems about destruction survive, such as the poem written by the young woman who, on her deathbed, declared bitterly that she had burned all her writings because poetry is no business of women (*fei furen shi ye*).[63] Not all deathbed poetry was morbid or sad. In one poem written as the poet lay dying, she reflects: "Who's to say that being dead isn't like being a bookworm? After death, your body may stay inside your books!"[64] Some deathbed poems were ironic, such as the one where the poet admonishes her readers to "save this one, and forget the catkin verses and rosy rhymes."[65] Poems addressed to parents as apologies from a poet on the verge of suicide depict the conflicting moral obligations that, as one young poet described it, tore them apart in an unendurable conflict from which death offered release. The poem "Comforting My Mother" says:

> Great principles are as weighty as a thousand years.
> This floating life is as light as a grain of rice.
> Your daughter leaves her purity and chastity to live on after her,
> Your daughter is better off dead than alive.[66]

The author of this poem was fifteen *sui* when she starved herself to death after her fiancé died. Another poem, titled "Parting from My Parents," reads:

> It was hard to live alone after my husband died.
> Your daughter is returning to the Yellow Earth.
> Father and mother, you nurtured me with kindness.
> Please wait for the next life, when I can repay you.[67]

This poem, mentioned in Chapter 3, was found in a chest of the writer's clothing after she succeeded in starving herself to death when her efforts to kill herself by drinking lye failed.

Yun Zhu's admiration for women whose moral conviction drove them to suicide explains why she went out of her way to include such poems in her anthology. By contrast, because of her bias against love poems in general and courtesans' poetry in particular, *Correct Beginnings* contains no love poetry apart from a handful of poems on the Double Seven Festival.[68] No sensual or erotic poems of the sort that might have been composed by courtesans appear. Her poetry collection therefore presents us with an excessively moralistic image of the female poet in the mid-Qing era. The main counterpoint to this overbearing moralism sounds in the poignant voices of young women as they mourn, suffer, and die. Their voices, of course, are intended to reinforce the moral code that Yun Zhu found so compelling. In our ears, though, they ring dissonantly as a critique that gains its power from the language of moralism even while attacking moralism's painful costs.

There can be no question, in any case, of the confident moral authority that mature women writers brought to their poetry. The moral voice of elite women writers in High Qing times sounds very much like the moral voice of church women in reform movements in the West. Like Christian temperance, Confucian wifehood reached beyond the domestic sphere to check men's behavior in public. It is worth noting here, however, that women poets of the High Qing era spoke through poetry alone. No church institution conveyed their voices into the public sphere, and no organizations drew their words to the attention of readers. Instead, in Chinese civic culture of the High Qing era, brush and paper, ink and print block conveyed the words and thoughts of individual women to the broadest possible reading audience—an audience trained by classical example to read women's words with care. Were they heeded? Yes, as the *querelle des femmes* demonstrates. Did they make a difference? Indeed, as the biographies of famous men and their mothers, aunts, sisters, and female cousins attest. We cannot understand eighteenth-century life without them.

Placing Women in the High Qing Era

What difference does it make to study the High Qing era by placing women at the center? With respect to the history of the Chinese family, placing women at the center of analysis invites a new appreciation of economic and demographic changes in the eighteenth century. Though direct demographic evidence is lacking, we can surmise that the expanding market for female labor, coupled with official programs to support it, enhanced the life chances for baby girls and increased the supply of women in the marriage market during the eighteenth century. The need for labor raised the value of female offspring, and the value of daughters as both workers and brides reduced the likelihood of female infanticide. Town markets and city pleasure quarters created a lively demand for female laborers, including courtesans and prostitutes, while the rising affluence of absentee landlords collecting rents on commercial cropland and the prominence of a commercial elite in the towns created new markets for employing females as domestic workers and servants and new resources for the purchase of concubines. This circular process in which demand induced supply, within the working classes and among the leisured elite as well, also suggests that the High Qing demographic explosion induced a more balanced sex ratio, at least in the Lower Yangzi region where economic transformation peaked.

If this is true, then the patrilineal family system gained ground in High Qing times because of the changing position of women and its impact on the marriage market. This same phenomenon is reflected in the success of Han Chinese hegemony abroad. Historians have shown that China's Confucian civilizing project in Korea and Vietnam displaced existing family structures and supplanted them with a patrilineal joint family system like the Chinese system.[69] The triumphs of Confucian hegemony remind us that elite women writers in High Qing times were not only part of a patrilineal family system, but they were also ruled by an expansionist state whose ideology empowered them even as they benefited from it. Yun Zhu's satisfied comments on the spread of her culture's values into the borderlands make her one of the most eloquent voices of Chinese chauvinism. She thus stands at the center of High Qing military adventures and pacification campaigns as well as at the center of the domestic realm. As wife, mother, and writer, she is an emblem of the civilizing process: the spread of the Confucian joint family system and its rituals beyond China's borders and the triumph of patrilineal kinship systems throughout East Asia.

Finally, placing women at the center of the High Qing era illuminates a neglected phenomenon for which the historical evidence is clear and abundant: the *querelle des femmes* that marked the age. Debates about women grew out of contradictions associated with the demographic transition, especially the spread of economic opportunity and rising aspirations, which sharpened competition for resources and status. These contradictions sparked arguments about women's education reminiscent of those that surfaced for the first time in the sixteenth century and continued in the seventeenth.[70] However, the reappearance of these arguments in the eighteenth century signals a new stage of the debate. In the High Qing era, markets for labor, sex, and marriage all called attention to the value of women, a value heightened by the continual pull of hypergamy favoring the families of the rich and by the wealth that captured widows and courtesans and kept them from entering the marriage market. Even among wealthy families, rising affluence drove up dowry costs and the price of attractive concubines. Grooming a daughter for marriage and enhancing her prospects increasingly required a proper "education," not only in the niceties of food preparation and ancestor worship or even in the basics of good manners and proper comportment, but also in the classical texts that a brilliant daughter should master to enhance her family's reputation and that a wise mother must know to rear a learned son who would heap glory on his ancestors.

Other contradictions that marked the eighteenth-century debates appear in lawsuits naming kidnappers, rapists, and wife sellers. The High Qing traffic in women fed an obsession with female seclusion and sexual segregation that did not sit well with erudite women, who were eager to display their talent and cultivate their knowledge by publishing and communicating with male and female peers. At the same time, educated elite women—the *guixiu*—wished to distinguish themselves from courtesan entertainers as learned women trained in the classics for future roles as mothers. They moved to marginalize learned courtesans within literati culture and to valorize their own roles as cultivated married women—wives and mothers. This shift within the ranks of educated womanhood in the eighteenth century marks a break with late Ming society, where courtesans played a central role in the literary and moral/ethical discourse and even in the political life of the literati classes, as Dorothy Ko has shown.[71]

We have reason to believe that Qing government programs to extend elite Confucian values into the villages were operating at peak efficiency during the eighteenth century. Newly constituted families received public instruction in the norms of the elite, including respect for elders, the importance of ancestor worship, the proper sequestering of women to keep them chaste, and so forth.[72] These ideas, together with beliefs in retribution, revenge in the afterlife, and salvation through faith in the bodhisattva Guanyin, doubtless contributed to the spiritual turmoil experienced by the thousands of young women reared to preserve their chastity who were forced to confront the demands of the marriage market and the job market, whether as widows, kidnap victims, or impoverished wage earners. Contradiction, indeed, seems to lie at the heart of every gender issue in the eighteenth century. No wonder men could not decide what to say about women during the High Qing era. Women were decadent and "mobile," in need of discipline and proper education. Women were frivolous and self-indulgent. Women were hardworking and highly skilled with spindle, loom, and needle. Women were learned in traditions of moral conduct that harked back to the golden age of the Duke of Zhou. Women were beautiful, cultivated, refined, elegant, talented, passionate, self-sacrificing, omnicompetent. Women in their contradictory roles became emblems of regional pride, as editors of the region's gazetteers published biographies and long lists of "martyred women" (*lienü*) who killed themselves to preserve their chastity, as travelers wrote their nostalgic memoirs of courtesan culture in Nanjing and Suzhou, as provincial governors touted plans to promote sericulture or cotton weaving in other regions so that women there could learn to work like Jiangnan women, and as Yuan Mei wrote admiringly of the cultivated women writers of Zhexi and Zhang Xuecheng eulogized the upright moral wives of Zhedong.

The traffic in women, spanning the range of criminal activity and reaching into the sordid realm of slavery and sexual abuse, raises other questions about economy and demographic change in the eighteenth century. Was it good or bad if more women survived to adulthood when the future that awaited them was sex work or servitude? Should the thirteen-*sui*-old courtesan admired by Suzhou literati be pitied or celebrated? Were many of these women better off dead than alive? What about suicide and early death, the self-destructive burning of creative work, the despairing tone of much of the poetry, the miserable marriages? Facing these questions brings us closer to the agony confronting fathers and brothers, mothers and sisters, as they lived through this age of hope and despair. We cannot answer; neither could they.

If our new picture of the High Qing era complicates our understanding of gender relations in Chinese history and the place of women in it, we need to ask one further question: What about the century that followed it? Conventional histories of Chinese women date the rise of "women's movements" to the antifootbinding societies and the promotion of women's education during the late nineteenth century, harking back occasionally to the critiques of footbinding by Yuan Mei and Yu Zhengxie and to the satiric novel *Romance of the Mirrored Flowers* (*Jinghua yuan*) as early waves in a tide that began to sweep China only in the twentieth century.[73] But what happened in the nineteenth? Can we really presume a teleological continuum in which consciousness about women and their changing roles propels history on a universal course of women's liberation?

Dorothy Ko has shown that gender relations in late Ming and early Qing times assumed a particular quality unique to the urban print culture of that age. I argue that Manchu conquest and the transformed cultural environment that Manchu rule produced caused the social relation of the sexes to shift again in High Qing times. The classical revival redefined the position of the moral wife and marginalized the courtesan. Qing statesmen amplified this effect with their concern about women's work in the household economy. Moreover, the power of women's writing and of women's religious practice means that women themselves participated in the reconstruction of gender relations. We cannot understand these changes in men's terms alone.

But there is every reason to expect that the end of the High Qing era derailed the historical processes this book has described, altering once again the social relation of the sexes. Recession in the 1820's eroded the markets for women's labor that had grown steadily throughout most of the eighteenth century.[74] The Opium War created military and foreign markets for prostitution that permanently altered classical courtesan culture and shifted its commercial nodes to the treaty ports, where under Western eyes courtesans acquired a new place in history.[75] The impact on gender relations of the Taiping Rebellion alone deserves a major study, for the Taipings decimated the region that stood at the vanguard of women's learning in the High Qing period. Ono Kazuko has described in detail the horror of Jiangnan women forced by the Taipings to unbind their feet and, worse, go out into the fields to work.[76] One can imagine that in the backlash against the Taiping occupation, during what Mary Wright so aptly called "the last stand of Chinese conservatism,"[77] women and men of the upper classes made a renewed commitment to images of womanhood that stood for an unproblematized Han Chinese essence: bound feet, the sequestering of women, their essential roles as wives and mothers, and their vulnerability to invasion. We should not be surprised to learn that by the time the collapse of Confucian education shut classical libraries up in camphor, the era we have been exploring—a juncture in the social relation of the sexes in China that shaped the thinking of its most prestigious elite—had been erased from memory.

By placing women at the center of High Qing history, then, we challenge a century and a half of scholarship (1843–1993) in which both Chinese radicals and Western missionaries saw Chinese women as oppressed victims of a "traditional culture" who were liberated only by education and values imported from the West. This assumption has locked the study of Chinese women in a response-to-the-West paradigm that most scholars in the China field thought they had long since cast aside. Worse, it has forced an Orientalist view of gender relations on students of Chinese history for which Western scholarship is largely to blame.[78] The study of women in High Qing times reveals, in short, that we have not yet freed the study of Chinese history from the lingering grip of ethnocentric theories. The modern history of Chinese women is still the story of how they were liberated by Western-style education and Western-inspired reform movements during the late nineteenth and early twentieth centuries.

A second misreading of Chinese history can result if we omit the eighteenth century from our understanding of gender relations. This misreading can be found in the recent debates about the rise of a "civil society" sometime in China's past or future.[79] These debates too smack of Orientalism—that is, they deploy a problematic Western standard to measure the historical progress of Chinese civilization. "Civil society," an invention of Western liberal political philosophy, distinguishes a "public" sphere from the "private" sphere of family and household. As Western feminist scholars have already noted, the entire conception of civil society is flawed because it systematically excludes women.[80] This flaw in the paradigm of civil society is dramatically illustrated by studying gender relations in the High Qing era. Qing writers had no conception of a "civil society" separated from domestic space.[81] On the contrary, the history of gender relations in the High Qing era shows clearly that in Chinese culture at that time, women's homely place in elite public discourse was recognized and articulated by leading intellectuals, as when the philosopher Zhang Xuecheng acknowledged the dependence of public man on cloistered woman by noting that her words, too, could be "everyone's" (*gong*). Based on a long history of moral philosophy placing women and the family at the center of political order, Zhang's understanding of women's public voice erases the line dividing public and private that Western political philosophy has canonized. In short, the historical record of Chinese women—both their placement in it and their consciousness as recorded there—shows a pervasive awareness of the intimate relationship between family life and public politics.

These features of Chinese intellectual life are dramatized by placing women at the center of historical analysis. They challenge efforts to impose the civil-society paradigm on late imperial Chinese history. They call our attention to Western habits of thinking that impede our understanding of Chinese culture and history. And they force a critical reflection on the gender bias in our own categories of analysis.

Historical shifts in gender relations are not easy to document. Evidence shows clearly that the High Qing was an era when gender relations were debated and subjected to new scrutiny. These debates produced changes in consciousness that are difficult to measure empirically. Yet poetry shows us how important they were to that tiny group that made up the empire's elite. Most of the poetic evidence comes from the Lower Yangzi region, where historians have already carefully charted the manifold economic, social, political, and cultural transformations of the High Qing era. Why, then, in the midst of all this scholarly attention, have debates about gender relations been so often overlooked, especially when contemporaries found them so obvious? Kang-i Sun Chang, pondering a similar question in her classic essay on anthologies of women's writing, attributes the neglect of gender in Chinese literary studies to a combination of factors. The main problem, she suggests, is the limited availability of texts, itself a function of anthologizing practice in late imperial China. Compilers of "standard" anthologies of men's writing tended to marginalize women's contributions by including few and placing them at the end, along with works by monks. At the same time, the major collections of women's writing were anthologized separately precisely because they comprised such a vast corpus of work that the existing format of conventional collections could not accommodate them. Thus, she argues, much of the blame for the neglect of these rich sources lies with twentieth-century literary critics and historians of literature, who failed to include them in their work and failed to recognize their place in late imperial literature.[82]

Unfortunately, these are excuses for ignoring women that China historians cannot comfortably use. All the evidence cited in this book comes from published—not archival—Chinese sources, many of them primary sources that were assiduously compiled, expensively printed, and widely read during the High Qing era by men and by women. Patricia Ebrey's historical study of marriage in the Song period and Dorothy Ko's analysis of women's culture in the seventeenth century have already demonstrated that the Chinese historical record is rich in evidence about gender relations and that Chinese women have a history of their own. In other words, although we will always need more and better sources, we cannot ignore the new ways to read the rich sources we already have.

What do our sources and new ways of reading tell us? Did women indeed "have a High Qing era"? Of course the question itself is flawed. "Chinese women" were a diverse population, crosscut by differences in region, status, and ethnicity.[83] Whereas elite women writers came into their own in the High Qing era, working women—confined increasingly to home industries and tied more closely than ever to the household economy as wives and mothers—were probably losing ground to men as the economy expanded. By the same token, while economic opportunities for women may have shrunk, relative to those for men, in High Qing Jiangnan, they seem to have expanded in frontier regions where sericulture was being promoted for the first time. Finally, we should note that Wanyan Yun Zhu's prominence as a spokeswoman for Qing imperialism may be the result of her Manchu marital ties. Perhaps Han Chinese women writers were far less interested in celebrating the imperium's civilizing project.

Most scholars who have assessed the role of women in Qing times have generalized about women as a category. Because of the Qing court's obsession with female purity and chastity, many have concluded that Manchu rule was especially oppressive to women. Frederic Wakeman, for example, has argued that the status of women under Qing rule declined because the Manchus so vehemently rejected late Ming urban culture and the "new female audience" it spawned.[84] Wakeman joins a host of harsh critics of the late imperial government when he labels Manchu policies a kind of "Neo-Confucian puritanism" that "strengthened patriarchal authority" and "curbed the independence of individual members of the lineage, especially women."[85] Evidence of women in servile positions, in arranged marriages, in economic production, and in the entertainment industry certainly lends support to Wakeman's conclusion. But evidence from women's writing shows that even "Neo-Confucian puritanism" could provide the basis for empowerment and that Buddhist and Daoist spirituality offered an autonomous sphere where women could escape patriarchy entirely. It may indeed have been the intention of the Manchu government, and of the officials and male commoners who supported Qing policies, to impose puritanical constraints on women to strengthen patriarchal authority. But women as writers and workers were part of the process of social and cultural production that reshaped gender relations in High Qing times. Elite women embraced the spirit of the age in their own terms and used their talents to empower themselves, especially within the family.

Paul Ropp's more sanguine view of the High Qing era stresses the "emergent discourse" of satire and criticism during the late eighteenth and early nineteenth centuries that called into question old Confucian morals. His analysis of satiric fiction in High Qing times posits that the particular conditions of the eighteenth century fostered incisive new critiques of gender roles. These critiques, he argues, are a mark of China's "early modernity," part of the "embryo of an emerging modern Chinese culture" that anticipates the women's liberation movements of the twentieth century.[86]

Evidence in this book complicates Ropp's optimistic reading as well. We have little to show that elite women heeded the calls for social change found in satire and fiction or in scholarly criticism. They did not, I believe, at least in part because of the remarkable satisfaction and gratification that women as writers enjoyed in High Qing times. Writing gave women the means to preserve what they valued, to celebrate what they admired, and to lament what they lost. Emotionally, writing offered solace in a world where no other source of comfort was forthcoming; socially, publishing provided recognition and prestige and opened a vast network of friendship and intellectual companionship far beyond the inner apartments. In their role as writing subjects who demanded and deserved an education, High Qing women writers are harbingers of China's modernity. In this respect, they anticipate the articulate, educated, independent women who so eagerly embraced revolutionary movements in the early twentieth century.

What became of educated women during the late-Qing reforms? What happened to the power of mothers during China's modern "family revolution"? And why have Chinese women not stood at the forefront of the global struggle for gender equality in the twentieth century? Perhaps the answer lies in the enormous gulf separating educated women from other women in Chinese culture, past and present. As Dorothy Ko has astutely observed, differences dividing Chinese women overrode any gender identity that might have united them. Although the numbers of learned women expanded continuously from the seventeenth century on, they derived their authority from classical learning and the power of writing. That power enabled the educated woman to create an identity that was both morally and humanly intelligible in the context of *wen*, Confucian high culture. The same power lost its meaning in the dramatic changes of the twentieth century, when the foundations of *wen* were rejected by revolutionary leaders, male and female alike. Consequently, in trying to understand gender relations in China's modern era, we must ask how and where educated women have repositioned themselves to retain or recover or remake their moral and cultural authority under new regimes.

APPENDIX

Appendix

THE SPATIAL DISTRIBUTION OF WOMEN WRITERS IN QING TIMES

TO ANALYZE THE SPATIAL distribution of women writers in Qing times, I have relied on data tabulated from Hu Wenkai's 1957 survey. I first supposed that the distribution of women writers corresponded to the distribution of the population, with the most densely populated areas having more women writers, and vice versa. The test of that hypothesis is displayed in Table A-1.

Table A-1 shows the spatial distribution of women writers in Qing times. Of the 3,181 Qing women writers for whom a native place is known, 2,258—or 70.9 percent—hailed from the Lower Yangzi region. In 1843 this entire macroregion accounted for 17 percent of the total population of the realm, excluding Manchuria.[1]

If the general distribution of the population is no guide to where women writers appeared, we might imagine instead that women writers came mainly from the most highly urbanized regions of China. The Lower Yangzi was by far the most densely populated region, having in 1843 an average density of 348, compared with an empirewide average of only 103, and an estimated urbanization rate of 7.9 percent, the highest of all macroregions.[2] But Table A-1 shows that urbanization rates cannot explain the prominence of women

TABLE A-1
Women Writers in Qing Times, by Region

Region	Urban population as percentage of regional population	No. of women writers	Regional women writers as percentage of all Qing women writers
Lower Yangzi	7.9	2,258	70.9
North China	4.2	213	6.7
Southeast Coast	5.9	191	6.0
Middle Yangzi	4.6	180	5.7
Lingnan	7.0	125	3.9
Gan Yangzi	—	81	2.5
Upper Yangzi	4.2	55	1.7
Northwest	4.9	46	1.4
Yungui	4.1	29	0.9
Manchuria	—	3	0.1

NOTE: Data on women writers are calculated from Hu Wenkai [1957] 1985. Calculations are based on the 3,181 Qing women writers whose native place Hu identifies. These figures span the entire Qing era and are not confined to the eighteenth century. Urbanization rates, however, are for 1843, following Skinner (1977: 235), who does not provide rates for the Gan Yangzi region or for Manchuria.

writers from that region, given that the Lingnan region, with an urbanization rate of 7 percent in the same period, produced only a small fraction of Qing women writers—125, or less than 4 percent of the total, ranking well below three other less urbanized regions.[3]

Population distribution and urbanization rates do not explain the exceptional concentration of women writers in the Lower Yangzi region. However, the localities where women writers were concentrated in Qing times were the same ones, by and large, that produced the highest numbers of male *jinshi* degree holders, suggesting a strong correlation between investment in men's education and women's learning. Table A-2 displays the seventeen leading Lower Yangzi prefectures that were home to women writers in Qing times. Prefectures are listed in order according to the proportion of the population accounted for by women writers. Of the first thirteen prefectures on this list, all but one (Anqing) were "leading culture areas" in Qing times, a term Ho Ping-ti uses to identify prefectures with high numbers of *jinshi* degree holders and first-class honors men.[4]

Table A-3 probes this regional concentration more closely by presenting a county-by-county tabulation of the native places of Qing women writers. These county-level data suggest that local cultural variations within the Lower Yangzi region may have affected the writing environment for women.

These subregional variations also appear in Map 2 (p. 6), which shows six different levels of women's literary productivity. The top nine counties listed in Table A-3 and shown in densest shading on Map 2 produced 86 or

TABLE A-2
Women Writers in Lower Yangzi Prefectures

Prefecture	No. of women writers	Women writers as percentage of prefectural population	Prefecture	No. of women writers	Women writers as percentage of prefectural population
Hangzhou	387	0.0121	Yangzhou	103	0.0031
Jiaxing	274	0.0098	Huizhou	72	0.0029
Suzhou	466	0.0085	Zhenjiang	55	0.0025
Songjiang	172	0.0065	Tongzhou	24	0.0025
Changzhou	248	0.0064	Hezhou	10	0.0023
Taicang	91	0.0051	Shaoxing	107	0.0020
Huzhou	121	0.0047	Quzhou	3	0.0020
Anqing	78	0.0044	Taizhou	33	0.0012
Jiangning	71	0.0038			

NOTE: Population data are from *Da Qing yitong zhi* [1820] 1966. Not listed are prefectures where women writers made up less than one-thousandth of 1 percent of the population. Data on women writers, from Hu Wenkai [1957] 1985, are for the entire Qing period.

TABLE A-3
Jiangnan Counties That Were Home to More Than One Qing Woman Writer

County no.[a]	County name	No. of Qing women writers[b]	County no.[a]	County name	No. of Qing women writers[b]
1447	Qiantang	276	1391	Songjiang	86
1370	Changzhou	213	1450	Shaoxing	72
1388	Wu	148	1360	Jiangdu	71
1398	Jiaxing	132	1350	Jiangning	70
1387	Changshu	106	1415	Xiuning	66
1395	Haining	96	1371	Wuxi	66
1401	Wuxing	94	1329	Tongcheng	60
1400	Wujiang	91			

NOTE: Data on women writers, from Hu Wenkai [1957] 1985, are for the entire Qing period.

[a] County numbers are from Skinner 1977.

[b] Numbers are for women writers whose native place could be identified at the county level. Despite a few scattered omissions in cases where a native place could not be specified to the county level, the figures are persuasive. More inclusive data would merely raise the numbers presented here.

more women writers during the Qing period.[5] These nine core counties all fall within the region known to eighteenth-century scholars as "West of the Zhe" (Zhexi), that is, those counties of Jiangnan that lay immediately west of the Qiantang River.[6] As a home for women writers in Qing times, Hangzhou and its environs (Qiantang county) take pride of place, followed by Changzhou (comprising the counties of Wujin and Yanghu), then Wu county (centered on Suzhou), then Jiaxing, and so on. These nine counties and their center cities were home to 1,242, or nearly 40 percent, of all the women writers of the Qing dynasty, as shown in Table A-4.

Thus whereas the Jiangnan, or Lower Yangzi, macroregion as a whole

TABLE A-4

Counties That Surpassed All Others in Claiming Women Writers as Native Daughters in Qing Times

County[a]	No. of women writers[b]	Percentage of all Qing women writers[b]	County[a]	No. of women writers[b]	Percentage of all Qing women writers[b]
Qiantang	276	8.6	Haining	96	3.0
Changzhou	213	6.7	Wuxing	94	3.0
Wu	148	4.6	Wujiang	91	2.9
Jiaxing	132	4.1	Songjiang	86	2.7
Changshu	106	3.3	TOTAL	1,242	39.0

NOTE: Data on women writers, from Hu Wenkai [1957] 1985, are for the entire Qing period.

[a] All counties are in Zhexi.

[b] Figures show the total number of writers from each county and then estimate that number as a percentage of the total number of Qing women writers whose place of birth can be identified. The method for calculating these figures is as follows. First, I assigned all native places named by Hu Wenkai ([1957] 1985) a county number, following the coding scheme used in the macroregional analysis by G. William Skinner (1977). Numbers assigned were based on the nearest identifiable county coded by Skinner. Where county names or local place names were not identical, I resolved the problem by consulting geographical dictionaries and Playfair [1910] 1968. Percentages were calculated by (1) aggregating all place names under the relevant county number; (2) summing where multiple numbers were found; (3) subtracting from the total number of Qing women writers (3,556) all those for whom place of origin could not be assigned (375); and (4) arriving at a total of 3,181 Qing women writers whose native place is identifiable. (Percentages do not add to total because of rounding.)

produced more than 70 percent of all Qing women writers, the region itself appears to have been divided into a "core" area, the Changzhou-Qiantang axis just described (Zhexi), and five satellite regions surrounding Shaoxing, Yangzhou [Jiangdu], Nanjing [Jiangning], Tongcheng, and Xin'an [Xiuning]. These microregional differences are briefly discussed in Chapter 8.

REFERENCE MATTER

Notes

1. Introduction

1. See Sung 1981.

2. See Spade 1979; also Tsai 1981.

3. Twitchett 1962: 108.

4. This convergence of assumptions is demonstrated most clearly in Patricia Ebrey's landmark study of marriage in the Song period (Ebrey 1993). Dorothy Ko, who focuses on women's subjectivity, also stresses the shared interests of elite men and women (see esp. Ko 1994: 260–61).

5. My approach owes much to work by contemporary feminist analysts of political economy. Sherry Ortner (1978), Cynthia Enloe (1990), and Nancy Folbre (1986; 1987; 1993) are among the social scientists who have drawn attention to the relationship between state policy and gender relations in societies past and present.

6. See Ko 1994.

7. Scholarship by non-Western feminists, especially critical theorists' studies of colonial discourse and research and writing on so-called Third World women, helped me question the utility of European models, however iconoclastic and inspiring, for the study of Chinese women. See especially Mohanty 1991 and Abu-Lughod 1986; 1993.

8. King 1980.

9. Findlen 1993.

10. The rare young women who managed to remain single were usually "married" first, either to a deceased fiancé or to a spouse who died prematurely. See the example of Tanyangzi discussed by Ann Waltner (1987).

11. Arthur Wolf uses the term "grand family," coined by Maurice Freedman, to specify the set of relationships implied in the Chinese joint family system (see Wolf and Huang 1980: 68). The classic historical essay on the Chinese family system is Ebrey 1990.

12. *HLM* 118.1,605; *Stone* 5: 318.

13. See Margery Wolf 1972 for the classic analysis.

14. See Chodorow 1978 for the definitive study of this traumatic pattern and its consequences in psychoanalysis.

15. Telford 1992b.

16. On the status of wives and concubines, see Rubie Watson 1991; on courtesans in High Qing times, see Chap. 5 of the present volume.

17. See Levy and Shih 1949.

18. Armstrong 1987.

19. The High Qing reading is different too, I would argue, from the conception of *nei* and *wai* posited in Dorothy Ko's study of the seventeenth century, where she identifies an expansion of the elite women's sphere—through reading, writing, and the emergence of talented women in companionate marriage—into spheres formerly dominated by men. See Ko 1994: 12–17 and chaps. 3–5.

20. Defined by Li Wai-yee as a "seamless continuity in inspiration, expression, and communication" (1993: 263).

21. Li Wai-yee 1993.

22. Edwards 1994: 59.

23. Bol 1992 explains the development of the idea of *wen* as culture, or what he calls "this culture of ours," during the Tang and Song periods. He examines its manifold meanings as a property of the elite, which they defined and redefined through their writings.

24. See Owen 1990 for a brief and insightful comparative analysis of the role of poetry in Chinese civilization and high culture.

25. The notion of a palace of memories is developed and explored in Spence 1985.

26. Ebrey 1993: 122–24.

27. See Abu-Lughod 1986: esp. pp. 255–59. Abu-Lughod identifies what she calls "two culturally elaborated discourses about the self and personal sentiments" in Bedouin society (255). But she points out that since one discourse is poetry, and poetry is art, the two discourses can be neither discrete and separate nor seamless and monolithic. Poetry mimics the hegemonic discourse, from which it derives its evocative power, and it creates a counterdiscourse that is autonomous and continually reinvented.

2. *Gender*

1. The term "High Qing" derives from the work of Ho Ping-ti, who in many studies of the Qing period underscored its unique importance in Chinese history and pointed to the eighteenth century as the peak of Qing rule (see Ho 1967; 1959). Ho called China's "long eighteenth century" the era of *Pax Sinica*—heralded by the pacification of the last stronghold of anti-Manchu resistance in 1683 and ending with the rise of rebellion and signs of corrupt administration in the 1790's. In his studies of China's population history, Ho cites qualitative evidence pointing to rising life expectancy and to retrospective assessments by writers of the early nineteenth century, a grimmer time; Yu Zhengxie, for example, looked back on the mid-eighteenth century as "the highest peak of peace and prosperity in history" (cited in Ho 1959: 214). In a later study of social mobility (Ho 1962), Ho also noted the paradoxical costs of demographic success in the High Qing: declining mobility rates

among the expanding educated classes, declining living standards, and "mounting economic strains," which, in his view, invited the Malthusian check supplied by the Taiping Rebellion. For another discussion of the High Qing, see Wakeman 1970. This book follows Wakeman's temporal boundaries of the period. Susan Naquin and Evelyn Rawski (1987), drawing on analyses by G. William Skinner, have argued that the "peak" and "decline" phases of the dynastic cycle can be identified only regionally and that the Lower Yangzi region remained untouched by problems that dramatically affected other areas during eighteenth-century disturbances. Their regional analysis is based on Skinner 1985 and articles in Skinner 1977. As readers will see, this book adopts a regional perspective.

2. The standard work is Ho 1959.

3. See Elman 1984; Guy 1987.

4. Will (1990), Will et al. (1991), and Perdue (1992) all point to successful state intervention in the grain economy to prevent famine and promote price stability and interregional price integration. Kung-chuan Hsiao (1960: 184–258) documents what he terms a pervasive system of "ideological control" instituted by Manchu rulers through propaganda, schools, and public rituals. The effects of Qing ideological control through education are examined in various essays in Elman and Woodside 1994.

5. Kuhn 1990: 30–48, quotation on p. 48.

6. Edwards 1994.

7. Mann 1992a, 1992b.

8. Ropp 1976 and 1981 are the classic works.

9. Mann 1992c.

10. See Ho 1962: 54–67, for a description of Ming status groups.

11. See Crossley 1987, 1989, 1990; Rawski 1991; and, for the seminal work on marriage customs and non-Han dynasties of conquest, Holmgren 1991 and literature cited therein.

12. Gulik 1961: 334–35.

13. McMahon 1988: 130–44, esp. p. 131n3.

14. McMahon 1994: 229.

15. The phrase "civilizing project" is borrowed from a recent essay by Stevan Harrell (1995). Harrell identifies a single "Confucian" civilizing project, but the reader will see that I share Pamela Crossley's conviction that the Manchus' civilizing project deployed their unique understanding of Confucianism (see esp. Crossley 1987).

16. Ko 1994.

17. Ebrey 1993.

18. Elvin 1984. Elvin's survey of "female virtue and the state" begins in the Han.

19. Elvin (1984: 123) dates the first records to 1304. Holmgren (1986) explains some of the reasons why conquerors who practiced the levirate had a political interest in chaste widowhood.

20. See Elvin 1984, Mann 1987, and T'ien 1988. For statistical data on the regional success of the cult in High Qing times, see Mann 1985, 1993.

21. An imperial decree of 1644 commanded that these shrines be constructed and maintained in every county. See Hsiao 1960: 226.

22. See Mann 1993: 97, which tabulates figures for Jiangnan and Zhejiang provinces.

23. Mann 1993: 91; Rowe 1992: 19. *A note on dates:* Dates in the Chinese calendar in my sources are generally marked by reference to the year of a reigning emperor—for instance, Qianlong 4, meaning the fourth year of the reign of the Qianlong emperor. Since the Chinese lunar calendar and the Western solar calendar do not exactly correspond, reign years

actually span two Western calendar years (Qianlong 4, for example, begins on February 8, 1739, and ends on January 28, 1740). Throughout this book, I use the first Western calendar year where the precise date within a reign year is unknown. Thus, Qianlong 4 is here referred to as 1739, not 1739/40 or 1740, since most of the year Qianlong 4 does in fact correspond to the Western calendar year 1739.

24. Imperial edicts from the Yongzheng and Qianlong emperors reiterate these concerns. See decrees issued in 1723, 1724, 1749, and 1755, in *Qinding Da Qing huidian zeli* (1748): 71/1a–b, 7a, 16–17.

25. See Mann 1987: 50. The wife, mother, and paternal grandmother of a successful official could each expect an honorific title, generally bestowed posthumously, based on the rank of her male kinsman. For titles, see Mayers [1897] 1966: 69–70.

26. The standard work on widow suicide is T'ien 1988. T'ien points to three areas where widow suicide was frequent and publicly acclaimed in Ming times. See esp. pp. 70–89.

27. T'ien 1988: 124–25. Margery Wolf (1975: 113–14) mentions similar beliefs in the twentieth century.

28. The most famous example is Gu Yanwu's foster mother, who starved herself to death in fifteen days to protest the Manchu conquest of her home region in 1645. Willard Peterson (1968: 144–45) notes that this act profoundly influenced Gu as a filial son and as a loyal subject; he refused to serve two rulers. On the suicide bans, see Elvin 1984: 127–28. On the government's success in curbing suicide, see Mann 1993. On female virtue and loyalism in the late Ming, see Kang-i Sun Chang 1991; on the Manchus' obsession with loyalism, see Crossley 1989: 88–91; see also Wakeman 1985, 2: 1,115–24.

29. T'ien 1988: 127.

30. Elvin 1984: 128, quoting an imperial edict of 1728. See also Mann 1985, 1993; T'ien 1988: 127–28.

31. See Will 1990; Perdue 1992; and Will et al. 1991. Qing policies in the eighteenth century were designed to ensure that grain stores leveled seasonal price fluctuations, protecting urbanites and farmers from the threat of grain shortages.

32. Leung 1993b: 154. Leung comments that the effect of this edict is not clear. Most construction of orphanages appears to have been private.

33. See Leung 1993a.

34. Ng 1987.

35. Ch'ü 1961: 25.

36. The impact of Qing law on gender relations is closely examined in Sommer 1994.

37. H. Levy 1966a.

38. H. Levy 1966a: 67–68. Levy's book includes photographs of the platform shoes favored by Manchu ladies, along with tantalizing notes about the history of Manchu attacks on the practice drawn from an array of obscure sources (see pp. 66–69).

39. Ko 1994: 150, 169–71, 263–64. Ko suggests that the erotic content of footbinding was especially attached to courtesans and concubines.

40. For High Qing examples, see H. Levy 1966a: 68–70; Ropp 1981: 146, 149–50.

41. Kai-wing Chow (1994: esp. 79–97) explains why Han Chinese constituents were especially sympathetic to Manchu policies affirming kinship obligations, concerned as they were about family rituals and kinship hierarchies in the transition to Qing rule.

42. Yin 1748: preface, p. 1.

43. See Mann 1991: 216–19, where this text is discussed.

44. The title of his family instruction book, *Shuangjietang yongxun* (Simple precepts

from the hall enshrining a pair of chaste widows), honors his father's second wife and a concubine, each a faithful widow.

45. See Mann 1991: 217.

46. The work was compiled in 1742, when Chen was serving as governor of Jiangxi province. It was reprinted at least twice after that time; I have used editions dated 1868 and 1895.

47. Rowe 1992: 10–18. See also examples and discussion in Mann 1991: 219–20.

48. Lan's work is described in *EC* 441 and discussed in Mann 1994: 21–22, quotation on p. 21. For a complete translation of the preface, see S. W. Williams 1900, 1: 574–76.

49. Huang's handbook figures prominently in the discussions in Chapter 7 of the present volume. On the chaste widow cult, see Huang Liuhong [1694] 1984: 44, 61, 499, 521.

50. See especially Chow 1994.

51. See Guy 1987.

52. Elman 1984, 1990.

53. My translation of the complete essay appears in Chang and Saussy (forthcoming 1997).

54. See the discussion of Wang Zhong's critique of widow chastity in Chap. 4, "Writing"; see also Ropp 1981: 128, 141, *et passim*. Mann 1991: 211–12 discusses Yu Zhengxie's critique of widow chastity as an outgrowth of his interest in philology.

55. Mann 1992a analyzes the debates; see also Chap. 4, "Writing."

56. G. William Skinner has noted that "the Qing pacification was but a perturbation in the upswing of the Suchou cycle that had begun a century earlier in the Lower Yangzi region," whereas in the Southeast Coast it was a major episode in a downswing set off in the last years of the Ming by a prohibition on coastal and overseas trade (1985: 281).

57. The changes are summarized in Naquin and Rawski 1987: 147–58.

58. See Chen Hongmou's complaints, translated in Mann 1991: 205.

59. Skinner 1987: 75.

60. James Lee and his collaborators have published tentative evidence suggesting that fertility as well as mortality was "highly responsive" to improved economic circumstances. Their data show that when food prices were high, people had fewer children, especially fewer girls (Lee, Campbell, and Tan 1992: 167). Moreover, they show, since sex-selective infanticide was a primary means of controlling fertility, decisions were made at the time of birth, not at the time of conception. They present evidence that the smaller and simpler the household, the more vulnerable it was to these economic pressures. Thus larger, more complex, wealthier families were less likely to kill baby girls even when times were bad unless they had been unsuccessful in producing sons (p. 169). Finally, they argue that because girls were such a luxury, once they survived infancy they were unlikely to be sold or given away because they were allowed to live only in families that were well able to support them (p. 175).

61. Japanese data show how this transformation occurred under comparable historical conditions but in the context of a very different family system. Thomas C. Smith's research presents convincing quantitative evidence that in Tokugawa Japan, where female infanticide was commonly practiced to control the size of offspring sets and the timing of births, prolonged peace and prosperity and an expanding secondary and tertiary economy caused a marked drop in female infanticide in the population of preindustrial Nakahara. See Smith 1977: esp. 147–56.

62. Some reports of female infanticide blame it on the high cost of dowries. Local literati even provided stipends to assist in rearing the infant daughters that might otherwise

have been put to death. For Jiangnan evidence, see the biography of Cao Zhixin of Jurong county, Jiangsu province, dated QL era, in *Xuzuan Jurong xian [Jiangsu] zhi* [1904] 1974: [10/13a–b] 816.

63. Liu Ts'ui-jung 1992b.

64. Telford 1992a, 1992b.

65. See Telford 1992b: 926, table 4, which shows that age at first marriage for women was highest in the first quarter of the eighteenth century, after which it gradually declined, dropping precipitously after 1820. For men, the scenario was slightly different, with age at first marriage peaking in the second quarter of the century, then declining steadily, with a sharp drop after 1839.

66. Widows moved from higher-status first marriages in one lineage to lower-status marriages as second wives or concubines, or to marriage as first wives in lower-class families (Telford 1992b: 932). As further evidence of worsening demographic conditions in the nineteenth century, Telford cites a rise in the proportion of males who never married. Here, he notes, the "elevated mortality of potential wives" (p. 937) created a shortage of marriage partners that even "recycling" widows could not alleviate. Moreover, those males lucky enough to acquire a spouse in this shrinking marriage market had to marry younger.

67. See Telford 1992a: 32, where he points out that whereas in preindustrial Western Europe "fluctuations in the age and proportion of married women constituted an important constraint on population growth," in China there was no such fertility restraint. In fact, the way the Chinese system operated, the only possible restraint on population growth would come from changes in the numbers and proportion of married men, and that effect would have been only "marginal at best."

68. Harrell 1985.

69. The most important study of migration and mobility is Kuhn 1990. His work underscores the deep contemporary concern within the elite about rootless people who were not safely anchored in families (pp. 42–43).

70. Ko 1994 (and some of my own evidence) shows that elite women did travel, both to fulfill family obligations and for pleasure. But see also Chap. 6 of the present volume, which stresses that even in farm families it was not considered respectable for a woman to work outside the home except on her own family's plot of land. Illustrations remind us that when women traveled, they were chaperoned and usually shielded from public view.

71. On guilds and sojourning in Qing times, see Skinner 1977: 538–46 and literature cited therein.

72. See Wang [1933] 1988; Yan 1992.

73. *GGZJ* 14/14a.

74. Ho 1962.

75. Kuhn 1990.

76. The early eighteenth-century Japanese intellectual Dazai Shundai (1680–1747) complained about fickle short-term (*dekawari*) servants, noting that in China one could still count on long-term servants, tantamount to slaves, who remained loyal to one master (Leupp 1992: 23–24). Of course, Dazai's observation may have been incorrect, but it echoes other statutory and anecdotal evidence for the persistence of long-term servitude in eighteenth-century Jiangnan.

77. Wei, Wu, and Lu (1982: 2–3) cite inventories of officials who were cashiered: over 1,000 servants in the household of the infamous Heshen; 140 in the estate of the father of Cao Xueqin, whose maternal grandfather employed 270.

78. Cited in Wei, Wu, and Lu 1982: 5.

79. Slaves and servile persons whose labor was bought and sold went by a number of

overlapping names in this period, including (following Wakeman 1985) *shipu* (hereditary servants, household serfs), *nu* (serfs, slaves), *nubei* (household slaves), *nuli* (slaves), *nupu* (serfs, bondservants), and *jiapu* (household servants). Jing (1993: 53) observes that most laws refer to slaves as *nubei*, a compound that conflates the terms for male slaves (*nu*) and female slaves (*bei*) as a single category, but generally refers to an unmarked male subject.

80. The population registered as pariah comprised not only slaves but also bondservants employed by Manchu families, persons who had indentured themselves as tenants or servants, yamen underlings, and various groups stigmatized by local custom or occupation, including the "lazy people" (*duomin*) of Ningbo and Shaoxing, the "boat people" (*danhu*) in the Canton delta, the "musicians" (*yuehu*) who served as entertainers at the court and in government yamens, and actors, courtesans, and ordinary prostitutes.

81. This hierarchy is described and analyzed in Jing 1993. Members of the Banner system were subject to a separate legal code.

82. In an edict of 1726, for example, the Yongzheng emperor expressed concern that the Han Chinese population did not preserve the proper distance between master and slave, which in Manchu custom was the foundation of social order. See Wei, Wu, and Lu 1982: 19. Most Manchu slaves were the descendants of war captives, although after the conquest of China untold numbers of persons were reduced to slave status as punishment for crimes. Manchu slaves included a range of status groups, from elite domestic bondservants to lowly agricultural workers. The heart of the Manchu slavery system was the Banner system; Bannermen referred to themselves as the slaves of the sovereign (Crossley 1990: 14–15).

83. To shore up the distinction between free commoners and slaves, Qing rulers passed a law in 1646, immediately after the conquest, threatening to punish persons who kept free commoners as slaves (Ch'ü 1961: 189n93). Early Qing laws protecting ordinary commoners from falling into slavery included a state regulation of 1658 that required any person who purchased a slave or an indentured servant (*nupu*) to take the contract to the magistrate's tribunal to be notarized. This same law stipulated that contracts signed since the conquest of 1644 were retroactively subject to this requirement. In actual practice, the effect of such regulations may have been limited, given that local officials were often accused of complicity in human trafficking (Wei, Wu, and Lu 1982: 49–50).

84. Exceptions were granted for persons who had lived for prolonged periods in dependency on another household and for persons whose marriages had been arranged for them by their masters but who had never been sold with a contract. They were to be treated as slaves, not as hired laborers, under the law. See Takahashi 1982: 73; Ch'ü 1961: 188.

85. Ch'ü 1961: 188n93. The definition of hired laborer here follows the Ming 1587 precedent. The Yongzheng emperor's contribution was to limit the sale of slaves to transactions involving red (officially certified) contracts, attempting thereby to bring the slave market entirely under the purview of local magistrates.

86. Takahashi 1982: 73. Thus, as scholars of Chinese law (Takahashi Yoshiro, Ch'ü T'ung-tsu, Jing Junjian) have noted, throughout the eighteenth century the laws on slaveholding derived from two contradictory propositions. On the one hand, the law forbade slave ownership by commoners and also provided strict punishments for persons who sold respectable commoners into slavery or who knowingly kept a respectable commoner as a slave. On the other hand, substatutes in the legal code and decisions in legal cases specified criteria for valid contracts involving the sale of persons, and county officials continued to validate such contracts with official seals. Moreover, the state protected the power of slave owners by maintaining not only that persons purchased with valid contracts were bound

in perpetuity, but also that their descendants were bound in service to the slave owner, provided the owner had arranged for the marriage of the slave couple in question.

87. Jing Junjian, who has analyzed these statutes, observes that these rulings were concentrated between the 1760's and the 1780's and that their major purpose was to move most hired laborers steadily into the ranks of ordinary commoners. See Jing 1981, 1993. He summarizes: "The clear trend in repeated revisions of Qing legislation concerning hired laborers was in the direction of removing certain workers from the legal category 'hired laborer.' However, the liberation of laborers from their inferior legal status was a rather slow and extremely convoluted historical process that commenced with the freeing from servile status of short-term laborers in the year 1588 (WL 16) and continued with the freeing of long-term laborers in 1788 (QL 53), a total of two hundred years. Even so, the process was not fully completed at the end of the Qing dynasty" (1981: 22; see also 1993: 39). Reforms in the legal status of hired laborers may be taken, according to Jing, as an index of the pace of change in economic relationships during that period. Takahashi (1982) has also briefly summarized these changes in the law, which he prefers to call "reorganizations" rather than "reforms."

88. The effect of new limits on male slavery is hinted at briefly in Jing 1993: 165 in a discussion of the status of female slaves, who were never classified as "hired laborers."

89. Jing 1993: 164–65.

90. A female slave's natal family, whether slave or free, had no legal say in marital arrangements (Ch'ü 1961: 189n98), although her family might be consulted or even permitted to take charge of them. See the next paragraph for an example from *HLM*.

91. Translated in Meijer 1980: 347–48.

92. *HLM* 21.290; *Stone* 1: 417. The body servant who attended a wealthy young woman stood in some respects at the apex of the employment hierarchy for working-class women. Selected for her learning, refinement, and comeliness, she had to see to her mistress's dress, hair, makeup, and moods, but was spared heavy labor. Such a female servant might be more secure and comfortable in her lowly position than a peasant wife from the same class. In one respect, however, the status of even the most refined servant resembled that of a slave or courtesan: all unmarried female servants were considered sexually accessible to the masters of the house, and some were assigned sexual service to a particular master.

93. Slaveholders expected to arrange marriages for "house-born" offspring of their own slaves; however, they might defer to the wishes of the family from whom a slave was purchased, if those wishes were known.

94. *HLM* 19.267–68; *Stone* 1: 385–87.

95. *HLM* 19.269–70; *Stone* 1: 388–89.

96. *HLM* 19.270; *Stone* 1: 389.

97. *HLM* 19.269; *Stone* 1: 388.

98. Commoners could beat their slaves freely, although if they killed a slave intentionally they were subject to a beating of 60 strokes and a year in prison (Ch'ü 1961: 192). Punishment for officials was less severe. An official who killed a slave with a knife received 100 strokes and was dismissed from office, but one who beat a slave to death was subject only to a fine or demotion. See Ch'ü 1961: 193.

99. The same rule had applied to grandmothers and mothers of officials (Ch'ü 1961: 194n134). On the continuing concern about abuse of servants and slaves by women who owned them, see Meijer 1980: 334, 348–52.

100. In 1673 a law forbade masters to have sexual intercourse with married female slaves or servants, specifying a penalty of 40 strokes if the offender was an ordinary commoner and a fine if the master was an official (Ch'ü 1961: 199). Meijer's study of the Qing code

points out that legally a son born to an unmarried female slave and her master could participate in the division of family property on an equal footing with offspring of wives and concubines (Meijer 1980: 333), though such cases, if they existed at all, must have been rare. By contrast, female slave owners were forbidden to have sexual relations with male slaves, married or unmarried. In cases where intercourse occurred, both slave and mistress were punishable by death (Ch'ü 1961: 199–200).

101. *HLM* 17.241–42; *Stone* 1: 350, cited in Wei, Wu, and Lu 1982: 44. When one took an artisan into one's household, this was called *mu* ("to hire"), but the persons so hired became permanent dependents. See also Clunas 1991: 67, citing a comment by Zhang Dai (1597?–1684).

102. Cited in Wei, Wu, and Lu 1982: 45.

103. Poem by Ji Yingzhong, recorded by Wei, Wu, and Lu 1982: 50.

104. Cited in Wei, Wu, and Lu 1982: 45; see also pp. 46–47, where the racket is described in detail. A buyer willing to pay high prices for a particular servant or slave would persuade local officials to intimidate the family into selling a wife or daughter.

105. Meijer 1980: 331.

106. Cited in Wei, Wu, and Lu 1982: 39.

107. See Wu's biography in *She xian [Anhui] zhi* [1937] 1975: [6/67b] 968.

108. Cited in Wei, Wu, and Lu 1982: 47–48.

109. Cited in Wei, Wu, and Lu 1982: 52; see also other reports from Zhejiang, Guizhou, Beijing, Sichuan, Shanxi, etc.

110. *HLM* 112.1: 542–43; *Stone* 5: 231–32 describes the drugging and kidnapping of the virgin nun Miaoyu. See also *HLM* 19.263; *Stone* 1: 378, where Baoyu warns his page that they should not sneak out of the mansion for a ride on their own because they might be kidnapped.

111. Leung 1993a: 6–8.

112. See the kidnap scene at the beginning of *Hong lou meng*, where the young girl who disappears later turns up as a slave in a distant household.

113. As in the case of Yuan Mei's sister, who was sold by her husband; see Wang Zhong [1815] 1970, "Nei bian" 1/15b.

114. A possible exception is the policy banning marriage between Han Chinese and Manchus, though this policy was inconsistent. During the early years of Qing rule, Han-Manchu intermarriage was recognized. See Wakeman 1985, 1: 478, esp. n. 159. At the start of the Qing era, to promote pacification and encourage interracial harmony, an order of 1649 permitted Han and Manchu officials and commoners to intermarry. As a dramatic gesture in that direction, in the year 1654 the emperor's fourteenth daughter was betrothed to the son of Wu Sangui. However, after 1655 Manchus were permitted to marry only those Han Chinese who belonged to one of the Banners. See Rawski 1991: 175, 181. From that time on, Qing policy with respect to marriage between Han Chinese and Manchus focused not on what we would term ethnic distinctions but rather on what the Manchus regarded as the crucial *political* distinction between those who submitted to or allied themselves with the Manchus and those who did not. Thus Manchu males intermarried freely with women in the Banners, whether they were of Manchu or Han or Mongol ethnicity. At the same time, the formal code published in the Regulations of the Board of Revenue stated that no female among the Banners resident in the capital could become the wife of a Han commoner. The heads of Manchu Banner households who contracted such marriages for their daughters were to be punished, with the same punishment extended to the head of the household of

the Han family in question, and the name of the female so betrothed was to be expunged from the Banner registers. A Manchu woman, or a Han Chinese woman affiliated with a Banner, who married a Han commoner was expelled from the Banner. One source argues that certain Han Chinese women were permitted to "marry up" through betrothal to a Bannerman. According to Chen Peng (1990: 496), if the daughter of a "famous" Han family was betrothed to a Bannerman, the company commander was to investigate the family's background and report his findings. If the report was positive, appropriate gifts of money were bestowed on the bride's family. If the investigation turned up some question or offense, the findings were publicized and the offending parties to the marriage punished.

115. The first edict—issued in 1723 by the Yongzheng emperor barely six months after he ascended the throne—formally abolished the hereditary status group known as *yuehu* and (perhaps inadvertently) opened the floodgates for a series of memorials and edicts clarifying the status of other *jianmin* groups around the country. During the first series of edicts, issued between 1723 and 1729, seven local pariah groups were named specifically as members of the "emancipated" groups: the *yuehu*, the "fisherfolk of the nine surnames" (found throughout Shaoxing prefecture); the *gaihu*, or beggars, of Suzhou prefecture; the *duomin* of Shaoxing and Ningbo; the boat people of the Canton delta; the shed people of Zhejiang, Jiangxi, and Fujian; and the hereditary bondservants of Huizhou, Ningguo, and Chizhou prefectures in Anhui province. The classic study of these edicts remains Terada 1959. See also Ch'ü 1961: 130–32n4.

116. Leung 1993b: 154–55. Leung notes that the first time separate categories are used to distinguish "rich" from "aristocratic" and "poor" from "pariah" is in the encyclopedic reference *Gujin tushu jicheng*, printed in 1728. The same work also for the first time collapses into one chapter titled "Arts and Technical Skills" ("Yishu dian") all nonscholarly occupations involving certain kinds of technical expertise, from merchants to beggars to hired laborers to courtesans, prostitutes, and actors. She takes this as a definitive measure of the blurred relationship between poverty and pariah status in the mid-Qing era and as a sign that social status did not necessarily follow the letter of the law with respect to pariahs.

117. See Rowe 1992: 13. See also p. 18, where Rowe notes that "Ch'en's efforts to implement the virtuous widow cult were concentrated in relatively frontier areas, rather than in core provinces such as Jiangsu and Jiangxi, where he also served."

118. For an analysis of the plan to build a multiethnic Manchu empire, see Crossley 1987, where she insightfully identifies the Qianlong emperor's concern with "harmonizing race and culture" by forcing "a comprehensive cultural structure upon the Qing polity, with the emperorship as its integrating center" (p. 779).

3. The Life Course

1. Standard accounts of the life course in Chinese society refer to the unmarked male subject. See, for example, Solomon 1971. In two lengthy footnotes (pp. 36–37nn14–15), Solomon acknowledges the problem. M. J. Levy (1949: 63–140) distinguishes between males and females and pays special attention to elderly women as *lao nian*. M. Wolf (1972) places the female life course at the center of her analysis, but because she uses family relationships as her reference point and because she was interviewing peasant women, she does not examine learning, spirituality, or other aspects of the female life course that emerge from a study of elite women's writings and festivals.

2. The numerical correspondences by which the number eight governed male physi-

cal development and seven, female first appear in *The Yellow Emperor's Classic of Internal Medicine* (*Huangdi neijing*). See Veith 1972: 98–99; see also Waltner 1986: 684–85.

3. On Xu's life, see *EC* 322–24 and Unschuld 1990. Unschuld translates Yuan Mei's epitaphs for Xu on pp. 37–42.

4. Veith 1972: 98–99.

5. Telford 1992b: 926.

6. Waltner 1986: 686.

7. The phrases *xiantian* ("what we are born with; what is innate") and *houtian* ("the things of this world; what is acquired"), literally translated, mean "the first" and "the last" part of the day; thus Hong uses them with a double meaning when he refers to the spirit one is born with (which is *xiantian*) and the food and drink of this world (which is *houtian*).

8. *Analects* XVI.7, translated in Legge [1893–95] 1991, 1: 312–13.

9. Hong Liangji [1793] 1969: 1/4a–5b. For a Shakespearean periodization of the life course of the Kangxi emperor, see Spence 1967.

10. *Book of Rites* 1, translated in Legge [1885] 1967, 1: 65–66.

11. See *Analects* II.4, translated in Legge [1893–95] 1991, 1: 146–47.

12. Legge's translation of the passage, slightly amended, is: "The way in which a man loses his proper goodness of mind is like the way in which the trees are denuded by axes and beaks. Hewn down day after day, can it—*the mind*—retain its beauty? But there is a development of its life day and night, and in the air of the peaceful dawn, the mind feels in a degree those desires and aversions that are proper to humanity; but the feeling is not strong, and it is fettered and destroyed by what takes place during the day" (*Mencius* VI.A.7, translated in Legge [1893–95] 1991, 2: 407–8).

13. Notice that Yuan Mei's ideas about a man's old age appear to tweak Hong's, for as an octogenarian Yuan had no intention of languishing in the women's apartments. He preferred to imagine himself roving in his garden or floating on West Lake in the company of erudite young poetesses, a number of whom wrote special verses honoring his eightieth birthday.

14. By embracing a notion of women as timeless and men as locked in cycles of time, Hong Liangji identified a gender difference that contrasts markedly with Emily Martin's 1988 analysis of gender ideologies in death rituals, in which she describes the women's world of pollution and death as transient and the men's world of social order as eternal. My evidence suggests that during the eighteenth century many elite men and women believed that women's purity made transcendence easier for them than it was for men.

15. As Thomas Metzger (1977) has shown, the learning process inculcating these values created enormous psychological pressures, which Metzger artfully examines as inescapable "predicaments."

16. Wu Pei-yi, analyzing late Ming and early Qing autobiographies written by men who scrutinized their own lives for signs of moral weakness and spiritual fulfillment, notes that moral pressures appear to have abated sometime around the year 1680. The confessional mode went out of style with the high tide of scholasticism that characterized the High Qing period, and in its place developed what Wu disparagingly calls "annalistic biography" (1990: 235–36). Wu attributes this shift to the rise of scholasticism, but it could also be explained as a pragmatic response to the increasingly competitive scholarly milieu of the High Qing era and perhaps to the manifest failure of Ming loyalism.

17. See Hsiung 1992: 204–11. Whereas classical texts specified that boys between the ages

of six and ten *sui* should receive preparatory instruction in good behavior and proper conduct at home before going out to formal schooling, Hsiung finds that in the Ming-Qing period it was common for boys as young as four *sui* to receive formal training in reading at home. She attributes this trend to pressure on parents to produce offspring who could succeed in the examinations.

18. *Hong lou meng* exposes a seamy underside of the upper-class clan school as an arena where homosexual liaisons flourish and verbal and physical abuse rules. A rich uncle preys on the young male cousins, dashing students seduce male servants, inkstones smash teabowls, and the repertoire of weapons runs from books to doorbars. See *HLM* 9.136–44; *Stone* 1: 205–16.

19. Skinner 1992. In *Hong lou meng* the hapless Baoyu would not have been singled out for a high-pressure academic career had it not been for the untimely death of his promising older brother.

20. This aspect of the scholar's life course is neglected in most standard biographies. A notable exception is the judicious treatment in Peterson 1979: 23–27, 141–45.

21. This instruction was available from maids, peers, elders, or courtesans. R. H. van Gulik remarks on the cleanliness of Chinese sexual practice, which required washing both before and after intercourse (Gulik 1961: 311). Pregnancy in the brothels may also have been reduced by the practice of *coitus reservatus* because many men were taught that ejaculation unnecessarily depleted the vital essence of the body. See Needham 1956: 149.

22. The best account of the elite male life course remains Peterson's 1979 biography of Fang Yizhi. Shen Fu ([1877] 1983) records the life of a young man who never seemed able to reach this stage, thereby straining his relationship with his parents.

23. See Chap. 5, "Entertainment," which is based on seven accounts—all anonymous—of the courtesans' quarters in three cities.

24. See Shen [1877] 1983.

25. Rubie Watson has observed that the many cycles of men's lives were "punctuated by the acquisition of new names, new roles, new responsibilities and new privileges; women's lives, in comparison, remain indistinct and indeterminate" (1986: 619). She points to rituals of naming as a hallmark of this difference, an observation to which I shall return in the concluding chapter.

26. See Ko 1994: 256–60.

27. Cormack ([1922] 1974: 18) describes a first-birthday ceremony in which the tray of objects for a girl is the same as that for a boy, with needlework accessories added. If a baby girl took hold of the brush, the silver shoe, or the official seal, it was taken as a sign of the career of her future husband.

28. See Wolf and Hanley 1985 and literature cited therein.

29. On the historically high rates of suicide among Chinese women of marriageable age, see M. Wolf 1975; on patterns of suicide in the Ming-Qing period, see T'ien 1988. Poems on illness and suicide are discussed later in this chapter.

30. Wu Pei-yi (1990: 64–67) cites the Song poetess Li Qingzhao as a notable exception.

31. At six years of age; *hui* for boys came one year later, at eight *sui*, or age seven.

32. Since virtually no written historical evidence for attitudes or methods of footbinding among any class exists for the eighteenth century, I base these comments and those that follow—unless otherwise indicated—on more recent ethnographic accounts. See the discussion on footbinding in Chap. 6, "Work."

33. But see Ko 1994: 169–71.

34. Yuan Mei (1716–98) and the novelist Li Ruzhen (c. 1763–c. 1830) are the most famous of these critics. See Levy 1966a: 69; Ropp 1981: 140–43, 149–50.

35. See Ko 1997.

36. Respectable young ladies mastered the *gu qin* but never danced; the pipa was the instrument of courtesans, who alone danced to music.

37. See Zhu Yun's epitaph for the mother of Zhang Xuecheng, where he describes her "emerging from the women's apartments and mingling with the guests" when her husband entertained (Zhu [1815] 1936: 328).

38. See Ko 1994; see also Chap. 5, "Entertainment."

39. See Rowe 1992; Mann 1994.

40. Relying on data from other premodern societies where nutrition and living standards were comparable, Telford suggests that the average age of menarche in China at this time was between 14 and 17 years (1992b: 926, 928). We would expect young women in elite families to reach menarche toward the early end of this range. Telford's age tables appear to be reckoned in Western, not Chinese, terms, using years and not *sui*. Hence, fourteen years might be fifteen *sui*; seventeen years, eighteen *sui*.

41. Telford 1992b: 926. In Qing times the legitimate age at marriage for both males and females fell even lower: sixteen *sui* for boys, fourteen for girls. The emperors married at an especially young age: Shunzhi at fourteen, Kangxi at twelve, Yongzheng at thirteen, and Qianlong relatively late (for an emperor) at seventeen. See Feng Erkang 1986: 308.

42. Hinsch (1990: 173–78) supplies a brief survey of allusions. See also Gulik 1961: 48, 109, 163, 274, 302; and Ko 1994: 266. Although reliable evidence of lesbian unions can be found in the Canton delta region in the twentieth century (see esp. Topley 1975), it would be unwise to infer anything about eighteenth-century Jiangnan from that evidence.

43. See the discussion in Ropp 1985.

44. In Qing society, as elsewhere, women tended to outlive men. Guo Songyi's sample from 33 genealogies shows that the modal age at death for males was between 50 and 69 years; for females, between 60 and 79 years (1987: 125–26).

45. Telford 1992b: 924. He does not elaborate, but the gap of an average of six years in the data must represent unreported births—perhaps female, perhaps stillborn, or perhaps deceased too young to be recorded in a genealogy.

46. Recall the case of Xiren, Baoyu's favored lady-in-waiting in *Dream of the Red Chamber*, discussed in Chap. 2, "Gender," esp. n. 92.

47. See, for example, Zhang Xuecheng [n.d.] 1922: 20/16b.

48. *Dream of the Red Chamber* supplies the famous example of marriage between cousins Xue Baochai and Jia Baoyu. See also the discussion of marriage alliances between the Zhuangs and the Tangs in eighteenth-century Changzhou (Elman 1990: 87), discussed in Chap. 8. The popularity of cousin marriage from Song through Qing times is discussed, with examples, by Ch'ü (1961: 95–96). He shows that legal proscriptions on cross-cousin marriage were routinely ignored or eventually rescinded.

49. Liu Ts'ui-jung 1985: 28, 31. Liu notes that this estimate is remarkably similar to marital fertility estimates derived from data collected in the late 1920's and early 1930's.

50. Furth 1994.

51. Furth 1987: 8.

52. Furth 1987: 16.

53. Dai Lanying's poem is recorded in *SNS* 5/21a. As Emily Martin remarked insightfully: "If there is a particularly female ideology of birth in China, perhaps it would stress . . . *conjunction* of the antitheses life and death in the same events" (1988: 169).

54. Temple 1986: 136–37; see also Unschuld 1990: 340n1. Variolation, called "planting the pox," used scabs from smallpox patients to inoculate children (Unschuld 1990: 339–40).

55. An account of such a crisis appears in *HLM* 21.294–96; *Stone* 1: 424–26.

56. See *GGZJ* 8/9a, 8/10a–b, 10/7a, 11/14a–b, 12/15b, 12/20b, 14/7b–8a, 14/13a, 14/20a, 16/22b, 17/18b, 18/6a, 18/17a, 19/22a.

57. *GGZJ* 10/7a.

58. *GGZJ* 11/14a–b.

59. *GGZJ* 12/20b.

60. On early death, see, e.g., poems and prefaces in *GGZJ* 4/19a, 5/7a–b, 6/22a–b, 9/5b, 11/6b. One talented young woman was tortured to death by her paranoid spouse, who locked her up whenever he left the house; see *GGZJ* 10/18a. Stories of suffering young wives are recounted in Zhang Xuecheng [n.d.] 1922: 20/16b–17a, 31b.

61. Yun Zhu's mid-Qing anthology of women's poetry includes many poems voicing the anguish and anger of young widows who took their own lives. See, for example, *GGZJ* 5/3a, 12/7a–b, 13/13a, 18/10a, 18/14b.

62. See *GGZJ* 19/21b. The poem appears in the present volume on p. 218.

63. See "Wang Mengji jiaxun" (The family instructions of Wang Mengji), reprinted in Chen Hongmou [1742] 1895, "Yu xia."

64. On women as "domestic bursars," see McDermott 1990: 15–16; McDermott 1991, esp. pp. 49–52.

65. For discussion and examples, see Robertson 1997.

66. Zhang Xuecheng [n.d.] 1922: 20/29a.

67. These ages assume an average interval of 6.5 years between marriage and the birth of the first son (Telford 1992b). Data in Telford 1992a show that 6.5 years was the average time between marriage and the birth of a first male child during the late imperial period.

68. I have just begun to notice the significance of this turning point in stories of women from earlier periods. For example, the twelfth-century Daoist adept and poet Sun Bu'er had three children and turned to Daoist meditation and practice when she was 51 years old, following her husband, who had entered a Daoist discipleship at age 45. The story makes one wonder whether women *had* to wait until the age of 50 *sui* to make this transition, whereas men were free to make it whenever they chose (see Cleary 1989: 21), but Ann Waltner, citing the case of Tanyangzi and her followers, assures me that this is not the case (personal communication, March 21, 1995).

69. These regulations are summarized in Mann 1987.

70. On pilgrimage and women's spiritual communities, see Chap. 7, "Piety." Today in Taiwan and in the People's Republic of China, sutra-chanting societies comprise mainly middle-aged and elderly women (Sangren 1983: 8; personal observation, Shanghai Jing'an Temple, October 1988).

71. *GGZJ* 8/18a; see also "Written to My Children," *GGZJ* 2/5a.

72. See Chap. 7, "Piety," for examples.

73. See the poem "Sitting in Silence," written by a woman at the age of 69, on p. 73.

74. *GGZJ* 13/14b–15a, 15/2a, 15/2b–3b, 2/18a.

75. See Sun Xingyan n.d.: 1/15a–b. A similar example appears in Chap. 4, "Writing."

76. In Shanghai in 1988, a Ningbo lady of 73 *sui* told me that she learned from her grandmother that she should plant a lot of flowers when she turned 50 so the Flower Goddess (Hua Shen) would look after her (interview 12/9/88, informant 5).

77. In some parts of China, on the twelfth day of the second lunar month a flower festival is celebrated by women and children as a kind of fertility rite. See C. A. S. Williams (1976: 191–92), who draws on a description of folklore in Shanghai published in 1902.

78. See C. A. S. Williams 1976: 155–56, esp. the drawing on 156.

79. Mayers, in his *Chinese Reader's Manual* ([1910] 1974: 338), translates a historical account of the Eight Immortals and their attributes by the eighteenth-century Jiangnan scholar Zhao Yi (1727–1814), whose research demonstrated that the legend did not predate the Yuan period. See Zhao Yi [c. 1775] 1957: 34/24a–26b.

80. Sangren (1983: 12) comments, perhaps without irony, that such rituals offered a "practical" new direction "for middle-aged and elderly women." He stresses that Buddhist piety offered personal spiritual solace to women who felt marginalized by the passage out of their reproductive years: "Buddhism's concern for individual salvation assures it an important role in the religious life not only of the socially anomalous, but also of others who see it as a necessary complement to the primarily social focus of the rituals of ancestor worship and territorial cults" (p. 17). For the notion of "rituals of post-parenthood," Sangren draws on work by Sherry P. Ortner (Sangren 1983: 18). In a similar vein, the historian Patricia Ebrey's research on women in the Song posits that a postmenopausal woman replaced in her husband's bed by a concubine would turn to Buddhist rituals to control her jealousy and find new sources of personal fulfillment beyond the family and outside the structure of Confucian meaning that informed the descent line and its rituals. See Ebrey 1993: 170–71, but see also 127–28.

81. Ethnographic evidence for these beliefs is rich. See especially Ahern's discussion of "the belief that women who have borne children (or, some say, who die in childbirth) are punished in the underworld for having produced polluting substances" (1975: 214). She quotes at length from an account translated from the work of Johannes Frick, whose informants told him that "women who die in childbed are sent to a special section of the underworld called *hsieh-k'eng*, blood pit. There the woman's soul is pinned down by a heavy stone." Frick's record of the soul's experience, quoted in Ahern, leaves little to the imagination: "The soul groans, yes, cries out in agony. As its eyes anxiously dart all around it sees only blood. It eats only blood clots; it drinks only bloody fluid. It is not the fresh blood of animals . . . but inevitably foul vaginal blood and fluid. The soul cannot rest in the dreadful torment that it endures. Incessantly it groans and cries, but no friendly spirit approaches to help it. All good spirits shun the soul of a woman who has died in childbed" (Johannes Frick, "Mutter und Kind bei den Chinesen in Tsinghai, I: Die Sozialreligiöse Unreinheit der Frau," *Anthropos* 50 [1955]: esp. 341–42; the last quotation appears on p. 358; translated in Ahern 1975: 214). Ahern explains that "Sometimes . . . a woman's sons will show their love and pity for her and attempt to lessen or eliminate this punishment by ritual means" (p. 214). On this ritual, called the Bloody Pond ceremony, see the description for Fuzhou in Doolittle 1867, 1: 196–97; for Taiwan, see Seaman 1981: 388–89. On Hong Kong, Elizabeth Johnson writes: "According to my older informants, when their own children were born the idea that a woman is unclean after childbirth was taken very seriously. They had to wear a hat if they went outdoors to avoid offending the gods. Their mothers-in-law made them stay in a bedroom, did not let them sit on chairs or eat with other people, or even serve rice

to themselves. These restrictions are no longer observed, but during the first month after childbirth women still do not worship the gods or ancestors, or enter anyone else's house without being specifically invited, because they are considered unclean" (1975: 234–35).

82. Not until Ming times was the mourning period for a mother changed to the three-year period equivalent for mourning a father and called by the same term, *zhancui*. In ancient times the period for mourning a mother (*ji*) was only one year; after bitter debates in the Tang it was extended to three years, but called by the special term *zicui* (Ch'ü 1961: 31, citing *Ming shi* 60/22b–23a).

83. See Freedman 1958: 45, 101. Arthur Wolf (1970: 201–3) found considerable disagreement among his informants in Taiwan with respect to a married woman's mourning obligations, a lack of consensus he attributes to ambiguity in the kinship system concerning what parents and parents-in-law should expect from a daughter or daughter-in-law. One would expect in families where daughters remained close to their parents after marriage that mourning would reflect that closeness, extending, perhaps, to mourning for maternal relatives as well as the paternal relatives to whom they had formal obligations.

84. Concubines, though "married," were still more marginalized in Confucian mourning rituals. A concubine's ties to her natal family were completely severed, the family into which she married having no ritual or legal relationship to her natal kin. This meant no ritual visits home and also no legitimate contact or support of any kind from her natal family. Therefore, although in theory a concubine retained her obligation to mourn her own parents for three years even after her marriage (since she was not a first wife), in practice she was unable to observe those rituals. Moreover, as a concubine she was required to mourn her husband's first wife in the same grade as she would mourn her husband, and in addition she assumed mourning obligations for her husband's parents as if she were a first wife), in practice she was unable to observe those rituals. Moreover, as a concubine she was required to mourn her husband's first wife in the same grade as she would mourn her husband, and in addition she assumed mourning obligations for her husband's parents as if she were a first wife. See Hoang 1916: "Annotations," pp. 36–39. A concubine's tablet, if it was installed on the ancestral altars at all, remained there until all of her husband's sons died. Of all the members of her husband's family, only they held mourning obligations toward her. Ann Waltner's forthcoming study of the Ming legal code points out that a concubine was mourned for one year by all of her husband's sons, regardless of who their mother was. A debate about the placement of concubines' tablets raged among scholars in the mid-Qing era—testimony to the emotional power of concubines as mothers or even surrogate mothers, to sons' devotion to them, and to the ambiguous status of concubines in the kinship system. See Chow 1994: 119; *JSWB* 67/19. Pierre Hoang shows that the offspring of concubines (sons and unmarried daughters) owed their mothers only 9 months of mourning (grade 3A), whereas the concubine herself was to mourn any children who predeceased her for a full 27 months (grade 1A); see Hoang 1916, "Annotations," p. 37.

86. Werner 1961: 164, 218, 535–36; Zong and Liu 1986: 418–25. Suzanne Cahill (1993: 229) discusses the Queen Mother (Xi Wang Mu) as a special protector of older women. Lady Hemp (Ma Gu) was the "personification of cosmic time" measured in cycles by the Eastern Sea, which continually drained to become mulberry fields and then filled once more. See Schafer 1985: 94–95; S. E. Cahill 1993: 62, 95. An illustrated biography of Lady Hemp appears in Kohn 1993: 355–58. She is also associated with Double Seven, according to one story. On the seventh day of the seventh month, she and her elder brother, the immortal Wang Fangping, descended to earth to attend a banquet at which she performed a purify-

ing miracle: encountering the matron of the house, who had just given birth, Lady Hemp scattered grains of rice that turned at once into cinnabar. The site is marked by a precipice on Mount Tiantai, the holy mountain in Zhejiang province (Schafer 1985: 94).

87. Peng Shaosheng 1872: *xia*/31a, 32b–33a. Elsewhere (e.g., *xia*/33b) the terms *chang zhai* and *xiu jing ye* appear to be synonymous.

88. On Ma Gu, see Werner 1961: 299–300; Zong and Liu 1986: 719–24. On He Xian Gu, see Zong and Liu 1986: 807–13; Werner 1961: 347–48.

89. Judith Boltz, in her discussion of women's *nei dan* texts, notes that references in the texts to embryonic respiration, refining the spirit, and avoidance of grains all "suggest that women of the Tao may have strived for purification through amenorrhoea or anorexia" (1987: 156).

90. San-pao Li points out the common ground between notions of chastity in neo-Confucianism and Daoist concepts of chastity in the *Yi jing* (*I-ching*): "The family prospers, according to the *I-ching*, when 'the females of the family behave properly' (*nü-chen*). . . . Based on Ch'eng I's commentary on the *I-ching*, *chen* (chastity) is, in actuality, synonymous with *cheng* (orthodox)" (1993: 123).

91. Wile (1992: 193) suggests that what he calls women's sexual yoga manuals may actually have been developed in Buddhist convents. See Paul (1985: 170–211) for a discussion of notions of sexual transformation in medieval Buddhism. Seaman (1981: 385) explains the "five obstacles," physical defects that prevented women from being reincarnated as higher beings.

92. The *Avatamsaka sutra* (*Hua yan jing*) sets forth the "totality of the design of Buddhism" by describing the Samantabhadra bodhisattvas, the universally good enlightening beings who have achieved immortality but remain on earth. See Cleary 1989: 5.

93. Wile 1992: 211.

94. See Schipper 1993: 124–29. Joseph Needham's analysis of Daoist sexual techniques notes: "The recognition of the importance of women in the scheme of things, the acceptance of equality of women with men, the conviction that the attainment of health and longevity needed the cooperation of the sexes, the considered admiration for certain feminine psychological characteristics, . . . reveal to us once more aspects of Taoism which had no counterpart in Confucianism or ordinary Buddhism" (1956, 2: 151).

95. Despeux (1990: 149) dates a version of this text to the late eighteenth century. She notes that "the appearance in the Qing, beginning in the eighteenth century, of a literature specifically devoted to women's alchemy . . . represents a new development in the history of Daoism" (p. 11).

96. Wile 1992: 193.

97. Wile 1992: 209.

98. On "slaying the red dragon," see Despeux 1990: 242–68.

99. Another text describes a successful practitioner emerging with the body of a man, her breasts flat and her menstrual blood purged (Wile 1992: 204).

100. In one text every manifestation of Guanyin becomes a metaphor for part of the process of achieving a yang state after slaying the dragon (Wile 1992: 217).

101. Wile 1992: 218.

102. Cleary (1989) translates many early surviving poems about women's *nei dan* techniques, including verse by an adept of the late nineteenth century. In one of the poems attributed to her, the twelfth-century Daoist adept Sun Bu'er describes "slaying the dragon" (p. 31).

103. On Yu Xuanji, see S. E. Cahill 1993: 234–36; on Xue Tao, Nienhauser 1986: 438–39. Wanyan Yun Zhu, whose anthology of women's poetry contains no poems alluding to *nei dan*, herself took a Daoist name at the age of 50 *sui*. Her silence on this subject may be the result of self-censorship or even of state attempts to suppress women's *nei dan* texts; further research is clearly needed in this area. For example, as I completed this chapter I discovered that the noted scholar Sun Xingyan published an edition of the *nei dan* text *Su nü jing* (Classic of the plain woman), which served as the reference for the standard modern edition edited by Ye Dehui in 1904. See Li and McMahon 1992: 148. Perhaps because women's *nei dan* texts were considered so seditious, Sun's biography in *Eminent Chinese* observes that he was interested in ancient texts, but fails to mention this one (*EC* 676–77). Needham (1956: 147n*c*) recalls that during his travels in China he was told by a noted authority that about half the men and women in Sichuan regularly consulted these texts, which were readily available from peddlers.

104. *GGZJ* 8/22a.

105. See *GGZJ* 12/19b–20a, 13/14b–15a, 15/2a.

106. Werner [1922] 1986: 274–87. See also Levering 1982.

107. *GGZJ* 16/11a.

108. As I was completing the manuscript of this book, Beata Grant published her illuminating study of the works of a lay Buddhist poet named Tao Shan. See Grant 1994. Many of Tao Shan's poems are included in Yun Zhu's collection.

109. Xu Kuichen [1804] 1914: 3a. Stories about Lady Zhang's life are collected in Hu Wenkai [1957] 1985: 533; and *QGSZ*, "Bu yi" 3b–4a (pp. 628–29).

4. Writing

1. The poet as divine woman, site of passion and source of transcendence, is elegantly described in S. E. Cahill 1993 (quotation on p. 243).

2. Louise Edwards (1994), in her analysis of gender in the novel *Dream of the Red Chamber*, analyzes tensions in gender relations along slightly different, but equally provocative, lines. She focuses in particular on the destructive potential of maternal love. I did not read her book until this manuscript was nearly finished, but she stimulated much of my thinking about the power of the mother as moral instructress—the "kindly mother [who] is my teacher too" (see Chap. 6, "Work").

3. Abu-Lughod's (1986) brilliant analysis of Bedouin women's poems illuminates the creative and subversive power of the female voice in the patriarchal family.

4. See, for example, discussions later in this chapter of Jin Wengying's remarks about Miaolianbao, p. 97; Yuan Mei's comments on the pitiful Miss Lu, p. 114; and Yun Zhu's description of herself in the preface to her anthology, quoted on p. 117.

5. See Handlin 1975 and Ko 1994.

6. This account of Ban Zhao's life is based on the excellent study by Nancy Lee Swann (1932).

7. The standard work on the Four Books for Women is Yamazaki 1986.

8. Zhang Xuecheng was perhaps less appreciative than most when he suggested dismissively that the intelligence of the alleged author of the *Nü lunyu*, Song Ruohua, did not save her from "a certain dullness and vulgarity" even though "the general direction of her work was near to refinement and correctness." "When those of us in the literary world cite her writing," he added, "we all acknowledge that her aspirations were worthy of praise." In a footnote he remarked that since the ancient tradition of women's learning had long since

disappeared by Song Ruohua's time, "under the circumstances, the best we could expect from women with aspirations was this sort of work" (Zhang Xuecheng [n.d.] 1922: "Fu xue" 5/34b). Yun Zhu was more laudatory, including in her anthology a poem celebrating the five Song sisters (*GGZJ* 8/12a).

9. Also known as the Former Qin, one of the sixteen kingdoms created in successive invasions by Xiongnu and other nomadic peoples from the steppe between the years 304 and 439. The story of Lady Song appears in *Jin shu* 96/17b–18b.

10. Zhang Xuecheng [n.d.] 1922: "Fu xue" 5/33b.

11. For the original text in translation, see Liu I-ch'ing [c. 430] 1976: 64. The catkin as symbol of the young femme fatale of letters figures in women's poetry as early as the Tang. See, for example, the preface to a poem by the distinguished Yu Xuanji, one of Zhang Xuecheng's controversial Tang female poets, translated in S. E. Cahill 1993: 236.

12. See Chow 1994, esp. pp. 204–14. Chow does not allude to the revival of interest in women's erudition that I believe was an important counterpoint to the concern with chastity he associates with classical ritualism.

13. *JSWB* 67/16a–b.

14. Wang Zhong [1815] 1970: "Nei bian" 1/14a–15b.

15. See the detailed discussion in Chow 1994: 204–7.

16. *Analects* XVII.8. I have followed the translation by D. C. Lau 1982: 144. My thanks to Philip J. Ivanhoe for reminding me of this allusion.

17. Wang Zhong [1815] 1970: "Nei bian" 1/15b. Quoted in Hu Shi 1931b: 117; see also Chow 1986: 307. Waley (1956: 36–38) discusses this essay, since one of the cases Wang cites involves the tragic misalliance of Yuan's younger sister; see also Nivison 1966: 262nj.

18. See Mann 1992a, 1992b.

19. See the examples discussed later in this chapter, pp. 101–2. Benjamin Elman's study of classical learning in late imperial Changzhou identifies the term *jia xue* in two different contexts: it appears, he says, as a general term referring to a "school" of learning marking scholars who share a common philosophical orientation, master-disciple relations, native place, or other recognized affinity (Elman 1990: 2, 4); it may also be claimed by a particular family, as by the Zhuangs (pp. 100, 138, 199). As will be clear in what follows, when women are identified with a *jia xue*, it is always the *jia xue* of their natal line. This association is significant, I think, because it shows that where learning was associated with a family, it could only be passed through the male line, and yet daughters could convey the learning of their natal families to the males of another line by teaching their sons. In these cases, as in the case of Zhang Xuecheng, a man's learning would be transmitted by his mother to his own line from another line's *jia xue*. Elman recognizes the importance of learned daughters-in-law in the marriage strategies of his subjects (see pp. 57–58, 71), but he does not acknowledge their participation in the transmission of a specific *jia xue*.

20. See Zhang Xuecheng [n.d.] 1922: 5/33a.

21. His first historical examples of women's voice were the palace instructresses described in the *Li ji*: "Among the government officials of the Chou state were a female libationer (*nü zhu*) and a female historian (*nü shi*). The Han statutes required that 'Diaries of Work and Rest' be kept for the women's apartments as well as for the court. Thus we see that women's literary skills had a use in ancient times. The term 'women's learning' (*fu xue*) can be found in references to women's posts in the Ministry of State found in the *Zhou li*." Zhang Xuecheng [n.d.] 1922: "Fu xue" 5/30b.

22. Zhang Xuecheng [n.d.] 1922: "Fu xue" 5/30b–31a.

23. Zhang Xuecheng [n.d.] 1922: "Fu xue" 5/32b.
24. See Nivison 1966: 201–2.
25. See her biography by Zhu Yun [1815] 1936: 327–28.
26. Nivison 1966: 83.
27. Zhang Xuecheng [n.d.] 1922: 16/70a–b. Both Zhang's mother and Shao Jinhan's mother are discussed in Mann 1996.
28. Nivison 1966: 128–30.
29. Zhang Xuecheng [n.d.] 1922: "Fu xue" 5/34b.
30. Preface to *SNS*.
31. The ode is "Zhou nan" 1.
32. A line from another section of the songs of the states, the ninth ode of Bei.
33. The story was preserved for Yuan Mei to record years later as a preface to two of Sun Yunfeng's poems included in his *Poetry Talks*. See *SS* 2, no. 31, p. 45. A biography of Sun Yunfeng appears in *QGSZ* 6/9a–10a (pp. 325–27). For another example, see *SSB* 2, no. 61, pp. 615–16.
34. *SSB* 5, no. 5, p. 679.
35. *QGSZ* 9/3b–4a (pp. 514–15); see also Liang Yizhen [1925] 1968: 230–31.
36. *SS* 3, no. 17, p. 74.
37. Clara Lau Ho's detailed review of the range of this controversy came to my attention just as I was finishing this manuscript. See Ho 1995.
38. *SS* 3, no. 20, pp. 75–76.
39. In the fighting during the Manchu conquest of the south, Yun Shouping's two brothers were killed. His father, who joined the resistance, escaped capture. In 1648, after the fall of the city of Jiangning, where he had taken refuge, Shouping himself was taken captive by the Manchus and imprisoned. At the age of sixteen, he was ordered released by the wife of the Han Banner general Chen Jin (d. 1652), who wanted him to draw jewelry designs for her. She subsequently adopted him. Meanwhile, Yun Shouping's father managed by a ruse to reclaim his son, who eventually rejoined his natal family in Changzhou. See Tong 1989: 210. A slightly different account of these events can be found in Wakeman 1985, 2: 732, 749–54; see also *EC* 46, 960. Evelyn Rawski (personal communication, Dec. 7, 1992) points out that an adoptive tie with a Han Bannerman would have lent legitimacy to Yun Zhu's marriage to the Manchu Tinglu (1772–1820), who was a member of the Imperial Household Bondservant Division of the Bordered Yellow Banner. See *EC* 507. See also Rawski 1991: 175, on "political endogamy" under the Manchus. Marriage between Manchus and Han Chinese women (to be taken as wives, not as concubines) was briefly encouraged as part of the pacification effort between 1648 and 1655. See Rawski 1991: 181.
40. As the reader will have surmised, Wanyan is Yun Zhu's married name and Yun Zhu is her maiden name (surname Yun, given name Zhu). All Manchus inherited a traditional clan name, which, in the case of Yun Zhu's husband, was Wanyan. But Manchus did not use formal surnames, regarding the surname as a mark of Chinese ethnicity. In writing and in public communication, as Pamela Crossley has pointed out, Manchus favored personal names alone. Even members of the Chinese-martial banners omitted mention of their lineage names "as part of their cultural solidarity with the Manchus" (Crossley 1990: 38). For this reason, Wanyan Yun Zhu is often identified simply as Yun Zhu and her son as Linqing; I follow that practice here.
41. Linqing [1897] 1981: 148a/16.
42. Linqing [1897] 1981: 151b/4–5, 151b/13. Linqing's work covers the years 1806–43, from

the time he was seventeen *sui* until three years before his death. The 1897 text is the unillustrated version first printed between 1839 and 1841, according to Fang Zhaoying [Fang Chao-ying], whose elegant biography of Linqing appears in *EC* 506–7. Illustrations reproduced here are from the complete illustrated text of *Hongxue yinyuan tuji*, with a preface by Ruan Yuan, Taibei (n.d.).

43. Ellen Widmer (personal communication, March 1996) points out that this claim is probably disingenuous, since Yun Zhu herself actively collected and even purchased the poems she eventually anthologized.

44. *GGZJ*, preface, 2a.

45. Yilanbao edited chaps. 1, 4, 7, 10, 13, 16, and 19; Jinsubao, chaps. 2, 5, 8, 11, 14, 17, and 20; and Miaolianbao, chaps. 3, 6, 9, 12, 15, and 18.

46. *GGZX*, second preface, 1b–2a.

47. Whether Yun Zhu's interest in women's learning and the erudition of the women in her family was influenced by Manchu culture is still an open question. Crossley notes that among the Manchu elite, female education was "not new or unusual" in the nineteenth century (1990: 155). She also points out that Manchu families were leaders in the movement to promote women's education in Hangzhou during the late Qing reform era (p. 195).

48. Yun Zhu wrote such remarks as prefaces to poems in her collection. On a poem by a woman from a tribal area, see *GGZJ* 5/3b; on the commoner poet from Yunnan, see 8/22b; on the chaste-widow poet from the borders of Guangxi, 10/21b; on Hami, Gansu, see 17/1a; on the Hunan border with the Miao tribal lands, see 17/21b.

49. *GGZJ*, "Li yan" 4b.

50. *GGZJ*, "Li yan" 5a. The women mentioned in the last paragraph are famous as lovers, not as wives. On Liu Shi (Liu Rushi), see Chang 1991 and Ko 1994.

51. For example, see *GGZJ* 10/5a.

52. To my knowledge, only Wang Zhaoyuan produced a noted work of philology in the Han learning tradition: appropriately enough, it was an annotated edition of Liu Xiang's *Lienü zhuan*. See Zurndorfer 1992 and literature cited therein.

53. My analysis of Hu Wenkai's survey of women writers ([1957] 1985) shows that of 3,556 women writers of the Qing period whose work he was able to locate, only 50 are known to have written in genres other than poetry.

54. *GGZJ* 16/9b.

55. *GGZJ* 9/14b–15a. The phrase "dashed off" (*ou cheng*) conveys an air of casual spontaneity, as if the poem had been composed by accident.

56. *GGZS* 8/8a.

57. *GGZJ* 9/1a, 9/5b, 16/14b.

58. *GGZJ* 2/19a.

59. *QGSZ* 5/14b (p. 288); *GGZJ* 11/19.

60. See the case of Wu Si, the only child of a provincial naval commander in Fujian, in *GGZJ* 5/18a–b.

61. *GGZJ* 7/12b–13a. Wen Pu's father was a low-ranking bureaucrat (with the title Storehouse Commissioner) who was perhaps overly eager that his offspring achieve greatness. His peculiar ambition for his scholarly daughter, however, is the only example of its kind that I have seen. The person challenging him mentions Ban Zhao for obvious reasons; Huang Chonggu was a gifted only child—poet, calligrapher, painter, and musician—who lived during the early third century (the Former Shu state). When the state fell, she went into hiding disguised as a man and was later arrested but released when she won the favor of the new prime minister by presenting him with a brilliant poem. Summoned to serve as an official, she was offered the hand of the prime minister's daughter. Her story thus

supplies the trope for a famous contemporary *tanci* (a story told to the accompaniment of stringed instruments), "Zai sheng yuan," and other stories about the romantic adventures of gifted girls who rise to high office disguised as men. Yun Zhu's comments on other cases of poet-daughters who remain unwed to serve sonless parents do not elaborate on the circumstances. See *GGZJ* 16/9a, 20/9b.

62. *GGZJ* 7/13a–b. For help with this beautiful and difficult poem, I am grateful to Stephen West. He comments that this poem may encode Wen Pu's deep resentment that her scholarly work cannot develop further. Her studies are blocked, and her poems—like the lost goose—are mere fragments that will be lost forever. (The phrase *duan hong*—a wild goose cut off from the flock—also refers to odd poems or fragments of poems not included in anthologies.)

63. Personal communication, March 28, 1995.

64. See Edwards 1994 for an analysis of how writing confuses gender roles in *Dream of the Red Chamber.*

65. Yun Zhu's anthology is full of allusions to the willow catkin. See, e.g., *GGZJ* 5/20b, 9/9a, 10/13b, 12/4b, 15/12a, 15/21a, 17/4b.

66. Xu Shichang 1929: 187/31b.

67. See, e.g., the case of Wang Liang of Xiuning, Anhui, whose father was a well-known poet and painter (*GGZJ* 9/14a); and that of Wang Yunhui of Lou county, Jiangsu, who carried on her father's talent in poetry (*GGZJ* 18/5a).

68. See *QGSZ* 4/1b (p. 198). The poet's meaning here is that one should adhere closely to pre-Song (Confucian) models.

69. See *GGZJ* 9/5b; see also *EC* 544–45. *Jia xue* need not refer to a recognized person or school. Cao, for example, was the middle of three accomplished daughters; her father, whose name is unknown, was a Shanghai scholar of modest means. See *QGSZ* 4/1b (p. 198).

70. *GGZJ* 15/6b.

71. Perhaps the earliest use is in *Jin shu* 5: 55/1, 497–98.

72. Edwards 1994: 113–29.

73. For details of Bi's life, see *EC* 622–25.

74. The term *jing xun* might also be read as "classics and instructions," implying both textual learning in classical studies and moral instruction, both scholarly erudition and moral worth. Bi Yuan used this phrase when he named the studio in which he edited one of his most distinguished works—a compendium of ancient texts collated and edited with meticulous care by Sun Xingyan, Hong Liangji, and other leading experts of the time—which was compiled in the years following his mother's death. See *EC* 624.

75. Poems by Zhang Zao are introduced with a detailed preface by Yun Zhu in *GGZJ* 8/1a–3b. See also *QGSZ* 3/15a (p. 175). For the poem here, see *GGZJ* 8/1b–2b; quotations on pp. 2a–b.

76. It is probably no accident that evidence of Bi Yuan's corruption was made public only after the Qianlong emperor's death in 1799, given their close personal relationship and the emperor's obvious admiration for this personal favorite. For a discussion of contemporaries' ambivalent views of Bi Yuan, see Jones 1972: 77–78, 143n1. Bi's worst political errors occurred during his term as governor-general of Hubei and Hunan, when he failed to supervise and curb the corruption of high-ranking provincial officials in Hubei. One of his greatest admirers, Hong Liangji, considered him a model of Confucian ethical integrity but a weak politician, because he was so gullible (Jones 1972: 97).

77. *GGZJ* 8/10a.

78. *GGZJ* 3/12a–b. See also an excerpt from a letter from Jiang Lan to her husband, quoted on pp. 123–24. The tone of the letter suggests that this poem too may be sarcastic.

79. Like Yun Zhu, Zhang Xuecheng quoted from Jiang Lan's work to dramatize the wife's moral qualities and to criticize her husband; see p. 123.

80. Xie Daocheng, *jinshi* of 1661, was a native of Min county, the seat of Fuzhou prefecture. A member of the Hanlin academy, he rose to the position of grand secretary under the Kangxi emperor.

81. Zhang Yingchang [1869] 1983, 2: 803–4. Jiang Lan's husband would commonly be described by modern writers as "hen-pecked," Xie Daocheng's mother as "wise." Poetry helps us see that the woman's voice is the same moral voice; men's reaction shades its meaning.

82. *GGZJ* 18/14b–15a. Liu Wanhuai is referred to here by her *zi*, Zhuanfang. See also *GGZJ* 15/6a.

83. *GGZJ* 12/3b.

84. See *QGSZ* 4/21b (p. 238); see also *GGZJ* 13/13b–14a.

85. *GGZJ* 15/1a–2a. The poet, recalling her father's words, tells the girls clearly that their talent must have its own sphere.

86. *GGZJ* 15/6b.

87. *GGZJ* 19/4b; see also 8/20b–21a.

88. *SNS* 5/22a; see also Xi Peilan's lament for her son, 1/6b–8a.

89. *GGZJ* 7/4a, 11/3a–4a. For biographical notes on Qian Mengdian, see *QGSZ* 5/14a–16a (pp. 287–91). Herself the center of a circle of women "poet friends" (*shi you*), Qian had a daughter-in-law who was also a poet.

90. *GGZJ* 10/6b. Another of her elder sisters was the poet Hu Shenyi, who lost both her husband and her son while she was still very young and supported herself as a teacher for more than 40 years. Many of Shenyi's more than twenty female pupils became well-known poets themselves (*GGZJ* 10/5a).

91. See, for example, *GGZXB* 59a–60a, 60b–61a.

92. *GGZJ* 11/21a.

93. *GGZJ* 18/12b–13a.

94. *GGZJ* 10/14b–15a.

95. See Waltner 1987.

96. *SS* 2, no. 53, p. 54.

97. See *GGZJ* 2/4a–b, 12/8a, 18/22a. Recall that these are the same young women condemned by Wang Zhong for "misreading" the classics. In other words, misreadings—from a young woman's point of view—may have had a practical purpose.

98. *SSB* 8, no. 65, p. 789.

99. *QGSZ* 6/4b (p. 316).

100. So did the husband of Xue Qiong; see *GGZJ* 8/4b.

101. *GGZJ* 19/1a; see also 6/13b, 9/3a.

102. See, e.g., *SSB* 8, no. 11, p. 767.

103. The source of this version of the story is *GGZJ* 12/12a. Yuan Mei has the same story in his *Suiyuan shi hua*, but the differences in the telling are interesting. Yuan cannot recall the name of the woman; Yun Zhu gives it in full, along with her courtesy name and her literary name. She also makes her female subject speak in literary Chinese, replacing the flip, slangy tone so clear in Yuan Mei's reading with a humble suggestion (albeit offered with a smile). The husband in Yuan Mei's story emits a guffaw; in Yun Zhu's, he makes no response. See *SSB* 6, no. 3, p. 712. See also Yuan Mei's account of a brother who plagiarized his sister's work (*SS* 2, no. 46, pp. 50–51).

104. Quoted in *QGSZ* 9/3b–4a (pp. 514–15).

105. *GGZJ* 16/10a–b.

106. Poem by Zhai Jingyi, in Xu Kuichen [1804] 1914, 8: 4/2a.

107. *GGZJ* 13/2b–3a.

108. These long poems, revered for centuries, have been translated by Hawkes 1959. They are tragic because of their association with the life of the poet Qu Yuan, who committed suicide in despair after being banished by the ruler to whom he was devoted. See also L. A. Schneider 1980. To a young woman, the *Chu ci* would have been emblems of separation, loneliness, and longing for an unreachable beloved.

109. See *SS* 3, no. 5, pp. 69–70.

110. *SSB* 4, no. 52, pp. 669–70. Though he rarely mentions it, we know that Yuan Mei was well acquainted with the dark side of learned women's experience. See Waley 1956: 36–37 for an account of the tragic ruin of Yuan's talented sister Suwen as a result of an arranged marriage. Another gifted sister, who died in childbirth, left poems betraying her loneliness (*SSB* 9, no. 55, p. 813). Finally, the mother-in-law of his aunt, who served several wealthy families as a governess, once witnessed the murder by poison of two of her talented charges (*SS* 1, no. 53, p. 24).

111. *SS* 2, no. 67, p. 60.

112. Ye Shi, "Xie mu," *GGZX* 3/6a.

113. *GGZJ* 17/17b.

114. *GGZJ*, first preface, 1b.

115. Zhu Yun (1729–81), "Funeral Ode for the Mother of Zhang Xuecheng, Goodwife Shi," in Zhu Yun [1815] 1936: 327–28.

116. See Zhu Yun [1815] 1936: 327.

117. See Edwards 1994: 113–29, where she analyzes *Dream of the Red Chamber* as a discourse on maternal value that "perpetuate[s] and . . . generate[s] this distrust of women in power."

118. See Woloch 1984: chap. 3.

5. Entertainment

1. Kang-i Sun Chang 1991; Ko 1994.

2. This chapter is based on these seven primary sources, all accounts of the pleasure quarters of the Lower Yangzi region written between 1784 and 1841. In endnotes, I cite them by city and year of publication as follows (in chronological order): Nanjing 1784, Nanjing 1787, Suzhou 1803, Suzhou 1813, Nanjing 1817, Nanjing 1818, and Ningbo 1841. Full citations appear in the References. All are listed in the chronology of the women's movement in China reprinted in Zhang and Li 1975: 1,516–18. All were reprinted in *Xiangyan congshu* 1914. The seven works actually belong to two distinct eras in the history of Chinese prostitution. The first six fall properly in the period of my study, the High Qing, but the last, both in style and in content, is clearly the product of an emerging political economy of war in which courtesans served military men at the seaports where they congregated.

3. See Chang 1992 and Ko 1994. Since the time of the great Tang courtesan poet Xue Tao, a euphemism for an elite courtesan was *jiao shu* ("collator of books"); the extraordinary erudition of the medieval courtesan was recognized even by Zhang Xuecheng [n.d.] 1922: 5/35a–b.

4. See Chap. 4, p. 98, and Chang 1992: 145–46. Chang remarks that "by the middle Ch'ing, courtesans were no longer prominent in the world of refined letters and seldom published their poems," a stark contrast to the early seventeenth-century courtesans "who so often provided the popular model of the 'talented woman' " (p. 146). See also pp. 128–

33, where Chang identifies a shift in attitudes toward courtesan poets between late Ming and early Qing times. Wang Duanshu's anthology of women's poetry, printed in 1667, arranged the poems in order of the status of the poets, grouping gentry women in the category "proper" (*zheng*) and courtesans in the category "erotic" (*yan*) (Chang 1992: 137). An anthology of Ming poetry published in 1705 also carefully distinguished gentry women's poems from those of courtesans, in a clear departure from the practice in late Ming times. Chang observes that such practices, which marginalized courtesan poets, contributed to a "misreading" of the work of noted Ming poets in Qing times (p. 133).

5. See Chang 1992 and Ko 1994.

6. Zhang Xuecheng [n.d.] 1922: 30/109a–110a. See also Jiang Lan's poem exhorting her husband to study (translated from Yun Zhu's anthology) in Chap. 4, "Writing," pp. 103–4.

7. Suzhou 1803: 3/7b–8b.

8. See Ningbo 1841. It is not possible to pinpoint the precise moment when the High Qing years ended and the prelude to the Opium War began. High Qing courtesans filled their clients' pipes, perhaps with opium (Nanjing 1818: 1/25a); see also Wang Shunu [1933] 1988: 274. One recent study of courtesan culture has argued that Qing pleasure quarters never fully regained the heights of courtesan culture achieved in the Ming, partly because they were more dispersed, but mainly because of government repression. See Yan 1992: 125–26. Yan's view differs sharply from that of Wang Shunu, on whose work he may have relied but whom he does not cite.

9. Hucker 1985: no. 728.

10. Wang Shunu [1933] 1988: 261. See Fig. 2.

11. Zhong Qi [1897] 1970, 3: 1,331–32 (in original edition, 38/3a–b).

12. Hucker 1985: nos. 2183, 8269, 5173. Note that Hucker's account here is contradictory, sometimes stating that the new Board of Music was independent, other times placing the two new offices under the Board of Rites. On the origins of the Qing Yue bu, see *Qinding Da Qing huidian shi li* (Jiaqing ed.), 410/1–3a (8,483–87). In 1651 the Shunzhi emperor decreed that women from the Jiaofang si were no longer permitted to enter the palace in their official roles. Instead, 48 eunuchs would take their place. See *Qinding Da Qing huidian shi li* (Jiaqing ed.), 410/2a (8,485).

In 1723 the Yongzheng emperor commanded that others talented in music besides the people registered as *yuehu* take up positions in the Jiaofang si; six years later he changed the Jiaofang si to Hesheng shu (Office of Harmonious Sounds). See *Qinding Da Qing huidian shi li* (Jiaqing ed.), 410/2b (8,486). In 1742, the Qianlong emperor established the Yue bu. See *Qinding Da Qing huidian shi li* (Jiaqing ed.) 410/3a (8,487). Its charge was three areas: music for official sacrifices, which fell under the jurisdiction of officials in the Court of Imperial Sacrifices (Taichang si) and the Imperial Music Office (Shenyue guan); music for banquets and court audiences (*chao hui*), presided over by the Master of Ceremonies of the Office of Harmonious Sounds (Hesheng shu); and music required by the Imperial Procession Guard (Luanyi wei).

13. Yan 1992: 130–34.

14. Yu Huai [1697] 1966.

15. High Qing writers often compared courtesans of their acquaintance to a late Ming predecessor. See, for example, Nanjing 1817: 3/17b–18a, where the Master Who Offers a Flower likens the Nanjing courtesan Hu Baozhu to Li Shixiang, one of the *ming ji* celebrated by Yu Huai.

16. Here are some of the things the caterer would bring on board to prepare one's meal

al fresco: "basins and bowls, knives and chopping boards, vinegar gourds, ladles, cruets, soysauce pots, utensils, and all the other 'lovely little pieces'; slaughtered game birds and animals, and fruits, peppery pickles, salted black beans, scallions and shallots" to stuff the fowl and flavor the meats (Nanjing 1818: 1/25a).

17. Nanjing 1818: 1/25b–26a.

18. According to Clunas (1991: 118), a courtesan could cost 1,000 ounces of silver—at least, that's what Gong Dingzi paid for Gu Mei.

19. Nanjing 1818: 1/26a.

20. Suzhou 1803: 3/7b.

21. See Nanjing 1817: 3/15b. Suzanne Cahill (1993: 238) notes that "smashing the gourd" is a visual pun on the Chinese character for gourd, which, broken in half, looks like the number eight written twice. According to a folk etymology, twice eight is sixteen, the age (in Chinese years, *sui*) of sexual maturity and a euphemism for the first sexual intercourse. See also the note in Edwards 1994: 110–11.

22. Nanjing 1818: 1/26a; see also the description, translated from a late-nineteenth-century novel, in Byron 1987: 57.

23. See Clunas 1991 on this separation and taboo. Clunas cites the Ming connoisseur Wen Zhenheng, noting that Wen was anxious lest men appropriate or mistakenly use things that by decoration, design, or custom, were properly women's (pp. 54–56).

24. Clunas 1991: 43. Parrots, in fact, were ironic emblems in a courtesan's boudoir. The chatty parrot was thought capable of informing on a wayward wife; hence the presence of a parrot signified chastity.

25. See Li Dou's comments on the distinction between two types of clients at the pleasure boats: the *guan ke* (male) and the *tang ke* (female) ([1794–97] 1984: 241); see also Nanjing 1818: 1/25a–26b.

26. Nanjing 1787: 2/3a.

27. Nanjing 1787: 2/2b.

28. See Peterson 1979: 141; see also Yu Huai [1697] 1966: 78.

29. Nanjing 1787: 2/2a.

30. Ningbo 1841: 3/31a.

31. Nanjing 1817: 3/26b.

32. Wang Shunu ([1933] 1988: 253–57) has shown that syphilis was widespread in China by late Ming times and "rampant" (p. 255) as early as the sixteenth century. He relies on the authoritative account published in 1632. Howard Levy (1966b: 4) notes that Yu Huai did not mention venereal disease.

33. Nanjing 1817: 3/11b–12a.

34. Nanjing 1787: 2/2a–b.

35. Nanjing 1787: 2/2b.

36. Nanjing 1784: 1/8a.

37. Nanjing 1787: 2/4b. See also the story of Tang Qiushui, who was originally the wife of a person also surnamed Tang. After a career as a successful courtesan, she once again left the brothel, became a waitress, and married a merchant. See Nanjing 1817: 3/28a.

38. See Nanjing 1817: 3/29a–b.

39. Zhang Xiaoyun was the niece of Shao Suyun (a note explains that Zhang Xiaoyun's original surname was Shao). See Suzhou 1813: 3/34a, 32a.

40. The text says: "Fanglan was ranked second. She came from Beicang Bridge and was married into the Dan family" (*Fanglan hang er, yi zhi Beicangqiao ren, jia yu Dan shi*). See Nanjing 1817: 3/24a–b.

41. Nanjing 1817: 3/25a–b, 23a.

42. Suzhou 1813: 3/23b.
43. Cited in Wang Shunu [1933] 1988: 267.
44. Cited in Wang Shunu [1933] 1988: 267.
45. See, e.g., the story of the Nanjing courtesan Wenxin, who came originally from a respectable family (*liangjia*), in Nanjing 1817: 3/15b.
46. See Nanjing 1817: 3/24b.
47. Nanjing 1817: 3/26a.
48. Nanjing 1817: 3/25a.
49. Nanjing 1817: 3/15a.
50. Nanjing 1817: 3/18a.
51. Nanjing 1817: 3/20a.
52. Nanjing 1817: 3/14b.
53. Nanjing 1817: 3/21a–b.
54. Suzhou 1813: 3/24a.
55. Nanjing 1817: 3/21a.
56. Such adoptive families have been described in detail by Hershatter and others studying more abundant sources from the modern period (Hershatter 1989: 479–80; Hershatter 1991: 269–70). Wolfe (1980: 77–78 *et passim*) challenges the assumption that most prostitutes were "adopted daughters." Hershatter (1992) stresses the continuing family ties that bound prostitutes to parents, children, and in-laws in twentieth-century Shanghai. For similar organizations among the geisha of Tokugawa Japan, see Dalby 1983: 4–5.
57. See Nanjing 1817: 3/27a. Note that this may be a misprint for Yang Fuling (18b–19a); it is less likely that the given name is accurate and refers to a courtesan with a different surname, Ji Zhaoling (11a).
58. See Suzhou 1803: 3/15b.
59. See the case of Fang Youlan in Suzhou 1813: 3/25b, 27a.
60. Suzhou 1813: 3/33b–34a.
61. For Xu Suqin, see Suzhou 1803: 3/11a; for Xu Xiao'e, see Suzhou 1813: 3/24b. For another example, see the Shi sisters in Nanjing 1817: 3/25a.
62. See the example in Nanjing 1817: 3/30a.
63. See Suzhou 1813: 3/24a; see also 23a, 24b.
64. The only case I have found concerns Zhao Aizhu, who was concubine to the courtesan Zhao Tonghua. Aizhu's original surname was Wang; she took Tonghua's surname at the time she entered into the relationship. See Nanjing 1817: 3/21b. The meaning of such a relationship, unfortunately, is left to our imagination. If lesbian couples formed within the brothels, male writers were not in a position to comment. We are told only that Zhao Tonghua herself had two daughters who also became courtesans (28b).
65. Nanjing 1817: 3/25a.
66. Nanjing 1817: 3/15b.
67. See Suzhou 1803: 3/18a.
68. For examples, see Nanjing 1784: 1/8a–9b.
69. See also Dalby 1983: 4.
70. Suzhou 1813: 3/27a.
71. Suzhou 1813: 3/23b.
72. Suzhou 1813: 3/22a, 34a.
73. See the account of Qian Qiuting and her younger sister Qian Suyue in Suzhou 1813: 3/24a, 23a. For another set of sisters with the "same mother," see Zhou Xiaolian, rank seven, and her two elder sisters, ranks six and five. See Suzhou 1813: 3/24b.
74. The brothel itself where women lived together was sometimes called a *yuan* (court or garden). See Suzhou 1803: 3/10b.
75. See the story of Lu Shunqing and Zhao Yaojuan, in Suzhou 1803: 3/11a; Suzhou 1813: 3/25b.
76. For example, Tian Wanlan lived in the residence formerly occupied by Zhang Qingyun. See Suzhou 1813: 3/26b; Suzhou 1803: 3/16b. Cui Xiuying's successor, Cui Xiaoying,

took up residence in the Hall of Green Clouds. See Suzhou 1813: 3/32a. Chen Shuqin occupied the former residence of Ma Rulan. See Suzhou 1813: 3/35a.

77. Suzhou 1813: 3/25a; see also Suzhou 1803: 3/7a, 17b, 18b.

78. Suzhou 1813: 3/32b–33a.

79. Suzhou 1803: 3/8a.

80. Suzhou 1803: 3/8a–b.

81. Zhao Fu's own daughter subsequently became a courtesan. See Nanjing 1817: 3/22a–b.

82. See Nanjing 1817: 3/19a.

83. Nanjing 1787: 2/3b.

84. See Chang 1991, Ko 1994, and Yan 1992: 126–29.

6. Work

1. The arguments of this chapter were inspired by the work of Nancy Folbre and other scholars whose analyses of the modern welfare state have demonstrated that government policies regulating labor markets also shape gender relations. As historians of Europe have shown, the labor policies of preindustrial states informed gender relations in the same way, even though the power of preindustrial governments was less pervasive and coercive. Merry Wiesner's analysis of guild efforts to take over various stages of production from women in German towns shows that women were gradually excluded from most weavers', drapers', tailors', and cloth cutters' guilds in most cities beginning in the late medieval period (1986: 172–85). Jean Quataert's 1985 study of Prussian rule in early nineteenth-century Saxony reveals how the Prussian government confronted that city's craft guilds as members attempted to maintain their monopolies in the tailoring industry, opening up new markets for women's labor both inside and outside the home.

2. *Huangchao zhengdian leizuan* [1903] 1969: 23/5a–b (2: 747–48), reprinting a memorial by Yin Yuanfou, vice minister of the Board of Public Works, dated 1730.

3. Ebrey devotes a chapter to documenting the introduction of cotton spinning and weaving in Lower Yangzi households and exploring the implications of these economic changes for women in the family (1993: 131–51). The reader will find that Qing writers shared and probably imitated many of the moral presumptions of Song officials and literati.

4. On hereditary artisans in the Ming, see Xu and Wu 1985: 112–15. The early Ming state-sponsored system (*guan shougongye*) was developed at a time when the government assumed that the agrarian economy was a stable, fixed economy in which each peasant household would meet its own needs for food and clothing. In such a world, specialized artisans were required only to supply the consumption needs of the official elite. These craftsmen—who produced ceremonial garments, ritual vessels, army uniforms, weapons, pottery and utensils, ships and transport vehicles, and so forth—were registered as a hereditary class in a special section of the Ming population records (Xu and Wu 1985: 112–13). In 1393, registered artisans and their dependent workers comprised an estimated 3 percent of the population (p. 115).

5. Similar towns grew in Shanxi, Sichuan, and Fujian. See Xu and Wu 1985: 124.

6. Xu and Wu 1985: chap. 2 and pp. 127–28.

7. Xu and Wu 1985: 116–18.

8. Xu and Wu 1985: 313.

9. Between the Song and the Ming periods, the real price of silk in Jiangnan fell by nearly 60 percent. See Xu and Wu 1985: 124–25.

10. Xu and Wu 1985: 129.

11. Peng Zeyi 1984: 391.

12. See Tsing Yuan 1979.

13. *Da Qing Shizong Xianhuangdi shilu* 57: 2–3, cited in Peng 1984: 419.

14. This saying from the Early Han period (perhaps two centuries B.C.E.) is quoted in the oft-reprinted Ming dynasty agricultural handbook, *Nongzheng quanshu*; see Xu Guang-qi [1639] 1900: 7/40a. The translation here is from Lien-sheng Yang 1952: 101. The implication of one version of this text is that women who abandon their spindles and looms turn to singing and dancing, i.e., prostitution.

15. An essay written in 1776 by Gao Jin takes officials to task for their refusal to struggle against this aspect of peasant mentality. See *JSWB* 37/6a.

16. A folksong heard on the streets of Beijing (then Beiping) in the 1930's dramatizes the town dweller's dependency on the market: "When the door is opened every day, seven things are necessary: Coal, rice, oil, tea, soy sauce, vinegar, and salt" (K. Johnson [1932] 1971: 32).

17. Philip Kuhn's 1990 study of the queue-cutting scare in the Jiangnan area during the 1740's emphasizes the effect of these anxieties on popular perceptions of wandering monks and vagrants (see esp. pp. 105–18).

18. Zhang Ying (1637–1708), "Heng chan suo yan" (Remarks on real estate), in *JSWB* 36/46b. The complete essay is translated in Beattie 1979: 140–51; see p. 150 for this excerpt, slightly adapted.

19. *Guliang zhuan* 4/7b (fourteenth year of Duke Huan, eighth month).

20. The description that follows is drawn from E. Williams 1935; cf. Kuhn 1988: 265–72.

21. Discussions of the importance of moral education (*jiaohua*) appear throughout the *JSWB*, but see especially 54/20a–b. The program for moral education exalted the farm community, exhorted farmers to be frugal, and deplored decadence and idleness by promoting work and proper ritual practice in rural families. Though the targets of some of these discussions were clearly members of the elite, writers in the *Collected Essays on Statecraft* spoke eagerly of extending the rites into commoner households (lit., "into the neighborhoods"); see *JSWB* 54/24a–b.

22. These were first developed under the Song to promote sericulture. See Xu and Wu 1985: 123. High Qing proposals to "teach" sericulture or weaving through extension stations appear in *Huangchao zhengdian leizuan* [1903] 1969: 24/4b, 6b (2: 764, 766).

23. L. M. Li 1981: figs. 1–4. Sun (1972: 82) refers to the *Shou shi tong kao*, published early in the Qianlong period, which devoted one of its eight sections to instructions for cultivating mulberry trees and raising silkworms. *Tiangong kaiwu*, published in 1637, also provides detailed illustrations of the gender division of labor in sericulture. See Sung Ying-hsing [1637] 1966: 36–59.

24. Rich materials on household handicrafts appear in *JSWB* in its three chapters (36–38) on agricultural policy ("Nong zheng"). More than half of the 49 essays in these chapters refer to home weaving, and one entire chapter containing 19 essays (*juan* 37) focuses exclusively on cotton and silk home handicraft industries.

25. *JSWB* 28/16–18.

26. *JSWB* 28/12–15. Two of Chen's memorials promoting sericulture in Shaanxi, dated

1751 and 1757, respectively, are reprinted in *Huangchao zhengdian leizuan* [1903] 1969: 24/4b–5b (2: 764–66). The second emphasizes that all members of a peasant household—"male and female, young and old"—can contribute to the enterprise of silkworm rearing and silk weaving (24/5b).

27. *JSWB* 37/1a.

28. See *JSWB* 37/3–4, "Teaching Sericulture."

29. *JSWB* 37/3b. See also memorials by Chen Hongmou advocating the promotion of sericulture in Shaanxi province, in *JSWB* 37/8–13.

30. *GGZJ* 5/11a.

31. *GGZJ* 5/17a.

32. *GGZJ* 17/17a.

33. On Ming cotton production, see Xu Xinwu 1981: 34 *et passim*.

34. Dietrich 1972: 111.

35. Fang [1809] 1988: "Fan li" 1b.

36. See Dietrich 1972, where some of Fang's illustrations of cotton cultivation and manufacturing are reproduced in an English-language book.

37. See Dietrich 1972: 113–26.

38. Dietrich 1972: 127.

39. Dietrich 1972: 127, citing Amano Motonosuke, "Nō sō shū yō to monsaku no tenkai" (The "Summary of agriculture and sericulture" and the development of cotton culture), *Tōyō gakuhō* 37 (Sept. 1954): 78.

40. See L. M. Li 1981: 50–54.

41. L. M. Li 1981: 49–50. On guilds and strikes in the Suzhou textile industry, see Santangelo 1993: 90–116.

42. See Guo Qiyuan's essay "Bu bo ying shu shuo" (Cotton versus silk: shrinking profits), in *JSWB* 37/5a.

43. *JSWB* 37/6–7. Gao pointed out that successful cotton cultivation threatened household self-sufficiency by reducing the land available for grain production. By his estimate, no more than 20 or 30 percent of Jiangnan peasants grew rice; the rest grew cotton. Asked why, peasants explained that cotton was cheaper to plant and more profitable to sell than rice, owing to the high labor costs of rice growing (*JSWB* 37/6a).

44. *JSWB* 37/7a–b.

45. Japanese scholars have been particularly interested in demonstrating the viability of household industry in late imperial China. See essays by Nishijima Sadao and Tanaka Masatoshi, translated in Grove and Daniels 1984: 17–100.

46. See Scott 1986: 1,069, where she observes that "concepts of power, though they may build on gender, are not always literally about gender itself. . . . Established as an objective set of references, concepts of gender structure perception and the concrete and symbolic organization of all social life. To the extent that these references establish distributions of power (differential control over or access to material and symbolic resources), gender becomes implicated in the conception and construction of power itself."

47. See Herlihy 1990.

48. See Quataert 1985: 1,127–29 for a discussion of the superiority of wool to linen in Prussian weaving trades. To my knowledge, cotton weaving in China was not considered unclean or polluting, though in other respects the relative status of wool over linen and silk over cotton is strikingly similar in these two societies. On hierarchies of value in the cloth industries of India, see also Bayly 1988. In Tokugawa Japan, silk and cotton weav-

ing were also expressions of class: "The peasant wives and daughters spun cotton and the samurai women silk" (Hirschmeier 1964: 302n13).

49. See Stockard 1989: 141–51. On pollution, see pp. 249–50n81.

50. See documents quoted in Xu Xinwu 1981: 41–42.

51. Class hierarchies were apparent even in a survey of farm and nonfarm labor in the 1930's. Among tenant farm families, for example, the survey found no men working in government jobs and no women doing embroidery. Informants explained that tenant farmers could not get government jobs because they were illiterate; women in tenant households could not embroider because "this kind of manual art is not something that all women can be versed in" (*cizhong shouyi fei yiban funü zhi suo shanchang*). See Feng Hefa 1933, 1: 300–301. Similar associations appear in other cultures where women's embroidery is a mark of high status, as Jane Schneider's research on embroidery in Sicily shows (1985: 86–92). Schneider identifies a relationship between textile arts and the seclusion of women (pp. 92–99). As machine-made cloth replaced homespun and woven cloth, women turned to new needle arts, especially embroidery and lace making, which they applied to the new commercial cloth. Embroidery was "purer" than weaving and spinning because formerly spinners and weavers had gone into the fields to help cultivate and harvest fiber crops, and that brought them into contact with men. See also Wheeler (1921: 35) for a discussion of the status of embroidery in New England: "The possession of a good piece of old crewel work, done in the country, is as strong a proof of respectable ancestry as a patent of nobility, since no one in the busy early colonial days had time for such work save those whose abundant leisure was secured by ample means and liberal surroundings."

52. See Garrett 1987: 76–78. As she puts it: "By the middle of the [Qing] dynasty embroidery was an industry in its own right, with men, women and children engaged in its manufacture. Ladies in well-to-do households learnt to do embroidery as a feminine accomplishment, but such households would employ an embroiderer to produce the many articles they required. The task was left to the wives and daughters of tradesmen and artisans who learnt to embroider as a means of contributing to the family income. Almost every garment worn by a middle- and upper-class Chinese would be embellished with embroidery. There were the official robes and the badges of rank worn by the mandarins and their wives, jackets and skirts for women, clothing for children, headwear for adults and children, purses for a variety of uses, shoes, and all the necessary soft furnishings for middle- and upper-class homes" (p. 77).

53. Schneider (1985: 98–99), commenting on the association between purity and textiles in Christian traditions, notes that the term "spinster" reflected the relationship between virginity and "industrious dedication to spinning, weaving, and embroidery." In Christianity, devotion to weaving might even require postponing marriage (as in the story of Saint Agatha, who refused to marry, despite her father's insistence, until she finished weaving a certain piece of cloth). I know of no comparable story in China. In Sicily, embroidery was mainly for virgins: before marriage a young girl worked exclusively on her trousseau, whereas "after marriage she did little if any embroidery, except for the layettes and baptismal dresses of newborn children and, when time permitted, occasional pieces for girls" (p. 99).

54. Gulik (1961: 318) finds the phrase (lit., "to love shame") commonly used in Qing erotic prose and poetry. Ko (1994: 172–76) discusses embroidery at some length, but does not allude to these sensual meanings.

55. The patron deity of sericulture is the Lady of Xiling (Xiling shi), consort of the

Yellow Emperor. Under his reign in the mid-third century B.C.E., the annual festivals celebrating agriculture and sericulture began: "The reigning emperor ploughed a furrow, and the empress made an offering, at the altar of her deified predecessor, of cocoons and mulberry leaves" (C. A. S. Williams 1976: 359–60). The counterpart of the empress in popular culture was the celestial Weaving Maid, patroness of embroidery.

56. One version of this story appears in Meng 1989: 52. See also Dietrich 1972: 112; Ebrey 1993: 138; and Kuhn 1988: 212, 266.

57. Peng Zeyi 1984: 223–24.

58. Xu Xinwu 1981: 17.

59. *JSWB* 37/17a.

60. Xu Xinwu 1981: 22.

61. *JSWB* 37/26–32a contains three essays that Song Rulin composed around 1825; all describe his efforts to introduce Shandong sericulture to the Upper Yangzi region. Chen Hongmou wrote essays explaining in detail his program to import southern weaving technology into Shaanxi while he was in office there (*JSWB* 37/10a; see also 36/48a, 36/2a).

62. Quoted in Peng Zeyi 1984: 224. The reference to his salary tells us that he has used his *yang lian* ("nurturing honesty") allowance to finance the bureau—a statement about the magistrate's moral probity.

63. In that sense, policies promoting home handicrafts were closely related to policies promoting the cult of chaste widowhood. See Elvin 1984; Mann 1987.

64. *JSWB* 37/19a–22a.

65. Quoted in Zhou Kai, "Quan Xiang min zhong sang shuo san ze" (Three guidelines for exhorting the people of Xiang[yang] to plant mulberry), in *JSWB* 37/19a. See also Zhang Shiyuan, "Nongtian ýi" (Discourse on farming), in *JSWB* 36/3a, where the same adage is quoted in a slightly different form.

66. Here (*JSWB* 37/21a) silk and purity are linked apparently by Zhou's antipathy for women doing farm labor in the fields. He does not specify why; it may be because he believed men and women should not comingle outside the home.

67. Zhou Kai's allusions to the poems in the *Book of Odes* (*JSWB* 37/21b) invoke images of the faithful wife. The first refers to the title poem in the odes from the state of Bin. See Ode 154, trans. in Legge [1893–95] 1991, 4: 226–27. The second, which is the title poem in the collection of odes from the state of Qi, describes the good wife admonishing her husband to rise early and attend to his duties (rather than languishing in connubial bliss). See Ode 96, in Legge [1893–95] 1991, 4: 150. The third allusion, to a cedar vessel, is the title poem in the collection of odes from the state of Yong, in which a widow protests against those forcing her to remarry. See Ode 45, in Legge [1893–95] 1991, 4: 73.

68. A quotation from *Mencius* VI.A.6, as translated in Chan 1973: 54.

69. *JSWB* 37/21a–b.

70. Zhang concludes this section on "woman's work" (*nü gong*), part of a much longer treatise, with an ambiguous, apparently sarcastic, warning about too much womanly talent: "Excessive skill with embroidery is to be avoided" (*cixiu yin qiao zai suo dang jie*) (*JSWB* 36/27b–28a).

71. Peng Zeyi 1984: 224.

72. Headland [1914] 1974: 103–5.

73. See examples cited in Grove and Daniels 1984: 62, 107, 108.

74. The ideal of a peasant household supported by "men plowing, women spinning" was still alive in the 1930's, as Huang (1990) emphasizes. See, for example, the classic ethnography published in 1939, which asserts that agriculture is "chiefly men's occupa-

tion," while silk production by women makes it possible for small farmers to survive (Fei [1939] 1962: 170).

75. The earliest reference appears in *Yantie lun* (Treatise on salt and iron), dated 81 B.C.E.

76. See Zhang Yingchang [1869] 1983, 7: 180. The author of this poem, Yan Wosi, was awarded first place in the *jinshi* examinations of 1664–65. A native of Gui'an county, the seat of Huzhou prefecture, Zhejiang province, he eventually rose to the office of vice minister (*shilang*) in the Board of Rites.

77. See Ebrey 1993: 149–51; Elvin 1972: 159–60.

78. *GGZJ* 10/17b.

79. See, for example, *GGZJ* 8/13a, 13/19b.

80. See, for instance, *GGZJ* 8/12b (on paying taxes: "For the peasant, rice is precious treasure; / For the official, no more than dirt"); 7/6b (a weaver's lament); 5/21b (a poem about starving families during the Mid-Autumn Festival).

81. *A Glance at the Interior* 1849: 57.

82. Fortune [1847] 1972: 259–60.

83. By contrast, Adele Fielde noticed during her ten-year sojourn (1877–87) in Swatow, Guangdong, that only the rich could afford to incapacitate young daughters by binding their feet at the age of six or eight; poor families did not begin binding until thirteen or fourteen years. Nevertheless, she observed, "even middle-class bound-foot women sometimes had to walk four or five miles daily" (Quoted in H. S. Levy 1966a: 274). Testimonies collected by Howard Levy reveal that maids commonly had bound feet (one had to sweep the floor on her knees) and show that women with bound feet regularly staggered to the well to collect water or stood for hours pounding rice with a heavy mortar. He also describes a mother-in-law who was so proud of her daughter-in-law's tiny feet that she allowed the girl to "sit with guests" and made the servants do all the manual labor (H. S. Levy 1966a: 213, 224, 226, 230). Especially in north China, bound feet appear to have presented no barrier to working in the fields. In the south, however, bound feet appear to have been more closely associated with indoor work. See Justus Doolittle's observations on Fuzhou (1867, 1: 61; 2: 202).

84. In the middle of the nineteenth century, Robert Fortune noted the following about the cotton-growing regions around Shanghai: "Every small farmer or cottager reserves a portion of the produce of his fields for the wants of his own family. This the female members clean, spin, and weave at home. In every cottage throughout this district the traveller meets with the spinning-wheel and the small hand-loom. . . . These looms are plied by the wives and daughters, who are sometimes assisted by the old men or young boys who are unfit for the labours of the field. Where the families are numerous and industrious, a much greater quantity of cloth is woven than is required for their own wants, and in this case the surplus is taken to Shanghae [*sic*] and the adjacent towns for sale" ([1847] 1972: 276–77).

85. See Huang Yizhi 1934: 2.

86. *SS* 1, no. 2, pp. 47, 52.

87. Bredon and Mitrophanow [1927] 1982: 369.

88. Hodous [1929] 1984: 176.

89. *Xinxiu Yin xian zhi* 1877: 2/12b.

90. See Yuan Dinghua 1973.

91. Zhang Xingzhou 1973: 81. Johnston describes Double Seven not as a women's festival, but simply as a day "of good omen and suitable for fortune-telling and the drawing

of lots": "On the preceding evening (the sixth of the month) boys and girls put bowls of water on the window-sill and leave them standing all night. In the morning each child picks a bristle from an ordinary broom and places it carefully on the surface of the water. [A note here adds that brooms can terrify evil spirits.] The shadow made in the water by the bristle is supposed to indicate the child's future lot in life" ([1910] 1986: 190–91). Thus, for instance, if the bristle looks like a brush, it augurs a boy's success as a scholar. More research on local variations in the meaning of this festival is in order.

92. The definitive study of the Double Seven Festival is Hong 1988. For standard accounts in English, see Tun 1965: 59; and Bredon and Mitrophanow [1927] 1982: 369–74. See in particular the translation and comment on a seventh-night poem by Xu Quan in Robertson 1992: 95–96.

93. Poem by Wu Lingze, in Liu Yunfen [1673] 1936: 69.

94. Poem by Zhang Yuzhen, dated 1782, in *SNS* 3/10b.

95. Poem by Zhang Yuzhen, in *SNS* 3/12b.

96. Poem by Shen Yixiu, in Liu Yunfen [1673] 1936: 72.

97. Poem by Han Pei, in Liu Yunfen [1673] 1936, part 3 ("Xin ji"), p. 25.

98. *GGZJ* 9/2b.

99. *GGZJ* 11/6a.

100. *GGZJ* 18/24b.

101. See Li Bozhong 1984, 1985a, 1985b, 1986.

102. See Fig. 19, p. 134. Proverbs capture these sentiments: "A spinning wheel is a money tree; shake it daily and riches will come"; also, "If the man picks mulberry leaves and the woman raises silkworms, in 45 days they'll see money" (cited in Arkush 1984: 468).

103. Elvin 1972.

104. Dietrich 1972: 113. He mentions specifically the "Saxony" type of spinning wheel with a flyer and the flying shuttle on the loom.

105. Elvin 1972.

106. Elvin 1972.

107. This argument is more fully developed in Elvin 1973.

108. P. C. C. Huang 1990: 111. Schneider's work on Sicily (1985), while noting that "cultural patterns making female labor unavailable for income-producing activities have impeded agrarian transformation and economic development" (p. 81), documents the increasing commercialization of women's home embroidery as a source of income.

109. See Bray 1997. Bray was kind enough to share her manuscript with me while we were each revising drafts. I am grateful to her for calling into question my original reading of the sources.

110. See Bray 1997. This will remind European historians of Judith Brown's revisionist work on women's economic roles in the Renaissance. Brown (1986) shows that women in Renaissance Florence were moving into new economic roles, but only in sectors vacated by men who had gone on to higher-paying or more highly skilled jobs.

7. Piety

1. The bodhisattva Guanyin entered China as an Indian icon—originally a male deity called Avalokitesvara, the bodhisattva of mercy, sometimes portrayed with a thousand arms. Early iconography indicates that the figure of Guanyin was perhaps syncretized with the tantric female deity Tara and also with a local cult deity, a princess called Miao Shan.

According to a modern version of the Miao Shan legend, the princess was to inherit her father's kingdom provided that she married. She refused. "I know that it is wicked to disobey my honorable father," she said, "but the glory of being an Empress is like the light of the moon reflected in a stream. Morning comes and it is gone. I only wish to sit quiet and pray to the gods that I may become perfect. I wish to care for the sick and to help the poor. I do not wish to marry" (Carpenter 1945: 32). So her father took away all her fine clothes and cast her out, but the winds and the moon brought her food and warmth. She requested permission to go live in the Nunnery of the White Sparrow. Her father granted her request, then asked the nuns to give her all the hardest work to do. But the Emperor of Heaven looked down on her and pitied her, sending "dragons to carry her water, a tiger to bring her wood, and birds to gather vegetables for her from the garden" (p. 33). This made the father even angrier, so he burned the nunnery to the ground. The smoke from the fire, however, carried Miao Shan's prayers up to heaven, which rained and put the fire out. Finally the emperor tried to cut his daughter's head off with an ax, but she was again rescued by a tiger sent from the Emperor of Heaven. She was taken to the underworld, which she transformed into a kingdom of light. Then she returned to earth, leading all the souls in Hades with her. There she met the god of immortality, who gave her the peach of eternal life. At length she returned to earth, to Putuo Shan in the Chusan (Zhoushan) Islands off the coast of Zhejiang province, where she was worshiped in High Qing times. Some stories say she returned to earth to aid her father. In one version of the legend, her father fell ill, and she cut the flesh from her arms to make medicine to cure him, whereupon he gratefully commissioned a statue of her with completely formed arms and eyes. The sculptor misunderstood and made her statue with many heads and many arms. When she refused to leave earth for heaven, she was transformed into the bodhisattva Guanyin. See C. A. S. Williams 1976: 244. This version of Guanyin's story clearly syncretizes her Indian origins and Chinese ideals of the faithful and pure daughter (*zhen nü*). Reed (1992: 160) stresses yet another syncretic aspect of the Guanyin cult, namely, that it united the artistic images and devotional traditions of Pure Land Buddhism and the salvational Buddhism of the *Lotus sutra*.

2. Nanjing 1818: 1/25b.

3. Guanyin's birthdays fall on the nineteenth day of the second, sixth, and ninth months. The first is her physical birthday; the second celebrates the day she achieved enlightenment; the third is variously described as the day of her passage into Nirvana, the day of her death, or the day she first donned the string of pearls that symbolize her spiritual authority. See Doolittle 1867, 1: 261–62.

4. Li Dou [1794–97] 1984: 16/347.

5. For a complete translation of a reprinted version of this original text, see Dudbridge 1978: 40–42. A portion of the text appears in Zong and Liu 1986: 855.

6. This scripture has been studied by Junfang Yu (Chün-fang Yü 1990), on whose work I have primarily relied.

7. Dudbridge 1978: 85–98, esp. pp. 92–93.

8. See S. E. Cahill 1993.

9. Dudbridge 1978: 92.

10. Beata Grant (1994: 58–59) shows that the devout Tao Shan wrote only religious poetry after the death of her sister; she spent the years between her engagement and the consummation of her marriage absorbed in the study of Buddhist texts.

11. Peng Shaosheng 1872: *xia*/32a–b.

12. Peng Shaosheng 1872: *xia*/30b–31a.

13. Cited in the preface by Yang Lien-sheng (Yang Liansheng) in Yü Ying-shih 1987: 21–22. For the original text, see Qian 1939: 12, 15, 18.

14. *GGZJ*, "Bian yan" 1a.

15. *GGZJ* 8/18a. Qian Hui's portraits of Guanyin and of palace ladies doubtless were copies of handscrolls like the painting "Lady Guoguo and Her Sisters Setting Forth on an Outing," reproduced in J. Cahill 1960: 20. On Li Gonglin's skill as a copyist of old masters, see Sullivan 1967: 178–79.

16. Reed (1992: 163) saw this painting at an exhibit in the National Palace Museum in Taiwan in 1985.

17. *GGZJ* 2/7b.

18. *GGZJ* 14/17b.

19. On the festival's many names in Chinese, see Teiser 1988: 8; also below. Scholars have argued that the double meanings of Double Seven—death and rebirth, loss and renewal—represent a remnant of archaic rites that ultimately filled the entire seventh month. See Lagerway 1987: 18–24. Citing Rolf Stein, Lagerway notes that festivals associated with the so-called Three Days of Origin, celebrated on the fifteenth day of the first, seventh, and tenth months, were originally held on the seventh (or fifth) days of those months. Yü Ying-shih (1981) has shown that classical sources repeatedly use the phrase *ji sheng ba* (reading *ba* for *po*, or soul), meaning "after the birth of the crescent" (similarly, *ji si ba*, or "after the death of the crescent"). These phrases, he argues, represent the ancient association between the soul and the growing light of the new moon. Yü comments that the phrases are "a key to both the story of the Weaving Maid and the Oxherd and that of the Queen Mother of the West." Han myths describe Xi Wang Mu's meeting with Emperor Wu on the seventh day of the first month; the Weaving Maid meets the Cowherd on the seventh day of the seventh. The Queen Mother of the West appears often on Han tomb burial objects as the renewer of the cosmic cycle and the restorer of an order upset by death. Both myths play on themes of rebirth and sexuality familiar in Chinese death rites (Yü Ying-shih 1981: 84). Loewe argues in a similar vein that both the Queen Mother and the Weaving Maid stories are derived from the same master myth that "saw the continuity of the universe as depending on two annual meetings that took place in summer and winter" (1979: 119). See also Teiser's (1988) analysis of the prehistory of the Ghost Festival in medieval times, which underscores the importance of the 7/15 festival in both Buddhism and Taoism.

20. See Yuan Dinghua 1973. See also Zhang Xingzhou 1973: 82 for an account of the rituals in Ningbo.

21. See Tun 1965: 61 and the illustration on p. 60. The middle of the seventh month was a pivot point of the year, the transition between ripening, darkening, and decay. See Lagerwey on the Chinese festival calendar: "The seventh month is . . . the most crucial time for feeding all the solitary, untended, and hence famished souls of hell. This feeding—the festival of Universal Salvation [*pudu*]—goes on throughout the seventh month, but its high point, even where performed by Buddhist priests, remains the 15th of the month" (1987: 20). During the *pudu*, the living try to appease the resentment of hungry dead souls by making offerings and to liberate the obstructed souls (*hun*) whose ultimate destiny is heaven, freeing them to leave their earthly prisons. Historically, at least as early as Tang times, the fifteenth day of the seventh month was a day of renewal observed at all levels of society: emperors presented their ancestors with the first fruits of the harvest, and common people marked "the conjunction of death and rebirth" (Teiser 1988: 26). For Buddhist

monks in India, the fifteenth day of the seventh month marked the end of the summer retreat, a day of confession, the beginning of a new year, the donning of new robes. In Daoism, the same day was a day of judgment.

22. See Sangren 1983: 18.

23. Teiser comments: "The seventh month brings the Weaving Maiden her only chance to cross the celestial stream that separates her from the Cowherd, just as the ghost festival brings into being the bridge that allows the ghostly inhabitants of the *yin* world to return to their loved ones in the *yang* world" (1988: 30). He notes the similarity to feast days described by Mikhail Bakhtin (1984: 8–9) that celebrate the same connections between cosmic, biological, and historical time.

24. Chün-fang Yü notes that Dizang Wang and Guanyin are frequently paired in art motifs dating from the Dunhuang cave murals of the Tang period (1990: 229n1).

25. Quoted in Dudbridge 1978: 94.

26. The novel *Dream of the Red Chamber* describes in detail a great funeral mass conducted by the Jia household. On the thirty-fifth day of the mass, the chief celebrant monk opens the way for imprisoned souls by chanting spells and incantations to break open the gates of hell. He shines a small hand mirror for the souls in darkness, confronts Yama, the Judge of the Dead, and invokes the assistance of Dizang Wang to help him conduct the souls out of the depths of hell (*HLM* 14.189; *Stone* 1: 275). At the same time, the Daoist priests present a petition to the Three Pure Ones and the Jade Emperor; Zen monks swing censers and scatter little cakes for the hungry ghosts as they perform the great Water Penitential; and in the shrine itself, before the coffin, six young monks and six young nuns in elaborate robes sit before the spirit tablet "quietly murmuring the *dharani* that would assist the soul of the dead woman on the most difficult part of its journey into the underworld" (*HLM* 14: 189–90; *Stone* 1: 275).

27. Dudbridge 1978: 95–96.

28. Werner 1961: 497–99; Zong and Liu 1986: 489. The Mulian stories are extensively analyzed in D. Johnson 1989.

29. David Johnson notes that Mulian operas were performed throughout the year, frequently on the fifteenth day of the seventh month. He cites numerous examples of such performances in the Lower Yangzi region, particularly in the area around Shaoxing (1989: 8).

30. For an interpretation, see Seaman 1981; in rituals he observed, the "blood" was wine dyed with red coloring (p. 389).

31. Peng Shaosheng 1872: *xia*/33a.

32. Scholars have argued that territorial gods were worshiped exclusively by men and that women turned instead to deities whose domain spanned territorial and social boundaries. See especially Sangren 1983: 18, where he stresses that Guanyin, "in part because of her gender, . . . serves as a focal symbol for a social group not united by any formally sanctioned ties of kinship or territory in a way that patrilineal ancestors or the male deities of the territorial cults could not." The Privy Goddess shows that women too worshiped territorial gods. In fact, women's dual allegiance to deities of the household and to deities like Guanyin is reminiscent of the dual religious structure identified in Korean households by Laurel Kendall (1987). Quite possibly further research will show that exorcists and other female ritual specialists (who are mentioned only briefly in this chapter) were also important in Chinese domestic rites.

33. Chard 1990: 168. Later Chard discusses the paradox of women's exclusion from New Year stove rites and the scriptural authority of the Stove God, on the one hand, and, on the

other, their inclusion in domestic rituals as described in folktales and fictive genealogies linking gods and goddesses in the domestic realm (pp. 181–83).

34. According to some accounts, the Privy Goddess went by the name of Seventh Daughter (Qi Gu), a homonym for one of her apocryphal names in Han times. For accounts of the Privy Goddess, see Zong and Liu 1986: 418–25. See also Chard 1990.

35. Chün-fang Yü (1990: 223) notes that Chan practitioners preferred this text and the *Heart sutra* (*Xin jing*).

36. Translated in Gregory 1991: 217.

37. Gregory 1991: 150.

38. See Li Wai-yee 1993: 59, quoting an early eighteenth-century critic.

39. The practical tone of the text led Arthur Waley to call it an "applied epistemology" (Waley 1956: 78–79).

40. Luk 1966: 137–38, 142.

41. Luk 1966: 142–50; quotations on pp. 147, 149.

42. Luk 1966: 101.

43. H. S. Levy 1966b: 67. The self-conscious use of Buddhist metaphors for purity to describe the most appealing and inaccessible courtesans (see, e.g., Nanjing 1787: 2/3a) suggests that the Japanese sensibility associated with the "floating world" was part of the aesthetics of courtesan connoisseurship for men. However, women's relationship to Buddhist beliefs would have been entirely different from men's. The Queen Mother of the West was also a special patron of courtesans. See S. E. Cahill 1993: 234–36.

44. Peng Shaosheng 1872: *xia*/31a.

45. Peng Shaosheng 1872: *xia*/31a.

46. *HLM* 88.1,257; *Stone* 4: 178.

47. *GGZJ* 13/11a.

48. *GGZJ* 14/22a.

49. The *Tract* was reprinted numerous times during the Qing period. Two editions appeared under imperial sponsorship, the first in the Shunzhi reign and the second in the Yongzheng. In the eighteenth century, in addition to the imperially endorsed Yongzheng edition, new reprints with identifiable dates appeared in 1734 and 1758. Zhang Xuecheng himself financed the publication of an additional reprint in 1785, adding his own colophon (see Zhang Xuecheng [n.d.] 1922: 29/12b–14a). The term "ledgers of merit and demerit" was coined by Cynthia Brokaw in her 1991 study of these texts; see esp. pp. 110–11. According to one source, the *Tract* was one of the three most influential and widely read books among women in late imperial times. See Guo Licheng [1904] 1982: 6.

50. Brokaw 1991: 172, esp. n. 41.

51. Brokaw 1991: 195, 199.

52. Beata Grant (1989) discusses the relationship between morality books and sacred texts as a continuum joining texts that uphold Confucian family and social bonds with texts that enable women to transcend them (see pp. 229–30 *et passim*, esp. 293n10). The evidence in this book suggests that the dichotomy between family obligation and transcendence was not absolute, but rather a function of the life course, and that women tolerated the dissonance between these two types of texts as a necessary condition of their lives. I agree with Reed (1992: 169–77), who argues that Buddhism offered women a means of both coping with and escaping from the constraints of Confucian family roles.

53. See Shek 1993: 83, 88–89.

54. Huang refers here to the "six dames" or "six hags" (*liu po*), much maligned in mid-Qing moral texts for women. One locus classicus is Zhao Yi [c. 1775] 1957: [38/3b–4a] 832. Citing a Ming text titled *Zhuogeng lu* (Notes written during respite from farm labor),

Zhao actually lists nine dangerous women: the "three spinsters" (*san gu*) include nuns (*nigu*), Daoist adepts (*daogu*), and female diviners (*guagu*); the "six dames" (*liu po*) are the procuress (*yapo*), the marriage go-between or matchmaker (*meipo*), the female exorcist (*shipo*), the professional praying woman (*qianpo*), the female drug peddler or herbalist (*yaopo*), and the midwife (*wenpo*, "she who brings forth grain from the hull"). See also Furth 1986: 65; Ayscough 1937: 87.

55. Huang Liuhong [1694] 1984: 609.

56. *HLM* 29.403–13; *Stone* 2: 68–83. In 1845 the Reverend George Smith observed a few women of a "superior class, being arrayed in beautiful dresses, and attended by their ammahs," worshiping at a Daoist temple in Ningbo city. "As soon as I made my appearance," he wrote, "they affected great modesty, and, with half-turned faces and half-suppressed smiles, quietly took their departure, with as much haste as their tottering steps and limping gait permitted" (1847: 210).

57. *HLM* 13.177; *Stone* 1: 260. *HLM* 14.189; *Stone* 1: 275.

58. *HLM* 14.188; *Stone* 1: 274.

59. *HLM* 14.195; *Stone* 1: 284. When a coffin is first moved away from the home, the chief mourner must break a pottery bowl in front of it. This ritual act is interpreted variously as a signal to begin mourning, as a sign of separation between parent and child, the dead from the living, and as a symbol of the child's transformed relationship to the parent. See Naquin 1988: 42–43, 57; Thompson 1988: 75, 81.

60. *HLM* 7.110–111; *Stone* 1: 172.

61. *HLM* 7.110; *Stone* 1: 171.

62. *HLM* 15.204–5, 206–7; *Stone* 1: 295–96, 299.

63. *HLM* 16.201–11; *Stone* 1: 305.

64. *HLM* 17.242; *Stone* 1: 351. See also the discussion of the traffic in women in Chap. 2, "Gender."

65. *HLM* 17.242; *Stone* 1: 351, translation slightly modified.

66. *HLM* 17.242; *Stone* 1: 351.

67. *HLM* 17.242–43; *Stone* 1: 352.

68. *HLM* 87.1,250–55; *Stone* 4: 170–77. *HLM* 112.1,542–45; *Stone* 5: 231–33.

69. *HLM* 22.308–310; *Stone* 1: 442–43.

70. *HLM* 115.1,577–78; *Stone* 5: 278–79. The Jia family is dismayed by the prospect of one of their own entering a nunnery.

71. *HLM* 88.1,258; *Stone* 4: 179.

72. Peng Shaosheng 1872. For Peng's biography, see *EC* 614–15.

73. Peng Shaosheng 1872: *xia*/31a.

74. In this category I would also place fictional works such as the two chapters on pilgrimage translated by Glen Dudbridge (1992) from the seventeenth-century novel *Marriage That Awakens the World* (*Xingshi yinyuan zhuan*). This rich source lampoons pilgrimage as a status symbol for elite women and satirizes the plight of the central female figure's hen-pecked husband. As my analysis shows, I view such works as expressions of the literati's fear of the power and authority of Buddhist monks and Buddhist beliefs rather than as evidence of women's actual Buddhist practice. The fictional account probably comes closest to the truth about women's religious practice when it exposes the many schemes of pious women to siphon off the resources of the patriline for their own religious expenses or philanthropic projects. In fact, as we have already seen, women contributed generously to their favorite religious causes.

75. Kuhn 1990: 42–47.

76. Zhong Qi [1897] 1970, 1: 12/4a–b (pp. 523–24). For another eighteenth-century example from Guangdong province, see Lan Dingyuan, "Depraved Religious Sects Deceive People," translated in Ebrey 1981: 202–3.

77. Huang Liuhong [1694] 1984: 608–9.

78. Huang Liuhong [1694] 1984: 64.

79. Huang Liuhong [1694] 1984: 431.

80. Huang Liuhong [1694] 1984: 551, translation slightly revised. Brook (1993: 190) correctly terms these sorts of comments "male fantasies."

81. See n. 86 and the accompanying text discussion of these rituals of self-immolation. They are also associated with two other Buddhist ceremonies: The first is the Boat of the Law ceremony, in which each Buddhist temple makes a paper boat and burns it in the evening to help spirits who are homeless or drowned cross "the sea of want, hunger, thirst and torment into which their sins had gotten them when they were overcome by death, and so to enable them to reach Nirvana" (Tun 1965: 61). The second is the true All Soul's Day, or Yu Lan Hui. On this day each Buddhist temple forms a Yu Lan Hui (Yu Lan society) and members also light lanterns and recite sutras to lead across the sea those suffering in the underworld. This festival is associated with the Buddha's command to his disciple Mulian —whose mother had been reborn among the hungry ghosts in Hades, where she was not allowed to eat anything—to form the Yu Lan Pen Society, which on the fifteenth day of the seventh month would put all kinds of different-tasting fruits into basins and offer them "so as to nurture great virtue in the ten quarters" (Tun 1965: 61). The lantern rituals described later by Chen Hongmou are associated with these seasonal lantern rites. See a definition of the term *rou deng* ("lanterns hung from the body") using a fire radical for the gold radical in the character *deng* in the text, in Morohashi 1955–60: no. 29236.94. These flesh lanterns are reminiscent of the lighted fingers described by Zhang Dai ([1877] 1935: 47).

82. Chen Hongmou, "Some Comments on Local Customs," *JSWB* 68/4–6; quotation on p. 5b. For a slightly different translation, see Rowe 1992: 23–24.

83. On Chen's career, see *EC* 86–87. On his views on women's education, see Rowe 1992. Chen's handbook on women's education, *Bequeathed Guidelines for the Instruction of Women* (*Jiaonü yigui*), was first printed in 1742. Both Chen Hongmou and Lan Dingyuan published works on women's education as well as women's religious practice; each expressed the same concerns about female morality and sexual purity. See Chap. 2, "Gender."

84. See the poem "Shown to My Children" in Chap. 3, "The Life Course."

85. Wei, Wu, and Lu (1982: 5) cite the case of the wife of a wealthy Hangzhou merchant who went on pilgrimage to Tian Zhu saccompanied by "scores" of servants. Unfortunately the citation Wei, Wu, and Lu provide for this source is incorrect, and I have not been able to locate the original text.

86. Self-immolation by burning was part of the pilgrim's profession of faith. A ninth-century record of a miracle at the Putuo shrines recounts the pilgrimage of a foreign monk who, after burning his ten fingers in front of the Cave of Tidal Sound, was rewarded by a vision of the bodhisattva, who presented him with a seven-hued precious stone (Yü 1992: 215).

87. Zhang Dai [1877] 1935: 47. See also the translation in Yü 1992: 227. On Zhang's life and writings, see the biography by Fang Zhaoying in *EC* 53–54.

88. See Crossley 1990: 63.

89. Qin Yaozeng 1843: 15/18b, 15/21b, 15/23b, 20/22a–23a, *et passim*. See the insightful discussion of gender and male patronage of Buddhist shrines in the late Ming period in Brook 1993: 188–91. Brook notes that women were prevented from investing in monasteries during the late Ming period; instead, male donors adopted a Confucian posture by attributing their interest in Buddhism to the influence of female relatives. The Manchu emperors' personal devotion to Buddhism and evidence for female investment in Buddhist activities suggest that in Qing times the situation was changing.

90. Crossley (1990: 64) notes that the empresses dowager came "repeatedly" in the Kangxi and Qianlong eras.

91. See *EC* 329. On June 25, 1665, the Dutch fleeing Taiwan landed on Putuo, a reminder that the Kangxi emperor's interest in the island was partly strategic and may date from that time. See records of the landing in Qin Yaozeng 1843: 13/4a.

92. According to Jonathan Spence (1966: 130).

93. Harold L. Kahn (1971: 91–92) opines that pleasing the empress dowager in her old age was the primary reason the emperor undertook the tours at all.

94. Kahn 1971: 88, 93.

95. Kahn 1971: 96.

96. Kahn 1971: 96n28, citing Fuchs.

97. Cloud [1906] 1971: 60–61. Cloud observed that the prayerbook was still in daily use while he resided in Hangzhou.

98. Chün-fang Yü 1992: 210–14.

99. Chün-fang Yü 1992: 224. The poem appears in *GGZJ* 2/4b. Ann Waltner has pointed out to me that this iconographic rendering of the Nanhai Guanyin was not new in the eighteenth century, however.

100. In the mid-nineteenth century there remained only 150 monks in the Forward Temple (Xiansi) and about 80 in the Rear Temple (Housi), a total of 230, excluding the monks resident in the other 72 temples scattered around the island (Smith 1847: 308, 313–14).

101. Smith 1847: 314.

102. Smith 1847: 315. See also Franck 1926: 27, where he refers to "Pootoo" as the "Island Without Women."

103. How many women pilgrims actually made the trip to see the restored temples on Putuo during the High Qing era remains an open question. Chün-fang Yü presents accounts of female pilgrims, including Zhang Dai's record of 1638, discussed earlier in this chapter; but she notes as well that the journey was difficult and costly (1992: 227). We may presume that most female pilgrims traveled overland to worship, perhaps sailing to Putuo once in a lifetime. When I attempted to visit Putuo myself in 1988, I was told by the travel service operating the ferry that I must wait three days for a reservation. Even in the present, logistics make it difficult to plan trips to the island.

104. An early-twentieth-century observer (Franck 1926: 37–38) says that 70–80 percent of the people of Shaoxing made a living from the spirit money business at the time of his travels there. The tinfoil (made from ore imported from Yunnan) that decorated spirit money had first to be poured into ingots or bars about half an inch thick, then pounded with an anvil for ten to fifteen days until paper thin. Bundles of pounded tin were then loaded onto coolies' backs and distributed to rural households, where the final stages of production took place.

105. For this insight, I am indebted to a conversation with my colleague Beverly Bossler.

106. A notable exception is Brook 1993.

107. This point is well demonstrated in Ebrey 1993: 124–28.

8. Conclusion

1. See Hu Shih [1931a] 1992: 12.

2. Recall that Fang Bao upset a noted Zhexi scholar, Wang Zhong, because he refused to install women's ancestral tablets in the Fang family shrines, claiming that this was a violation of classical ritual codes.

3. The best example is Shang Jinglan; see Ko 1994: 226–32 *et passim.*

4. At 579.55 persons per square kilometer, Shaoxing prefecture was more densely populated than Hangzhou or Changzhou prefectures; in fact, it was the most densely populated prefecture in Zhejiang province after Jiaxing. See figures from *Da Qing yitongzhi* (1820), reproduced in Liang Fangzhong 1985: 275.

5. See the Appendix. Zhedong refers to the area east of the Qiantang River centered on Shaoxing, Yuyao, and Ningbo. The Qiantang flows at a slight south-north angle past the city of Hangzhou eastward into Hangzhou Bay. To the north and west of the Qiantang lay the region known as Zhexi, which included not only Hangzhou but also a network of Lower Yangzi towns and cities that spilled across the provincial boundary into Jiangsu, the most important being Jiaxing, Suzhou, and Changzhou.

6. See "Zhedong xueshu" (The scholarship of eastern Zhejiang), in Zhang Xuecheng [1832] 1964: 51–53. Zhang himself at times appeared reluctant to contrast the intellectual heritage of the regions too starkly, and the dichotomies he drew are difficult to defend when closely analyzed. See the literature reviewed in He 1991. A description in English of the Zhe schools appears in Elman 1981; see also Paul Demiéville 1961: 169–70. In a detailed study of leading Zhedong scholars, including Quan Zuwang, Lynn Struve singled out the following traits of the region's intellectual culture: "(1) philosophical independence, (2) a related tendency to find middle ground between Ch'eng-Chu and Lu-Wang positions on learning, (3) erudition and scholarly achievement, and (4) resistance to political cooptation, especially during turmoil and alien conquest" (1988: 116).

7. The notion of "imagined communities" is developed and explained in Anderson 1983.

8. See Cole 1986: 8, citing Li Ciming (1830–94), *Yueman tang wenji* 2/12b. Li Ciming, a native of Guiji (see *EC* 493), was a voluminous writer and astute observer who recorded his opinions and observations in detail. Of the difference between Zhedong and Zhexi culture, he had this to say: "Our Zhe area is divided into two regions, east and west. The mountains and rivers in each are not the same, and the climates also differ. Thus the literary culture nourished in west and east differs as well, along similar lines." Citing an earlier work, Li characterized the scholars of Zhexi as "refined and cultivated" (*xiu er wen*) and the scholars of Zhedong as "pure and simple" (*chun er pu*).

9. Elman 1990: 86.

10. Elman 1990: 87.

11. Elman 1990: 57–58.

12. Elman 1990: 71.

13. Elman argues that in Changzhou, at least from the time of Tang Shunzhi in the late Ming, prose was the literary genre that served as a vehicle for the Way (*wen yi zai Dao*) (Elman 1990: 291). Thus the great Changzhou scholars Zhao Yi and Zhang Huiyan wrote acclaimed verse, but regarded their poems as little more than embellishments on their scholarship (Elman 1990: 293).

14. The Zhuang lineage alone claimed 22 female poets in the Qing period, the most famous being Zhuang Panzhu. See Elman 1990: 57.

15. On the social and cultural importance of having a given name, see Watson 1986.

16. See *EC* 25–26.

17. Zhang Xuecheng [n.d.] 1922: 30/109a–110a.

18. Lerner 1986.

19. Ann Waltner made a similar observation during a discussion of women's consciousness of their own history at the Conference on Women and Literature in Ming-Qing China, June 23–26, 1993, at Yale University. See also the discussion in Ko 1994: 14–15.

20. For a biography of Wang Yun (born c. 1757, died after 1802), see Zheng Guangyi 1991: 1,667–72. Her discontent with her identity as a woman, her fantasies about becoming a scholar-official, and her admiration for ancient heroines civil and military—including Ban Zhao and Hua Mulan—fill her writings. Poems by Wang Yun are translated in Ropp 1994: 141–42. On Chen Duansheng, see M. H. Sung 1994 for the most recent study in English.

21. Edwards 1994: 97. See also her astute observation that women warriors do not display the "masculine" quality *yi*, or righteousness; they do not band together as brothers, but rather—if they unite at all—do so to serve a patriarch (pp. 101–2).

22. See Zhang Xuecheng's comments discussed earlier in this chapter; see also Edwards 1994: 105.

23. On the collectaneum as a hallmark of publishing in this period, see Elman 1984: 151–52. One version of the text *Lidai mingyuan tushuo* is Luo Wenzhao [1779] 1879. This text may be identical to the text of the same date that appeared in the *Zhi buzu zhai* collectaneum, which I have not seen. Carlitz (1991) describes an illustrated edition in sixteen chapters that appeared in 1779 in the *Zhi buzu zhai* collectaneum under the title *Huitu lienü zhuan*. An illustration of the wife of Liu Changqing cutting off her ear, reproduced from the *Zhi buzu zhai* edition in Carlitz 1991: 130 (fig. 2), also appears in Luo Wenzhao [1779] 1879: *shang*/27a. An illustrated text in my possession titled simply *Gu lienü zhuan* is a facsimile of the classic Song edition printed by the premier publishing house owned by the Yu family of Jian'an, Fujian (preface dated 1063). I am indebted to Cynthia Brokaw for recognizing its value. It was reprinted in 1825 and, according to some sources, was passed off as an original edition to wealthy collectors (see Carlitz 1991: 138n48). The *lienü* stories, as Carlitz points out, were illustrated with narratives reminiscent of dramatic plots from fiction. In fact, Carlitz has shown that publishing houses used the same illustrative motifs for both exemplary women and potboiler novellas and plays.

24. See *LGBL*. The preface is dated the first ten days of the second month of summer, 1831 (approximately mid-June).

25. *LGBL*, "Li yan" 1a–b.

26. Translations follow the felicitous wording of the Jesuit Reverend Alfred R. O'Hara (1945).

27. *LGBL* 1/27b–29a.

28. *LGBL* 4/49b–50a.

29. *LGBL* 5/28a.

30. *LGBL* 5/27a–29a.

31. *LGBL* 5/29a.

32. *LGBL* 1/30a.

33. *LGBL* 6/1a.

34. *LGBL* 6/1b–2a.

35. *LGBL* 6/4a–b.

36. *LGBL* 6/5a.

37. *LGBL* 6/6a–b.

38. *LGBL* 6/5b–6a.

39. *LGBL* 6/9a–10a.

40. *LGBL* 6/10b.

41. *LGBL* 6/9a–b. This poem has been reprinted countless times, including by Yuan Mei in his collection of comments on poetry.

42. Ebrey 1993: 120–24.

43. See, respectively, *GGZJ* 12/2b, 13/9a, 14/1a. Other poems by Manchu women in Yun Zhu's poetry anthology may be found in *GGZJ* 9/1b, 12a; 10/13b; 11/6a; 16/11b; 18/16b, 23b–24a; 19/3a; 20/10a.

44. *GGZJ* 18/23b–24a.

45. See, respectively, *GGZJ* 4/16b, 5/3b, 10/21b, 8/22b, 17/1a, 17/21b.

46. *GGZJ* 8/22b.

47. *GGZJ* 10/21b.

48. *GGZJ* 17/1a.

49. *GGZJ* 17/21b.

50. *GGZJ*, "Li yan" 4a–b.

51. *GGZJ* 9/5b.

52. *GGZJ* 13/14a, 15/6b, 18/15a.

53. *GGZJ* 14/8b (mother-daughter poems); 8/20b–21a, 9/3b (poems to brothers); 10/6a, 19/14b (to sisters); 11/3a–4a (to sister-in-law).

54. *GGZJ* 11/21a.

55. E. L. Johnson 1988.

56. *GGZJ* 11/1a.

57. *GGZJ* 11/4b.

58. *GGZJ* 11/6b–7a.

59. *GGZJ* 15/6b.

60. Recall the story of Tan Guangyao's dowry (*GGZJ* 16/14b), mentioned in Chap. 4, "Writing."

61. McMahon 1994.

62. See the dramatic moment when Lin Daiyu burns her poems in *HLM* 97.1,368–69; *Stone* 4: 353.

63. *GGZJ* 4/19a.

64. *GGZJ* 5/12a.

65. *GGZJ* 6/6a.

66. *GGZJ* 13/13a.

67. *GGZJ* 19/21b.

68. See *GGZJ* 7/19b; 8/16a–b; 9/2b, 18b–19a; 10/12b; 11/6a; 13/22a; 15/19a–b; 17/15b; 18/24b; 19/17b. See also Harrell 1995.

69. See Deuchler 1992; Woodside 1971: 5, 21, 27, 44–45.

70. See Handlin 1975; Ko 1994.

71. Ko 1994; see also Kang-i Sun Chang 1991.

72. Chow 1994.

73. See Ropp 1976, 1981; see also Lin Yü-t'ang [1935] 1992; Li Ruzhen [1828] 1965.

74. For an analysis of the monetary crisis of the early nineteenth century, see Lin Man-houng 1991.

75. Hershatter 1997.

76. Ono [1978] 1989: 11–13.

77. Wright 1957.

78. On Orientalism, the classic is Said 1978.

79. See "Symposium" (1993) for articles by the leading contributors to this debate, especially William T. Rowe and Frederic Wakeman.

80. See Pateman 1988.

81. Ko makes this point elegantly in her introduction (1994: 12–17).

82. See Kang-i Sun Chang 1992: 120–21.

83. Ko (1994) sounds this diversity as a major theme of her study of women in the seventeenth century; for a twentieth-century example, see Honig 1986.

84. See Wakeman 1985, 2: 1,094n47. The phrase "new audience" refers to Handlin's

(1975) classic analysis of the emergence of a female reading audience in the sixteenth century.

85. Wakeman 1985, 2: 1,094n47. Other critics range from leading contemporary scholars like T'ien Ju-k'ang (1988: esp. 135, 147) to reform-minded Chinese writers in the early twentieth century, such as Liu Jihua (1934).

86. See Ropp 1976, 1981; quotations from 1976: 19–23.

Appendix

1. See Skinner 1977: 213.

2. See Skinner 1977: 213, 235.

3. Wing-kai To has pointed out to me that these figures may simply represent the bias of the compiler of the data, who would be predisposed to discount or ignore writings from regions outside the Lower Yangzi (personal communication).

4. See Ho Ping-ti 1962: 246–49, 250–54.

5. My measures are admittedly crude: figures are gross totals from the entire Qing period and include only those women writers from the Lower Yangzi for whom native places could be identified at the county level. Nonetheless, the patterns permit some confident generalization.

6. On the boundaries of Zhexi, see Chap. 8, n. 5.

CHARACTER LIST

This list includes all Chinese titles, names, and terms that do not appear in References.

ai xiu 愛繡
Amidha 阿彌陀
Anhui 安徽
Anqing 安慶
A'quan 阿全
a'yi 阿姨

"Bai nian" 百年
Baili Xi 百里奚
Baishan shi chao 白山詩鈔
Baiyun waishi 白雲外史
Ban Gu 班固
Ban Jieyu 班倢伃
Banqiao 板橋
Bao Zhihui 鮑之蕙
Baochai 寶釵
baojuan 寶卷
Baoyu 寶玉
Bei (state) 邶
Beijing 北京
beinü 婢女
ben liangjia nü 本良家女
ben wu 本務
ben ye 本業
Bi Fen 畢汾
Bi Yuan 畢沅
"Bian yan" 弁言
bie 別
Bin 豳
bin xun ci wei 稟訓慈闈
bing qi 病起
Biqiuni zhuan 比丘尼傳
bo 帛
Bo Juyi 白居易
"Bu bo ying shu shuo" 布帛贏縮說
Bufeiqian gongde li 不費錢功德例

Cai Run 蔡閏
Cai Wenji 蔡文姬
Cai Yan 蔡琰
cainü 才女
Cao Cao 曹操
Cao Dagu 曹大家
Cao Huangmen 曹黃門
Cao Xishu 曹錫淑
Cao Zhixin 曹之辛
ce 廁
Chan 禪
chang zhai 長齋
Chang'e 嫦娥
Changshu 常熟
changzhi 常知
Changzhou 常州
chao hui 朝會
chao shan jin xiang 朝山進香
Chaozhou 潮州
chen 臣
Chen Anzi 陳安茲
Chen Duansheng 陳端生
Chen Jin 陳錦
Chen Qiongpu 陳瓊圃
Chen Shu 陳書
Chen Shuqin 陳疏琴
Chen Xigu 陳錫嘏
Chen Zilong 陳子龍
Cheng (brothers) 程
Cheng (emperor) 成
cheng (inherit) 承
cheng ci xun 承慈訓
cheng mu jiao 承母教
cheng qi jia xue 承其家學
cheng ting xun 承庭訓
Chizhou 池州
Chu 楚
Chu ci 楚辭
chu piao qiang yao 出票強要
chuan 傳
chun er pu 醇而樸
Chun qiu 春秋
ci (lyric) 詞
ci (maternal kindness) 慈
cixiu yin qiao zai suo dang jie 刺繡淫巧在所當戒
cizhong shouyi fei yiban funü zhi suo shanchang 此種手藝非一般婦女之所擅長
cong gu wenren de gong yu mujiaozhe duo 從古文人得功於母教者多
cong liang 從良
cong liang wei sui 從良未遂
Cui Xiaoying 崔小英
Cui Xiuying 崔秀英

da 大
"Da ya" 大雅
Dahong 大洪
Dai Lanying 戴蘭英
Dai Yunyu 戴韞玉
Daiyu 黛玉
Dalei 大雷
Daming 大明
Dan Fanglan 單芳蘭
danhu 蛋戶
Dao, dao 道
Dao de jing 道德經
daogu 道姑
de qiao 得巧
de, yan, rong, gong 德言容功
deng 燈
Dezong 德宗
Dinghai 定海
Dizang Wang 地藏王
Dong Zhongshu 董仲舒
Du Fu 杜甫
Du Jin 杜堇
Du Ningfu 杜凝馥
"Du shi ou cheng" 讀史偶成
du shu po wan juan xia bi ru you shen 讀書破萬卷下筆如有神
duan hong 斷鴻
duan yan ru liangjia fu 端妍如良家婦
duo 墮
duomin 墮民

duozhe, jiang zhi; shaozhe, jie zhi; feizhe, cheng zhi 多者獎之少者戒之廢者懲之

"Er nan" 二南
Er ya 爾雅
erhu 二胡

fan li 凡例
fang 房
Fang Bao 方苞
fang huai 放懷
Fang Jing 方靜
fang shui pei tou 放水轡頭
Fang Xuan 方璇
Fang Yao 方曜
Fang Yizhi 方以智
Fang Youlan 方友蘭
Fang Yunu 方玉奴
Fang Zhaoying [Fang Chao-ying] 房兆楹
fangju 紡局
Fanglan hang er, yi zhi Beicangqiao ren, jia yu Dan shi 芳蘭行二邑之北倉橋人嫁於單氏
"Fangzhi zhi li" 紡織之利
fei furen shi ye 非婦人事也
Feng 豐
feng (air, style) 風
fu 府
fu ke 婦科
Fu Qin 苻秦
"Fu ren wu zhu da wen" 婦人無主荅問
Fu Sheng 伏生 (勝)
"Fu xue" 婦學
Fujian 福建
Fuzhou 福州

Gai Qi 改琦
gaihu 丐戶
gaitu guiliu 改土歸流
Gan Yangzi 贛揚子
Gansu 甘肅
Gao 高
Gao Guizi 高桂子
Gao Jin 高晉
Gao Shunlin 高薙林
gong 公
Gong Dingzi 龔鼎孳
Gongyang 公羊
gu hun 孤魂
Gu Kaizhi 顧愷之
Gu lienü zhuan 古列女傳
Gu Mei 顧媚
gu qin 古琴
Gu Ruoxian 顧若憲
Gu Yanwu 顧炎武
gu zuo 枯坐
guagu 卦姑
Guan Daosheng 管道昇
guan guan ju jiu 關關雎鳩
"Guan ju" 關雎
guan ke 官客
guan shi yin 觀世音
guan shougongye 官手工業
Guangdong 廣東
Guangxi 廣西
Guangzhou 廣州
guanji 官妓
guanxi 關係
Guanyin 觀音
gubei 錮婢
gugong ren 雇工人
gui yue 鬼月
Gui'an 歸安
guige 閨閣
Guiji 會稽
guixiu 閨秀
Guizhi 桂枝
Guizhou 貴州
guo feng 國風
Guo Qiyuan 郭起元
Guoguo 郭郭
Gutan heshang 古潭和尚
guwen 古文

Haining 海寧
Hami 哈宓
Han (Lady) 韓
Han (dynasty) 漢
Han Pei 韓佩
Han shu 漢書
hang 行
hang da 行大
hang san 行三
hang yi 行一
Hangzhou 杭州
Hanlin 翰林
Hao 鎬
hao 號
he 和
He Xian Gu 和仙姑
hehu shu shizhi 闔戶數十指
Heilongjiang 黑龍江
heng chan 恆產
"Heng chan suo yan" 恆產瑣言
Heshen 和珅
Hesheng shu 和聲署
Hezhou 和州
hongfen zhiji 紅粉知己
Hou Cheng'en 侯承恩
Hou Shuangling 侯雙齡
Housi 後寺
houtian 後天
Hu Baozhu 胡寶珠
Hu Junsheng 胡駿聲
Hu Shenrong 胡慎容
Hu Shenyi 胡慎儀
hua cong 花叢
hua lan 花籃
Hua Mulan 花木蘭
Hua Shen 花神
Hua Xian 花仙
Hua yan jing 華嚴經
huafang 畫舫
Huai 淮
Huan 桓 (duke)
Huang Chonggu 黃崇嘏
Huang Cui'er 黃翠兒
Huang Daopo 黃道婆
Huang Jingren 黃景仁
Huangdi neijing 黃帝內經
Huangqi 黃溪
Huayan 華嚴
Hubei 湖北
Hufu 虎阜
hui 毀
Huitu lienü zhuan 繪圖列女傳
Huizhou 徽州
hun 魂
Hunan 湖南
Huzhou 湖州

Ji 紀
ji (cycle) 紀
ji (mourning term) 期
ji fu 繼婦
ji hu 機戶
ji nü 繼女
ji sheng ba 既生魄
ji si ba 既死魄
ji wai 寄外
Ji Yingzhong 紀映鍾
Ji Zhaoling 紀招齡
Jia 賈
jia (false) 假
jia (house) 家
jia mei 假妹
jia mu 假母
jia ou! 佳耦
jia pin si xianqi, guo luan si liangxiang 家貧思賢妻國亂思良相
jia xue 家學
jia yu 家語
Jiading 嘉定
jian (frugal) 儉
Jian'an 建安
Jiang (prostitute) 姜
Jiang Biqin 江碧岑
Jiang Lan 江蘭
Jiang Yuzhen 蔣玉珍
Jiangbei 江北
Jiangdu 江都
Jiangnan 江南

Jiangning 江寧
Jiangsu 江蘇
Jiangxi 江西
Jiangyin 江陰
jianmin 賤民
jiao shu 校書
Jiaofang si 教坊司
jiaohua 教化
jiapu 家僕
Jiaqing 嘉慶
jiasheng nupu 家生奴僕
Jiaxing 嘉興
jie 節
jie fu 節婦
jie jiming 戒雞鳴
jiji 唧唧
Jilin 吉林
Jin (dynasty) 晉
Jin Tingbiao 金廷標
Jin Wengying 金翁瑛
Jin Yi 金逸
Jinan 濟南
jing 靜
jing biao 旌表
jing kou shou 經口授
Jing xun ke jia 經訓克家
jing yang 靜養
Jing'an 靜安
Jinhua 金華
Jinling 金陵
Jinshan 金山
jinshi 進士
Jinsubao 金粟保
jiong 窘
"Jiu shi zi shou" 九十自壽
jiu yu 九漁
Jizhou 濟州
jun 君
junzi 君子
juren 舉人
Jurong 句容

Kangxi 康熙
kaozheng xue 考證學
Keng San Guniang 坑三姑娘
Kong Jiying 孔繼英
Kong Qinxiang 孔琴香
Kong Rongxian 孔蓉仙
kuan, ren, ci, hui 寬仁慈惠
kuisi 窺伺

lai erji zuo sheng ya 賴二姬作生涯
Lai'an 來安
Lan Caihe 藍采和
lao nian 老年
laofu 老夫
laoren 老人
Lei Zu 嫘祖
Leng yan jing 楞嚴經
Li 李
li 里
Li Ba 李拔
Li Ciming 李慈銘
Li Dayi 黎大宜
Li Gonglin 李公麟
Li Hanzhang 李含章
Li ji 禮記
Li Qingzhao 李清照
li qiu 立秋
Li Shixiang 李十孃
"Li yan" 例言
Li Ye 李冶
Li Yu 李漁
Li Zhi 李贄
lian li 廉吏
liang (measure for thread) 兩
liang (respectable) 良
Liang Lan'e 梁蘭猗
liangjia 良家
liangmin 良民
lienü 列女
Ling 凌
Lingnan 嶺南
lingzhi 靈芝
Linqing (port city) 臨淸
Liu 劉
Liu Changqing 劉長卿
Liu Fulin 劉馥林

liu po 六婆
Liu Rushi 劉如是
Liu Ruzhu 劉如珠
Liu Shi 柳是
Liu Wanhuai 劉琬懷
Liu Zhuanfang nü shi 劉撰芳女史
Lohan 羅漢
Long Nü 龍女
Lou (county) 婁
Lu (Lady) 祿
Lu (surname) 陸
Lu Danrong 陸淡容
Lu Guanlian 陸觀蓮
Lu Qiqin 陸綺琴
Lu Shunqing 陸順卿
Lu Xixiong 陸錫熊
Lü 呂
Lü Kun 呂坤
Lü Zhangcheng 呂章成
Luanyi wei 鑾儀衛
Lun yü 論語
Luping 綠萍

Ma Gu 麻姑
Ma Gu xian shou 麻姑仙壽
Ma Ji 馬姬
Ma Rulan 馬如蘭
Mai Yinggui 麥英桂
Mang shen 芒神
Mao 毛
Mao shi 毛詩
meipo 媒婆
Mi Manyun 宓鬘雲
mi xi tu 秘戲圖
Mianhua tu 棉花圖
Miao 苗
Miao Shan 妙善
Miaoyu 妙玉
Micheng 糜城
Min 閩
ming ji 名妓
Ming shi 明史
mo 末
Mulian 木蓮

nan geng nü zhi 男耕女織
Nanhai 南海
Nanjing 南京
nei 內
nei dan 內丹
nei yan buchu men wai 內言不出門外
Neijing 內經
nian fu po gua 年甫破瓜
nigu 尼姑
Ningbo 寧波
Ningguo 寧國
Nishijima Sadao 西島定生
Niulang 牛郎
nong 農
nong sang 農桑
"Nong shu" 農書
"Nong zheng" 農政
"Nongtian yi" 農田議
nu 奴
nubei 奴婢
nuli 奴隸
nupu 奴僕
nü 女
nü gong 女工 (紅)
nü gong zhi yi qin ye 女工之宜勤也
nü mensheng 女門生
nü shi (female scholar) 女士
nü shi (female scribe or historian) 女史
nü xiansheng 女先生
Nü xiaojing 女孝經
nü zhu 女祝
nüyue 女樂
"Nüzi xu jia er xu si congsi ji shouzhi yi" 女子許嫁而婿死從死及守志議

Ouyang Xiu 歐陽修

peng 蓬
pengpai 泙湃
pin 品
pipa 琵琶
Potalaka 寶陀巖
pudu 普度

Putian 莆田
Putuo 普陀
Putuo shan 普陀山
Puyuan 濮院

Qi (ancient state) 齊
qi 氣
qi bi ye yu 其蔽也愚
Qi Gu 七姑
qi qiao 乞巧
qi xiang 七襄
Qian Chenqun 錢陳群
Qian Hui 錢蕙
Qian Mengdian 錢孟鈿
Qian Qiuting 錢秋婷
Qian Suyue 錢素越
Qian Weicheng 錢維城
qiang mai 強賣
qiang shui 搶水
Qianlong 乾隆
qianpo 虔婆
Qiantang 錢塘
qie (concubine) 妾
Qin (dynasty) 秦
qin (industrious) 勤
qin (instrument) 琴
Qinding siku quanshu 欽定四庫全書
Qing 清
qing 情
qing lou 青樓
Qinshi 秦氏
qinying 親迎
qiyue ban 七月半
Qu Yuan 屈原
Quan Tang shi 全唐詩
"Quan Xiang min zhong sang shuo san ze" 勸襄民種桑說三則
Quan Zuwang 全祖望
Quzhou 衢州

Ronghu daoren 蓉湖道人
rou deng 肉燈
Ruan Yuan 阮元
Ruiyun 瑞芸
rulaizang 如來藏
Ruobing 若冰

Samantabhadra 三曼多跋陀
San Gu 三姑
san gu 三姑
san yan kong zhong cha ke ni 撒鹽空中差可擬
sang 桑
Shaanxi 陝西
Shandong 山東
Shang (ancient dynasty) 商
Shang Jinglan 商景蘭
Shang shu 尙書
Shanghai 上海
Shangyu 上虞
Shanxi 山西
Shao Jiayun 邵佳鈗
Shao Jinhan 邵晉涵
"Shao nan" 召南
Shao Suyun 邵素筠
Shaoxing 紹興
she huo 社火
Shen Yixiu 沈宜修
sheng shi 盛世
Shengze 盛澤
Shenyue guan 神樂觀
Shenyue shu 神樂署
Shi (surname) 史
shi (poetry, poem) 詩
shi (scholars) 士
shi (show, display) 示
Shi Baochang 釋寶唱
shi bozhou 矢柏舟
Shi hua 詩話
Shi ji 史記
Shi jing 詩經
Shi Qianxian 史倩仙
Shi Xiangxia 史湘霞
shi you 詩友
shilang 侍郎
shinüzhong zhi gaoda fu 詩女中之高達夫
shipo 師婆

shipu 世僕
shirenzhe bushi qi chizi zhi xinzhe ye 詩人者不失其赤子之心者也
Shou shi tong kao 授時通考
shoupin 受聘
Shu (state) 蜀
Shuanglin 雙林
Shui (surname) 水
shui xie 水榭
Shunde 順德
Shunzhi 順治
si de 四德
Sichuan 四川
Siku 四庫
Siku quanshu qinding tiyao 四庫全書欽定提要
Sima Qian 司馬遷
Song 宋
Song Rulin 宋如林
Song Ruohua 宋若華
Song Shanggong 宋尙宮
Songjiang 松江
Songling nü shi 松陵女史
Su Hui 蘇蕙
Su nü jing 素女經
Su Shi 蘇軾
su xin 素心
Subei 蘇北
Sui 隨
sui 歲
Sun Bu'er 孫不二
Sun Yunfeng 孫雲鳳
suo jian jue wu jiazhe 所見絕無佳者
sushan 宿山
Suzhou 蘇州
Swatow (Shantou) 汕頭

tai jiao 胎教
Tai'an 泰安
Taicang 太倉
Taichang si 太常寺
Taiping 太平
Taishang ganying pian 太上感應篇
Taizhou 泰州
Tan Guangyao 覃光瑤
Tanaka Masatoshi 田中正俊
tanci 彈詞
Tang (lineage) 唐
Tang Chao 湯朝
tang ke 堂客
Tang Qiushui 唐秋水
Tang Shunzhi 唐順之
Tang Xiao 唐小
Tang Zhen 唐甄
Tangshan 唐山
Tanyangzi 曇陽子
Tao Shan 陶善
"Tao yao tu zan" 桃夭圖贊
Tian Wanlan 田宛蘭
Tian Wen 田雯
Tian Zhu 天竺
Tiangong kaiwu 天工開物
Tiantai 天台
tiaoling 髫齡
Tinglu 廷鑅
tong cheng ci xun 同承慈訓
Tongcheng 桐城
tongju 同居
tongmu 同母
tongmu jie 同母姊
tongshu 通書
Tongxiang (Zhejiang) 桐鄉
tongyangxi 童養媳
Tongzhou 通州
tou'an 偷安
tun hu 囤戶

wai 外
Wanli 萬歷
Wang 王
Wang Dao 王導
Wang Duanshu 王端淑
Wang Fangping 王方平
Wang Feiqiong 王飛瓊
Wang Fen 王芬
Wang Liang 汪亮
Wang Long 王瓏
Wang Mengji jia xun 王孟箕家訓

Wang Ren 汪紉
Wang Si 王四
Wang Su'e 王素娥
Wang Suzhen 王素貞
Wang Xiaoheng 王小荇
Wang Xizhi 王羲之
Wang Yingfu 汪英福
Wang Yun 王筠
Wang Yunhui 王韞徽
Wang Zhaoyuan 王照圓
Wangjiangjing 王江涇
Wanyan 完顏
Wei (Lady) 衛
Wei (dynasty) 魏
Wei (state) 衞
Wei Cheng 韋逞
wei ji 未笄
Wei Rongxiang 衛融香
wei ruo liu xu yin feng qi 未若柳絮因風起
wei wang ren 未亡人
Wen (king) 文
wen 文
Wen Pu 聞璞
wen xing 文星
wen yi zai Dao 文以載道
Wen Zhenheng 文震亨
wenjiao hua 文教化
wenpo 穩婆
Wenxin 文心
Wu (empress) 武
Wu (king) 武
Wu (region, surname, county) 吳
Wu Enzhao 吳恩詔
Wu Lan 吳蘭
Wu Lingze 吳令則
Wu Ruoyun 吳若雲
Wu Sangui 吳三桂
Wu Si 吳絲
wu yi zhuan qi zhiye er yi qi xin zhi 無以專其執業而壹其心志
Wujiang 吳江
Wuxi 無錫
Wuxing 吳興
Xi Peilan 席佩蘭
Xi Wang Mu 西王母
Xia Longyin 夏龍隱
xian (fall) 陷
xian (practical wisdom) 賢
xian cao 仙草
xian mu 賢母
Xiang 襄
xiang hui 香會
xiang ke 香客
Xiang Yun 湘雲
Xiangshan baojuan 香山寶卷
Xiangyang 襄陽
Xianlai 姍來
Xiansi 先寺
xiantian 先天
Xiao jing 孝經
xiao lian 孝廉
xiaomin wei li shi tu 小民惟利是圖
Xichun 惜春
Xie (Pure Daughter) 謝
Xie An 謝安
Xie Daocheng 謝道承
Xie Daoyun 謝道韞
"Xie mu" 謝母
xifu 媳婦
Xiling shi 西陵氏
Xin jing 心經
Xin'an 新安
Xinghua 興化
Xinglian 星聯
Xingshi yinyuan zhuan 醒世姻緣傳
Xiongnu 匈奴
Xiren 襲人
xiu (embroidery) 繡
xiu (shame) 羞
xiu er wen 秀而文
Xiu Fo Nü Shi 繡佛女史
xiu jing ye 修淨業
Xiuning 休寧
xiuwu zhi xin 羞惡之心
Xu 徐
xu 絮
Xu Dachun 徐大椿

Xu Quan 許權
Xu Suqin 徐素琴
Xu Xiao'e 徐小娥
Xu Yingyu 徐映玉
xue 血
Xue Qiong 薛瓊
Xue Tao 薛濤
xueshi 學士
Xun (Lady) 荀
xun si 殉死

ya 雅
ya ya 啞啞
Yama 閻羅
yan (erotic) 豔
yan (speech) 言
yan (strict) 嚴
yan fu ci mu 嚴父慈母
Yan Jing 嚴靜
Yan Wosi 嚴我斯
Yan'an 延安
yang 陽
Yang Baoqin 楊寶琴
Yang Fuling 楊福齡
yang lian 養廉
yang mu 養母
Yang Youhuan 楊又環
Yang Yuxiang 楊玉香
Yang Zhaoling 楊拐齡
Yang Zhi 楊枝
Yanghu 陽湖
"Yangmin sizheng" 養民四政
Yangzhou 揚州
Yangzi 揚子
"Yantie lun" 鹽鐵論
Yanzhou 嚴州
Yao 堯
Yao Yundi 姚允迪
yaopo 藥婆
yapo 牙婆
Ye Dehui 葉德輝
ye gui 野鬼
Ye Shi 葉氏
"Ye zuo ou cheng" 夜坐偶成
yi 義
yi ji wei qian shuzi 以姬爲錢樹子
yi jie 義姊
Yi jing 易經
Yi Jingzhu 弋鏡珠
yi mei 義妹
"Yi mu quan xue shi" 憶母勸學詩
yi nü 義女
Yilanbao 伊蘭保
Yin 鄞
yin 陰
Yin Yuanfou 尹元孚
Yingzhou 穎州
yinqi 印契
Yishu dian 藝術典
Yong 鄘
yong yong ming yan 雝雝鳴鴈
Yongji 用濟
Yongzheng 雍正
"Youxing laoren" 獨醒老人
Yu 余
Yu Lan Hui 盂蘭會
Yu Xiefan 虞叶蘩
Yu Xuanji 魚玄機
Yu Youlan nü shi 虞友蘭女史
Yu Yuzi 喻玉子
Yu Zhengxie 俞正燮
Yuan 袁
yuan (court, garden) 園
Yuan Biao 袁表
Yuan Susheng 袁蘇升
Yuan Suwen 袁素文
Yuan Tingtao 袁廷檮
Yue 越
Yue bu 樂部
yuehu 樂戶
Yueman tang wenji 越縵堂文集
yueshang qian feng jing 月上千峰靜
yun qi sheng 隕其生
Yun Shouping 惲壽平
Yun Zhenpu 惲珍浦
Yun Zhu 惲珠
Yungui 雲貴
Yunnan 雲南

Yuyao 餘姚

za geng'ou 雜耕耦
"Zai sheng yuan" 再生緣
zangfu 傖父
zao duo feng chen 早墮風塵
zao hui 早慧
Zhai Jingyi 柴靜儀
zhancui 斬衰
Zhang (Lady) 張
Zhang (river) 漳
Zhang Baoling 張寶齡
Zhang Foxiu 張佛繡
Zhang Huiyan 張惠言
Zhang Lunying 張綸英
Zhang Lüxiang 張履祥
Zhang Qi 張琦
Zhang Qingyun 張輕雲
Zhang Shiyuan 張士元
Zhang Shulian 張淑蓮
Zhang Wanying 張紈英
Zhang Xiaoyun 張小雲
Zhang Xinglin 張杏林
Zhang Xiuqin 張繡琴
Zhang Yin 張因
Zhang Ying 張英
Zhang Youxiang 章有湘
Zhang Yuesun 張曜孫
Zhang Yuzhen 張玉珍
Zhang Zao 張藻
Zhang Zhao 張照
zhangfang 賬房
Zhao Aizhu 趙愛珠
Zhao Fu 趙福
Zhao Tonghua 趙桐華
Zhao Yaojuan 趙瑤娟
Zhe 浙
zhe 柘
Zhedong 浙東
"Zhedong xueshu" 浙東學術
Zhejiang 浙江
zhen nü 貞女
Zheng 鄭
zheng (correct) 正
zheng (musical instrument) 箏
Zheng Huwen 鄭虎文
zheng shi 正始
Zhenhai 鎮海
Zhenpu, *see* Yun Zhenpu
Zhenyang 鎮洋
Zhenze 震澤
Zhexi 浙西
Zhi buzu zhai 知不足齋
zhi ji 知己
zhi yin 知音
zhijizhe 知己者
Zhinü 織女
zhinü 志女
Zhiping 治平
Zhou 周
Zhou Cuiling 周翠齡
Zhou Kai 周凱
Zhou li 周禮
"Zhou nan" 周南
Zhou Xiaolian 周小蓮
Zhou Yubu 周羽步
Zhoushan 舟山
Zhu Lanyun 朱蘭雲
Zhu Shuzhen 朱淑眞
Zhu Wenyu 朱文毓
Zhu Xi 朱熹
Zhu Yunguan 朱芸官
Zhuang (Duke) 莊
Zhuang (lineage) 莊
Zhuang Panzhu 莊盤珠
Zhuang zi 莊子
Zhuogeng lu 輟耕錄
Zhuxi 竹西
zi (marriage name) 字
zi (purple) 紫
zicui 齊衰
Ziyuan 子元
zu shi 足食
Zuo Muguang 左慕光
Zuo zhuan 左傳

REFERENCES

SOURCES CITED BY ABBREVIATION

EC Hummel, Arthur W., ed. 1943. *Eminent Chinese of the Ch'ing Period.* Washington, D.C.: U.S. Government Printing Office.

GGZJ Wanyan Yun Zhu 完顏惲珠, comp. 1831. *Guochao guixiu zhengshi ji* 國朝閨秀正始集 (Correct beginnings: Women's poetry of our august dynasty). Hongxiangguan edition.

GGZX Wanyan Miaolianbao 完顏妙蓮保, comp. 1836. *Guochao guixiu zhengshi xuji* 國朝閨秀正始續集 (Correct beginnings: Women's poetry of our august dynasty, continued). Hongxiangguan edition.

GGZXB Wanyan Miaolianbao 完顏妙蓮保, comp. 1836. *Guochao guixiu zhengshi xuji buyi* 國朝閨秀正始續集補遺 (Supplement to Correct beginnings: Women's poetry of our august dynasty, continued). Hongxiangguan edition.

HLM Cao Xueqin 曹雪芹 and Gao E 高鶚. [1791] 1988. *Hong lou meng* 紅樓夢 (Dream of the Red Chamber). 3 vols. Beijing: Renmin wenxue chubanshe.

JSWB He Changling 賀長齡, comp. [1826] 1963. *Huangchao jingshi wenbian* 皇朝經世文編 (Collected essays on statecraft of our august dynasty). Reprint, Taibei: Guofeng chubanshe.

LGBL Wanyan Yun Zhu 完顏惲珠, comp. 1831. *Langui baolu* 蘭閨寶錄 (Precious record from the maidens' chambers). Hongxiangguan edition.

Nanjing 1784 "Zhuquan jushi" 珠泉居士 (The recluse of the pearl spring). *Xu Banqiao za ji* 續板橋雜記 (Scattered records of Banqiao, continued). Reprinted in *Xiangyan congshu* 1914, 18: 1/1a–17b.

Nanjing 1787 "Zhuquan jushi" 珠泉居士 (The recluse of the pearl spring). *Xue hong xiao ji* 雪鴻小記 (A little record of the wild goose in snow). Reprinted in *Xiangyan congshu* 1914, 19: 2/1a–8a.

Nanjing 1817 "Penghua sheng" 捧花生 (The master who offers a flower). *Qinhuai huafang lu* 秦淮畫舫錄 (The painted boats of Qinhuai). Reprinted in *Xiangyan congshu* 1914, 14: 3–4.

Nanjing 1818 "Penghua sheng" 捧花生 (The master who offers a flower). *Qinhuai huafang yutan* 秦淮畫舫餘譚 (Afterthoughts on the painted boats of Qinhuai) [Continuation of the *Qinhuai huafang lu*]. Reprinted in *Xiangyan congshu* 1914, 18: 1/18a–36b.

Ningbo 1841 "Er shi sheng" 二石生 (The master of the two stones). *Shizhou chun yu* 十洲春語 (Spring words from Shizhou). Reprinted in *Xiangyan congshu* 1914, 15:3.

QGSZ Shi Shuyi 施淑儀, comp. [1922] 1987. *Qingdai guige shiren zhenglüe* 清代閨閣詩人徵略 (Brief lives of women poets of the Qing dynasty). Reprint, Shanghai: Shanghai shudian.

SNS Yuan Mei 袁枚. 1796. *Suiyuan nüdizi shixuan* 隨園女弟子詩選 (Collected poems by the women pupils of [Yuan] Suiyuan [Mei]).

SS Yuan Mei 袁枚. [1793–96] 1982. *Suiyuan shihua* 隨園詩話 (Poetry talks). Gu Xuexie 顧學頡, ed. Reprint, 2 vols., Beijing: Renmin wenxue chubanshe.

SSB Yuan Mei 袁枚. 1793–96. *Suiyuan shihua buyi* 隨園詩話補遺 (Supplement to Poetry talks). Reprinted as volume 2 of *SS*.

Stone *The Story of the Stone*, a translation of *HLM* by David Hawkes (vol. 1, 1973; vol. 2, 1977; vol. 3, 1980) and John Minford (vol. 4, 1982; vol. 5, 1986). New York: Penguin Books.

Suzhou 1803 "Xiqi shan ren" 西溪山人 (The mountain dweller of the western stream). *Wumen huafang lu* 吳門畫舫錄 (The painted boats at the "Gateway to Wu"). Reprinted in *Xiangyan congshu* 1914, 17: 3/7a–19a.

Suzhou 1813 "Gezhong xiansheng" 箇中先生 (An Insider). *Wumen huafang xulu* 吳門畫舫續錄 (The painted boats at the "Gateway to Wu," continued). Reprinted in *Xiangyan congshu* 1914, 17: 3/20a–42b.

OTHER SOURCES

Abu-Lughod, Lila. 1986. *Veiled Sentiments: Honor and Poetry in a Bedouin Society*. Berkeley: University of California Press.

———. 1993. *Writing Women's Worlds: Bedouin Stories.* Berkeley: University of California Press.

Ahern, Emily M. 1975. "The Power and Pollution of Chinese Women." In Margery Wolf and Roxane Witke, eds., *Women in Chinese Society.* Stanford: Stanford University Press.

Anderson, Benedict. 1983. *Imagined Communities: Reflections on the Origin and Spread of Nationalism.* London: Verso.

Arkush, R. David. 1984. "'If Man Works Hard the Land Will Not Be Lazy': Entrepreneurial Values in North Chinese Peasant Proverbs." *Modern China* 10.4: 461–80.

Armstrong, Nancy. 1987. *Desire and Domestic Fiction: A Political History of the Novel.* New York: Oxford University Press.

Ayscough, Florence [Mrs. Harley Farnsworth MacNair]. 1937. *Chinese Women Yesterday and To-day.* Boston: Houghton Mifflin.

Bakhtin, Mikhail. 1984. *Rabelais and His World.* Trans. Helene Iswolsky. Bloomington: Indiana University Press.

Ban Zhao 班昭. [1624] 1893. *Nü jie* 女誡 (Instructions for women). In *Nü sishu* 女四書 (Four Books for Women). Annotated by Wang Xiang 王相. Imperially commissioned edition.

Bayly, C. A. 1988. "The Origins of Swadeshi (Home Industry): Cloth and Indian Society, 1700–1930." In Arjun Appadurai, ed., *The Social Life of Things: Commodities in Cultural Perspective.* Cambridge: Cambridge University Press.

Beattie, Hilary J. 1979. *Land and Lineage in China: A Study of T'ung-ch'eng County, Anhwei, in the Ming and Ch'ing Dynasties.* Cambridge: Cambridge University Press.

Bol, Peter K. 1992. *"This Culture of Ours": Intellectual Transitions in T'ang and Sung China.* Stanford: Stanford University Press.

Boltz, Judith M. 1987. *A Survey of Taoist Literature: Tenth to Seventeenth Centuries.* Berkeley: Center for Chinese Studies, Institute of East Asian Studies, University of California.

Bray, Francesca. Forthcoming 1997. *Inner States: Domestic Technologies and the Social Order in Late Imperial China.* Berkeley: University of California Press.

Bredon, Juliet, and Igor Mitrophanow. [1927] 1982. *The Moon Year: A Record of Chinese Customs and Festivals.* Reprint, New York: Oxford University Press.

Brokaw, Cynthia. 1991. *The Ledgers of Merit and Demerit: Social Change and Moral Order in Late Imperial China.* Cambridge, Mass.: Harvard University Press.

Brook, Timothy. 1993. *Praying for Power: Buddhism and the Formation of Gentry Society in Late-Ming China.* Cambridge, Mass.: Harvard University Press.

Brown, Judith C. 1986. "A Woman's Place Was in the Home: Women's Work in Renaissance Tuscany." In Margaret W. Ferguson, Maureen Quilligan, and Nancy J. Vickers, eds., *Rewriting the Renaissance: The Discourses of Sexual Difference in Early Modern Europe.* Chicago: University of Chicago Press.

Byron, John. 1987. *Portrait of a Chinese Paradise: Erotica and Sexual Customs of the Late Qing Period.* London: Quartet Books.

Cahill, James. 1960. *Chinese Painting.* Skira edition. Cleveland: World Publishing Company.

Cahill, Suzanne E. 1993. *Transcendence and Divine Passion: The Queen Mother of the West in Medieval China.* Stanford: Stanford University Press.

Carlitz, Katherine. 1991. "The Social Uses of Female Virtue in Late Ming Editions of *Lienü Zhuan.*" *Late Imperial China* 12.2: 117–48.

Carpenter, Frances. 1945. *Tales of a Chinese Grandmother.* New York: Doubleday, Doran.

Chan, Wing-tsit. 1973. *A Source Book in Chinese Philosophy.* Princeton: Princeton University Press.

Chang, Kang-i Sun. 1991. *The Late-Ming Poet Ch'en Tzu-lung: Crises of Love and Loyalism.* New Haven: Yale University Press.

———. 1992. "A Guide to Ming-Ch'ing Anthologies of Female Poetry and Their Selection Strategies." *The Gest Library Journal* (special issue) 5.2: 119–74.

Chang, Kang-i Sun, and Haun Saussy, eds. Forthcoming 1997. *Chinese Women Poets: An Anthology of Poetry and Criticism from Ancient Times to 1911.* Stanford: Stanford University Press.

Chard, Robert L. 1990. "Folktales on the God of the Stove." *Chinese Studies* 8.1: 149–82.

Chen Hongmou 陳宏謀, comp. [1742] 1868; 1895. *Jiaonü yigui* 教女遺規 (Bequeathed guidelines for instructing women). In *Wuzhong yigui* (Five sets of bequeathed guidelines).

Chen Peng 陳鵬. 1990. *Zhongguo hunyin shi gao* 中國婚姻史稿 (A draft history of marriage in China). Beijing: Xinhua shudian.

Chodorow, Nancy. 1978. *The Reproduction of Mothering: Psychoanalysis and the Sociology of Gender.* Berkeley: University of California Press.

Chow, Kai-wing. 1986. "Scholar and Society: The Textual Scholarship and Social Concerns of Wang Chung (1745–1794)." *Hanxue yanjiu* 4.1: 297–312.

———. 1994. *The Rise of Confucian Ritualism in Late Imperial China: Ethics, Classics, and Lineage Discourse.* Stanford: Stanford University Press.

Ch'ü T'ung-tsu. 1961. *Law and Society in Traditional China.* Paris: Mouton.

Chūgoku rekidai josei zōten 中國歷代女性像展 (Exhibit of portraits of Chinese women through history). 1987. Tokyo: Center for Pan-Asian Cultural Exchange.

Cleary, Thomas, ed. and trans. 1989. *Immortal Sisters: Secrets of Taoist Women.* Boston: Shambhala.

Cloud, Frederick D. [1906] 1971. *Hangchow: The "City of Heaven."* Shanghai: Presbyterian Mission Press. Reprint, Taibei: Chengwen.

Clunas, Craig. 1991. *Superfluous Things: Material Culture and Social Status in Early Modern China.* Cambridge, Eng.: Polity Press.

Cole, James H. 1986. *Shaohsing: Competition and Cooperation in Nineteenth-Century China.* Tucson: University of Arizona Press.

Cormack, Mrs. J. G. [1922] 1974. *Chinese Birthday, Wedding, Funeral and Other Customs.* Shanghai: Kelly and Walsh. Reprint, Taibei: Chengwen.

Crossley, Pamela Kyle. 1987. "*Manzhou yuanliu kao* and the Formalization of the Manchu Heritage." *Journal of Asian Studies* 46.4: 761–90.

———. 1989. "The Qianlong Retrospect on the Chinese-Martial (*Hanjun*) Banners." *Late Imperial China* 10.1: 63–107.

———. 1990. *Orphan Warriors: Three Manchu Generations and the End of the Qing World*. Princeton: Princeton University Press.

Da Qing Shizong Xianhuangdi shilu 大清世宗憲皇帝實錄 (Veritable records of the Yongzheng reign). [1937] 1964. Facsimile reprint of Da Manzhou diguo guowuyuan edition, Taibei: Huawen shuju.

Da Qing yitong zhi 大清一統志 (Comprehensive gazetteer of the realm). [1820] 1966. Jiaqing edition. Reprint, Taibei: Taiwan shangwu yinshuguan.

Dalby, Liza Crihfield. 1983. *Geisha*. Berkeley: University of California Press.

Demiéville, Paul. 1961. "Chang Hsueh-ch'eng and His Historiography." In W. G. Beasley and E. G. Pulleyblank, eds., *Historians of China and Japan*. London: Oxford University Press.

Despeux, Catherine. 1990. *Immortelles de la Chine ancienne: Taoïsme et alchimie féminine*. Puiseaux: Pardès.

Deuchler, Martina. 1992. *The Confucian Transformation of Korea: A Study of Society and Ideology*. Cambridge, Mass.: Harvard University Press.

Dietrich, Craig. 1972. "Cotton Culture and Manufacture in Early Ch'ing China." In W. E. Willmott, ed., *Economic Organization in Chinese Society*. Stanford: Stanford University Press.

Doolittle, Rev. Justus. 1867. *Social Life of the Chinese*. 2 vols. New York: Harper.

Dudbridge, Glen. 1978. *The Legend of Miao-shan*. London: Ithaca Press.

———. 1992. "Women Pilgrims to T'ai Shan: Some Pages from a Seventeenth-Century Novel." In Susan Naquin and Chün-fang Yü, eds., *Pilgrims and Sacred Sites in China*. Berkeley: University of California Press.

Ebrey, Patricia Buckley, ed. 1981. *Chinese Civilization and Society: A Sourcebook*. New York: Free Press.

———. 1990. "Women, Marriage, and the Family in Chinese History." In Paul S. Ropp, ed., *Heritage of China: Contemporary Perspectives on Chinese Civilization*. Berkeley: University of California Press.

———. 1993. *The Inner Quarters: Marriage and the Lives of Chinese Women in the Sung Period*. Berkeley: University of California Press.

Edwards, Louise P. 1994. *Men and Women in Qing China: Gender in "The Red Chamber Dream."* Leiden: E. J. Brill.

Elman, Benjamin A. 1981. "Ch'ing Dynasty 'Schools' of Scholarship," *Ch'ing-shih wen-t'i* 4.6: 1–44.

———. 1984. *From Philosophy to Philology: Intellectual and Social Aspects of Change in Late Imperial China*. Cambridge, Mass.: Council on East Asian Studies, Harvard University.

———. 1990. *Classicism, Politics, and Kinship: The Ch'ang-chou School of New Text Confucianism in Late Imperial China*. Berkeley: University of California Press.

Elman, Benjamin A., and Alexander Woodside, eds. 1994. *Education and Society in Late Imperial China, 1600–1900*. Berkeley: University of California Press.

Elvin, Mark. 1972. "The High-Level Equilibrium Trap: The Causes of the Decline of Invention in the Traditional Chinese Textile Industries." In W. E. Willmott, ed., *Economic Organization in Chinese Society*. Stanford: Stanford University Press.

———. 1973. *The Pattern of the Chinese Past*. Stanford: Stanford University Press.

———. 1984. "Female Virtue and the State in China." *Past and Present* 104: 111–52.

Enloe, Cynthia. 1990. *Bananas, Beaches, and Bases: Making Feminist Sense of International Politics*. Berkeley: University of California Press.

Fang Guancheng 方觀承. [1809] 1988. *Qinding shouyi guangxun* 欽定授衣廣訓 (Imperially commissioned edition of wide-ranging instructions on the provision of clothing). Facsimile reprint, Shanghai: Guji chubanshe.

Fei, Hsiao-tung. [1939] 1962. *Peasant Life in China*. London: Routledge and Kegan Paul.

Feng Erkang 馮爾康. 1986. "Qingdai de hunyin zhidu yu funü de shehui diwei shulun" 清代的婚姻制度與婦女的社會地位述論 (Monograph on the marriage system in the Qing dynasty and the social status of women). In Zhongguo renmin daxue Qing shi yanjiusuo (Institute for Research on Qing History, China People's University), comp., *Qingshi yanjiu ji* (Collected research on Qing history), vol. 5. Beijing: Guangming ribao chubanshe.

Feng Hefa 馮和法, ed. 1933. *Zhongguo nongcun jingji ziliao* 中國農村經濟資料 (Source materials on China's agricultural economy). 2 vols. Shanghai: Liming shuju.

Findlen, Paula. 1993. "Science as a Career in Enlightenment Italy: The Strategies of Laura Bassi." *Isis* 84: 441–69.

Folbre, Nancy. 1986. "Cleaning House: New Perspectives on Households and Economic Development." *Journal of Development Economics* 22.1: 5–40.

———. 1987. "The Pauperization of Motherhood: Patriarchy and Public Policy in the United States." In Naomi Gerstel and Harriet Engel Gross, eds., *Families and Work*. Philadelphia: Temple University Press.

———. 1993. *Who Pays for the Kids? Gender and the Structure of Constraint*. London: Routledge.

Fortune, Robert. [1847] 1972. *Three Years' Wanderings in the Northern Provinces of China, Including a Visit to the Tea, Silk, and Cotton Countries*, 2d ed. London: John Murray. Reprint, Taibei: Chengwen.

Franck, Harry A. 1926. *Roving Through Southern China*. London: T. Fisher Unwin.

Freedman, Maurice. 1958. *Lineage Organization in Southeastern China*. London: University of London, Athlone Press.

Fu Yiling 傅衣凌. 1956. *Ming Qing shidai shangren ji shangye ziben* 明清時代商人及商業資本 (Merchants and commercial capital during the Ming and Qing dynasties). Beijing: Renmin chubanshe.

Furth, Charlotte. 1986. "Blood, Body, and Gender: Medical Images of the Female Condition in China." *Chinese Science* 7: 53–65.

———. 1987. "Concepts of Pregnancy, Childbirth, and Infancy in Ch'ing Dynasty China." *Journal of Asian Studies* 46.1: 7–35.

———. 1994. "Rethinking van Gulik: Sexuality and Reproduction in Traditional Chinese Medicine." In Christina K. Gilmartin, Gail Hershatter, Lisa Rofel, and Tyrene White, eds., *Engendering China: Women, Culture, and the State*. Cambridge, Mass.: Harvard University Press.

Garrett, Valery M. 1987. *Chinese Clothing in Hong Kong and South China, 1840–1980*. Hong Kong: Oxford University Press.

A Glance at the Interior of China Obtained During a Journey Through the Silk and Green Tea Districts. 1849. Shanghai: n.p.

Grant, Beata. 1989. "The Spiritual Saga of Woman Huang: From Pollution to Purification." In David Johnson, ed., *Ritual Opera, Operatic Ritual: "Mu-lien Rescues His Mother" in Chinese Popular Culture*. Berkeley: Chinese Popular Culture Project, University of California.

———. 1994. "Who Is This I? Who Is That Other? The Poetry of an Eighteenth Century Buddhist Laywoman." *Late Imperial China* 15.1: 47–86.

Gregory, Peter N. 1991. *Tsung-mi and the Sinification of Buddhism*. Princeton: Princeton University Press.

Grove, Linda, and Christian Daniels, eds. 1984. *State and Society in China: Japanese Perspectives on Ming-Qing Social and Economic History*. Tokyo: University of Tokyo Press.

Guisso, Richard W., and Stanley Johannesen, eds. 1981. *Women in China: Current Directions in Historical Scholarship*. Historical Reflections, Directions Series 3. Youngstown, N.Y.: Philo Press.

Gujin tushu jicheng 古今圖書集成 (Completed collection of graphs and writings of ancient and modern times) [1728] 1985. Reprint, Beijing: Zhonghua shuju.

Guliang zhuan 穀梁傳 (*Guliang* commentary on the Spring and Autumn Annals). [1927–28] 1965. Sibu beiyao edition. Reprint, Taibei: Zhonghua shuju.

Gulik, R. H. van. 1961. *Sexual Life in Ancient China*. Leiden: E. J. Brill.

Guo Licheng 郭立誠. [1904] 1982. "Xie zai *Nü ren jing* qianye" 寫在女人經前頁 (Written as a foreword to the *Classic for Women*). In *Nü ren jing* 女人經 (Classic for women). Reprint, Taibei: Dali chubanshe.

Guo Songyi 郭松義. 1987. "Qingdai renkou wenti yu hunyin zhuangkuang de kaocha" 清代人口問題與婚姻狀況的考察 (A study of population and marital status in the Qing dynasty). *Zhongguo shi yanjiu* 3: 123–37.

Guy, R. Kent. 1987. *The Emperor's Four Treasuries: Scholars and the State in the Late Ch'ien-lung Era*. Cambridge, Mass.: Council on East Asian Studies, Harvard University.

Handlin, Joanna F. 1975. "Lü K'un's New Audience: The Influence of Women's Literacy on Sixteenth-Century Thought." In Margery Wolf and Roxane Witke, eds., *Women in Chinese Society*. Stanford: Stanford University Press.

Harrell, Stevan. 1985. "The Rich Get Children: Segmentation, Stratification, and Population in Three Chekiang Lineages, 1550–1850." In Susan B. Hanley and

Arthur P. Wolf, eds., *Family and Population in East Asian History*. Stanford: Stanford University Press.

———. 1995. "Introduction: Civilizing Projects and the Reaction to Them." In Harrell, ed., *Cultural Encounters on China's Ethnic Frontiers*. Seattle: University of Washington Press.

Hawkes, David. 1959. *Ch'u Tz'u: The Songs of the South*. London: Oxford University Press.

He Guanbiao 何冠彪. 1991. "Qingdai 'Zhedong xuepai' wenti pingyi" 清代「浙東學派」問題評議 (A critical assessment of the controversy surrounding the Zhedong school of scholarship). In *Mingmo Qingchu xueshu sixiang yanjiu* 明末清初學術思想研究 (Studies of scholarship and thought in the Ming-Qing transition). Taibei: Taiwan xuesheng shuju.

Headland, Isaac Taylor. [1914] 1974. *Home Life in China*. London: Methuen. Reprint, Taibei: Chengwen.

Herlihy, David. 1990. *Opera Muliebria: Women and Work in Medieval Europe*. New York: McGraw-Hill.

Hershatter, Gail. 1989. "The Hierarchy of Shanghai Prostitution, 1870–1949." *Modern China* 15.4: 463–98.

———. 1991. "Prostitution and the Market in Women in Early Twentieth-Century Shanghai." In Rubie S. Watson and Patricia Buckley Ebrey, eds., *Marriage and Inequality in Chinese Society*. Berkeley: University of California Press.

———. 1992. "Sex Work and Social Order: Prostitutes, Their Families, and the State in Twentieth-Century Shanghai." In Institute of Modern History, Academia Sinica, eds., *Family Process and Political Process in Modern Chinese History*, vol. 2. Taibei: Institute of Modern History, Academia Sinica.

———. Forthcoming 1997. *Dangerous Pleasures: Prostitution and Modernity in Twentieth-Century Shanghai*. Berkeley: University of California Press.

Hinsch, Bret. 1990. *Passions of the Cut Sleeve: The Male Homosexual Tradition in China*. Berkeley: University of California Press.

Hirschmeier, Johannes. 1964. *The Origins of Entrepreneurship in Meiji Japan*. Cambridge, Mass.: Harvard University Press.

Ho, Clara Wing-chung [Liu Yongcong 劉詠聰]. 1995. "The Cultivation of Female Talent: Views on Women's Education in China During the Early and High Qing Periods." *Journal of the Economic and Social History of the Orient* 38.2: 191–223.

Ho Ping-ti. 1959. *Studies on the Population of China*. Cambridge, Mass.: Harvard University Press.

———. 1962. *The Ladder of Success in Imperial China: Aspects of Social Mobility, 1368–1911*. New York: Columbia University Press.

———. 1967. "The Significance of the Ch'ing Period in Chinese History." *Journal of Asian Studies* 26.2: 189–95.

Hoang, Pierre. 1916. *Le mariage chinois au point de vu légal*. 2d ed., rev. and corrected. Variétés sinologiques no. 14. Shanghai: Catholic Mission.

Hodous, Lewis. [1929] 1984. *Folkways in China*. Reprint, Taibei: Orient Cultural Service.

Holmgren, Jennifer. 1986. "Observations on Marriage and Inheritance Practices in Early Mongol and Yuan Society, with Particular Reference to the Levirate." *Journal of Asian History* 20.2: 127–92.

———. 1991. "Imperial Marriage in the Native Chinese and Non-Han State, Han to Ming." In Rubie S. Watson and Patricia Buckley Ebrey, eds., *Marriage and Inequality in Chinese Society*. Berkeley: University of California Press.

Hong Liangji 洪亮吉. [1793] 1969. "Yi yan ershi pian" 意言二十篇 (Opinions: Twenty essays). *Juanshige wen, jia ji* 卷施閣文甲集 (Essays from the Pavilion of the Juanshi Plant, first collection), *juan* 1. In *Hong Beijiang xiansheng yiji* 洪北江先生遺集 (The bequeathed works of Hong Liangji). Shoujing tang edition, vol. 1. Reprint, Taibei: Huawen shuju.

Hong Shuling 洪淑苓. 1988. *Niulang zhinü yanjiu* 牛郎織女研究 (A study of the folktale of "The Cowherd and the Weaving Maid"). Taibei: Taiwan xuesheng shuju.

Honig, Emily. 1986. *Sisters and Strangers: Women in the Shanghai Cotton Mills, 1919–1949*. Stanford: Stanford University Press.

Hsiao, Kung-chuan. 1960. *Rural China: Imperial Control in the Nineteenth Century*. Seattle: University of Washington.

Hsiung Ping-chen [Xiong Bingzhen] 熊秉真. 1992. "Hao de kaishi: Jinshi shiren zidi de younian jiaoyu" 好的開始: 近世士人子弟的幼年教育 (A good start: childhood education of scholars in modern history). In Institute of Modern History, Academia Sinica, eds. *Family Process and Political Process in Modern Chinese History*, vol. 1. Taibei: Institute of Modern History, Academia Sinica.

———. 1994. "Constructed Emotions: The Bond Between Mothers and Sons in Late Imperial China." *Late Imperial China* 15.1: 87–117.

Hu Shih [Hu Shi 胡適]. [1931a] 1992. "Women's Place in Chinese History." In Li Yu-ning, ed. *Chinese Women Through Chinese Eyes*. Armonk, N.Y.: M. E. Sharpe.

———. 1931b. *Zhang Shizhai xiansheng nianpu* 章實齋先生年譜 (Yearly chronicle of the life of Zhang Shizhai [Xuecheng]). Expanded and amplified by Yao Mingda 姚名達. Shanghai: Shangwu yinshu guan.

Hu Wenkai 胡文楷, ed. [1957] 1985. *Lidai funü zhuzuo kao* 歷代婦女著作考 (A survey of women writers through the ages). Shanghai: Shanghai guji chubanshe.

Huang Liu-hung [Huang Liuhong 黃六鴻]. [1694] 1984. *Fuhui quanshu* 福惠全書. Translated as *A Complete Book Concerning Happiness and Benevolence, Fu-hui ch'üan-shu, A Manual for Local Magistrates in Seventeenth-Century China.* Trans. and ed. Chu Djang. Tucson: University of Arizona Press.

Huang, Philip C. C. 1990. *The Peasant Family and Rural Development in the Yangzi Delta, 1350–1988*. Stanford: Stanford University Press.

Huang Yizhi 黃逸之. 1934. *Huang Zhongze nianpu* 黃仲則年譜 (A chronological biography of Huang Jingren). Shanghai: Commercial Press.

Huangchao zhengdian leizuan 皇朝政典類纂 (Sources on governmental institutions of the reigning dynasty, arranged by category). [1903] 1969. Reprint, Taibei: Chengwen chubanshe.

Hucker, Charles O. 1985. *A Dictionary of Official Titles in Imperial China*. Stanford: Stanford University Press.

Jin shu 晉書 (History of the Jin dynasty). [646–48] 1974. Reprint, 10 vols., Beijing: Zhonghua shuju.

Jing Junjian 經君健. 1981. "Lun Qingdai shehui de dengji jiegou" 論清代社會的等級結構 (The structure of stratification in Qing dynasty society). *Jingji yanjiusuo jikan* 3: 1–64.

———. 1993. *Qingdai shehui de jianmin dengji* 清代社會的賤民等級 (The status of pariah populations in Qing society). Hangzhou: Zhejiang renmin chubanshe.

Johnson, David, ed. 1989. *Ritual Opera, Operatic Ritual: "Mu-lien Rescues His Mother" in Chinese Popular Culture*. Berkeley: Chinese Popular Culture Project, University of California.

Johnson, Elizabeth L. 1975. "Women and Childbearing in Kwan Mun Hau Village." In Margery Wolf and Roxane Witke, eds., *Women in Chinese Society*. Stanford: Stanford University Press.

———. 1988. "Grieving for the Dead, Grieving for the Living: Funeral Laments of Hakka Women." In James L. Watson and Evelyn S. Rawski, eds., *Death Ritual in Late Imperial and Modern China*. Berkeley: University of California Press.

Johnson, Kinchen. [1932] 1971. *Folksongs and Children-Songs from Peiping*. Taibei: Orient Cultural Service.

Johnston, Reginald F. [1910] 1986. *Lion and Dragon in Northern China*. New York: John Murray. Reprint, Hong Kong: Oxford University Press.

Jones, Susan Mann. 1972. "Hung Liang-chi (1746–1809): The Perception and Articulation of Political Problems in Late Eighteenth-Century China." Ph.D. diss. Stanford University.

Jones, Susan Mann, and Philip A. Kuhn. 1978. "Dynastic Decline and the Roots of Rebellion." In John K. Fairbank, ed. *The Cambridge History of China*. Vol. 10: *Late Ch'ing, 1800–1911*, part 1. New York: Cambridge University Press.

Kahn, Harold L. 1971. *Monarchy in the Emperor's Eyes: Image and Reality in the Ch'ien-lung Reign*. Cambridge, Mass.: Harvard University Press.

Kelly, Joan. 1984. *Women, History, and Theory: The Essays of Joan Kelly*. Chicago: University of Chicago Press.

Kendall, Laurel. 1987. *Shamans, Housewives, and Other Restless Spirits: Women in Korean Ritual Life*. Honolulu: University of Hawaii Press.

King, Margaret L. 1980. "Book-Lined Cells: Women and Humanism in the Early Italian Renaissance." In Patricia H. LaBalme, ed., *Beyond Their Sex: Learned Women of the European Past*. New York: New York University Press.

Ko, Dorothy Y. 1994. *Teachers of the Inner Chambers: Women and Culture in China, 1573–1722*. Stanford: Stanford University Press.

———. Forthcoming 1997. "The Body as Attire: Footbinding and the Boundaries of Alterity in Seventeenth-Century China." *Journal of Women's History*.

Kohn, Livia, ed. 1993. *The Taoist Experience: An Anthology*. Albany: State University of New York Press.

Kuhn, Dieter. 1988. *Science and Civilisation in China.* Vol. 5: *Chemistry and Chemical Technology*, part 9, *Textile Technology: Spinning and Reeling*. Cambridge: Cambridge University Press.

Kuhn, Philip A. 1990. *Soulstealers: The Chinese Sorcery Scare of 1768*. Cambridge, Mass.: Harvard University Press.

Lagerwey, John. 1987. *Taoist Ritual in Chinese Society and History*. New York: Macmillan.

Lan Dingyuan 藍鼎元. [early eighteenth century] 1977. *Nü xue* 女學 (Women's learning). Reprint, Taibei: Wenhai chubanshe.

Lau, D. C., trans. 1982. *Confucius: The Analects*. New York: Penguin Books.

Lawton, Thomas. 1973. *Chinese Figure Painting*. Washington, D.C.: Freer Gallery of Art.

Lee, James, Cameron Campbell, and Guofu Tan. 1992. "Infanticide and Family Planning in Late Imperial China: The Price and Population History of Rural Liaoning, 1774–1873." In Thomas G. Rawski and Lillian M. Li, eds., *Chinese History in Economic Perspective*. Berkeley: University of California Press.

Legge, James, trans. [1885] 1967. *Li Chi: Book of Rites*. Ed. Ch'u Chai and Winberg Chai. 2 vols. New Hyde Park, N.Y.: University Books.

———, trans. [1893–95] 1991. *The Chinese Classics*. Vol. 1, *"Confucian Analects," "The Great Learning," and "The Doctrine of the Mean."* Vol. 2, *The Works of Mencius*. Vol. 4, *"The She King."* Vol. 5, *"The Ch'un Ts'ew with The Tso Chuen."* Taibei: SMC Publishing. Reprint of the last editions, Oxford: Oxford University Press.

Lerner, Gerda. 1986. *The Creation of Patriarchy*. New York: Oxford University Press.

Leung, Angela Ki Che [Liang Qizi 梁其姿]. 1993a. "To Chasten Society: The Development of Widow Homes in the Qing." *Late Imperial China* 14.2: 1–32.

———. 1993b. "'Pinqiong' yu 'qiongren' guannian zai Zhongguo sushi shehuizhong de lishi yanbian" 「貧窮」與「窮人」觀念在中國俗世社會中的歷史演變 (The historical transformation of concepts of "poverty" and "the poor" in Chinese popular culture). In Huang Yinggui 黃應貴, ed., *Renguan, yiyi, yu shehui* 人觀, 意義, 與社會 (Perception, meaning, and society). Taibei: Zhongyang yanjiuyuan minzuxue yanjiusuo.

Leupp, Gary P. 1992. *Servants, Shophands, and Laborers in the Cities of Tokugawa Japan*. Princeton: Princeton University Press.

Levering, Miriam L. 1982. "The Dragon Girl and the Abbess of Maoshan: Gender and Status in the Ch'an Buddhist Tradition." *Journal of the International Association of Buddhist Studies* 5.1: 19–35.

Levy, Howard S. 1966a. *Chinese Footbinding: The History of a Curious Erotic Custom*. New York: Walton Rawls.

———, trans. 1966b. *A Feast of Mist and Flowers: The Gay Quarters of Nanking at the End of the Ming*. Yokohama: privately printed.

Levy, Marion J., Jr. 1949. *The Family Revolution in Modern China*. London: Oxford University Press.

Levy, Marion J., Jr., and Kuo-heng Shih. 1949. *The Rise of the Modern Chinese Business Class: Two Introductory Essays*. New York: Institute of Pacific Relations, International Secretariat.

Li Bozhong 李伯重. 1984. "Ming Qing shiqi Jiangnan shuidao shengchan jiyue chengdu de tigao—Ming Qing Jiangnan nongyejingji fazhan tedian tantao zhi yi" 明清時期江南水稻生產集約程度的提高—明清江南農業經濟發展特點探討之一 (The rising intensification of rice production in Jiangnan during the Ming-Qing period—the first inquiry into the special characteristics of the development of Jiangnan's agricultural economy during the Ming-Qing period). *Zhongguo nongshi* 1: 24–37.

———. 1985a. "'Sang zheng daotian' yu Ming Qing Jiangnan nongye shengchan jiyue chengdu de tigao—Ming Qing Jiangnan nongyejingji fazhan tedian tantao zhi er" "桑爭稻田" 與明清江南農業生產集約程度的提高—明清江南農業經濟發展特點探討之二 ("Mulberry versus paddy fields" and the rising intensification of agricultural production in Jiangnan during the Ming-Qing period—a second inquiry into the special characteristics of the development of Jiangnan's agricultural economy during the Ming-Qing period). *Zhongguo nongshi* 1: 1–12.

———. 1985b. "Ming Qing Jiangnan nongye ziyuan de heli liyong—Ming Qing Jiangnan nongyejingji fazhan tedian tantao zhi san" 明清江南農業資源的合理利用—明清江南農業經濟發展特點探討之三 (The rational use of agricultural resources in Ming-Qing Jiangnan—a third inquiry into the special characteristics of the development of Jiangnan's agricultural economy during the Ming-Qing period). *Nongye kaogu* 2: 150–163.

———. 1986. "Ming Qing Jiangnan zhongdao nonghu shengchan nengli chutan—Ming Qing Jiangnan nongyejingji fazhan tedian tantao zhi si" 明清江南種稻農戶生產能力初探—明清江南農業經濟發展特點探討之四 (A preliminary study of the productivity of peasant rice cultivators in Ming-Qing Jiangnan—the fourth inquiry into the special characteristics of the development of Jiangnan's agricultural economy during the Ming-Qing period). *Zhongguo nongshi* 3: 1–12.

Li Dou 李斗. [1794–1797] 1984. *Yangzhou huafang lu* 楊州畫舫錄 (Guide to the pleasure quarters of Yangzhou). Yangzhou: Jiangsu guangling guji keyinshe.

Li, Lillian M. 1981. *China's Silk Trade: Traditional Industry in the Modern World, 1842–1937*. Cambridge, Mass.: Harvard University Press.

Li Ling and Keith McMahon. 1992. "The Contents and Terminology of the Mawangdui Texts on the Arts of the Bedchamber." *Early China* 17: 145–185.

Li Ruzhen 李汝珍. [1828] 1965. *Jinghua yuan* 鏡花緣. Translated as *Flowers in the Mirror*. Trans. and ed. Lin Tai-yi. Berkeley: University of California Press.

Li, San-pao. 1993. "Ch'ing Cosmology and Popular Precepts." In Richard J. Smith and D. W. Y. Kwok, eds., *Cosmology, Ontology, and Human Efficacy: Essays in Chinese Thought*. Honolulu: University of Hawaii Press.

Li Wai-yee. 1993. *Enchantment and Disenchantment: Love and Illusion in Chinese Literature*. Princeton: Princeton University Press.

Liang Fangzhong 梁方仲, ed. 1985. *Zhongguo lidai hukou, tiandi, tianfu tongji* 中國歷代戶口,田地,田賦統計 (Population, land, and tax data through Chinese history). Shanghai: Renmin chubanshe.

Liang Qizi. *See* Leung, Angela Ki Che.

Liang Yizhen 梁乙真. [1925] 1968. *Qingdai funü wenxue shi* 清代婦女文學史. Reprint, Taibei: Zhonghua shuju.

Lin Man-houng. 1991. "Two Social Theories Revealed: Statecraft Controversies over China's Monetary Crisis, 1808–1854." *Late Imperial China* 12.1: 1–35.

Lin Yü-t'ang. [1935] 1992. "Feminist Thought in Ancient China." In Li Yu-ning, ed., *Chinese Women Through Chinese Eyes*. Armonk, N.Y.: M. E. Sharpe.

Linqing 麟慶. [1897] 1981; n.d. *Hongxue yinyuan tuji* 鴻雪因緣圖記 (Sketches of a wanderer's fortune). Reprint, Wang Xiqi 王錫祺, comp. *Xiaofanghu zhai yudi congchao* 小方壺齋輿地叢鈔, portfolio 5, no. 3: 144–58. Shanghai: Zhuyitang. Reprint (3 vols., unpaginated [vol. 3, illustrations]), Taibei: Guangwen shuju.

Liu I-ch'ing [Liu Yiqing 劉義慶]. [c. 430] 1976. *Shishuo xinyu* 世說新語. Translated as *"Shih-shuo Hsin-yü": A New Account of Tales of the World*. Trans. and ed. Richard B. Mather. Minneapolis: University of Minnesota Press.

Liu Jihua 劉紀華. 1934. "Zhongguo zhenjie guannian de lishi yanbian" 中國貞節觀念的歷史演變 (Historical change in the concept of chastity in China). *Shehui xuejie* 8: 19–35.

Liu Ts'ui-jung [Liu Cuirong 劉翠溶]. 1985. "The Demography of Two Chinese Clans in Hsiao-shan, Chekiang, 1650–1850." In Susan B. Hanley and Arthur P. Wolf, eds., *Family and Population in East Asian History*. Stanford: Stanford University Press.

———. 1992a. "Formation and Function of Three Lineages in Hunan." In Institute of Modern History, Academia Sinica, eds., *Family Process and Political Process in Modern Chinese History*. Taibei: Institute of Modern History, Academia Sinica.

———. 1992b. *Lineage Population and Socio-economic Changes in the Ming-Ch'ing Periods*. 2 vols. Nangang, Taibei: Institute of Economics, Academia Sinica, Economic Studies Series no. 15.

Liu Xiang 劉向. [16 B.C.E.] 1966. *Lienü zhuan* 列女傳 (Biographies of exemplary women). Reprint, Taibei: Sibu beiyao edition.

Liu Yunfen 劉雲份, comp. [1673] 1936. *Cui lou ji* 翠樓集 (Collected poems from azure chambers). Yexiangtang edition. Shanghai: Zazhi gongsi.

Loewe, Michael. 1979. *Ways to Paradise: The Chinese Quest for Immortality*. London: Allen & Unwin.

Lou Shou 樓璹. [1696] 1808. *Yüzhi gengzhi tu* 御製耕織圖 (Imperially commissioned illustrations of plowing and weaving). Illustrated by Jiao Bingzhen 焦秉貞. N.p.

Luk, Charles [Lu K'uan Yu], trans. 1966. *The Surangama Sutra (Leng Yen Ching)*. London: Rider.

Luo Wenzhao 羅文昭, comp. [1779] 1879. *Lidai mingyuan tushuo* 歷代名媛圖說 (Illustrated tales of famous beauties throughout history). 2 vols. Reprint, Shanghai: Dianshizhai.

McDermott, Joseph P. 1981. "Bondservants in the T'ai-hu Basin During the Late Ming: A Case of Mistaken Identities." *Journal of Asian Studies* 40.4: 675–701.

———. 1990. "The Chinese Domestic Bursar." *Ajia bunka kenkyū* (November): 15–32.

———. 1991. "Family Financial Plans of the Southern Sung." *Asia Major*, 3d ser., 4.2: 15–52.

McMahon, Keith. 1988. *Causality and Containment in Seventeenth-Century Chinese Fiction*. Leiden: E. J. Brill.

———. 1994. "The Classic 'Beauty-Scholar' Romance and the Superiority of the Talented Woman." In Angela Zito and Tani E. Barlow, eds., *Body, Subject, and Power in China*. Chicago: University of Chicago Press.

Mann, Susan. 1972. *See* Jones, Susan Mann.

———. 1985. "Historical Change in Female Biography from Song to Qing Times: The Case of Early Qing Jiangnan," *Transactions of the International Conference of Orientalists in Japan*, no. 30: 65–77.

———. 1987. "Widows in the Kinship, Class, and Community Structures of Qing Dynasty China." *Journal of Asian Studies* 46.1: 37–56.

———. 1991. "Grooming a Daughter for Marriage: Brides and Wives in the Mid-Ch'ing Period." In Rubie S. Watson and Patricia Buckley Ebrey, eds., *Marriage and Inequality in Chinese Society*. Berkeley: University of California Press.

———. 1992a. "Classical Revival and the Gender Question: China's First Querelle des Femmes." In Institute of Modern History, Academia Sinica, eds., *Family Process and Political Process in Modern Chinese History*, vol. 1. Taibei: Institute of Modern History, Academia Sinica.

———. 1992b. "'Fuxue' (Women's Learning) by Zhang Xuecheng (1738–1801): China's First History of Women's Culture." *Late Imperial China* 13.1: 40–63.

———. 1992c. "Household Handicrafts and State Policy in Qing Times." In Jane Kate Leonard and John R. Watt, eds., *To Achieve Security and Wealth: The Qing Imperial State and the Economy, 1644–1911*. Cornell East Asia Series no. 56. Ithaca: Cornell University East Asia Program.

———. 1993. "Suicide and Survival: Exemplary Widows in the Late Empire." In *Chūgoku no dentō shakai to kazoku: Yanagida Setsuko sensei koki kinen ronshū* 中國の傳統社會と家族:柳田節子先生古稀記念論集 (Family and society in traditional China: Essays in honor of Professor Yanagida Setsuko). Tokyo: Kyūko shoin.

———. 1994. "The Education of Daughters in the Mid-Ch'ing Period." In Benjamin A. Elman and Alexander Woodside, eds., *Education and Society in Late Imperial China, 1600–1900*. Berkeley: University of California Press.

———. 1996. "Women in the Life and Thought of Zhang Xuecheng." In Philip J. Ivanhoe, ed., *Chinese Language, Thought and Culture: Nivison and His Critics*. La Salle, Ill.: Open Court Press.

Mann, Susan, and Philip A. Kuhn. 1978. *See* Jones, Susan Mann and Philip A. Kuhn.

Martin, Emily. 1988. "Gender and Ideological Differences in Representations of

Life and Death." In James L. Watson and Evelyn S. Rawski, eds., *Death Ritual in Late Imperial and Modern China*. Berkeley: University of California Press.

Mayers, William Frederick. [1897] 1966. *The Chinese Government: A Manual of Chinese Titles, Categorically Arranged and Explained, with an Appendix*. Shanghai: Kelly & Walsh. Reprint, Taibei: Chengwen.

———. [1910] 1974. *The Chinese Reader's Manual*. Shanghai: American Presbyterian Mission Press. Reprint, London: Probsthain.

Meijer, Marinus J. 1980. "Slavery at the End of the Ch'ing Dynasty." In Jerome Alan Cohen, R. Randle Edwards, and Fu-mei Chang Chen, eds., *Essays on China's Legal Tradition*. Princeton: Princeton University Press.

Meng Fanke 孟繁科, ed. 1989. *Zhongguo funü zhi zui* 中國婦女之最 (China's greatest women). Beijing: Zhongguo liuyou chubanshe.

Metzger, Thomas A. 1977. *Escape from Predicament: Neo-Confucianism and China's Evolving Political Culture*. New York: Columbia University Press.

Mohanty, Chandra Talpade. 1991. "Under Western Eyes: Feminist Scholarship and Colonial Discourses." In Chandra Talpade Mohanty, Ann Russo, and Lourdes Torres, eds., *Third World Women and the Politics of Feminism*. Bloomington: Indiana University Press.

Morohashi Tetsuji 諸橋轍次. 1955–1960. *Dai Kan-Wa jiten* 大漢和辭典 (Comprehensive Chinese-Japanese dictionary). Tokyo: Taishukan shoten.

Nakagawa Tadahide 中川子信. [1799] 1983. *Shinzoku kibun* 清俗紀聞 (Travelers' accounts of Qing customs). Reprint, Taibei: Dali chubanshe.

Naquin, Susan. 1988. "Funerals in North China: Uniformity and Variation." In James L. Watson and Evelyn S. Rawski, eds., *Death Ritual in Late Imperial and Modern China*. Berkeley: University of California Press.

Naquin, Susan, and Evelyn S. Rawski. 1987. *Chinese Society in the Eighteenth Century*. New Haven: Yale University Press.

Needham, Joseph. 1956. *Science and Civilisation in China*. Vol. 2: *History of Scientific Thought*. Cambridge, Eng.: Cambridge University Press.

Ng, Vivien. 1987. "Ideology and Sexuality: Rape Laws in Qing China." *Journal of Asian Studies* 46.1: 57–70.

Nienhauser, William H., Jr., ed. and comp. 1986. *The Indiana Companion to Traditional Chinese Literature*. Bloomington: Indiana University Press.

Nivison, David S. 1966. *The Life and Thought of Chang Hsueh-ch'eng (1738–1801)*. Stanford: Stanford University Press.

O'Hara, Rev. Alfred R. 1945. *The Position of Woman in Early China According to the Lieh Nü Chuan, "The Biographies of Eminent Chinese Women."* Washington, D.C.: Catholic University of America Press.

Ono Kazuko 小野和子. [1978] 1989. *Chūgoku josei shi* 中國女性史. Trans. as *Chinese Women in a Century of Revolution, 1850–1950*. Ed. and trans. Joshua A. Fogel. Stanford: Stanford University Press.

Ortner, Sherry. 1978. "The Virgin and the State." *Feminist Studies* 14.3: 19–35.

Overmyer, Daniel L. 1985. "Values in Chinese Sectarian Literature: Ming and Ch'ing

Pao-chüan." In David Johnson, Andrew J. Nathan, and Evelyn S. Rawski, eds., *Popular Culture in Late Imperial China*. Berkeley: University of California Press.

Owen, Stephen. 1990. "Poetry in the Chinese Tradition." In Paul S. Ropp, ed., *Heritage of China: Contemporary Perspectives on Chinese Civilization*. Berkeley: University of California Press.

Pateman, Carole. 1988. *The Sexual Contract*. Stanford: Stanford University Press.

Paul, Diana Y. 1985. *Women in Buddhism: Images of the Feminine in Mahayana Tradition*. 2d ed. Berkeley: University of California Press.

Peng Shaosheng 彭紹昇, comp. 1872. *Shan nüren zhuan* 善女人傳 (Biographies of female lay devotees). 2 *juan*. N.p.

Peng Zeyi 彭澤益. 1984. *Zhongguo jindai shougongyeshi ziliao* 中國近代手工業史資料 (Materials on the history of China's modern handicraft industries). Vol. 1. Beijing: Zhonghua shuju.

Perdue, Peter. 1992. "The Qing State and the Gansu Grain Market, 1739–1864." In Thomas G. Rawski and Lillian M. Li, eds., *Chinese History in Economic Perspective*. Berkeley: University of California Press.

Peterson, Willard J. 1968. "The Life of Ku Yen-wu (1613–1682)." Part 1. *Harvard Journal of Asiatic Studies* 28: 114–56.

———. 1979. *Bitter Gourd: Fang I-chih and the Impetus for Intellectual Change*. New Haven: Yale University Press.

Playfair, G. M. H. [1910] 1968. *The Cities and Towns of China: A Geographical Dictionary*. 2d ed. Reprint, Taibei: Chengwen.

Qian Xiao 錢曉, comp. 1939. *Tingwei za lu* 庭幃雜錄 (Scattered records of the home life of Yuan Zhong and his brothers). Changsha: Shangwu shudian.

Qin Yaozeng 秦耀曾, comp. 1843. *Chongxiu Nanhai Putuo shan zhi* 重修南海普陀山志 (Gazetteer of Mount Putuo in the Southern Seas, revised).

Qinding Da Qing huidian shi li 欽定大清會典事例 (Imperially endorsed edition of the statutes and precedents of the Qing dynasty). [Jiaqing edition] 1991/92. Reprint, Taibei: Wenhai chubanshe.

Qinding Da Qing huidian zeli 欽定大清會典則例 (Imperially endorsed edition of the regulations and precedents of the Qing dynasty). 1748. Qianlong edition.

Qingdai hua falang tezhan mulu 清代畫琺瑯特展目錄 (Catalog of a special exhibition of Qing dynasty painted enamels). 1984. Taibei: Guoli gugong bowuyuan.

Quataert, Jean H. 1985. "The Shaping of Women's Work in Manufacturing: Guilds, Households, and the State in Central Europe, 1648–1870." *American Historical Review* 90.5: 1,122–48.

Rawski, Evelyn S. 1991. "Ch'ing Imperial Marriage and Problems of Rulership." In Rubie S. Watson and Patricia Buckley Ebrey, eds., *Marriage and Inequality in Chinese Society*. Berkeley: University of California Press.

Reed, Barbara E. 1992. "The Gender Symbolism of Kuan-yin Bodhisattva." In José Ignacio Cabezón, ed., *Buddhism, Sexuality, and Gender*. Albany: State University of New York Press.

Robertson, Maureen. 1992. "Voicing the Feminine: Constructions of the Gendered

Subject in Lyric Poetry by Women of Medieval and Late Imperial China." *Late Imperial China* 13.1: 63–110.

———. Forthcoming 1997. "Changing the Subject: Gender, Representation, and Self-Inscription in Author's Prefaces and 'Shi' Poetry by Women in Ming-Qing China." In Ellen Widmer and Kang-i Sun Chang, eds., *Writing Women in Late Imperial China*. Stanford: Stanford University Press.

Ropp, Paul S. 1976. "The Seeds of Change: Reflections on the Condition of Women in the Early and Mid Ch'ing." *Signs: Journal of Women in Culture and Society* 2.1: 5–23.

———. 1981. *Dissent in Early Modern China: "Ju-lin wai-shih" and Ch'ing Social Criticism*. Ann Arbor: University of Michigan Press.

———. 1985. "Between Two Worlds: Women in Shen Fu's *Six Chapters of a Floating Life*." In Anna Gerstlacher, ed., *Women and Literature in China*. Bochum, Germany: Brockmeyer.

———. 1994. "Vehicles of Dissent in Late Imperial Chinese Culture." In Léon Vandermeersch, ed. *La société civile face à l'Etat: dans les traditions chinoise, japonaise, coréenne et vietnamienne*. Etudes thématiques 3. Paris: Ecole Française d'Extrême-Orient.

Rowe, William T. 1992. "Women and the Family in Mid-Qing Social Thought: The Case of Chen Hongmou." *Late Imperial China* 13.2: 1–41.

Said, Edward. 1978. *Orientalism*. New York: Pantheon Books.

Sangren, P. Steven. 1983. "Female Gender in Chinese Religious Symbols: Kuan Yin, Ma Tsu, and the 'Eternal Mother.'" *Signs: Journal of Women in Culture and Society* 9.11: 4–25.

Santangelo, Paulo. 1993. "Urban Society in Late Imperial Suzhou." In Linda Cooke Johnson, ed., *Cities of Jiangnan in Late Imperial China*. Albany: State University of New York Press.

Schafer, Edward H. 1985. *Mirages on the Sea of Time: The Taoist Poetry of Ts'ao T'ang*. Berkeley: University of California Press.

Schipper, Kristofer. 1993. *The Taoist Body*. Trans. Karen C. Duval. Berkeley: University of California Press.

Schneider, Jane. 1985. "Trousseau as Treasure: Some Contradictions of Late Nineteenth-Century Change in Sicily." In Marion A. Kaplan, ed., *The Marriage Bargain: Women and Dowries in European History*. New York: Haworth Press.

Schneider, Laurence A. 1980. *A Madman of Ch'u: The Chinese Myth of Loyalty and Dissent*. Berkeley: University of California Press.

Scott, Joan W. 1986. "Gender: A Useful Category of Historical Analysis." *American Historical Review* 91.5: 1,053–75.

Seaman, Gary. 1981. "The Sexual Politics of Karmic Retribution." In Emily Martin Ahern and Hill Gates, eds., *The Anthropology of Chinese Society*. Stanford: Stanford University Press.

She xian [Anhui] zhi 翕縣 [安徽] 志 (Gazetteer of She county [Anhui]). [1937] 1975. Reprint, Taibei: Chengwen chubanshe.

Shek, Richard. 1993. "Testimony to the Resilience of the Mind: The Life and Thought of P'eng Shao-sheng (1740–1796)." In Richard J. Smith and D. W. Y. Kwok, eds., *Cosmology, Ontology, and Human Efficacy: Essays in Chinese Thought*. Honolulu: University of Hawaii Press.

Shen Fu 沈復. [1877] 1983. *Fusheng liu ji* 浮生六記. Trans. as *Six Records of a Floating Life*. Trans. Leonard Pratt and Chiang Su-hui. Harmondsworth, Eng.: Penguin Books.

Shen Yizheng 沈以正. 1984. *Lidai meiren huaxuan* 歷代美人畫選 (Collected paintings of beauties through the ages). Taibei: Yishu tushu gongsi.

Shinü hua zhi mei 仕女畫之美 (Glimpses into the Hidden Quarters: Paintings of Women from the Middle Kingdom). 1988. Taibei: National Palace Museum.

Skinner, G. William, ed. 1977. *The City in Late Imperial China*. Stanford: Stanford University Press.

———. 1985. "Presidential Address: The Structure of Chinese History." *Journal of Asian Studies* 44.2: 271–92.

———. 1987. "Sichuan's Population in the Nineteenth Century: Lessons from Disaggregated Data." *Late Imperial China* 8.1: 1–79.

———. 1992. "'Seek a Loyal Subject in a Filial Son': Family Roots of Political Orientation in Chinese Society." In Institute of Modern History, Academia Sinica, eds., *Family Process and Political Process in Modern Chinese History*, vol. 2. Taibei: Institute of Modern History, Academia Sinica.

Smith, George. 1847. *A Narrative of an Exploratory Visit to Each of the Consular Cities of China and to the Islands of Hong Kong and Chusan*. London: Seeley, Burnside & Seeley.

Smith, Thomas C. 1977. *Nakahara: Family Farming and Population in a Japanese Village, 1717–1830*. Stanford: Stanford University Press.

Solomon, Richard H. 1971. "Confucianism and the Chinese Life-Cycle." In *Mao's Revolution and the Chinese Political Culture*. Berkeley: University of California Press.

Sommer, Matthew. 1994. "Sex, Law, and Society in Late Imperial China." Ph.D. Diss., University of California, Los Angeles.

Song Ruozhao 宋若昭 [1624] 1893. *Nü lunyu* 女論語. In *Nü sishu* 女四書 (Four books for women). Wang Xiang 王相, annot. Imperially commissioned edition.

Spade, Beatrice. 1979. "The Education of Women in China During the Southern Dynasties." *Journal of Asian History* 1.13: 15–41.

Spence, Jonathan. 1966. *Ts'ao Yin and the K'ang-hsi Emperor: Bondservant and Master*. New Haven: Yale University Press.

———. 1967. "The Seven Ages of K'ang-hsi (1654–1722)." *The Journal of Asian Studies* 26.2: 205–12.

———. 1985. *The Memory Palace of Matteo Ricci*. New York: Penguin Books.

Stockard, Janice. 1989. *Daughters of the Canton Delta*. Stanford: Stanford University Press.

Struve, Lynn A. 1988. "The Early Ch'ing Legacy of Huang Tsung-hsi: A Reexamination." *Asia Major*, 3d ser., 1.1: 83–122.

Sullivan, Michael. 1967. *A Short History of Chinese Art*. Berkeley: University of California.

Sun, E-tu Zen. 1972. "Sericulture and Silk Textile Production in Ch'ing China." In W. E. Willmott, ed., *Economic Organization in Chinese Society*. Stanford: Stanford University Press.

Sun Xingyan 孫星衍. n.d. "Zhenjietang ji" 眞節堂記 (Record of the Hall of Purity and Chastity). In *Wusongyuan wen gao* 五松園文稿 (Manuscripts from the Garden of Five Pines), 1/15a–b. In *Sun Yuanru shi wen ji* 孫淵如詩文集 (The collected poetry and prose of Sun Xingyan). Sibu congkan edition.

Sung, Marina H. 1981. "The Chinese Lieh-nü Tradition." In Richard W. Guisso and Stanley Johannesen, eds., *Women in China: Current Directions in Historical Scholarship*. Youngstown, N.Y.: Philo Press.

———. 1994. *The Narrative Art of "Tsai-sheng-yüan": A Feminist Vision in Traditional Chinese Society*. Taibei: Chinese Materials Center Publications.

Sung Ying-Hsing. [1637] 1966. *T'ien-kung K'ai-wu: Chinese Technology in the Seventeenth Century*. Trans. E-tu Zen Sun and Shiou-chuan Sun. University Park: Pennsylvania State University Press.

Swann, Nancy Lee. 1932. *Pan Chao: Foremost Woman Scholar of China*. New York: Century.

"Symposium: 'Public Sphere'/'Civil Society' in China?" 1993. *Modern China* 19.2.

Takahashi Yoshiro 高橋芳郎. 1982. "Minmatsu-Shinshoki nuhi kokōjin mibun no saihen to tokushitsu" 明末清初期奴婢雇工人身分の再編と特質 (The reorganization and special characteristics of the status of slaves and hired laborers during the late Ming and early Qing period)." *Tōyōshi kenkyū* 41.3: 60–85.

Tan Danjiong 譚旦冏. 1987. *Taozhen hui lu* 陶瓷彙錄 (Survey of ceramic arts). Taibei: Guoli gugong bowuyuan.

Tan Qixiang 譚其驤, ed. 1982. *Zhongguo lishi ditu ji* 國中歷史地圖集 (The Historical Atlas of China). vol. 8. Shanghai: Ditu chubanshe.

Teiser, Stephen F. 1988. *The Ghost Festival in Medieval China*. Princeton: Princeton University Press.

Telford, Ted A. 1992a. "Covariates of Men's Age at First Marriage: The Historical Demography of Chinese Lineages." *Population Studies* 46: 19–35.

———. 1992b. "Family and State in Qing China: Marriage in the Tongcheng Lineages, 1650–1880." In Institute of Modern History, Academia Sinica, eds., *Family Process and Political Process in Modern Chinese History*, vol. 2. Taibei: Institute of Modern History, Academia Sinica.

Temple, Robert. 1986. *The Genius of China: 3,000 Years of Science, Discovery, and Invention*. New York: Simon & Schuster.

Terada Takanobu 寺田隆信. 1959. "Yōseitei no semmin kaihōrei ni tsuite 雍正帝の賤民開放令について (Concerning the emancipation of the *jianmin* in the Yongzheng reign). *Tōyōshi kenkyū* 18.3: 124–41.

Thompson, Stuart E. 1988. "Death, Food, and Fertility." In James L. Watson and Evelyn S. Rawski, eds., *Death Ritual in Late Imperial and Modern China*. Berkeley: University of California Press.

T'ien Ju-k'ang. 1988. *Male Anxiety and Female Chastity: A Comparative Study of Chinese Ethical Values in Ming-Ch'ing Times*. Leiden: E. J. Brill.

Tong, Ginger. 1989. "Yün Shou-P'ing and His Patrons." In Li Chu-tsing, ed., *Artists and Patrons: Some Social and Economic Aspects of Chinese Painting*. N.p.: Kress Foundation Department of Art History, University of Kansas, and Nelson-Atkins Museum of Art, Kansas City, in association with University of Washington Press.

Topley, Margery. 1975. "Marriage Resistance in Rural Kwangtung." In Margery Wolf and Roxane Witke, eds., *Women in Chinese Society*. Stanford: Stanford University Press.

Tsai, Kathryn A. 1981. "The Chinese Buddhist Monastic Order for Women: The First Two Centuries." In Richard W. Guisso and Stanley Johannesen, eds., *Women in China: Current Directions in Historical Scholarship*. Youngstown, N.Y.: Philo Press.

Tun Li-Ch'en. 1965. *Annual Customs and Festivals in Peking*. Trans. and ed. Derk Bodde. Hong Kong: Hong Kong University Press.

Twitchett, Denis. 1962. "Chinese Biographical Writing." In W. G. Beasley and E. G. Pulleyblank, eds., *Historians of China and Japan*. Oxford: Oxford University Press.

Unschuld, Paul U., trans. and annot. 1990. *Forgotten Traditions of Ancient Chinese Medicine: The "I-hsüeh Yüan Liu Lun" of 1757, by Hsü Ta-Ch'un*. Brookline, Mass.: Paradigm Publications.

Veith, Ilza, trans. and ed. 1972. *The Yellow Emperor's Classic of Internal Medicine*. Berkeley: University of California Press.

Wakeman, Frederic, Jr. 1970. "High Ch'ing, 1683–1839." In James B. Crowley, ed., *Modern East Asia: Essays in Interpretation*. New York: Harcourt, Brace & World.

———. 1985. *The Great Enterprise: The Manchu Reconstruction of Imperial Order in Seventeenth-Century China*. 2 vols. Berkeley: University of California Press.

Waley, Arthur. 1956. *Yuan Mei: Eighteenth Century Chinese Poet*. New York: Grove Press.

———. 1961. *Chinese Poems*. London: Unwin Books.

Waltner, Ann. 1986. "The Moral Status of the Child in Late Imperial China: Childhood in Ritual and in Law." *Social Research* 53.4: 667–87.

———. 1987. "T'an-yang-tzu and Wang Shih-chen: Visionary and Bureaucrat in the Late Ming." *Late Imperial China* 8.1: 105–33.

———. Forthcoming. "Breaking the Law: Family Violence, Kinship and Gender in the Legal Code of Ming Dynasty China." *Ming Studies*.

Wang Chun 王純, comp. 1816. *Er Nan xunnü jie* 二南訓女解 (Instructions for women from the "Er Nan," explained).

Wang Huizu 汪輝祖. [1794] 1970. *Shuangjietang yongxun* 雙節堂庸訓 (Simple precepts from the Hall Enshrining a Pair of Chaste Widows). Reprint, Taibei: Huawen shuju.

Wang Shunu 王書奴. [1933] 1988. *Zhongguo changji shi* 中國娼妓史 (The history of prostitution in China). Shanghai: Sanlian shudian.

Wang Zhong 汪中. [1815] 1970. *Shu xue* 述學 (An account of learning). Reprint, Taibei: Guangwen shuju.

Watson, Rubie S. 1986. "The Named and the Nameless: Gender and Person in Chinese Society." *American Ethnologist* 13: 619–31.

———. 1991. "Wives, Concubines, and Maids: Servitude and Kinship in the Hong Kong Region, 1900–1940." In Rubie S. Watson and Patricia Buckley Ebrey, eds., *Marriage and Inequality in Chinese Society*. Berkeley: University of California Press.

Wei Qingyuan 韋慶遠, Wu Qiyan 吳奇衍, and Lu Su 魯素, comp. 1982. *Qingdai nubei zhidu* 清代奴婢制度 (The slavery system in the Qing dynasty). Beijing: Zhongguo renmin daxue chubanshe.

Werner, Edward T. C. [1922] 1986. *Ancient Tales and Folklore of China*. London: Bracken Books. Originally published as *Myths and Legends of China*.

———. 1961. *A Dictionary of Chinese Mythology*. New York: Julian Press.

Wheeler, Candace. 1921. *The Development of Embroidery in America*. New York: Harper.

Widmer, Ellen. 1989. "The Epistolary World of Female Talent in Seventeenth-Century China." *Late Imperial China* 10.2: 1–43.

———. 1992. "Xiaoqing's Literary Legacy and the Place of the Woman Writer in Late Imperial China." *Late Imperial China* 13.1: 111–55.

Wiesner, Merry E. 1986. *Working Women in Renaissance Germany*. New Brunswick, N.J.: Rutgers University Press.

Wile, Douglas. 1992. *Art of the Bedchamber: The Chinese Sexual Yoga Classics, Including Women's Solo Meditation Texts*. Albany: State University of New York.

Will, Pierre-Etienne. 1990. *Bureaucracy and Famine in Eighteenth-Century China*. Trans. Elborg Forster. Stanford: Stanford University Press.

Will, Pierre-Etienne, and R. Bin Wong, with James Lee. 1991. *Nourish the People: The State Civilian Granary System in China, 1650–1850*. Ann Arbor: Center for Chinese Studies, University of Michigan.

Williams, C. A. S. 1976. *Outlines of Chinese Symbolism and Art Motives*. 3d rev. ed. New York: Dover.

Williams, Edward T. 1935. "The Worship of Lei Tsu, Patron Saint of Silk Workers." *Journal of the North China Branch, Royal Asiatic Society*, n.s. 66: 1–14.

Williams, S. Wells. 1900. *The Middle Kingdom*. 2 vols. New York: Scribner's.

Wolf, Arthur P. 1970. "Chinese Kinship and Mourning Dress." In Maurice Freedman, ed., *Family and Kinship in Chinese Society*. Stanford: Stanford University Press.

Wolf, Arthur P., and Susan B. Hanley. 1985. "Introduction." In Hanley and Wolf, eds., *Family and Population in East Asian History*. Stanford: Stanford University Press.

Wolf, Arthur P., and Chieh-shan Huang. 1980. *Marriage and Adoption in China, 1845–1945*. Stanford: Stanford University Press.

Wolf, Margery. 1972. *Women and the Family in Rural Taiwan*. Stanford: Stanford University Press.

———. 1975. "Women and Suicide in China." In Margery Wolf and Roxane Witke, eds., *Women in Chinese Society*. Stanford: Stanford University Press.
Wolfe, Barnard. 1980. *The Daily Life of a Chinese Courtesan: Climbing Up a Tricky Ladder*. Kowloon, Hong Kong: Learner's Bookstore.
Woloch, Nancy. 1984. *Women and the American Experience*. New York: McGraw-Hill.
Woodside, Alexander Barton. 1971. *Vietnam and the Chinese Model: A Comparative Study of Vietnamese and Chinese Government in the First Half of the Nineteenth Century*. Cambridge, Mass.: Harvard University Press.
———. 1983. "Some Mid-Qing Theorists of Popular Schools: Their Innovations, Inhibitions, and Attitudes Toward the Poor." *Modern China* 9.1: 3–36.
Wright, Mary Clabaugh. 1957. *The Last Stand of Chinese Conservatism: The T'ung-Chih Restoration, 1862–1874*. Stanford: Stanford University Press.
Wu Pei-yi. 1990. *The Confucian's Progress: Autobiographical Writings in Traditional China*. Princeton: Princeton University Press.
Xiangyan congshu 香艷叢書 (Collection of feminine fragrance). 1914. Guoxue fulunshe edition. Shanghai: Zhongguo tushu gongsi.
Xinxiu Yin xian zhi 新修鄞縣志 (Gazetteer of Yin county, newly compiled). 1877.
Xiong Bingzhen, *see* Hsiung Ping-chen.
Xu Dixin 許滌新 and Wu Chengming 吳承明, eds. 1985. *Zhongguo zibenzhuyi de mengya* 中國資本主義的萌芽 (The sprouts of capitalism in China). Beijing: Renmin chubanshe.
Xu Kuichen 許夔臣, comp. [1804] 1914. *Xiangke ji xuancun* 香咳集選存 (Collection of selected "fragrant writings"). Reprinted *Xiangyan congshu* 1914, 8: 4/1a–40b.
Xu Guangqi 徐光啓. [1639] 1900. *Nongzheng quanshu* 農政全書 (The complete book of agricultural policy). Reprint, Shanghai: Wenhai shuju.
Xu Shichang 徐世昌. 1929. *Wanqing yishi hui* 晚晴簃詩匯 (The Wanqing poetry anthology).
Xu Xinwu 徐新吾. 1981. *Yapian zhanzhengqian Zhongguo mianfangzhi shougongye de shangpin shengchan yu ziben zhuyi mengya wenti* 鴉片戰爭前中國棉紡織手工業的商品生產與資本主義萌芽問題 (Commercial production in China's cotton spinning and weaving protoindustry before the Opium War and the problem of the sprouts of capitalism). Yangzhou: Jiangsu renmin chubanshe.
Xuzuan Jurong xian [Jiangsu] zhi 續纂句容縣 [江蘇] 志 (Gazetteer of Jurong county [Jiangsu], continued). [1904] 1974. Reprint, Taibei: Chengwen chubanshe.
Yamazaki Jun'ichi 山崎純一. 1986. *Kyōiku kara mita Chūgoku joseishi shiryō no kenkyū* 教育から見た中國女性史資料の研究 (A documentary study of Chinese women's history as seen from education). Tokyo: Meiji shoin.
Yan Ming 嚴明. 1992. *Zhongguo mingji yishu shi* 中國名妓藝術史 (A history of the courtesan's art in China). Taibei: Wenjin chubanshe.
Yan Xiyuan 顏希源, comp. 1755. *Huapu baimeitu bing xinyong hebian* 畫譜百美圖併新詠合編 (Combined edition of the illustrated register of one hundred beauties with new verses). Prefaces dated 1787, 1790, 1792, 1804.

Yang, Lien-sheng [Yang Liansheng 楊聯陞]. 1952. *Money and Credit in China: A Short History*. Cambridge, Mass.: Harvard University Press.

Yin Huiyi 尹會一, comp. 1748. *Sijian lu* 四鑑錄 (Record of four mirrors). Reprint, Congshu jicheng jianbian edition. Vol. 148. Taibei: Shangwu yinshuguan.

Yü, Chün-fang [Yu Junfang 于君方]. 1990. "Images of Kuan-yin in Chinese Folk Literature." *Hanxue yanjiu* 8.1: 222–85.

———. 1992. "P'u-t'o Shan: Pilgrimage and the Creation of the Chinese Potalaka." In Susan Naquin and Chün-fang Yü, eds., *Pilgrims and Sacred Sites in China*. Berkeley: University of California Press.

Yu Huai 余懷 [1697] 1966. *A Feast of Mist and Flowers: The Gay Quarters of Nanking at the End of the Ming*. Trans. Howard Levy. Yokohama: published privately. Originally titled *Banqiao za ji* 板橋雜記 (Diverse records of Banqiao).

Yü Ying-shih [Yu Yingshi 余英時]. 1981. "New Evidence on the Early Chinese Conception of Afterlife—A Review Article." *Journal of Asian Studies* 41.1: 81–85.

———. 1987. *Zhongguo jinshi zongjiao lunli yu shangren jingshen* 中國近世宗教倫理與商人精神 (Religious ethics and the entrepreneurial spirit in modern China). Taibei: Lianjing chubanshiye gongsi.

Yuan Dinghua 袁定華. 1973. "Ningbo qixi de qili fengguang" 寧波七夕的綺麗風光 (The beautiful atmosphere in Ningbo on Seventh Night). In Zhang Xingzhou 張行周, ed., *Ningbo xisu congtan* 寧波習俗叢談 (Collected anecdotes about the customs of Ningbo). Taibei: Minzhu chubanshe.

Yuan, Tsing. 1979. "Urban Riots and Disturbances." In Jonathan D. Spence and John E. Wills, Jr., eds., *From Ming to Ch'ing: Conquest, Region, and Continuity in Seventeenth-Century China*. New Haven: Yale University Press.

Zhang Dai 張代. [1877] 1935. *Langxuan wen ji* 瑯嬛文集 (The Langxuan prose collection). Reprint, Shanghai: Shanghai zazhi gongsi.

Zhang Xingzhou 張行周. 1973. "Dinghai qiuling xisu" 定海秋令習俗 (Autumn festival customs in Dinghai). In Zhang, ed., *Ningbo xisu congtan*. Taibei: Minzhu chubanshe.

Zhang Xuecheng 章學誠. [n.d.] 1922. *Zhangshi yishu* 章氏遺書 (The bequeathed works of Master Zhang). Jiayetang edition.

———. [1832] 1964. *Wen shi tong yi* 文史通義 (A comprehensive analysis of literature and history). Reprint, Hong Kong: Taiping shuju.

Zhang Yingchang 張應昌, comp. [1869] 1983. *Qingshi duo* 清詩鐸 (Anthology of Qing poetry, classified by topic). First printed under the title *Guochao shi duo* 國朝詩鐸. Reprint (2 vols.), Beijing: Zhonghua shuju.

Zhang Yufa 張玉法 and Li Youning 李又寧, eds. 1975. *Jindai Zhongguo nüquan yundong shiliao* 近代中國女權運動史料 (Documents on the feminist movement in modern China, 1842–1911). 2 vols. Taibei: Zhuanji wenxueshe.

Zhao Yi 趙翼. [c. 1775] 1957. *Gaiyu congkao* 陔餘叢考 (The step-by-step collection of studies). Reprint, Shanghai: Shangwu yinshuguan.

Zheng Guangyi 鄭光儀, comp. 1991. *Zhongguo lidai cainü shige jianshang cidian* 中國歷代才女詩歌鑒賞辭典 (A connoisseur's dictionary of poems and songs by talented women writers through Chinese history, arranged by dynasty). Beijing: Zhongguo gongren chubanshe.

Zhong Qi 鍾琦, comp. [1897] 1970. *Huangchao suoxie lu* 皇朝瑣屑錄 (Recorded fragments of our time). Jindai Zhongguo shiliao congkan edition, no. 532. 3 vols.

Zhou Wu 周蕪, comp. 1988. *Zhongguo banhua shi tu lu* 中國版畫史圖錄 (Illustrated record of the history of Chinese woodcut illustrations). 2 vols. Shanghai: Renmin meishu chuban she.

Zhou Xun 周汛 and Gao Chunming 高春明. 1988. *Zhongguo lidai funü zhuangshi* 中國歷代婦女妝飾 (Adornments of women throughout Chinese history). Hong Kong: Sanlian chubanshe.

Zhu Yun 朱筠. [1815] 1936. *Sihe wenji* 笥河文集 (The collected writings of [Zhu] Sihe [Yun]). Reprint, Shanghai: Shangwu yinshuguan.

Zong Li 宗力 and Liu Qun 劉群. 1986. *Zhongguo minjian zhu shen* 中國民間諸神 (Popular gods in China). Shijiazhuang: Hebei renmin chubanshe.

Zurndorfer, Harriet T. 1992. "The 'Constant World' of Wang Chao-Yuan: Women, Education, and Orthodoxy in Eighteenth-Century China—A Preliminary Investigation." In Institute of Modern History, Academia Sinica, eds., *Family Process and Political Process in Modern Chinese History*, vol 1. Taibei: Institute of Modern History, Academia Sinica.

Index

In this index an "f" after a number indicates a reference on the next page, and an "ff" indicates separate references on the next two pages. A continuous discussion over two or more pages is indicated by a span of page numbers, e.g., "57–58." *Passim* is used for a cluster of references in close but not continuous sequence.